THE CIVIL LAW TRADITION
IN
SCOTLAND

THE STAIR SOCIETY

THE CIVIL LAW TRADITION
IN SCOTLAND

by

VARIOUS AUTHORS

edited by

ROBIN EVANS-JONES

EDINBURGH
THE STAIR SOCIETY
1995

Published by

The Stair Society
Saltire Court
20 Castle Terrace
Edinburgh
EH1 2ET

First published 1995

ISBN 1 872517 08 0

British Library Cataloguing-in-Publication Data

A catalogue record for this book is available from the British
Library.

Typeset in the ITC Garamond Book face by the Computer
Publishing Unit of the University of Glasgow.

Printed in Great Britain by Antony Rowe Ltd, Chippenham,
Wiltshire.

CONTENTS

THE STAIR SOCIETY

Supplementary Volumes

ACKNOWLEDGEMENTS

This book has been made possible by contributors who provided their essays notwithstanding the demands of extremely busy schedules. To them I offer my thanks. I should also like to thank Bill Gordon, Geoffrey MacCormack and Niall Whitty who all cheerfully gave their time, support and help in the production of this volume to a degree which it was unreasonable of me to ask. My thanks also go to Philip Simpson who shouldered much of the burden which should properly have been borne by the editor. Lastly, I should like to thank Frank Lyall, the Dean of Aberdeen Law Faculty, who supported this project when others did not. Thereby he earns a little forgiveness for his forthcoming book entitled "British Law".

LIST OF CONTRIBUTORS

Robin Evans-Jones LL.B., Ph.D., is a Senior Lecturer in Law in the University of Aberdeen.

William M. Gordon, M.A., LL.B., Ph.D., F.R.S.E., is Douglas Professor of Civil Law in the University of Glasgow.

Reinhard Zimmermann, Dr.Iur., LL.D., is Professor of Civil Law, Roman Law and Comparative Law in the University of Regensburg.

Peter Birks, Q.C., D.C.L., LL.D., F.B.A., is Regius Professor of Civil Law in the University of Oxford.

Douglas J. Osler, M.A., LL.B., Ph.D., D.Phil., is an academic fellow of the Max-Planck-Institut für Europäische Rechtsgeschichte, Frankfurt am Main.

David L. Carey Miller, B.A., LL.B., LL.M., Ph.D., is a Professor of Law in the University of Aberdeen.

David Johnston, M.A., Ph.D., Advocate, is Regius Professor of Civil Law in the University of Cambridge.

Alan Rodger, The Rt Hon. Lord Rodger of Earlsferry, Q.C., D.C.L., F.B.A., is the Lord Advocate of Scotland.

Geoffrey MacCormack, B.A., M.A., LL.B., D.Phil., is Professor of Jurisprudence in the University of Aberdeen.

Donna McKenzie, LL.B., Dip.L.P., N.P., is a Lecturer in Law in the University of Aberdeen.

LIST OF ABBREVIATIONS

Aberdeen Univ. Rev.	*Aberdeen University Review*
A.c.P.	*Archiv für die civilistische Praxis*
Am.J.Comp.L.	*American Journal of Comparative Law*
Am.J.L.H.	*American Journal of Legal History*
A.P.S.	*Acts of the Parliaments of Scotland*, edd. T. Thomson and C. Innes. 12 vols. (Edinburgh, 1814–75)
Australian L.J.	*Australian Law Journal*
Bankton	Lord Bankton, *An Institute of the Laws of Scotland*, (Edinburgh, 1751–3, reprinted, Stair Society, vols. 41–43, Edinburgh, 1993–95)
Bell, *Comm.*	G. J. Bell, *Commentaries on the Law of Scotland*, (Edinburgh, 2nd ed., 1810, 5th ed. 1825, 7th ed. by J. McLaren, 1870, reprinted 1990)
Bell, *Prin.*	G. J. Bell, *Principles of the Law of Scotland*, (Edinburgh, 4th ed. 1839, 10th ed. by W. Guthrie, 1899, reprinted, 1989)
B.G.B.	Bürgerliches Gesetzbuch
B.G.H.Z.	Entscheidungen des Bundesgerichtshofs in Zivilsachen
B.I.D.R.	*Bullettino dell' Istituto di diritto romano*
Bing.	Bingham's Reports
Boston Univ. L.R.	*Boston University Law Review*
B.S.	Brown's *Supplement* to *Morison's Dictionary*
Butterworth's S.A.L.R.	*Butterworth's South African Law Review*
C.	*Codex* of Justinian
Canadian Y.I.L	*Canadian Yearbook of International Law*
C.I.L.S.A.	*Comparative and International Law Journal of Southern Africa*
C.L.P.	*Current Legal Problems*
C.L.R.	Commonwealth Law Reports
Co. Rep.	Coke's Reports

Craig	Sir Thomas Craig, *Jus Feudale*, (Edinburgh, 1655, 3rd ed. by J. Baillie 1732)
D.	*Digest* of Justinian
Duke L.R.	*Duke Law Review*
E.R.	English Reports
Erskine, *Inst.*	J. Erskine, *An Institute of the Law of Scotland* (Edinburgh, 1773, ed. J. B. Nicolson, 1871, reprinted, 1990)
Erskine, *Prin.*	J. Erskine , *Principles of the Law of Scotland* (Edinburgh, 4th ed. 1769)
Gaius, *Inst.*	*The Institutes* of Gaius
H. & N.	Hurlstone & Norman
Harv. L.R.	*Harvard Law Review*
Hume	Hume's *Decisions*
Hume, *Comm.*	D. Hume, *Commentaries on the Law of Scotland* (4th ed. by B. R. Bell, 1844, reprinted, Edinburgh, 1986)
Hume, *Lectures*	*Baron David Hume's Lectures 1786–1822,* ed. G.C.H. Paton, 6 vols. (Stair Society, vols. 5, 13, 15, 17-19, Edinburgh, 1939, 1949, 1952, 1955, 1957-58)
Hume, *Treatise*	D. Hume, *A Treatise of Human Nature*, (London, 1739-40)
I.C.L.Q.	*International and Comparative Law Quarterly*
Irish Jur.	*Irish Jurist*
J.L.S.S.	*Journal of the Law Society of Scotland*
Jour. Comp. Legis.	*Journal of Comparative Legislation*
Jour. of Jurisprudence	*Journal of Jurisprudence*
J.R.	*Juridical Review*
Justinian, *Inst.*	*The Institutes* of Justinian
Law & Hist. Rev.	*Law and History Review*
Lesotho L.J.	*Lesotho Law Journal*
Louisiana L.J.	*Louisiana Law Journal*
L.Q.R.	*Law Quarterly Review*

M. & W.	Meeson & Welsby
Mackenzie	G. Mackenzie, *Institutions of the Law of Scotland* (Edinburgh, 1684, 2nd ed. 1688)
M.L.R.	*Modern Law Review*
Mor.	Morison's *Dictionary of Decisions*
Oxford J.L.S.	*Oxford Journal of Legal Studies*
RabelsZ.	*Rabels Zeitschrift für ausländisches und internationales Privatrecht*
R.P.C.	*Register of the Privy Council of Scotland*, edd. J. H. Burton *et al.* (Edinburgh, 1877–)
S.A.	South African Law Reports
S.A.L.J.	*South African Law Journal*
S.C.	Session Cases; Cape Supreme Court
Sc. Hist. Rev.	*Scottish Historical Review*
Sc.Jur.	*Scottish Jurist*
Scottish Law Commision, *Recovery of Benefits*	Scottish Law Commission, *Recovery of Benefits Conferred under Error of Law* (Discussion Paper no. 95). 2 vols. (September, 1993)
S.C.L.R.	Scottish Civil Law Reports
S.D.H.I.	*Studia et documenta historiae et iuris*
S.L.J.	*Scottish Law Journal*
S.L.R.	*Scottish Law Review*
S.L.T.	Scots Law Times
Stair	James Dalrymple, Viscount Stair, *Institutions of the Law of Scotland* (Edinburgh, 1681, 2nd ed. 1693, Tercentenary ed. by D. M. Walker, Edinburgh and Glasgow, 1981)
Stair Memorial Encyclopaedia	*The Laws of Scotland. Stair Memorial Encyclopaedia*, gen. edd. the late Sir Thomas Smith and R. Black. 25 vols. (Edinburgh, 1987-95)
Swaziland L.R.	Swaziland Law Reports
T.H.R.H.R.	*Tydskrif vir Hedenaagse Romeins-Hollandse Reg*
Tulane L.R.	*Tulane Law Reivew*

T.v.R.	*Tijdschrift voor Rechtsgeschiedenis*
Virginia LR.	*Virginia Law Review*
Walker, *Principles*	D. M. Walker, *Principles of the Law of Scotland*, (Edinburgh, 1970, 2nd ed. 1975, 3rd ed. 1983, 4th ed. 1988)
W. & S.	Wilson and Shaw
Z.Eu.P.	*Zeitschrift für Europäisches Privatrecht*
Z.N.R.	*Zeitschrift für neuere Rechtsgeschichte*
Z.S.S. (GA)	*Zeitschrift der Savigny-Stiftung für Rechtsgeschichte (germanistische Abteilung)*
Z.S.S. (KA)	*Zeitschrift der Savigny-Stiftung für Rechtsgeschichte (kanonistische Abteilung)*
Z.S.S. (RA)	*Zeitschrift der Savigny-Stiftung für Rechtsgeschichte (romanistische Abteilung)*
Zimmermann, *Obligations*	R. Zimmermann, *The Law of Obligations. Roman Foundations of the Civilian Tradition* (Cape Town, etc. , 1990)

Section One:
Introductory

1. CIVIL LAW IN THE SCOTTISH LEGAL TRADITION

By ROBIN EVANS-JONES

Lord Cooper, in his celebrated essay on the Scottish legal tradition,[1] concluded his treatment of the historical background about 1820. He observed that while that may seem a long time ago "we are still too near the trees of the 19th century to see the wood". Lord Cooper published his essay in 1949. Therefore it is now time that an attempt is made to see that part of the wood which concerns the Civil law.

Law has long been regarded (by some) as a manifestation of the spirit of a people and it is therefore natural that the Scots should view their legal system with pride. It is also perhaps understandable that this pride should sometimes shade into romanticism because the union with England left its legal system as one of the few reminders that Scotland was once an independent nation. The romantic picture is further enhanced by the image of the Scottish legal system as a small "mixed" jurisdiction standing between the two giants of western civilisation, the Civil and the Common law. Scots are portrayed as having a pronounced talent for law, which, founding on an eclectic tradition, has allowed them to choose what is best from the competing influences of their neighbouring giants.

These positive images of the Scottish legal system originate from a legal establishment which has a clear self-interest in the result. Therefore, once in a while, it is sensible to consider whether the picture really is so bright. In this essay I shall focus on the Scots' perception of one feature of the past; namely their civilian tradition which is commonly referred to in Scotland as "Roman law". I shall identify some themes which concern the Scottish legal system as a whole, especially its so-called "mixed" nature.

When assessing the position of "Roman law" in the modern Scottish legal system one is immediately struck by the strength and diversity of opinion which is held by Scottish lawyers on the subject. At one extreme Roman law has been, or is at least thought to have been, portrayed by a few as the path to a golden future in which the Scottish legal system looks once more for its inspiration exclusively to the civilian legal tradition. The impression is that this legal renaissance is seen as part of a more wide-ranging spiritual, cultural and political revival in Scotland of which the central goal is independence from England

---

1   Republished in *The Scottish Legal Tradition*, ed. S.C. Styles (Edinburgh, 1991), 65ff. The quotation is at p.71.

3

almost at any cost. At the other extreme the idea that Scotland had a legal culture which in matters of private law was extensively drawn from the Roman legal tradition is dismissed as a figment of the imagination of misguided souls.

One encounters a number of other approaches to "Roman law", including that of the modernising functionalists. The modernising functionalists are people who see that a legal system is largely about solving real problems for ordinary people. Part of the composition of Scots law is seen to be "Roman law" which is necessarily perceived as a different system fashioned for a very different age. "Roman law" is also often still transmitted in Latin which presents an unnecessary barrier to the proper identification and elucidation of the pressing problems of a modern legal system. In the place of this "Roman law" and its Latin terms are substituted modern notions and translations which have logic and sound function as their purpose. There is something to be said for this approach, I suppose.

The problem with the approach of the modernising functionalists is that it is based upon two misperceptions which are aggravated by the self-confidence which so often goes with a modernising zeal. The first misperception is to present legal rules, principles and causes of action of Scots law which may in origin have been derived from Roman law as "Roman law". Once it has been received in Scotland "Roman Law" becomes Scots law to which this "Roman law" is therefore not foreign. Do we, for example, persist in calling a legal rule derived from the Common law "English law" once it has become part of Scots law? Secondly, it was not, as the term "Roman law" suggests, directly the law of Justinian's *Corpus Iuris Civilis* which made an important contribution to the formation of Scottish private law, but the civilian legal tradition. There was a succession of schools of legal scholars which grew up during and after the renaissance of civilian studies which exerted a profound influence on the substance of, and attitudes towards, Roman law. Of the Commentators, for example, H. D. Hazeltine, drawing on Gierke, in an often quoted passage, says:[2]

> (Their) great achievement ... was in fact the transformation of Roman law into a medieval Italian law. It was the living Romano-Italian law of the Commentators and not the pure Roman law of Justinian which crossed the Alps into Germany in the age of the Reception.

Roman law started a second life which is thought to have commenced about 1100 at the University of Bologna. Five hundred and eighty one years elapsed before the publication of the foundation of the modern Scottish legal system, Stair's *Institutions of the Law of Scotland*, during which sometimes the substance, certainly the perceptions of the

---

2   In his introduction to W. Ullmann, *The Medieval Idea of Law* (London, 1946) at p.xix.

authority of Roman law, and ideas on the very function of law itself underwent major revision.

The modernising functionalists think of the "Roman" part of Scots law mainly in terms of the law of the *Corpus Iuris Civilis*. This permits an unwarrantable degree of freedom when it comes to the "modernisation" of Scots law since, not only can the law of Justinian often be shown to be ill-suited to the modern age, but it is also perceived to be essentially an anachronistic component in the modern legal system. The continuity that modern Scots law has with its own legal history is also broken by this approach to the modernisation of "Roman law". Once the parameters of a legal institution have been fixed in the mind's eye by reference to the *Corpus Iuris Civilis* what the Scottish institutional writers or the early case law understood by the same institution is often completely ignored.

In the middle ground as regards their attitudes to the civilian part of Scotland's legal tradition stand those people who rightly perceive that the quality of "function", like beauty, is usually open to debate. These people see that a mature legal system must have one eye to function but also an equally sound eye to its own traditions.

Lawyers who have a sense of the traditions of Scots law will, on occasion, have to evaluate Roman law and what has been made of Roman law by the *ius commune*. They should do the latter primarily by reference to the institutional writers because it was by incorporation in these works that the law of the *ius commune* became Scottish. A study of what modern civilian systems have made of the same law can also be highly instructive. There is, however, too often a very real difficulty experienced by Scots law in understanding the Scottish institutional writers. For example, the House of Lords in *Cantiere*[3] made a genuine attempt to apply the *condictio causa data causa non secuta* in conformity with the statements of the institutional writers and early case law. They were partly led astray by the perception that they were dealing with "Roman" and not Scots law which led them to rely on H. J. Roby's textbook, *Roman Private Law*.[4] As a result conceptions of classical Roman law, albeit in a rather distorted fashion, were substituted in place of the different Scots law developed from the *ius commune;* a sign of the third, but erratic, reception of Roman law in Scotland[5]. An additional problem was that, as regards the civilian tradition, the institutional writers were viewed by the House of Lords in a cultural vacuum. The judges were wholly unaware of the fact that with changing

---

3   *Cantiere San Rocco SA* v. *Clyde Shipbuilding and Engineeering Co.* 1922 S.C. 723; 1923 S.C. (H.L.) 105; see the contribution by G.D. MacCormack in this volume.

4   *Roman Private Law in the Times of Cicero and of the Antonines.* 2 vols. (Cambridge, 1902).

5   See R. Evans-Jones, "Unjust Enrichment, Contract and the Third Reception of Roman Law in Scotland", (1993) 109 *L.Q.R.* 663.

conceptions of contract in the *ius commune* the role of the *condictio*
had itself altered and that it was this developed law which had been
received in Scotland. The famous *dictum* of Lord President Inglis in
Watson v. *Shankland*[6] was also mis-read to conform with the judges'
own different cultural perceptions. Modern Scots is now grappling
with the consequences which include nice conflicts of principle
between the law of contract and the law of unjustified enrichment.

Examples of the failure to understand the institutional writers
abound. A recurring feature of these misunderstandings is that the
propositions which need to be understood are usually simple, yet, if
approached from a wholly different cultural perspective, they are
impossibly remote. For example, Scots law we are told rejects the *actio
quanti minoris*.[7] The institutional writers do not wholly bear this out,
however. The problem stems from the fact that due to the influence of
the *ius commune* two claims are referred to as *actio quanti minoris:*
one derived from the old Justinianic rules on *laesio enormis* is clearly
rejected and one, apart from a doubt expressed by Erskine, clearly
accepted. Scots law then confused one with the other. The result, once
one has analysed what is meant by the term *actio quanti minoris,* is
that the modern law in principle does not allow a buyer of heritage a
claim of damages under the contract of sale in respect of material
defects, including defects of title, in what he bought. This is certainly a
remarkable, if not unique, proposition and one which cannot be desirable since the Law Society of Scotland now recommends that solicitors
acting for a buyer of heritage should insert a statement in the missives
to the effect that the *actio quanti minoris* shall be available.[8]

The cultural vacuum in Scotland regarding the civilian tradition
results in extremes. Occasionally its contribution is over-stated.
Normally it is understated, misdirected or even lampooned, usually, but
not always, because it is largely unknown. Established Scots law is
replaced by the prevailing ideas of what is thought to be best. However,
in practice, it is usually not what is best that is adopted; merely what is
known. Functionalism is thereby undermined because the quality of
the new "functional" institution is never fully tested by debate before
its incorporation into the modern legal system.

What is known is now usually English law. It is in fact those parts of
Scottish private law which are most "civilian" in character that are
undergoing the strongest reception of English law in a manner which
shows all the hallmarks of a classical reception. English law is accessible

6   (1871) 10 M. 142.
7   See R. Evans-Jones, "The History of the *actio quanti minoris* in Scotland",
     1991 *J.R.* 190.
8   *The House Purchase and Sale Guideline and Standard Clauses*, B12. But
     see now the elegant treatment in *Scottish Law Commission, Contract Law:
     Extrinsic Evidence, Supersession, and the Actio Quanti Minoris*
     (Discussion Paper no. 97) (April, 1994).

at all levels, including most importantly, language. It has its own power-ful culture which is brought to Scotland by university teachers and by students returning from study in England. They apply their training in the courts and in the academic literature. Indigenous Scots seek out English law in the case reports, textbooks, and in their personal con-tacts.

A strong medium through which the influence of English law is now being felt is in translations of Scottish legal institutions from Latin into English. Translation is a desirable but profoundly delicate exercise which should seek to reproduce the essence of an institution after a process of careful study. If it is merely shot from the hip of an inventive mind it can effect, not a translation but a transformation. Two examples will serve as an illustration. *Condictio indebiti* has recently been ren-dered as "mistake",[9] which is straight out of the English law book, *The Law of Restitution* by Goff and Jones. Even the most convinced innno-cent must suspect that, under the guise of the pursuit of what is func-tionally best, there is something odd in the rendition of *"condictio indebiti"* as "mistake" or "error"[10] and that the translator is imposing his own cultural perceptions on something which clearly signals in a differ-ent direction. If either of these translations is accepted[11] it has very major consequences for the manner is which the law of unjustified enrichment will develop in Scotland. Scots law received two traditions from Roman law on the *condictio indebiti:* the tradition which sees the cause of action, in effect, as a transfer "without a legal basis" subject to a defence of knowledge and the tradition founding on Gaius[12] which sees "error" as a positive feature of the claim. The translation "mistake" forces the Scottish *condictio indebiti* into the latter camp favoured by English law even although the twentieth century civilian systems, and in fact the early Scottish institutional writers, all chose the former as functionally better. Also, although sound function was the justification for the introduction of "mistake", it failed at the hurdle presented by the recent *Woolwich* case decided in the House of Lords[13] where an approach based on an alternative Scottish understanding of *condictio indebiti* as the claim to recover an "undue transfer" would not have failed.[14] Equally distorting, *condictio causa data causa non secuta,*

---

9   See P. B. H. Birks, "Restitution: A View of Scots Law", (1985) 38 *C.L.P.* 57; "Six Questions in Search of a Subject", 1985 *J.R.* 227.
10 See Scottish Law Commission, *Recovery of Benefits.*
11 "Mistake" was immediately presented as Scots law with no evaluation of its merits by W. J. Stewart, *The Law of Restitution in Scotland* (Edinburgh, 1992), 67.
12 Gaius, *Inst.* 3,91, aided and abetted by Justinian's interpolation of D.22.3.25*pr.*
13 *Woolwich Equitable Building Society* v. *I.R.C.* [1992] 3 W.L.R. (H.L.(E)) 366; [1993] 1 A.C. 70 (C.A.) and (H.L.(E)).
14 These issues are dealt with in greater detail in my contribution on the *con-dictio indebiti* in this volume.

since the intervention of the House of Lords,[15] is "the claim to recover what was given for a consideration which failed". This translation has created a complete muddle by obscuring the operation of the mutuality principle within the law of contract and the *condictio* within the law of unjustified enrichment.[16]

English law is both politically and culturally strong in Scotland. By contrast, the culture which supports the civilian parts of Scots law is weak and has been for nearly two hundred years. This culture has been remote from Scotland and is transmitted in languages other than English which has rendered it inaccessible to most Scots. However, Roman law has always been a culture fostered and transmitted by the universities. At first sight it therefore seems rather strange that the civilian culture in Scotland should be so weak since the Scottish universities recently have had a healthy tradition in this field. The explanation for the paradox lies in the fact that teaching in modern times in the Scottish universities has itself been a reflection of particular cultural perceptions. Many teachers have adopted an exclusively archaeological approach in order to unearth that product of genius, classical Roman law, from the miasmatic *Corpus Iuris Civilis*. In comparison with classical Roman law, Scots law derived from the *ius commune* has often been treated as unworthy of serious attention.

Teaching of civil law in the Scottish universities for the last thirty years has been an antiquarian science concerned with the study of a legal system which, albeit unsuited to the modern legal system in many respects, is nevertheless seen by its proponents as intrinsically superior to Scots law. Thus, when some of these lawyers do turn their attention to the "civilian" Scots law we can understand why they think so directly in terms of "Roman Law". This either engenders the modernising zeal which normally founds on English law; or, less often, it results in what I have called the third reception of Roman law.[17] This occurs when classical or Justinianic law is imported into modern Scots law at the expense of the developed civilian law derived from the *ius commune.* The third reception is fostered by the overwhelming concentration on the law of the *Corpus Iuris Civilis* in university education. Classical Roman law is admired and, since it is translated into plain English and commented upon in numerous fine textbooks, like that of Roby, it is accessible. By contrast, Scots law derived from the *ius commune* is not admired. It is to be found in the works of the institutional writers but they are in difficult English, and because they are rarely taught, they remain largely unknown. The decision of the House of Lords in *Cantiere* is an example of the third reception. A new example, just beginning, is the resurrection, partly on the authority of Roman law, of the *condictio ob turpem*

---

15   In *Cantiere, cit. sup.,* n.3.
16   See J. A. Dieckmann and R. Evans-Jones, "The Dark Side of *Connelly* v. *Simpson*", 1995 *J.R.* 90.
17   See n.5 above.

vel iniustam causam which the Scottish judiciary, quite rightly, has effectively killed.

The Scottish "civilian" culture is being squeezed at both ends by English and Roman law. Although the former is overwhelmingly the more powerful, these systems have in common the fact that they are regarded as superior and are known. Does it really matter? The modern history of the rule that payments in error of law are irrecoverable is a good illustration of the consequences. The rule, which arises in respect of *condictio indebiti* and was a feature of the law of Justinian, was never part of Scots law, as the institutional writers and early case law make perfectly clear. In the face of one, or was it two, *obiter dicta* of Lord Chanceller Brougham[18] the Scots abandoned their law, and, with the zeal of the converted, gave what they received a particular severity in *Glasgow Corporation* v. *Lord Advocate*.[19] Now English law has decided to abandon the error of law rule, so, with this imprimatur, Scots law wishes to revert to the position which it abandoned in the face of the formidable Lord Brougham.[20] On one level it is quite amusing but, on another, one loses respect for a legal system which has such a little sense of its own direction. It may be argued that Lord Brougham was seeking the most rational solution and had no desire to impose English law on Scotland. However, it is clear that his perception of what was best was entirely circumscribed by his own later training which led him to disregard an immensely longer tradition on the subject than that of English law. In short, lawyers, no doubt like others, have a pre-disposition to see as best what they know best.

Scottish private law was created on a base which was extensively civilian in character and thereafter it came under the formative influence of the English Common law. The result is now portrayed as the mixed hybrid which falls between the Civil and Common law worlds. However, when one views the effects of this Scottish cultural re-orientation, which gained particular strength at the beginning of the nineteenth century, one is struck by the fact that the Scottish mixed legal system is not a static entity. If things continue as they are, the present "mixed" character of Scots law represents a transitory stage of its development into a pure Common law jurisdiction heavily under the influence of English law. The development of Scots law in this direction suggests that social and political factors - power in a broad sense - has been the critical element weighing against the Scottish civilian tradition.[21]

And yet the idea that Scots law has developed in response to such social and political factors does not entirely conform to the traditional

---

18 *Wilson and McLellan* v. *Sinclair* (1830) 4 W. and S. 398 at 409; *Dixon* v. *Monkland Canal Co.* (1831) 5 W. and S. 445 at 452.
19 1959 S.C. 203; but cf. now *Morgan Guaranty Trust Co.* v. *Lothian Regional Council* 1995 S.L.T. 299.
20 Scottish Law Commission, *Recovery of Benefits*.
21 In this regard the observations of R. C. Van Caenegem, *An Historical Introduction to Private Law* (Cambridge, 1992), 180ff. are of interest.

image of the Scottish mixed jurisdiction. Eclecticism of outlook is always presented as the central characteristic of the Scots lawyer who, from a vantage point between the Civil and the Common law, is portrayed as choosing what is best from alternative approaches. The Scots lawyer is seen to be the master of comparative law who transcends earthly limitations like cultural orientation and training to produce the functional, elegant legal system of which he is so proud. The problem with this perception is that it simply is not true. Law is the product of culture and the quality of the law will always be informed by the quality of the culture. Since the appropriate cultural support for important parts of Scottish private law has been removed it comes as no surprise that, instead of the best of all worlds, Scots law now too often seems to end up with the worst.

If, especially within parts of the law of obligations, the interaction between the Civil and Common law has been so unfruitful, it may seem to give some legitimacy to those who are of the view that it would be better to dispose of all reminders of Scotland's civilian tradition as soon as possible. The alternative to such a vision of "progress" is to strive to build a culture which lends proper support to those parts of Scots law derived from the Civil law. Two reasons in particular may be identified why this is a preferable approach.

The civilian tradition is an international and European tradition. These are two characteristics which, due to the influence of the European Union, can increasingly be detected in the Scottish political and cultural outlook. An example of this new re-orientation is the ERASMUS scheme. At the university of Aberdeen approximately one fifth of the present yearly intake of Scottish students now spend up to a year of their studies at one of the universities of either Freiburg, Regensburg, Lyon, Grenoble, Brussels or Palermo. Most importantly, as a result of this development, instead of the LL.B. degree in Scots law, a number of students at Aberdeen are taking a new degree of LL.B. in which Scots law is combined with German, French or Belgian law. The LL.B. is also now offered with German, French or Spanish language. The civilian tradition was brought to Scotland by students studying on the European mainland and this tradition has re-commenced. In a quite new development European students are also coming to study in Scotland; in Aberdeen law faculty each year there are of the order of forty European students studying Scots law. Although the student exchanges have only been running for a short time there has already been a series of articles published by scholars from the university of Regensburg on Scots private law.[22] The signs are that the cultural, political,

---

22   J. Faber, "*Rückforderung wegen Zweckverfehlung - Irrungen und Wirrungen bei der Anwendung römischen Rechts in Schottland*", (1993) 1 *Z.Eu.P.* 279; J. E. du Plessis and H. Wicke "*Woolwich Equitable Building Society* v. *I.R.C.* and the *condictio indebiti* in Scots Law", 1993 S.L.T. (News) 303; J. A. Dieckmann and R. Evans-Jones, "The Dark Side of *Connelly* v. *Simpson*", 1995 *J.R.* 90.

and linguistic isolation of Scotland from Europe which undermined the former's civilian tradition may now be coming to an end. This year two Aberdeen students returning from a year's study in Regensburg drew the conclusion that the *Leistungskondiktion* has quite a lot in common with the Scottish *condictio indebiti*. That is an important observation! In future the manner in which Scotland approaches its civilian tradition, quite rightly, will lie in the hands of people like these. It depends to a large extent on what they make of the European experience.

A second factor that argues in favour of developing a healthy civilian legal culture in Scotland relates to the *"Qualitätsfrage"*; to the fact that the strengths of the mixed legal system, as presented by the classical image, really are well worth achieving. The Scottish legal system should indeed occupy a challenging position at the interface of the Civil and Common law where it will be well placed, when appropriate, to select what is best from each. Like all mixed systems, however, Scotland's is a small jurisdiction. A central and absorbing question presented to the Scots is this: how does such a system maintain its vigour and capacity for change without merely succumbing to the power of its neighbours? One should not question the continuing value of English law, or for that matter, on occasion, Roman law. For example, the English notion of "mistake" suggested for *condictio indebiti* raises the important point that there is no good reason why repetition should be limited to cases of error as to liability. In an uncodified system it is also possible, and sometimes helpful, to draw directly from Roman law. For instance, those who are interested in a contractual approach to the problems dealt with in *Cantiere* should note Stair's approval of Cujas on D.19.2.33.[23] I do not question the value of outside influence where it is appropriate but suggest that in its pursuit of what is best Scots law always needs to be able properly to evaluate what is offered by other legal systems against what it has already. For the health of its own traditions this means that Scotland arguably needs to maintain, not just one, but at least two distinct legal cultures of high quality. Since mixed legal systems are invariably small systems this poses a difficulty which has yet fully to be met in modern times.

The idea that the Scots should have a full command of that part of their own law which is derived from the Civil law, that this is a tradition which looks forward and not just back, and that the Scots can continue to derive great benefit from this tradition seems entirely self-evident, but these are propositions which have become clouded by distortion and prejudice. In such circumstances it can be a grave error to take the self-evident for granted. Especially in a small jurisdiction where the number of lawyers is small there is a responsibility on the Scottish "Civil" lawyer to address Scottish private law drawn from the civilian tradition. This book is an effort to do precisely that. It contains an

---

23   Stair, 1,14,7.

introductory section which shows how the civilian culture was brought to Scotland and why it declined, and a chapter which examines the nature of the mixed legal system from the perspective of South Africa, where a greater degree of equilibrium has been achieved than in Scotland between the influences of the Civil and the Common law. The main section of the book examines aspects of the Scottish civilian tradition falling mainly within the law of property and obligations but also including a contribution on the importance of the civilian legacy of "system" for Scots law and Scottish legal education. A central purpose of this main section is to show how the Civil law tradition can contribute to a better understanding and sounder development of modern Scots law. The book concludes with a bibliography compiled by Professor W. M. Gordon of writings on Civil law in Scotland. Roman law is the foundation of the civilian tradition but it is not the end. Similarly, this book seeks to be a new beginning and not to celebrate the end of the Civil law tradition in Scotland.

2. ROMAN LAW IN SCOTLAND

By WILLIAM M. GORDON

I Introduction

Scots law in the course of its history has had much closer contact with the European civilian tradition than has the English Common law but there have also been significant influences from the Common law. This essay explores the civilian influence but in the course of doing so it must also look at the effect which contact with the Common law has had, especially since 1707. As backgound to discussion of Roman influence on Scots law some brief account of the demarcation of the boundaries of what was the kingdom and is now the jurisdiction within which Scots law operates is desirable.[1]

The modern border between Scotland and England runs along a line from the river Solway on the west to the river Tweed on the east, excluding Berwick-upon-Tweed at the mouth of the Tweed which became an English possession finally in 1482. Modern Scotland includes, besides the mainland, the Western Isles and the northern islands of Orkney and Shetland. However, Scotland became a single kingdom only in the early eleventh century and the somewhat artificial boundary between Scotland and England[2] was drawn in the twelfth century, settling the disputed claims of the kings of Scotland to territory in northern England.

Little is known with certainty of the laws applied among the various peoples who were brought under a single rule in the eleventh century – the Picts, the Scots, the Britons and the Angles. The same may be said of the Scandinavian settlements in the north and south-west but Scandinavian influence clearly predominated in the northern and western

---

1   On the history of Scotland reference may be made e.g. to M. Lynch, *Scotland: A New History,* (2nd ed., London etc., 1992), the most modern single volume history, and for fuller treatments to the multi-volume *Edinburgh History of Scotland,* gen. ed. G. Donaldson. 4 vols. (Edinburgh, 1965–75) and *The New History of Scotland,* gen. ed. J. Wormald. 8 vols. (London, 1981–84, now being reissued by the Edinburgh University Press, with some volumes in revised editions). D. M. Walker offers a synthesis with particular emphasis on the law in *A Legal History of Scotland,* of which vols. 1 (The Beginnings to A.D. 1286), 2 (The Later Middle Ages), and 3 (The Sixteenth Century) (Edinburgh, 1988, 1990 and 1995) have appeared to date.

2   See the comment in H. Summerson, "The Early Development of the Laws of the Anglo-Scottish Marches, 1249–1449" in *Legal History in the Making,* edd. W. M. Gordon and T. D. Fergus (London and Rio Grande, 1991), 29–42 at 33.

islands which were brought within the Scottish kingdom at later dates – the thirteenth century in the case of the Western Isles and the fifteenth century in the case of Orkney and Shetland.[3] It would be reasonable to assume a diversity of law, customary or other, among them and there is some firm evidence of that diversity, and indeed of some continuity of diverse custom and law, in references to special customs of Galloway in the south-west,[4] to Celtic law in the Highlands and Western Isles[5] and to Scandinavian law in Orkney and Shetland.[6] But the scanty early sources of Scots law assume in general a common law for Scotland. They may give a misleading picture and the possibility that they do so must be kept in mind. Nevertheless the question what Roman influence there has been in Scots law has to be addressed in the light of what sources there are and these allow us to speak of "Scots law" even although there may be a suspicion that to do so imposes a uniformity which did not in fact exist and perhaps indeed reflects a later imposition of uniformity, of which imposition there is certainly some trace.[7]

Although the Romans penetrated into Scotland and for a period occupied the southern part of modern Scotland between Hadrian's Wall, running from the Solway to the Tyne, and the Antonine Wall, running from the Clyde to the Forth, there is no clear evidence that that occupation continued into the third century. It cannot, therefore, be stated with certainty that even southern Scotland was still part of the Roman empire when in A.D. 212 the Edict of Caracalla extended Roman citizenship to almost all inhabitants of the empire.[8] The Roman occupation of Scotland, such as it was, was limited and the Roman forces were withdrawn from the whole of Britain in the early fifth century. In these circumstances it seems unlikely that Roman occupation left any traces in the law even of southern Scotland. It has been stated confidently that

---

3   The Western Isles were brought in by treaty with Norway in 1266. Orkney and Shetland were pledged for the dowry of Margaret, daughter of Christian I of Denmark, who married James III of Scotland in 1468. They were forfeited to the Scottish crown in 1472 for non-payment of the dowry and redemption was never conceded.

4   See H. L. MacQueen, "The Laws of Galloway: a Preliminary Study" in *Galloway: Land and Lordship*, edd. R. D. Oram and G. P. Stell (Edinburgh, 1991), 131–43.

5   W. D. H. Sellar, "Celtic Law and Scots Law: Survival and Integration (The O'Donnell Lecture 1985)", (1989) 29 *Scottish Studies* 1–27.

6   W. J. Dobie, "Udal law" in *An Introductory Survey of the Sources and Literature of Scots Law*, (Publications of the Stair Society, 1, Edinburgh, 1936), 445–60.

7   See e.g. Statutes of Iona (Icolmkill) in 1609, recorded in the register of the Privy Council in 1610 – *R.P.C.*, 1st ser., ix (Edinburgh, 1889), 26–30.

8   On the Roman occupation of Scotland see e.g. P. Salway, *Roman Britain*, (Oxford, 1981); G. S. Maxwell, *The Romans in Scotland*, (Edinburgh, 1989).

it did not.[9] It is also very doubtful whether there was any influence, or any substantial influence, through contact with Rome by the peoples who came together to form the Scottish nation, even if in the present state of research it may be unwise to deny that possibility categorically.[10] Influence through the Roman church would come into the reckoning.

But whatever early traces may be found by further research it is safe to say that in so far as Scotland has and has had a share in the civilian tradition it has acquired that share essentially from later influence, initially through Canon law and then directly through contact with the Roman law taught in the universities. The Roman law which has helped to shape the development of modern Scots law is mainly, if not exclusively, Roman law as revived and understood by the Glossators and thereafter as understood by the successive schools of Roman lawyers who applied themselves to study and application of the texts which survived from antiquity. In Scotland, as elsewhere in Europe, the Roman law which influenced the native rules was not a fixed body of doctrine. What was known of Roman law and how what was known was understood and applied varied over the centuries. The authority given to it or the inspiration derived from it also varied at different periods. This is not always as clearly understood as it might be as "Roman law" tends to be equated simply with the rules embodied in the *Corpus Iuris Civilis* and to be thought of as ascertainable by consultation of the sources of the ancient Roman law or modern manuals thereof. These rarely consider the post-Justinianic developments of Roman doctrines. The richness and complexity of the Roman heritage is thereby and therefore underestimated.

II The Period up to the Sixteenth Century

There are not many traces of Roman law in the early material on Scots law. What traces there are seem to derive from the use of Canon law rather than from use of Roman law direct. This is true both of the occasional references in early collections of legal materials such as the Laws of the Four Burghs and the *Liber de iudicibus*[11] and the more extensive passages relating to Roman law in the treatise known as *Regiam*

---

9   J. Dove Wilson, "The Sources of the Law of Scotland", (1892) 4 *J.R.* 1–13 at 4; Walker, *Legal History, cit. sup.*, n.1, vol. 1, 5.

10   See T. G. Watkin, "Saints, Seaways and Dispute Settlements" in *Legal History in the Making, cit. sup.*, n.2, 1–9, esp. at 4–9.

11   Laws of the Four Burghs, c. 101 (*A.P.S.*, i,41; red pagination, 353) – *cum necessitas non habet legem* from the *Decretum*; *Liber de iudicibus*, cc. 36–44 with extracts from Ivo of Chartres, including *Inst.*, 2.1.12–16 on acquisition of wild animals. See Stein, *Ius Romanum Medii Aevi*, Pars V, 13b (Milan, 1968) reprinted as "Roman Law in Medieval Scotland" in *The Character and Influence of the Roman Civil Law. Historical Essays* (London and Ronceverte, 1988), 269–317 at 275ff.

Majestatem.[12] The latter have been shown by Stein to come from Goffredus de Trano's *Summa in titulos decretalium*, which was written between 1241 and 1246.[13] Such records of litigation and other documents as survive from the thirteenth century and contain references to Roman law show the same connection, although it has to be said that this may reflect their provenance which is commonly the records of the Church. Where the Church was involved, skilled lawyers were available, although they would have been trained abroad, because there was no Scottish university until the foundation of St. Andrews in 1413. These lawyers used their learning in court actions and arbitrations and the procedure of the church courts was the Romano-canonical procedure found in church courts generally, at least from the twelfth century. Thus in 1233 judges-delegate hearing a dispute between Paisley Abbey and one Gilbert of Renfrew decided the case on the advice of men skilled both in Canon and Civil law[14] and in 1288 there is recorded the cautionary tale of Adam Urry a cleric of the diocese of Glasgow who had learned the Civil law. He, it is said, cared more for the court of riches than the cure of souls but repented on his deathbed and damned thoroughly the lawyers' court.[15] The tale implies that Roman law, or at least the skills learned from the study of Roman law, were useful in the secular courts as well as the church courts. A spectacular example of reference to Roman law in a thirteenth century legal dispute is the reference to Paris lawyers for advice in the Great Cause of Scotland, the dispute over the succession to the Scottish crown after the death of the Maid of Norway in 1290, which was settled by Edward I of England, although it does not appear that Roman law was actually applied.[16]

Documents drawn by notaries, who are found in Scotland from the thirteenth century, also show both a connection with the church and a knowledge of Canon and Roman law. About half the notaries identified

---

12   *A.P.S.,* i, 597 ff. (red pagination); also edited and translated with an introduction and notes by Lord Cooper, using a text based on Skene's edition, in *Regiam Majestatem and Quoniam Attachiamenta,* (Publications of the Stair Society, 11, Edinburgh, 1947). The relevant passages are 1.29–2.7 and 2.10–12 (*A.P.S.,* i, 605–8) and in Cooper's edition 1.28–2.10 and 2.13–15. See Stein, *Historical Essays, cit. sup.,* n.11, 280ff.
13   P. G. Stein, (1969) 48 *Scot. Hist. Rev.* 107–23.
14   *Register of Paisley Abbey* (Publications of the Maitland Club, 17, Edinburgh, 1832 and of the New Club, 1, Paisley, 1877), 159; also in *A.P.S.,* i, 97.
15   *Chronicon de Lanercost* (Publications of the Bannatyne Club, 65 and the Maitland Club, 46, Edinburgh, 1839), 124 under the year 1288; Stein, *Historical Essays, cit. sup.,* n.11, 293–94.
16   E. L. G. Stones and G. G. Simpson, *Edward I and the Throne of Scotland: an Edition of the Record Sources for the Great Cause* (Oxford, 1977–78); Stein, *Historical Essays,* 294ff.

are Papal notaries, the others being imperial notaries.[17] As part of their training they picked up some knowledge of Roman law and early Scottish documents, like documents from elsewhere in Europe in this period prepared by notaries, show the practice of renouncing rights, privileges and defences which might be available under Roman law.[18] Whether there was any real risk that Roman law might be appealed to is unclear but notarial documents prepared by a papal notary could be used as a basis of a claim to jurisdiction by the church courts and so the renunciations were not necessarily a mere show of learning. From this evidence it is clear that by the end of the thirteenth century Roman law was being used, sometimes perhaps directly but more often indirectly as a source of ideas. In the church courts it was used as subsidiary authority where it did not conflict with Canon law.

The evidence of use of Roman law continues throughout the fourteenth century and there is greater evidence of its use in the secular courts as well as in the church courts in addition to the evidence of its use derived, for example, from documents. To some extent the increase in the evidence available may simply result from the survival of a greater quantity of material. There is no magic in 1301 as the start of a new era but it is a fact that more evidence survives as we come closer to the present day. One example is the increase in the number of notaries who can be identified in the fourteenth century, thirty-five as against five so far for the earlier period.[19] No doubt more notaries can be identified simply because we have more notarised documents. On the other hand there is some evidence that there actually were more notaries acting because a diocesan system of admission of papal notaries is found operated by the bishops, acting under delegated powers. This indicates that there was a greater need for control of admission arising from greater numbers seeking admission. As well as a greater quantity of evidence there is an indication that Roman law was being used in a sophisticated way implying a sure grasp of it rather than its use as a show of learning. This indication comes from two cases,

---

17   J. Durkan, "The Early Scottish Notary" in *The Renaissance and Reformation in Scotland. Essays in Honour of Gordon Donaldson*, edd. I. B. Cowan and D. Shaw (Edinburgh, 1983), 22–40.

18   *Liber Sancte Marie de Melros.* 2 vols. (Publications of the Bannatyne Club, 56, Edinburgh, 1837), vol. 1, 288, No. 327, a composition between the Knights of St. John of Torphichen and Reginald Cheyne and his wife Eustachia, to be dated after 1272/3 - D. B. Smith, "A Note on Roman Law in Scotland", (1921) 18 *Scot. Hist. Rev.* 66–68. The composition contains renunciations of *restitutio in integrum* and the *condictiones ex lege, sine causa* and *ex iniusta causa* and, on the part of Eustachia, of the benefit of the *S.C. Vellaeanum* and the *lex Julia de fundo dotali*. See also *Liber Sancte Marie de Calchou.* 2 vols. (Publications of the Bannatyne Club, 82, Edinburgh, 1846), vol. 1, 181, No. 223, dated 1287, an agreement between Kelso Abbey and the Knights Templar, and Stein, *Historical Essays, cit. sup.*, n.11, 293–94.

19   Durkan, *loc. cit.*, n.17.

Abbey of Lindores v. *Earl of Douglas* recorded in the cartulary of the abbey[20] and *Bishop of Aberdeen* v. *Crab* recorded in the register of the diocese of Aberdeen.[21]

In the former case the abbey had been summoned to appear before the court of the earl to do homage for lands which he claimed that the abbey held from him. The abbey appeared but disclaimed him as superior and took the case to the king's court on the basis that the land was held of the king and not of the earl having been excepted from the grant on which the earl relied. Both Roman law and Canon law were cited in the elaborate arguments presented for the abbey, with Azo and Pierre de Belleperche among the civilian authorities quoted. In the latter case a charter granted to Crab and his wife by a former bishop was challenged by the bishop in a court held by him as feudal superior of the disputed lands requiring his vassals to show that they had good title.[22] The decision of the bishop that the charter had not been validly granted was challenged in the court of the sheriff on the basis that the bishop had been judge in his own cause. Again an elaborate argument relying on both Roman and Canon law was presented and although it may be that the arguments in both cases were prepared by the same man, William de Spynie, a clerical lawyer who died as bishop of Moray in 1406,[23] the fact that such arguments could be presented in secular courts suggests that expertise in Roman law was not confined to clerics and the church courts. Other evidence that the king had access to lawyers knowledgeable in Roman law is found in an account of a dispute between David II and the earl of Ross whom the king confounded by citing civilian authorities.[24]

In the fourteenth century we also have more definite evidence of how a knowledge of Roman law was obtained in that the careers of Scots who went to continental universities to study can be traced.[25] William de Spynie was one of them, having studied arts and Canon law in Paris and Roman law elsewhere, perhaps in Avignon.[26] Those who studied law predominantly studied Canon law[27] and in so doing would acquire some knowledge of Roman law but some made more advanced study of Roman law. The most favoured universities were Orléans,

---

20   *Cartulary of the Abbey of Lindores* (Publications of the Scot. Hist. Soc., 1st ser., 42, Edinburgh, 1903), No. CXLIX (200-12) and Appendix V (314-25).
21   *Registrum Episcopatus Aberdonensis* 2 vols. (Publications of the Maitland Club, 63 and the Spalding Club, 13 and 14, Edinburgh, 1845), vol. 1, 143-55. See on both cases Stein, *Historical Essays, cit. sup.* n.11, 299-305.
22   R. M. Graham, "Showing the Holding", 1957 *J.R.* 251-69.
23   Stein, *Historical Essays*, 305.
24   Lord Saltoun, *The Frasers of Philorth* 2 vols. (Edinburgh, 1879), vol. 2, Appendix, charter no. 12; Stein, *Historical Essays*, 298.
25   D. E. R. Watt, *A Biographical Dictionary of Scots Graduates to 1410* (Oxford, 1977).
26   *Ibid.*, s.v. Spyny, William de, 503-6.
27   Stein, *Historical Essays, cit. sup.*, n.11, 327, referring to information given to him by D. E. R. Watt.

where there was a Scottish nation from the early fourteenth century,[28] Paris and Avignon. The preference for French universities is easily explained by the close ties between Scotland and France through the "Auld Alliance". The Scots also supported the Avignon papacy during the Great Schism. If the *Regiam Majestatem* is correctly dated to the early fourteenth century we have evidence of some use of Roman law in a treatise on Scots law, albeit through Canon law, and it is clear that there is still a close connection between Roman and Canon law in the fourteenth century. What is difficult to assess, given the fragmentary nature of our evidence, is the extent to which Roman law competed with native authority in the secular courts.

When we enter the fifteenth century we are better supplied with legal source materials and have a still wider range of evidence of the use of Roman law, including knowledge of the content of cathedral libraries. One of the important indications of the value of Roman and Canon law in legal practice is the foundation of universities which had as one of their specific aims the provision of legal education. The earliest was St Andrews founded in 1413 by the efforts of Bishop Wardlaw who had studied Roman and Canon law at Orléans and Avignon. The bull of foundation provided for the teaching of both Civil and Canon law but only the teaching of Canon law seems to have begun.[29] In 1432 the university petitioned Pope Eugenius IV for a dispensation for beneficed clergymen to study both laws to help the provision of legal expertise in the secular courts, alleging that few took up the study of Civil law.[30] The university of Glasgow was founded some forty years later in 1451 through the efforts of Bishop Turnbull who had studied at Louvain and Pavia. There is some evidence of the teaching of both Civil and Canon law in the 1450s although it is not clear how long it continued.[31] However long it did continue the foundation is significant as is the third foundation of the fifteenth century, the university of Aberdeen.

---

28 J. Kirkpatrick, "The Scottish Nation in the University of Orléans 1336-1538", in *Second Miscellany of the Scottish History Society* (Publications of the Scottish History Society, 1st ser., 44, Edinburgh, 1904), 47-102; T. B. Smith, "The Influence of the 'Auld Alliance' with France on the Law of Scotland" in *Studies Critical and Comparative* (Edinburgh, 1962), 28-45.

29 *Acta Facultatis Artium 1413-1588*, ed. A. I. Dunlop (Publications of the Scottish History Society, 3rd ser., 54-55, Edinburgh, 1964), cli ff.

30 *Ibid.*, cliii; *The Saint Andrews Formulare, 1514-1546*, edd. G. Donaldson and C. Macrae. 2 vols. (Publications of the Stair Society, 7 and 9, Edinburgh, 1942 and 1944), vol. 2, 310, No. 525 gives a style for a licentiate in Civil law, dating from the early sixteenth century.

31 *Munimenta Universitatis Glasguensis.* 4 vols. (Publications of the Maitland Club, 72, Glasgow, 1854), vol. 2, 67. There was no provision for the teaching of law in the *Nova Erectio* of 1577 when new provision was made for teaching after a period of decline - J. Durkan and J. Kirk, *The University of Glasgow 1451-1577* (Glasgow, 1977), 328 and 331.

The man responsible for the creation of a university in Aberdeen is Bishop Elphinstone who studied arts in Glasgow and began teaching Canon law there and who then studied Canon law in Paris and Civil law at Orléans . He became bishop of Aberdeen in 1483 and chancellor of Scotland in 1488 and obtained the bull of foundation of a university in Old Aberdeen in 1495. The bull again made provision for the teaching both of Canon and Civil law but it made more adequate arrangements for payment of the professors than was made in the earlier foundations and it contained from the start a dispensation for clerics to study Civil law. The university did not in fact operate until the beginning of the sixteenth century but the foundation recognised that a need for it already existed in the fifteenth.[32]

Important as the foundation of the three oldest Scottish universities is as an indication of the relevance of Roman and Canon law to practice in the Scottish courts, it is not clear that they contributed many law graduates or trained lawyers for those courts. It appears that study abroad was still found attractive whether for its own sake or because the Church was an international institution and those whose first choice was Canon law might have better hope of advancement if they had attended continental universities many of which were longer established and better endowed.[33] Many Scots students went to Cologne and, after its foundation in 1425, to Louvain.[34] Some went to Italy[35] but France was less popular in the fifteenth century because Paris was occupied by the English and the French took a different view of papal politics. Orléans still had its attraction and Bishop Elphinstone, who had studied there, prescribed the Orléans course in Civil law for Aberdeen.[36] What is clear is that there was legally trained manpower in Scotland even if the training was not done as often in Scottish universities as had been hoped. The contents of cathedral libraries are evidence of the availability of Canon and Roman law literature.[37]

---

32 L. J. Macfarlane, *William Elphinstone and the Kingdom of Scotland 1431–1514: The Struggle for Order* (Aberdeen, 1985), esp. ch. 1 on Elphinstone's education and ch. 7 on the foundation of the university. Lectures delivered by William Hay in 1533 have survived and were published by the Stair Society – *William Hay's Lectures on Marriage*, ed. J. C. Barry (Publications of the Stair Society, 24, Edinburgh, 1967).

33 A. I. Dunlop, *Scots Abroad in the Fifteenth Century*, Historical Association Pamphlet No. 124 (London, 1942), 13–19.

34 J. H. Baxter, "Scottish Students at Louvain University", (1928) 25 *Scot. Hist. Rev.* 327–34.

35 R. J. Mitchell, "Scottish Law Students in Italy in the Later Middle Ages", (1937) 49 *J.R.* 19–24.

36 Macfarlane, *William Elphinstone, op. cit.*, n.32, 345.

37 A list of books in Aberdeen in 1436 in the *Registrum Episcopatus Aberdonensis, op. cit.*, n.21, vol. 2, 127 at 129–32 names fifty-eight books on Canon law and at 132 nine on Civil law with seven not found and at 133–34 missing volumes of Canon and Civil law, three of the Canon law and one of the Civil law books being noted as found; a list of those in Glasgow made in 1432, *Registrum Episcopatus Glasguensis* 2 vols. (Publications of the

Lawyers in the fifteenth century continued to serve the Church in its courts and administration and the Church regularly supplied literate members of the secular administration but there is fuller evidence of the effects of Roman law on the secular law also. In addition, in conveyancing practice there is evidence of the existence of skilled lawyers not operating entirely in the sphere of the Church, although it is true that the Church was a great landholder and may well have helped to supply the expertise which is evidenced. For example, there is a great increase in the number of notaries known in the period 1400–1600 – at the very least 1500 altogether.[38] The Act 1424 c.45 (*A.P.S.* ii, 8, c.24), the earliest Scottish statute on legal aid for the poor, requires judges to find "lele and wyse" advocates to plead the causes of those unable to pay the normal fees and implies the existence of lawyers in the secular courts as well as in the church courts. The Education Act of 1496, the Act 1494 c.53 in Glendook's quarto edition, (*A.P.S.* ii, 238, c.3), the inspiration for the passing of which is attributed to William Elphinstone, the founder of Aberdeen University, requires substantial freeholders to send their sons to the grammar schools to learn Latin perfectly and then to send them for three years to the schools of arts and law. The stated purpose is that they may have knowledge and understanding of the laws and so be better prepared to do justice in the courts which they hold. The consequence hoped for is that this will relieve the central courts from concerning themselves with "ilk small Iniure". This indicates that the Roman and Canon law which would be learned in the universities was seen as being of value in the secular courts also.

From the fifteenth century come the first surviving originals of the records of the Scottish parliament and the King's council. The extant series of parliamentary records dates from 1466 and the extant council records from 1478.[39] From these, and from such evidence as we have of

---

Bannatyne Club, 75 and the Maitland Club, 61, Edinburgh, 1843), vol. 2, 335 at 335 names three Civil law books and three Canon law ones and at 338 a further five Civil law (all the *Corpus Iuris*) and seven Canon law.

38   This figure, based on his unpublished researches, was given to me by Professor R. Lyall of Glasgow University. I am grateful for his permission to quote it; see also J. J. Robertson, "The Development of the Law" in *Scottish Society in the Fifteenth Century*, ed. J. M. Brown (London, 1977), 136–52.

39   Lord Thankerton, "The Statutory Law", in *Sources and Literature, cit. sup.*, n.6, 1–15 at 5; The *Parliaments of Scotland. Burgh and Shire Commissioners*, ed. M. D. Young. 2 vols. (Edinburgh, 1992 and 1993), Introduction; R. K. Hannay, "Early Records of Council and Session, 1466–1659" in *Sources and Literature*, 16–24; the parliamentary record as then known is published in *A.P.S.*; the records of Council have been published up to 1503 in *The Acts of the Lords of Council in Civil Causes*, edd. T. Thomson and others (Edinburgh, 1839 and 1918–) [*A.D.C.*, i to iii], now 3 vols., the last in 1993 with an introduction by A. L. Murray, clarifying the original arrangement of the records before T. Thomson's editorial interventions. There is a rather less satisfactory version of the Council record from 1501–1503 in the Publications of the Stair Society, 8, (Edinburgh, 1943).

the activity of parliament and council from sources other than the official records before these dates, we have some indication of what at least seems to be evidence of the use of Roman law in contexts not involving the Church. Examples of statutes are the Tutors Act of 1474 (the Act 1474 c.51; *A.P.S.* ii, 106–7, c.6) providing that the tutor to a pupil child shall be the nearest agnate (relative through a male) aged twenty-five and possibly the Prescription Act of the same year (the Act 1474 c.54; *A.P.S.* ii, 107, c.9) introducing a forty year prescription. There is express reference to the Civil and Canon law as authorising the revocation of acts done to their prejudice by those "constitute in youtheid and tender age" in the Act of 1493 setting aside acts done to the prejudice of the Crown during the minority of James IV (*A.P.S.* ii, 236, c.22); there are less clear allusions to these laws in the similar laws passed by James III's parliament in 1464 in relation to acts done during the minority of James II (*A.P.S.* ii, 84). The Liferent Caution Act of 1491 (the Act 1491 c.25; *A.P.S.* ii, 224–25, c.6) providing for security against waste or destruction of lands held in ward or under a liferent right seems to be inspired by the *cautio usufructuaria* of Roman law.

In the conduct of judicial business in council and parliament the procedure used appears to be derived from the Romano-canonical procedure of the church courts.[40] Certainly it closely resembles that procedure, with the defender required to appear by a summons stating the basis of the claim made by the pursuer against him, the defender appearing either personally or by a procurator, allegations and reasons being propounded by the parties to the court and the decision taking the form of a decreet issued by the court which had heard the case. Roman ideas appear in the record, sometimes in Scots dress, as on 13 March 1482/83 where an obligation is challenged as having been made "be force and dreid", i.e. *vi ac metu*.[41] The records do not disclose, and given their nature and purpose, could not be expected to disclose, a high proportion of decisions based on legal as opposed to factual issues or to reveal much direct evidence of the use of Roman law where a legal issue did arise. They do provide clear evidence of a sophisticated treatment of the issues to be dealt with. Careful provision is made for the trial of any issues of fact and for discussion of points of law by men who were certainly aware of the possibility of the use of Roman law.[42] In short, it is clear that by the end of the fifteenth century at least, and probably long before, Scots law was a legal system mature enough to be able to take advantage of the

---

40 *A.D.C.*, *passim*. H. L. MacQueen, "Pleadable Brieves, Pleading and the Development of Scots Law", (1986) 4 *Law and Hist. Rev.* 403–22 is more cautious and suggests (at 420–22) that the direct influence may have come from England.

41 *A.D.C.*, ii, CX, 13 March 1482/3.

42 See W. M. Gordon, "The Acts of the Scottish Lords of Council in the Late Fifteenth and Early Sixteenth Centuries – Records and Reports" in *Proceedings of the 11th British Legal History Conference*, July 1993, forthcoming.

learned laws for its development, at least in respect of cases dealt with in the courts of highest instance. It was also a system operated by men who were willing and able to take advantage of these laws.

III   The Sixteenth and Seventeenth Centuries

The evidence from the sixteenth century then confirms the picture emerging from what we know of earlier development. Roman law and Canon law are established as subordinate persuasive authorities in the secular courts and Canon law is being applied in the Church courts as authority binding on these courts. The binding authority of Canon law ended with the Reformation when Papal authority was rejected in 1560[43] but where Canon law was already accepted as part of Scots law it continued to be applied in courts dealing with matters, such as status, which had been regulated by Canon law before the Reformation, in so far as Canon law did not conflict with Reformed doctrine. Canon law could also be referred to on questions not already settled but technically it was now only of persuasive authority.[44]

The creation of the College of Justice in 1532 by legislation confirmed in 1541[45] both settled the jurisdiction exercised by the king's council as a central court and indirectly led to its extension.[46] Exercise of its jurisdiction increasingly influenced the direction taken by the law where direction was given to it by decisions of the courts rather than by legislative act. The judges in the College of Justice, the Senators of the College, or Lords of Council and Session as they were known, formed what was called the Session and may somewhat anachronistically be called the Court of Session.[47] They commonly had resort to Roman law to assist them in the decision of the legal questions which came before them. This is sometimes presented as a new development or the impression is given that there was a major change in 1532 (or 1541) but, although it must be accepted that the foundation of the

---

43   *A.P.S.*, ii, 534–35, c.2; confirmed after the deposition of Mary in 1567 by the Act 1567 c. 2 (*A.P.S.*, iii, 14, c.3 and *A.P.S.*, iii, 36).

44   See Craig, 1,2,24; Stair, 1,1,14 and 16.

45   The Act 1537 cc.36–41 (in Glendook's quarto edition) (*A.P.S.*, ii, 335–36, cc.1–2); the Act 1540 c.93 (*A.P.S.*, ii, 371, c.10).

46   A. L. Murray, "Sinclair's Practicks" in *Law Making and Law Makers in British History. Papers presented to the Edinburgh Legal History Conference, 1977*, ed. A. Harding (Royal Historical Society Studies in History Series, 22, London, 1980), 90–104 at 98–100; H. L. MacQueen, "Jurisdiction in Heritage and the Lords of Council and Session after 1532" in *Miscellany II*, ed. D. Sellar (Publications of the Stair Society, 35, Edinburgh, 1984), 61–85; *Common Law and Feudal Society in Medieval Scotland* (Edinburgh, 1993), ch. 8.

47   H. L. MacQueen, "Stair's Later Reputation as a Jurist: the Contribution of William Forbes" in *Miscellany III*, ed. W. M. Gordon (Publications of the Stair Society, 39, Edinburgh, 1992), 173–94 at 186 n.26. The term "Court of Session" comes into common use only in the eighteenth century.

College was significant, neither the reorganisation nor the use of
Roman law represented a complete innovation. The use of Roman law
in particular, as has been seen, was the continuation of an older tradition.

In the sixteenth century the records of the Council become differentiated. The series of acts of council continues until 1559; in the records
the name was changed from *Acta Dominorum Concilii* to *Acta
Dominorum Concilii et Sessionis* as from 1532 by the nineteenth century
Keeper of the Records, Thomas Thomson, but there is no contemporary
warrant for the change.[48] A new series of Acts and Decreets starts from
1542 and records the decrees of the Court of Session; the Books of
Sederunt recording the sederunts of the court, acts of sederunt regulating procedure, and the admission of judges to the bench and advocates to
practice before the court, start from 1553; a register of deeds for preservation and execution – a deed could and can be recorded to maintain an
official record of its terms and to obtain warrant to enforce an obligation
contained in it – starts from 1554 and is referred to as the Books of
Council and Session. A new register of the activities of the Council as the
royal privy council dealing with public affairs, including the supervision
of the administration of justice in other courts, begins from 1545.[49]

Publication of these records, other than the records of the privy
council dealing with public affairs, which are printed up to 1691, is not
far advanced. Nor is exploration of the records to help elucidate the
development of the law, except on particular points,[50] but cases dealing
with what were regarded, or appear to have been regarded, as questions of importance were recorded in collections described as
"practicks". Some of these contain decisions only and are hence
referred to as "decision practicks"; others are more of the nature of
handbooks containing references to decisions and other authorities
and are referred to as "digest practicks".[51] It is not altogether clear
whether the collections of decisions which have survived were made
for the private purposes of the collector or to help inform the court of
the course of past decisions. If they circulated they circulated in
manuscript and although the extant collections give an almost continu-
ous record of decisions from 1540 onwards, which is available in the
surviving manuscripts, few have been printed.[52] None of the decision

48   A. L. Murray, *A.D.C.* iii, Introduction.
49   R. K. Hannay, "Early Records of Council and Session, 1466-1659" in *Sources
     and Literature, cit. sup.,* n.6, 16-23.
50   E.g. H .L. MacQueen, "Jurisdiction in Heritage", *cit. sup.,* n.46.
51   H. McKechnie, "Practicks" in *Sources and Literature, cit. sup.,* n.6, 25-41.
52   Two collections of digest practicks have been published or, in the case of
     Balfour, republished by the Stair Society – Hope's *Major Practicks
     1608-1633*, ed. J. Avon Clyde. 2 vols. (Publications of the Stair Society, 3
     and 4, Edinburgh, 1937 and 1938); *The Practicks of Sir James Balfour of
     Pittendreich*, ed. P. G. B. McNeill. 2 vols. (Publications of the Stair Society,
     21 and 22, Edinburgh, 1962 and 1963). The text of Balfour's *Practicks* is
     reproduced from the edition published in 1754.

practicks are among these although work is being done on them.[53] Like the original records the practicks would repay more detailed examination than they have been given hitherto but the studies which have been made of them,[54] and even unsystematic examination of those which have been printed,[55] provides increasing evidence of familiarity with and application of Roman law or of ideas derived from Roman law. The evidence of the records thus supports the remark of John Lesley (1527–96), a Lord of Session from 1564, that Roman law was turned to whenever there was a difficult case on which there was no native authority.[56]

---

53   A. L. Murray has published a study of the earliest decision practicks, Sinclair's *Practicks,* in the article cited in n.46 above. An edition of Maitland's *Practicks* is being prepared by R. Sutherland.

54   See, e.g., A. L. Murray, in the study of Sinclair's *Practicks* cited above, at pp. 103–4:

> Some written pleadings of 1503 refer to the *Institutes* and *Codex* and to the commentaries of Nicholas de Tudeschis, John de Ferrariis and Johannes Andreae. From Sinclair's *Practicks* it appears that citation of such authorities must have been the common currency of those who pleaded before the lords of council.

> Sinclair's citations of legal authorities, which were in the usual highly abbreviated form, have suffered more than the rest of his text from careless and uninformed copyists. However, it is possible to identify numerous references to Civil and Canon law texts. He also cites from a range of jurists, Panormitanus, Bartolus, Jason de Mayno, Johannes Andreae and even the relatively obscure Johannes Monachus.

> Some of the cases cited to illustrate these points are printed in Morison's *Dictionary,* e.g. *Keir* v. *Marjoribanks* (1546) Mor. 5036; *Kirkcaldy* v. *Pitcairn* (1542) Mor. 9367. In a case in 1548 it is argued that "an omitted case remains at the disposal of the common law" meaning by "common law" the Civil and Canon law, the *ius commune* – Murray, *op. cit.,* at 101–2.

55   See e.g. in Balfour's *Practicks,* vol. 1, 198 the case of *Balfour* v. *Pitcairne* decided in 1540 where it was held that goods deposited which had been stolen along with the depositee's own property need not be restored to the depositor "*quia neque dolum neque lata culpa commisit et depositarius solum tenetur de dolo et lata culpa*" (because he committed neither fraud nor serious fault and the depositee is liable for fraud and serious fault); Hope's *Major Practicks,* II.9.2 : "the wed [i.e. the pledge] being stolln or reft or lost be any violent chance without the keeper's negligence, *cui resisti non potuit,* the creditor is not oblidged to the restitution thereof, and yet hes good action for his debt".

56   *De origine moribus et rebus gestis Scotorum* (Rome, 1576) at 71 and (Rome, 1578) at 76: "*nos ita lege municipali teneri ut si causa multis controversiis implicata quod saepe fit incidat quae legibus nostratibus non possit dirimi statim quicquid ad hanc controversiam decidendam necessariam censetur ex civilibus Romanorum legibus promatur*". Cf. also the Scots version by Dalrymple in the Publications of the Scottish Text Society, 1 (Edinburgh, 1888) at 120, quoted by Stein, *I.R.M.A.E.* V, 13b, 49 [= *Historical Essays, cit. sup.,* n.11, 315] in the Latin and in "The Influence of Roman Law on the Law of Scotland", 1963 *J.R.* 205–45 at 216 [= *Historical Essays,* 319–59 at 330] in the Scots.

By the beginning of the seventeenth century we have the start of what can properly be described as a literature of Scots law and this also testifies to familiarity with and use of Roman law. The first substantial treatise on Scots law is Craig's *Jus feudale* which was finished around 1606,[57] although first printed in 1655. As the title indicates, Craig's main concern is the feudal law and hence he deals primarily with land law. But, in the first place, his work shows some evidence of the influence of Roman law in its structure (and, of course, the *Books of the Feus* were part of the medieval *Corpus Iuris Civilis* and were still included in editions in Craig's day). In the second place, Craig explicitly discusses the place of Roman law among the sources of Scots law and its authority in Scotland and, in the third place, there is ample evidence throughout the *Jus feudale* of the use of Roman law and of writers on Roman law, past and contemporary, to assist with the treatment of Scots law, especially on general points.

So far as structure is concerned Craig begins with titles on the origin of law and appears to have had at least some regard to the institutional scheme of persons, things and actions, although the *Books of the Feus* probably also exercised some influence on his presentation. In his discussions of the use of Roman law in Scotland Craig, in the second and eighth chapters of his first book, refers to the wide use made of Roman law in western Europe and says that where no answer to a legal problem is to be found in Scottish legislation or judicial decisions or the feudal law recourse is had to Roman law (and to Canon law, which is preferred in case of conflict with Roman law).[58] Examples which

---

57 J. W. Cairns, T. D. Fergus and H. L. MacQueen, "Legal Humanism in Renaissance Scotland", (1990) 11 *Jour. Leg. Hist.* 40–69 at 49 (also in *Humanism in Renaissance Scotland*, ed. J. MacQueen (Edinburgh, 1990)); J. W. Cairns, "The *breve testatum* and Craig's *Jus feudale*", (1988) 56 *T.v.R.* 311–32 at 317.

58 Craig, 1,8,17:

> *Si neque ex actis Parliamentorum, neque consuetudine judiciali, neque jure Feudali, quid sit faciendum in quavis quaestione occurrat, ad jus Civile recurrendum est. Nam jus Civile hominum societatem respicit, & quomodo in repub. seu communi societate civium ex aequo & bono res adminstretur, docet: cujus juris maximus usus & omnibus seculis & apud omnes gentes fuit. Et licet singulae gentes formulas suas judiciorum usurparint, tamen hoc jus Civile omnibus negotiis & circa res omnes ita diffunditur, ut nulla fere quaestio, nulla facti species occurrat, in qua ejus singularis usus non sit manifestus. Et in foro nostro si quid arduum, si quid difficile interveniat, ex jure Civili ejus solutio petenda est: si tamen in aliquibus per jus Canonicum sive Pontificium sit innovatum (& sunt qui ea omnia colligerunt in quibus jus Canonicum a Civili dissentit), in eis jus Pontificium a nostris praefertur, praecipue ubi Ecclesiae administratio, vel scandalum (ut Canonistae loquuntur) ubi animae periculum versatur*

and cf. 1,2,14 where he specifies the areas in which Roman law is particularly used as:

show Craig's familiarity with Roman law, which he had perhaps learned in Paris, and his knowledge of current views on questions of Roman and feudal law are to be found in his discussion of what objects can be granted in feu,[59] of the effect of the wrong designation of the granter of a feu charter[60] and of the question whether the right of a feudal vassal is a kind of *dominium* or merely a usufruct, as held by Cujas.[61] Craig, therefore, is using Roman law in much the same way as the judges were using it in the sixteenth century.

What we find in Craig is, if anything, even more clear in the later institutional writers until Bell and Hume who were writing at the end of the eighteenth century and the beginning of the nineteenth when the influence of the English Common law becomes more evident. For the institutional writers Roman law is a guide and an inspiration but it is not necessarily to be followed at all or in detail. It is also to be noted that from the seventeenth century onwards Roman law in Scotland, as elsewhere, had to compete with rational natural law as a model and Roman rules might be referred to and relied on not simply because they were Roman but because they were seen as "natural". Conversely Roman rules might be rejected as not being in conformity with natural law even if there was no conflicting native authority to rely on where previously, in such circumstances, it would have been normal and natural in another sense to turn to Roman law for guidance. In other words natural law provided an alternative source of general authority at a time when, not only in Scotland, but throughout Europe writers were seeking to present accounts of their own systems breaking away from the *ius commune* and were encouraged to give greater emphasis to native

---

> *in rerum praecipue mobilium administratione, licet judiciorum proprias & peculiares formas unaquaeque gens usurpaverit. Et nos etiam nostris formis actionum non omnino a jure Civili abhorrentibus utimur, tamen in pactis, transactionibus, restitutionibus in integrum, arbitriis, sive (ut hodie loquimur) arbitramentis, servitutibus, contractibus tam bonae fidei quam stricti juris, tam non nominatis, quam nominatis, evictionibus, pignoribus, tutelis, legatis, actionibus, exceptionibus, obligationibus, denique in delictis puniendis, jus Civile sequendum omnino proponimus: et ut vere dicam, in rebus omnibus nostris, & circa omnes res, hoc jus Civile ita diffunditur, ut nulla fere quaestio, nulli facti species occurrat, in quo ejus vis & usus singularis non appareat manifeste: in foro sive judiciis, quoties quid arduum occurrit, ejus solutio inde est petenda.*

Craig's *Jus feudale* was translated, along with the *Libri feudorum* in Cujas's recension, by J. Avon Clyde and published in two volumes, (Edinburgh, 1934). The translation is a free one and needs to be compared with the Latin.

59 1,15.

60 2,3,14.

61 1,9,10ff.; see also Cairns, *et al*, n.57 above, at 48–49 and Cairns, "Craig, Cujas and the Definition of *feudum*: is a Feu a Usufruct?" in *New Perspectives in the Roman Law of Property*, ed. P. B. H. Birks (Oxford, 1989), 75–84.

sources by the approach of the Humanists in the sixteenth century to
Roman law.[62] The Humanists saw Roman law itself as a historical system
which was not necessarily applicable in the different circumstances of
their own times.[63]

In Stair, the earliest of the Scottish institutional writers to give a
conspectus of the whole of the private law, both the use of Roman law
as a source of ideas and as persuasive authority and the competition
between Roman and natural law can be seen. Indeed, close reading of
Stair's text shows that even where he might appear at first sight to be
relying on Roman law he is in fact testing it against natural law.[64] He is
critical of the arrangement of treatises on Civil, in the sense of Roman,
law[65] and even of the clearer institutional order of persons, things and
actions,[66] although he makes a concession towards that order in his
second edition of 1693 by arranging his work in four books, with the
last devoted to actions.[67] Stair is also quite clear that Roman law is not
used as binding authority in Scotland[68] although he himself makes

---

62   See O. F. Robinson, T. D. Fergus and W. M. Gordon, *European Legal
     History. Sources and Institutions* (2nd ed., London etc., 1994), para. 14.2.2;
     K. Luig, "The Institutes of National Law in the Seventeenth and Eighteenth
     Centuries", 1972 *J.R.* 193-226 (a revised version of "*Institutionen-
     lehrbücher des nationalen Rechts im 17. und 18. Jahrhundert*", (1970) 3
     Ius Commune 64-97); J. W. Cairns, "Institutional Writings in Scotland
     Reconsidered", (1983) 4 *Jour. Legal Hist.* 76-117 [= *New Perspectives in
     Scottish Legal History*, edd. A. Kiralfy and H. L. MacQueen (London, 1984),
     76-117].
63   Robinson, Fergus and Gordon, *European Legal History, cit.*, paras. 10.2 to
     10.5.
64   See his treatment of *negotiorum gestio* in Stair, 1,8,3ff.
65   Stair, 1,1,17: "There is little to be found among the commentaries and trea-
     tises upon the civil law, arguing from any known principles of right: but all
     their debate is a congestion of the contexts of the law: which exceedingly
     nauseates delicate ingines [minds]".
66   Stair, 1,1,23: "...these are only the extrinsic object and matter, about which
     law and right are versant. But the proper object is the right itself, whether
     it concerns persons, things or actions". His order is to treat of the constitu-
     tion and nature of rights, their conveyance or translation *inter vivos* or
     mortis causa and the remedies for their enforcement.
67   This was perhaps a response to Mackenzie's *Institutions* which follows
     Justinian more closely – see Watson, "Some Notes on Mackenzie's
     Institutions and the European Legal Tradition", (1989) 16 *Ius Commune*
     303-13.
68   Stair, 1,1,16: "Our customs, as they have arisen mainly from equity, so they
     are also from the Civil, Canon and feudal laws, from which the terms,
     tenors and forms of them are much borrowed; and therefore these (espe-
     cially the civil law) have great weight with us, namely, in cases where a
     custom is not yet formed. But none of these have with us the authority of
     law: and therefore are only received according to their equity and expedi-
     ency, *secundum bonum et aequum*"; cf. also Stair, 1,1,12: "...the Civil law of
     the Roman commonwealth or empire, as the most excellent...the affinity
     that the law of Scotland hath with it...and its own worth...though it be not

considerable use of it in the first and second books (following the order of the second edition), which deal with obligations and property, and in the third book when he is dealing with succession. He makes particularly generous use of it when he is dealing with general questions and with testamentary succession. References are more sporadic in the treatment of the law of actions in the fourth book because Stair is there dealing with Scottish practice but even in this book it is clear that the Roman law was at least at the back of his mind.[69] It is not true to say, as is sometimes done, that he filled gaps in Scots law by incorporating Roman law[70] but he did use it to suggest questions and possible solutions to problems on which there was no native authority, as on the law of risk in sale.[71]

Mackenzie's *Institutions* were first published in 1684 and passed through eight editions by 1758. After that they were supplanted as a student textbook by Erskine's *Principles* which were first published in 1754. They follow the Roman institutional order more closely than Stair's *Institutions* although Mackenzie does adapt that order to Scottish needs, for example, in dealing with the division between heritable and moveable property which is foreign to Roman law. It is suggested by Erskine[72] that Mackenzie regarded Roman law as part of the written law of Scotland but this seems to be inaccurate. Of Roman law generally he says, "...as this Civil law is much respected generally, so it has great influence in Scotland except where our own express Laws or Customs have receded from it"[73] but Erskine may be referring to Mackenzie's

---

acknowledged as a law binding for its authority, yet being, as a rule, followed for its equity, it shall not be amiss here to say something of it". In this latter passage "as a rule" does not mean "generally" as it would in modern English but "as a guide" or the like, see A. Watson, "The Rise of Modern Scots Law" in *La formazione storica del diritto moderno in Europa. Atti del III congresso internazionale della società Italiana di storia del diritto.* 3 vols. (Florence, 1977), vol. 3, 1167–76 at 1176.

69   W. M. Gordon, "Roman Law as a Source" in *Stair Tercentenary Studies,* ed. D. M. Walker (Publications of the Stair Society, 33, Edinburgh, 1981), 107–12.

70   W. M. Gordon, "Stair's Use of Roman Law" in *Law-making and Law-makers in British History, cit. sup.,* n.46, 120–26 and "Roman Law as a Source", *cit.,* at 111.

71   Stair, 1,14,7. His treatment of this topic, as of *arra,* may have been inspired by Vinnius's *Partitiones.* He also used Gudelinus, *De iure novissimo* and Vinnius's commentary on the *Institutes of Justinian* – see W. M. Gordon, "Stair, Grotius and the Sources of Stair's *Institutions*" in *Satura Roberto Feenstra sexagesimum quintum annum aetatis complenti ab alumnis collegis amicis oblata,* edd. J. A. Ankum, J. E. Spruit and F. B. J. Wubbe (Fribourg, 1985) 571–83.

72   Erskine, *Inst.,* 1,1,41.

73   Mackenzie, 1,1,7.

(too general) remark that "...by the common Law in our Acts of Parliament is meant the *Civil Law*".[74]

Mackenzie's *Institutions* give a much more succinct account of the law than Stair's, which explains their adoption as an elementary student textbook, and he is much more sparing in his references, except to statutes. However, it is clear in reading through his book that he writes as one familiar with Roman law and he does make some express comparisons with or comments on the relevance of Roman law, for example, in dealing with persons under age and with obligations.[75] Scots law comes first but he finds Roman law helpful in exposition of Scots law by suggesting a structure and questions to be addressed whether or not Roman law has already been incorporated into the fabric of Scots law.

In the seventeenth century the decision practicks, which give details of cases alone, and the digest practicks, which give details of or references to cases and other legal authorities found to be useful in practice, begin to be superseded by the closer ancestors of law reports. These reports are more like modern law reports than the practicks but they do not yet give the opinion of the court or the opinions of individual judges. Decisions of the Court of Session were decisions of the court and individual opinions were not delivered as nowadays although the views of individual judges who contributed to the decision may be indicated in the course of reporting the contentions of parties. Although Roman law was still not regarded as having binding authority[76] there are cases in which it appears in fact to have settled an issue.[77] Even where it was not decisive or not expected to be decisive it was nevertheless cited to the courts and this was at least partly because Scottish advocates who pleaded in the higher courts had normally received their academic training in Roman law, usually at a continental university and commonly, at this time, in the Netherlands. They were also required to display some competence in Roman law as one of the formal requirements of admission to the bar in the ordinary way.[78] An

---

74   *Ibid.,* citing James IV, c.51 (1493 c.51, *A.P.S.,* ii, 236, c.22); James V, c. 80 (1540 c.80, *A.P.S.,* ii, 360, c.15); Queen Mary, c. 22 (1551 c.22, *A.P.S.,* ii, 487, c.17); James VI, Parl. I, c. 31 (1567 c.31, *A.P.S.,* ii, 548, c.2). The reference may be to the Civil law in these instances but there are others in which the reference is to the common law of Scotland as opposed to local laws, e.g. *A.P.S.,* ii, 252, c.24 (1503) and iii, 41, c.48 (1567) and ii, 360, c.15 (1540) – "be disposition of the common law baith *canone ciuile* and statutes of the realm" – is somewhat ambiguous.

75   Mackenzie, 1,7, 2 and 23; 3,1.

76   E.g. *Pinkill* v. *Lord Balcarras* (1649) 1 B.S. 441.

77   E.g. *Ballenden* v. *Macmath* (1628) 1 B.S. 155; numerous other examples are given in D. Baird Smith, "Roman law" in *Sources and Literature, cit. sup.,* n.6, 171–82 at 174 n.2.

78   See *The Minute Book of the Faculty of Advocates. Vol. I, 1661–1712,* ed. J. M. Pinkerton (Publications of the Stair Society, 29, Edinburgh, 1976), Introduction, ix–x; J. W. Cairns, "John Spotswood, Professor of Law: a Preliminary Sketch" in *Miscellany III, cit. sup.,* n.47, 131–59 at 132–33.

examination in Scots law was introduced for such "ordinary" applicants for admission only in 1750[79] and, significantly, the number of advocates who went abroad for their academic education declined quite sharply thereafter.[80] This decline can also to be explained by the revival of law teaching in the Scottish universities, and especially in Edinburgh and Glasgow, in the eighteenth century but the relation with the new style of examination does seem significant. The extent to which Roman law was cited and found helpful no doubt depended on the knowledge of it held by both advocates and judges[81] and it is reasonable to assume that this varied but, as the Court of Session was a collegiate court, it is unlikely that there were many occasions on which no expertise on Roman law was available on the bench.

IV The Eighteenth and Nineteenth Centuries

Erskine in his *Principles* which appeared in 1754 and in his *Institute,* which was published posthumously in 1773, follows the scheme adopted by Mackenzie in his presentation of the law. He continues the pattern of exposition of Scots law with the assistance of Roman law but he cites Roman law in his *Institute* much more frequently than did Mackenzie in his much slighter work. Like Mackenzie, he mentions cases in which statutes have justified the exercise of powers by reference to Roman law[82] and he notes that it was felt necessary to pass a statute abrogating doctrines of Roman and Canon law repugnant to Protestant doctrine after the Reformation[83] but he draws from these evidences of use of or reference to Roman law the conclusion that, while Roman law is very useful in determining controversies where there is no fixed rule of Scots law, there is no case for applying any rules special to that system.[84] In his treatment of individual topics he is

---

79   See *The Minute Book of the Faculty of Advocates. Vol. 2, 1713–1750*, ed. J. M. Pinkerton (Publications of the Stair Society, 32, Edinburgh, 1980), 241.

80   N. Phillipson, *The Scottish Whigs and the Reform of the Court of Session, 1785–1830* (Publications of the Stair Society, 37, Edinburgh, 1990), Appendix A, giving figures for Leiden, Utrecht and Groningen which show a drop in the 1740s and a very sharp drop from the 1760s.

81   Reference may be made in this connection to J. W. Cairns, "The Formation of the Scottish Legal Mind in the Eighteenth Century: Themes of Humanism and Enlightenment in the Admission of Advocates" in *The Legal Mind. Essays for Tony Honoré*, edd. N. MacCormick and P.B.H. Birks (Oxford, 1986), 253–77.

82   Erskine, *Inst.,* 1,1,41.

83   *Ibid.,* referring to the Act 1567 c.31 (*A.P.S.,* ii, 548, c.2).

84   *Ibid.:*

> These observations prove at least that great weight is to be laid on the Roman law in all cases not fixed by statute or custom, and in which the genius of our law will suffer us to apply it; and as we have few statutes in the matter of contracts, transactions, restitutions, servitudes, tutories and obligations, the knowledge of it must be singularly useful in determining controversies arising from those heads of the

in some respects closer to Roman law than Stair in that he cites Roman texts explicitly and more freely but he does not follow Roman law exactly even when he draws heavily on it, as in his discussion of possession in his second book. For example, he says that the liferenter (who is more or less equivalent to the Roman usufructuary) and the tenant both have possession in Scots law which they did not have in Roman law (albeit the usufructuary had possessory remedies by extension of the possessory interdicts). He leaves it unclear whether the borrower has possession or not in Scots law although he follows Roman law in denying possession to the depositary.[85]

Andrew McDouall, Lord Bankton, in his *Institute*, which was published in three volumes between 1751 and 1753 and is now being republished by the Stair Society,[86] explicitly follows the order of Stair's *Institutions*. However, he modifies it in certain respects to make it conform even more closely to the order of Justinian's *Institutes* than Stair himself had done in his second edition. For example, he adds titles on the state and distinction of persons and on the division and quality of things,[87] although the latter comes in the first rather than in the second book and so corresponds rather to the placing of the title on the division and quality of things in the *Digest* (D.1.8). His general attitude is similar to that of Erskine[88] and throughout his work he refers frequently to

---

law. Yet where any rule of the Roman law appears to have been founded on a subtilty peculiar to their system, it were absurd to pay the smallest regard to it.

In his list of areas in which there were few statutes he might have included moveable property. In dealing with that in *Inst.*, 2,1 and with possession at *Inst.*, 2,1,20ff., he refers to many Roman law texts and virtually bases his account on Roman law in the absence of much Scottish material on which to draw.

85   Erskine, *Inst.*, 2,1,20 and 22 respectively.
86   Volumes I and II have appeared as volumes 41 (Edinburgh, 1993) and 42 (Edinburgh, 1994), respectively, and volume III will appear as volume 43 in 1995.
87   Bankton, 1,2 and 3; cf. D.1.8.
88   Bankton, 1,1,42:

From many of our statutes it appears, that our legislators had great regard to the Civil and Canon laws, which therein are termed *the common law* [he cites the Acts 1493 c.51 (*A.P.S.*, ii, 236, c.22), 1540 c.69 (*A.P.S.*, ii, 356, c.1) and c.80 (*A.P.S.*, ii, 360, c.15), and 1551 c.22 (*A.P.S.*, ii, 487, c.17)] as being common to most nations; this indeed shews, that our lawgivers followed these laws as an example, in framing those statutes for their reasonableness and expediency; and therefore, it may from thence be concluded, that our judges ought to direct themselves by the civil and canon laws, as a rule, where our own statutes and customs fail, or where the question, tho' concerning a feudal subject, is not decided by our feudal customs.

In such case the civil law most commonly takes place, unless we have entirely rejected it in matters of that kind. Thus, for example, it were absurd to argue from the civil law, in favour of adoption of slavery, and other matters, which are entirely abolished by universal custom of nations.

Roman texts.[89] As in Stair the references do not necessarily mean that he thinks that Roman law does or should apply. Roman law is there rather as a framework of discussion, whether or not it is applicable. For example, he is ambiguous on the acceptance of the *actio de effusis vel deiectis* in Scots law.[90]

In the eighteenth century as in the seventeenth there are many cases in which Roman law was cited to or by the courts and we are still better informed of decisions as a result of improvement in the reporting of the activity of the courts. However, the original records have still to be fully explored for the light which they may cast on the use of Roman law in cases which were not reported or which were reported but in which the report is not full enough to disclose all the authorities which were relied on.[91] Roman law might still be decisive although not applied as binding authority[92] but equally a Roman rule might be rejected if it was seen as unsuitable for application in Scotland.[93] However, by the end of the eighteenth century we have to reckon with three limiting factors affecting recourse to Roman law – first, the increasing availability of English authority on points undecided in Scotland; secondly, the perception (which might or might not be accurate) that at least in some areas such as mercantile law English law ought to be applied as persuasive authority because of the greater experience of English lawyers in dealing with new problems in the relevant area; and, thirdly, the increasing settlement of Scots law by decision or legislation, making it less necessary to refer to Roman law for guidance. So far as the last point is concerned, even where Roman law had had a hand in settling the Scots law in the first place the Scottish authorities might be referred to in preference to the relevant Roman ones if a new point developing the basic rules should arise.

Reference to English authority does not begin with Bell but probably the most familiar evidence of the existence of and preference for English authority is found in Bell's reliance on English cases in his *Commentaries,* which appeared first as a treatise on bankruptcy law in 1800 but ended as *Commentaries on the Law of Scotland and on the*

---

89 See, e.g., the distinction of public and private law in Bankton, 1,1,54 and the rules of interpretation and the effect of statutes in Bankton, 1,1,61–70.

90 Bankton, 1,4,31; see *Gray* v. *Dunlop,* 1954 S.L.T. (Sh. Ct.) 75 where it was held that it was not received into Scots law.

91 See the Scottish Law Commission, *Recovery of Benefits*, vol. 2, (Background Research Papers), 19ff., an extract from the pleadings in *Stirling* v. *Earl of Lauderdale* (1733) Mor. 2930, contained in SRO 228/5/2/92.

92 E.g. *Sword* v. *Sinclair* (1771) Mor. 14241 – in sale risk passes, in principle, when the contract is concluded.

93 *Allan* v. *Cleghorn's Creditors* (1713) Mor. 11835 – a widow had no tacit hypothec for her marriage contract provisions on analogy of the tacit hypothec to secure her dowry given to a wife by Roman law.

Principles of Mercantile Jurisprudence.[94] Bell alleges in his preface (at
viiiff.) that the progress of Scots mercantile law was hindered by the
concentration of lawyers on questions of land law arising out of the for-
feitures imposed on those who were convicted criminally for their support of the Jacobite risings in 1715 and 1745 and that it might have
seemed better simply to adopt English mercantile law "which had
already made great progress towards perfection". He himself regarded
such a course as premature and he claimed that he had extracted the
principles of the law merchant from the English and foreign authorities
and not simply followed English cases some of which, he says (at
xiii–xiv):

> ...contain so strong an infusion of common law [i.e. English
> Common law, not the *ius commune*] intimately blended in the
> judgment, that without a careful comparison of them with the great
> principles of jurisprudence delivered in the Roman law, and recog-
> nised in the Scottish authorities, or commented on by foreign writ-
> ers of credit, there was much hazard of impairing what it was my
> design to clear, and of substituting, in the place of mere obscurity,
> corrupted doctrine and mistaken principles.

Bell hoped to bring the two systems closer together and to bring Scots
law to the attention of English lawyers some of whom he had "...been
mortified to find ignorant on this subject, and in no degree aware of the
admirable principles and comprehensive views by which the law of
Scotland is distinguished".[95] What is not clear is that others used
English authorities with the same discrimination or that he was successful in persuading English lawyers who were not already so persuaded of the virtue of paying attention to the distinctive virtues of
Scots law. Despite his close attention to English authorities Bell does
still refer to Roman law both in his *Commentaries* and in his *Principles*
but he does not discuss Roman law as a source in the body of either
work and his view of Roman law as well as his actual use of it has to be
deduced from the references made to it rather than from a programmatic statement. This task is made less easy than it might have been by
the absence of any entry relating to Roman law as such in the index to
either work.

   Hume, Bell's predecessor in the chair of Scots law in the university
of Edinburgh, does discuss the use of Roman law as a source of Scots
law. In his *Lectures,* published by the Stair Society long after his death,[96]
he refers to the usefulness of the study of Roman law as part of legal
education but he also stresses (in the first volume, at 1–4) the need to
know Scots law and while acknowledging the contribution of Roman
law to the development of Scots law he rejects the idea that Roman law

---

94   See Introduction by R. Black to the reprint (Edinburgh, 1990), 1–2.
95   Preface, xiv.
96   Hume, *Lectures.*

is authoritative.[97] In his *Commentaries on the Law of Scotland respecting Crimes,* the first version of which appeared in 1797, he also rejects the authority of Roman law but, in addition, he states that, because of the wide differences between Rome and Scotland in circumstances relevant to the application of criminal law,[98] he has not looked very frequently or extensively into Roman law except where Roman law has actually been taken into account in Scottish practice[99] and he has paid even less attention to modern commentators on it. He acknowledges that their observations are "just and rational" but says that they are generally "...nothing more than any man of plain sense, with a little attention to the subject, will readily, and to as good purpose, make out for himself".[100] On the other hand he has found that if authorities are needed the works of English lawyers are to be preferred because English practice offers a closer analogy and English writers are as good in explaining and illustrating doctrines as the writers of other countries.[101] Hume does look primarily to Scottish practice as illustrated not only from reported cases but from the records of the criminal courts but his preference for English persuasive authority over the persuasive authority of Roman law is significant.

In matters of private law and public law (other than criminal law, in respect of which the House of Lords had no jurisdiction), some influence from English law was almost inevitable by reason of the exercise by the House of Lords of the appellate jurisdiction which it was not explicitly granted in the Treaty and Acts of Union of 1707 but which it

---

97   *Ibid.,* vol. 1, 13: "...the obeisance we pay to the Civil [law] is now, and always has been, a voluntary obeisance, and matter of courtesy – such as depends, in the main, on its agreement with equity and reason, its analogy to the rest of our practice, and its suitableness to our state of things and kinds of business". Cf. also Appendix A to that volume, giving additional material derived from student notes, at 357.

98   *Ibid.,* vol. 1, 15 and 16: "Because in any country, the frame and character of this part of its laws, has always a much closer dependence on the peculiar circumstances of the people, than the detail of its customs and regulations in most of the ordinary affairs of civil life...", adding that the law of crimes "...has a near relation to the distinctions of rank among the people, the functions of their Magistrates, their institutions and national objects, their manners and habits, their religion, their state of Government, and their position with respect to others" and in all these respects there is a difference between Rome and Scotland.

99   *Ibid.,* vol. 1, 17: "For these reasons, though I have not neglected the authorities of the Roman system, in cases where I find that they have actually been regarded in our practice; yet I have not engaged in frequent or very extensive inquiries with respect to them".

100 *Ibid.,* vol. 1, 17.

101 *Ibid.*

assumed or accepted soon after as a matter of practice.[102] The House of Lords had a majority of English peers and there was no requirement that a member familiar with Scots law should sit on Scottish appeals. This meant that it was unlikely that Scots law would be dealt with in Scottish appeals by judges with an intimate knowledge of that system. Although litigants were willing enough to take advantage of the right of appeal it is not surprising to find that little attention was paid to decisions of the House of Lords as precedents in the Court of Session in the eighteenth century.[103] Nevertheless the existence of the House of Lords as the ultimate appeal court was an obvious encouragement to the greater use of English law, the effects of which become apparent later. There was also a considerable body of opinion favourable to the adoption of English ideas and English law as models;[104] criticism of the anglicisation of Scots law and of the baneful influence of English law exercised through the House of Lords has not been the only view of the relationship between Scots and English law taken over the years. At the beginning of the nineteenth century the House of Lords was more concerned to stem the tide of litigious Scotsmen exercising their rights to approach it in the hope of obtaining a favourable decision (and meanwhile postponing execution of an adverse decree in the Court of Session) than seeking opportunity to accept cases and thereby increase its influence on the development of Scots law.[105]

Roman law clearly was important in the creation of Scots law but as Scots law became established with an increasing quantity of source material in the form of legislation and court decisions and with its own legal literature, both in the form of the institutional writings already referred to[106] and in the form of other treatises on particular topics, there was less need to look to Roman law for solutions to legal problems. Again, doctrines, principles or rules derived in whole or in part from Roman law when once incorporated into Scots law could and did take on a life of their own in which the Roman element might no longer play an essential role. For example, the so-called *conditio si institutus sine liberis decesserit*, which is read into testamentary provisions with the effect of allowing the children of a beneficiary instituted to take the provision in preference to a substitute named even if there is no

---

102 See A. J. MacLean, "The 1707 Union: Scots Law and the House of Lords", (1984) 4 *Jour. Leg. Hist.* 50-75 (= *New Perspectives in Scottish Legal History*, edd. A. Kiralfy and H. L. MacQueen (London, 1984), 50-75) and most recently R. S. Tompson, "James Greenshields and the House of Lords: a Reappraisal" in *Legal History in the Making, cit. sup.*, n.2, 109-24. There was no appeal on criminal matters – see MacLean at 60 n.48 and Tompson, 119-20.
103 Tompson, *op. cit.*, at 116-17. Erskine, *Inst.*, 1,1,47 is clear that individual decisions of the House of Lords are not binding precedents.
104 See N. T. Phillipson, *The Scottish Whigs, cit. sup.*, n.80, 90ff. and 177-79.
105 See Tompson, *op. cit.*, n.102, at 120ff.
106 See sections III and IV above.

express destination to the children of the institute, has its roots in Roman law. There it could be implied for the benefit of descendants of the testator. Once adopted into Scots law it was extended to the children of collateral institutes as well as to the children of descendants if it appeared that a family provision was intended.[107] However, as the law developed it gradually lost contact with the Roman basis of the principle as the courts were able to refer to earlier cases rather than to the Roman texts for authority on its application and in a case in 1891[108] the Roman contribution was dismissed in argument as "three obscure passages in the *Corpus Iuris*". In *Farquharson* v. *Kelly*[109] the court did not apply the *conditio* in the case of an illegitimate child although some support for its application could have been found in Roman texts applying it to natural children. These Roman texts do not appear to have been cited to the court.

From the nineteenth century onwards there is also evidence that to some extent Roman law was less used because it was less well understood or where understood it was seen as a historical system rather than a living source of ideas which could still be applied even in changed circumstances. Roman law did keep a place in legal education but its relative share of attention tended to diminish as other subjects claimed a place in the teaching of law in the Scottish universities. The examination in Roman law required of intrants to the Faculty of Advocates seems to have become less rigorous in that the theses prepared were not necessarily the unaided work of the intrant and this particular part of the admission requirement was dropped in 1966.[110]

Evidence on the question of the competence of judges and advocates in Roman law in the nineteenth century is somewhat impressionistic but there are undoubtedly negative impressions in some cases, as in *Gowans* v. *Christie*[111] where what appear to be several citations of writers on Roman law turn out to be essentially a citation of Voet, with writers quoted by him, and where, moreover, full advantage of the arguments which might have been derived from Roman law, had it been used as well as it might have been, was not taken.[112] That Voet was relied on in that case is indicative of a view that the Roman law to be

---

107 *Walker* v. *Walker* (1744) Mor. 10328; see W. M. Gordon, "Roman and Scots Law – the *conditiones si sine liberis decesserit*", 1969 *J.R.* 108–27 at 115ff.
108 *Hall* v. *Hall* (1891) 18 R. 690 at 691.
109 (1900) 2 F. 863; the actual decision, which is hardly surprising at its date, is now superseded by legislation equalising the rights of legitimate and illegitimate children for almost all purposes – the Law Reform (Miscellaneous Provisions) (Scotland) Act 1968 (c.70) and the Law Reform (Parent and Child) (Scotland) Act 1986 (c.9).
110 D. A. O. Edward, "Faculty of Advocates. Regulations as to Intrants", 1968 S.L.T. (News) 181–3 at 181.
111 (1871) 9 M. 485 and (1873) 11 M. (H.L.) 1.
112 See W. M. Gordon, "Roman Law in a Nineteenth Century Scottish case: *Gowans* v. *Christie*" in *Sodalitas. Scritti in onore di Antonio Guarino,* ed. V. Giuffrè. 10 vols. (Naples, 1984–85), vol. 7, 3371–87.

looked at was the law as understood at a time when Roman law was having considerable influence on the development of Scots law. The opinion that it is Roman law as understood at the time of the institutional writers which alone is relevant when Roman law is looked at in modern times was explicitly stated by Lord President Clyde in the more recent case of *McDonald* v. *Provan (of Scotland St.) Ltd.*[113] But in fact there has been no clear policy with regard to the citation of Roman law as persuasive authority in cases from the nineteenth and twentieth centuries. Sometimes only texts are cited;[114] sometimes there is a range of writers from medieval times onwards;[115] sometimes modern textbooks are cited, using "modern" here to mean contemporary, at least in terms of use, with the case in which the citation appears;[116] sometimes writers contemporary with the Scottish institutional writers of the seventeenth and eighteenth centuries, as in the cases mentioned above and sometimes a range of writers both modern and contemporary with the institutional writers.[117] There seems to have been no clear consciousness that Roman law as applied in Roman times is one thing and Roman law as an influence on the development of western European legal thought is another; that the Roman law applied in Rome and the Roman empire itself has a history of over a thousand years and Roman law scholarship has approached that history in various ways; that there have been various approaches to Roman law since Justinian; and that inspiration can be derived from a range of material all of which can claim some relevance to the question how a particular question should be decided. Sometimes it may be suspected that judges have been happy to find reasons not to go into Roman law and explore the range of material available.[118]

The argument that Roman law is no longer of the same service as in earlier periods of Scots law has also been used to reduce the scope for reliance on Roman law. It has been said that Roman law is not as well adapted to an industrial as to an agricultural society[119] and it can be argued that English law has become more appropriate as a source of

---

113 1960 S.L.T. 231.
114 See e.g. *Douglas' Executors* (1869) 7 M. 504; *Magistrates of Kilmarnock* v. *Mather* (1869) 7 M. 548.
115 See e.g. *Thompson* v. *Whitehead* (1862) 24 D. 331.
116 See e.g. *Waygood & Co.* v. *Bennie* (1885) 12 R. 651; *Glasgow Corporation* v. *Lord Advocate* 1959 S.C. 203.
117 See e.g. *Sloans Dairies Ltd.* v. *Glasgow Corporation* 1977 S.C. 223, where the modern authors Moyle and de Zulueta were cited along with Voet and Pothier.
118 See *Sloans Dairies, cit., per* L. J.-C. Wheatley at 235: "I have been able to [reach my conclusion] without a detailed examination of the writings of the civilians and the commentators thereon and the works of the institutional writers and textbooks which were so extensively canvassed before us".
119 P. G. Stein, "The Influence of Roman Law", *cit. sup.*, n.56, 243 (= *Historical Essays*, cit. sup., n.11, 357).

inspiration. English law is also the system with which most of the judges in the House of Lords are familiar and it is to the House of Lords that civil appeals may ultimately be brought (where no reference to the European Court of Justice is involved); those judges are likely to be more receptive to arguments presented in terms with which they are familiar. The relevance of this last consideration was apparent in *Gowans* v. *Christie*[120] where the judges in the House of Lords were clearly uneasy with the civilian concepts and terminology used in argument, although it must be said that this sort of reaction has become uncommon nowadays.[121] It has also been argued that it is now too late to import wholly new ideas from Roman law, as in *Drummond's Judicial Factor* v. *H.M. Advocate*,[122] where the use of the survivorship presumptions of Roman law in a case in which two persons who had left reciprocal wills had been killed simultaneously was rejected, leaving the law to be settled considerably later by legislation.[123] All this has led to a decline in the continuing influence of Roman law, without necessarily diminishing the actual importance of keeping contact with the civilian elements of the law.

V The Present Day

Roman law is still referred to in twentieth century cases but it has not been decisive in any of those in which it has been cited. It has been used rather to support a decision in areas in which Roman law has already been used in the past, as for example in *Sloans Dairies*.[124] Examination in the Roman law of property and obligations is still required of those entering the Faculty of Advocates; it is not, however, required of those solicitors who are permitted to plead in the Court of Session and the High Court of Justiciary under the provisions for extending rights of audience contained in the Law Reform (Miscellaneous Provisions) (Scotland) Act 1990 s.24. Only Aberdeen of the Scottish universities which teach law has kept a compulsory course in Civil law for all students and that course was shortened in 1990-91. As an option Roman law is under pressure from other options in the law curriculum perceived by some students and their advisers as more relevant to practice and, in particular, to practice as solicitors. The Scottish Law Commission tends to look to modern systems and especially to Common law jurisdictions for comparative material when considering reform. The common ground which Roman law and, more particularly, the Civil law could offer to European lawyers is not at present appreciated as much as the common ground of the latest directive

---

120 *cit. sup.*, n.111.
121 Cf. *Will's Trs.* v. *Cairngorm Canoeing and Sailing School Ltd.* 1976 S.C.(H.L.) 30.
122 1944 S.C. 298.
123 Succession (Scotland) Act 1964 (c.41), s.31.
124 *Cit. sup.*, n.117.

or regulation from the European Union[125] but it has also to be said that Roman law is not universally appreciated as a foundation of legal studies even in civilian jurisdictions. There remains the hope that a more enlightened view will ultimately prevail.

---

125 See, however, D. A. O. Edward, "Scots Law and Six Heresies", (1994) 39 *J.L.S.S.* 159-62 at 161 for a warning against exaggeration of the importance of the common civilian heritage as a bridge between Scots law and European law.

3. ROMAN LAW IN A MIXED LEGAL SYSTEM
– THE SOUTH AFRICAN EXPERIENCE

By REINHARD ZIMMERMANN

I

1. Codification, it was realised dimly in nineteenth-century Germany, might mark the end of the exalted status of the Roman law professor as the leader of the legal world. No longer would he be an "Angel of the Empire", no longer the high priest of scholarship conjuring up the legal spirit of the nation.[1] What would his new role be? Bernhard Windscheid addressed himself to this question as early as 1858:

> And when this work is achieved the science of Roman law shall not perish, but shall bloom in a new glory. For our discipline shall have the opportunity to give itself wholly to the contemplation of Roman law as such, of pure Roman law, without any extraneous thoughts...And this too will be a practical task, the most practical of tasks, the task of education. When the authority of the *Corpus Iuris* is put aside in Germany, then, for the first time, the lecture halls of the teachers of Roman law shall truly fill; and the rising generations shall sit at their feet, to learn...what beauty is.[2]

Somehow, this is not quite the experience of the modern German Roman law professor. The neo-humanistic, purely antiquarian approach of twentieth century Roman legal scholarship[3] has resulted, by and large, in only a few scattered specialists still sitting at his feet,[4] and the

---

1   For details and references cf. the fascinating study by J.Q. Whitman, *The Legacy of Roman Law in the German Romantic Era*, 1990.

2   Bernhard Windscheid, "Das römische Recht in Deutschland", in *Gesammelte Reden und Abhandlungen*, 1904, at 48.

3   Cf. already P. Koschaker, *Europa und das römische Recht*, 4th ed., 1966, 290ff.

4   Still, however, at all the bigger German law faculties there is at least one, and in many cases there are even two professors of Roman law. At some of the younger (and smaller) law faculties, one professor has to be responsible for legal history at large. Every German Roman law professor, whether at a bigger or smaller, a newly established or old faculty, also carries responsibility for (the teaching of) modern private law – there are no chairs purely of Roman law (or legal history). Generally, Roman law is one of a variety of *"Grundlagenvorlesungen"* which first or second year students may take to acquire their *"Grundlagenschein"* (a certificate in a "basic" subject which is a requirement for admission to the first state examination in law). Specialised instruction in Roman law tends to be confined to "seminars" (small group research classes).

Roman heritage has thus been fading rapidly from the average lawyer's consciousness. He does not seem to want to know what beauty is.

Obviously, under these circumstances, a German Roman lawyer will look with interest and curiosity, perhaps even with a sense of enchantment, at legal systems where a more utilitarian approach to Roman law, the Bartolist as opposed to the Cujacian tradition, still prevails. There are no longer many systems of this kind. Too pervasive has been the influence of the idea that the private law of a proper modern nation state should be contained in a clear, well-structured and easily accessible codification. In continental Europe only San Marino springs to mind as a country where the Roman-Canon *ius commune* is still applicable.[5] Italian law professors are appointed as appellate judges, and they decide the disputes brought before them, to this day, ultimately on the basis of the *Corpus Iuris Civilis*. Of greater European significance is Scotland where, however, the Roman heritage survives in a much more diluted version. Outside Europe, South Africa presents the major example of a jurisdiction where the civilian tradition still survives in its original, uncodified form. How did this come about and what is the significance of Roman law in such a jurisdiction?

2. At the outset, two points have to be remembered. Scotland and South Africa not only share in the civilian heritage, they also belong to what are commonly termed "mixed" legal systems.[6] To some extent, of course, all the major legal systems of the Western world are mixed. They have grown together from various roots, and they have, over the centuries, been subject to many different influences. The history of a system of law, in the words of Roscoe Pound,[7] is largely "a history of borrowings of legal materials from other legal systems and of assimilation of materials from outside of the law". In central and western Europe, Roman law has played the major role, but the church, the merchants and the local communities, for instance, also had considerable influence on European private law with their specific legal rules and customs. The great success of the Roman-Dutch jurisprudence of the seventeenth century is largely attributable to the integration of contemporary legal practice, of the "*mores hodierni*" or "*consuetudines nostrae*" into the learned law.[8] Even the English Common law has never "flourished in noble isolation from Europe";[9] throughout the centuries continental jurisprudence has exercised a considerable, and characteristic,

---

5   See P.G. Stein, "Civil Law Reports and the Case of San Marino", in *The Character and Influence of the Roman Civil Law*, 1988, 126ff.

6   Cf. e.g. T.B. Smith, *Studies Critical and Comparative*, 1962; Joseph Dainow (ed.), *The Role of Judicial Decisions and Doctrine in Civil Law and in Mixed Jurisdictions*, 1974.

7   As quoted by A. Watson, *Legal Transplants*, 1974, at 22.

8   For details cf. R. Feenstra and R. Zimmermann (edd.), *Das römisch-holländische Recht. Fortschritte des Zivilrechts im 17. und 18. Jahrhundert*, 1992.

9   J.H. Baker, *An Introduction to English Legal History*, 3rd ed., 1990, at 35.

influence on its rules and institutions.[10] In spite of these historical connections and in spite of the fact that Common law and Civil law can
therefore be regarded as emanations of one and the same, of a
"Western", legal tradition,[11] they are emanations with their own distinctive features; and they are thus widely regarded as constituting two distinct legal families.[12] Due, largely, to historical accident, a new
interrelation has in certain places come about between the two; and it
is for those jurisdictions that the term "mixed" is usually reserved.
Apart from Scotland and South Africa, we are dealing here with
Quebec, Louisiana, Sri Lanka, Botswana, Lesotho, Swaziland, Namibia
and Zimbabwe. In all these territories, civilian jurisprudence has, to a
larger or lesser extent, survived within a Common law environment.
Depending, however, on the way in which the Civil law has been preserved, they can again be subdivided. In Quebec a codification, based
on the *Code Napoléon*, was adopted in 1866. It has tended to shield the
substantive Civil law against Common law influences, but it has also put
an end to the use of Roman law as a living source of law.[13] In Louisiana
a Civil Code had already been promulgated in 1825. It had even been
preceded by a compilation referred to as the Digest of 1808, which in
turn had drawn from Roman, French and Spanish law. Again, the civilian heritage was thus preserved, but at the expense of a further organic
development of Roman law.[14] In all the other jurisdictions mentioned
above there has never been a codification, and the Roman sources have
therefore retained a somewhat different status. This paper will focus on

---

10   Cf. recently Richard H. Helmholz, "Continental Law and Common Law:
     Historical Strangers or Companions?", 1990 *Duke L.J.* 1207ff.; C. Donahue,
     Jr., *"Ius commune*, Canon Law, and Common Law in England" (1992) 66
     Tulane L.R. 1685ff.; and my own attempts to substantiate this thesis: "Der
     europäische Charakter des englischen Rechts. Historische Verbindungen
     zwischen Civil law und Common law", 1993 *Z.Eu.P.* 4ff.; "'Heard melodies
     are sweet, but those unheard are sweeter...'. *Condicio tacita,* Implied
     Condition und die Fortbildung des europäischen Vertragsrechts" (1993)
     193 *A.c.P.* 121ff.
11   H.J. Berman, *Law and Revolution. The Formation of the Western Legal
     Tradition,* 1983.
12   Cf. e.g. F.H. Lawson, *A Common Lawyer Looks at the Civil Law,* 1953, 1ff.;
     R. David, *Les grands systèmes de droit contemporains,* 8th ed., 1982; A.G.
     Chloros, "Common Law, Civil Law and Socialist Law: Three Leading
     Systems of the World, Three Kinds of Legal Thought", in C. Varga,
     Comparative Legal Cultures, 1992, 83ff.; A.T. van Mehren and J.R. Gordley,
     The Civil Law System, 2nd ed., 1977, 3ff.
13   For an overview cf. K. Zweigert and H. Kötz, *Einführung in die
     Rechtsvergleichung auf dem Gebiete des Privatrechts,* 2nd ed., 1984, vol. 1,
     135ff.; J.-L. Baudouin, "The Impact of the Common Law on the Civilian
     Systems of Louisiana and Quebec", in Dainow, *op. cit.,* n.6, at 1ff.
14   On Louisiana cf. the works mentioned in n.13; also e.g. A. N. Yiannopoulos,
     "The Civil Codes of Louisiana", in *Louisiana Civil Code,* 1991 edition,
     XXIIIff.

South African law, which, Scotland apart, must be regarded as the leading one among this group of mixed legal systems. Botswana, Lesotho[15]
and Swaziland have all inherited their private law from the Cape of
Good Hope and still display such uniformity that they have even been
grouped together as the "Southern African Law Association".[16] The
same can be said about Namibia (which was administered by South
Africa until independence in 1990)[17] and Zimbabwe (which eventually
retained the private law of its predecessor, Southern Rhodesia).[18] Even
during the period of political hostility between Zimbabwe and her
southern neighbour, South African precedents enjoyed considerable
persuasive authority; at the same time, however, as was the case already
in Southern Rhodesia, English law tends to be more readily resorted
to.[19] Even more marked has been the influence of English law in Sri
Lanka, which also shares a common legal heritage with South Africa.
Decisions of South African courts regarding core areas of private law
are "though not absolutely binding,...treated with great respect".[20]

   3. The second point that must be mentioned relates specifically to
South Africa. It is, of course, in itself somewhat ironic that the southern
tip of Africa should have become one of the last strongholds in the
modern world of European jurisprudence in its original uncodified
form. Access to law is certainly not facilitated by the multiplicity of

---

15 The one hundredth anniversary of the introduction of Roman-Dutch law
    in Lesotho was commemorated with an international conference in May
    1984. The papers presented at this conference constitute vol. 1 (1985) of
    the *Lesotho Law Journal.*
16 A term used by Schreiner, J.A., in: *Annah Lokudzinga Mathenjwa* v. *R,*
    (1970–1976) Swaziland L.R. 25, at 29H. For general comment, cf. the
    entries under the various countries in the *International Encyclopedia of
    Comparative Law*, vol. I (S. Roberts, Botswana, B–39ff.; S.M. Poulter,
    Lesotho, L–23ff.; N. Rubin, C. B. O'Beirne, Swaziland, S–153ff.); J.H. Pain,
    "The Reception of English and Roman-Dutch Law in Africa with Reference
    to Botswana, Lesotho and Swaziland" (1978) 11 *Comparative
    International Law Journal of Southern Africa* (sic!) 137ff.; A.J.G.M.
    Sanders, "The Characteristic Features of Southern African Law" (1981) 14
    C.I.L.S.A. 328ff.
17 When South Africa was entrusted, after the First World War, with the
    power to administer South West Africa, the Roman-Dutch law as applied in
    the province of the Cape of Good Hope on 1 January 1920 was introduced
    as common law of the territory. Roman-Dutch law continues to apply after
    independence (20.3.1990) in terms of art. 140 I of the Constitution of the
    Republic of Namibia.
18 For details, see R. Zimmermann, "Das römisch-holländische Recht in
    Zimbabwe" (1991) 51 *RabelsZ.* 505ff.
19 For details, see the article mentioned in the previous note.
20 I. Jennings and H.W. Tambiah, *The Dominion of Ceylon. The Development
    of its Laws and Constitution*, 1970, at 188; cf. further H.W. Tambiah, "Sri
    Lanka", in *International Encyclopedia of Comparative Law*, vol. I, S–125ff.;
    T. Nadaraja, *The Legal System of Ceylon in its Historical Setting*, 1977;
    M.H.J. van den Horst, *The Roman-Dutch Law in Sri Lanka*, 1985.

legal sources, some of them in ancient, some in modern, none in indigenous languages. As is well-known, the South African government for
many years pursued policies that, in the eyes of many South Africans,
deeply affected the legitimacy of the legal system. Not even a subject
such as Roman law remained unaffected at a time when all traditional
values got caught up in a maelstrom of partisanship and intolerance.
This raises the question as to whether it is both suitable and feasible to
retain a legal system rooted in, and still intimately related to, centuries
of European history. The "Africanisation" of the legal professions, a dramatic extension of tertiary education for those who were hitherto
underprivileged and the facilitation of access to justice on all levels are
among the matters requiring urgent consideration; widespread poverty
provides a sombre background.[21] And although the African National
Congress endorsed the retention of the present private law,[22] the basis
for its application may soon be widely eroded. This is, in fact, already
happening in Zimbabwe.[23] Any discussion of Roman law in South
Africa therefore has to be aware of the fact that one is dealing with an
intellectually stimulating and instructive, but at the same time – in a
broader, practical perspective – highly problematic, some will even say
frivolous, topic.

II.

1. During the seventeenth century the Republic of the United
Netherlands experienced its Golden Age. Economically it was among
the most important world powers, the achievements of its artists, scien-
tists and philosophers were renowned, and Roman-Dutch jurisprudence was in full bloom.[24] Those were the days of Grotius and Voet, of
Vinnius, Ulrich Huber, Van Groenewegen and Van Leeuwen, writers
who rendered a major contribution towards making this particular variant of the European *ius commune* the most modern legal system of its

---

21   I have tried to provide a detailed assessment of the situation in 'Turning
     and Turning in the Widening Gyre ... Gegenwartsprobleme der
     Juristenausbildung in Südafrika', in *Gedächtnisschrift für W.K. Geck*, 1989,
     985ff.
22   A. Sachs, *The Future of Roman-Dutch Law in a Non-Racial Democratic
     South Africa, Some Preliminary Observations*, 1989; *idem*, *Protecting
     Human Rights in a New South Africa*, 1990, at 94. Sachs, however, argues
     that "if Roman Dutch Law is to survive, it must...proclaim itself for what it
     is, South African law...What is needed is a self-consciously South African
     law for an emerging South African nation". He also contemplates a fusion
     between Roman-Dutch and African law. Cf. also, in this context, the
     remarks by H.J. Erasmus, "Roman Law in South Africa Today" (1989) 106
     S.A.L.J. 670ff.
23   Cf. (1991) 51 *RabelsZ.* 528ff.
24   For details, cf. Feenstra and Zimmermann, *op. cit.*, n.8, 9ff. Generally on this
     phase of European legal development, K. Luig, "The Institutes of National
     Law in the Seventeenth and Eighteenth Centuries", 1972 *J.R.* 193ff.

time.[25] In the same year in which the last mentioned of these authors coined the term *Rooms-Hollands-Regt*[26] (usually translated, less precisely, Roman-Dutch law[27]), a seemingly unimportant event occurred which guaranteed the survival of this legal system to this day: on 6 April 1652, three ships of the *Vereenigde Geoctroyeerde Oost-Indische Compagnie* (V.O.C.) arrived in Table Bay in order to establish a supply base for ships on their way to the Indies. This supply station was soon turned into a more permanent settlement. The Dutch settlers brought with them their own, native legal system and transplanted[28] it into the new environment.[29] The question why they should have lived at the Cape of Good Hope under a different legal system than at home probably did not even occur to them. What precisely had to be applied, however, was never quite clearly spelt out. The United Netherlands, after all, consisted of seven different provinces, each with its own (though, of course, very closely related) legal system. Yet in practice it was accepted, from the beginning, that the law of Holland had to be applied, since it was by far the wealthiest and most powerful of all the provinces and, moreover, boasted the most influential contemporary centres of legal learning and legal practice.[30]

Ironically, the continued existence of Roman-Dutch law at the Cape can be ascribed exactly to the same event which initially seemed to signal its downfall. For whereas the mother country was forced to adopt the French *Code Napoléon*, the Cape of Good Hope was occupied by the British and slowly turned, from 1806, into an integral part of their worldwide Empire. In accordance with British constitutional practice,[31] however, Roman-Dutch law remained the common law of

---

25   For an analysis of the relevant factors cf. R. Zimmermann, "Roman-Dutch Jurisprudence and its Contribution to European Private Law", (1992) 66 *Tulane L.R.* 1685ff., 1711ff.

26   *Paratitula juris novissimi, dat is, Een kort begrip van het Rooms-Hollandts-Reght*, 1652. This was a predecessor to Van Leeuwen's more famous work *Het Rooms-Hollands-Regt*, 1664.

27   Cf. E. Kahn, "The Role of Doctrine and Judicial Decisions in South African Law", in Dainow, *op. cit.*, n.6, at 225.

28   Cf. M. Rheinstein, "Types of Reception", in *Gesammelte Schriften*, ed. H.G. Leser, vol. 1, 1979, 261ff.

29   On the early legal history of the Cape after the arrival of the Dutch settlers, cf. H.R. Hahlo and E. Kahn, *The Union of South Africa. The Development of its Laws and Constitution*, 1960, 1ff.; H.R. Hahlo and E. Kahn, *The South African Legal System and its Background*, 1968, 566ff.; G.G. Visagie, *Regspleging en Reg aan die Kaap van 1652 tot 1806*, 1969, 24ff.; D.H. van Zyl, *Geskiedenis van die Romeins-Hollandse Reg*, 1979, 420ff.; R. Zimmermann, *Das römisch-holländische Recht in Südafrika*, 1983, 1ff.; J.C. de Wet, *Die Ou Skrywers in Perspektief*, 1988, 1ff.; W. de Vos, *Regsgeskiedenis*, 1992, 226ff.

30   Cf. Feenstra and Zimmermann, *op. cit.*, n.8, 19ff.

31   *Campbell* v. *Hall* (1774) 1 Cowper 204; 98 E.R. 1045 at 1047, *per* Lord Mansfield.

the country; a position that was retained by the First and Second Charters of Justice in 1827 and 1832.[32] Within the next few decades the territorial sphere of influence of Roman-Dutch law grew considerably, for it was adopted in the three independent Republics (Natal, Orange Free State, Transvaal) created by the "Boers" who emigrated from the Cape Colony; and as in the Cape, it remained in force even when these Republics became British territories.[33] It is therefore not surprising that after the South Africa Act of 1909 had brought about the unification of the four colonies in 1910, Roman-Dutch law was generally taken to have become the common law of the new Union of South Africa.[34] This position was perpetuated under the constitutions of the Republic of South Africa of 1961 and 1983.

2. It was, however, no longer the pure Dutch variant of the European *ius commune* that was thus adopted in South Africa. In the course of the nineteenth century, English law had started to infiltrate and a process was set in motion that ultimately transformed South

---

32 On the early legal history under British rule cf. C. Graham Botha, "The Early Influence of the English Law upon the Roman-Dutch Law in South Africa" (1923) 40 *S.A.L.J.* 396ff.; P.J. van der Merwe, *Regsinstellings en die Reg aan die Kaap 1806 tot 1834*, unpublished LL.D. thesis, University of the Western Cape, 1984; De Vos, *op. cit.*, n.29, 242ff.; S.D. Girvin, "The Establishment of the Supreme Court of the Cape of Good Hope and its History under the Chief Justiceship of Sir John Wylde", (1992) 109 *S.A.L.J.* 293ff. and (1992) 109 *S.A.L.J.* 652ff.

33 For details, see Hahlo and Kahn, *Union, op. cit.*, n.29, 21ff.; Van Zyl, *op. cit.*, n.29, 459ff.; Zimmermann, *op. cit.*, n.29, 20ff.; De Wet, *op. cit.*, n.29, 34ff.; De Vos, *op. cit.*, n.29, 250ff. On the legal history of Natal cf. P.R. Spiller, *A History of the District and Supreme Courts of Natal (1846–1910)*, 1986; *idem*, "Hendrik Cloete, Recorder of Natal: as Revealed in his Judgments", (1982) 45 *T.H.R.H.R.* 148ff.; *idem*, "The 'Romodutchyafricanderenglander' law of nineteenth-century Natal", (1985) 48 *T.H.R.H.R.* 164ff.; cf. also, for the time immediately after Union, S.D. Girvin, "John Dove Wilson as Judge President of the Natal Provincial Division 1911–1930: his Approach to Legal Authorities and their Influence in Cases involving Black Litigants", (1988) 105 *S.A.L.J.* 479ff.; *idem*, "An Evaluation of the Career of a Scots Colonial Judge: John Dove Wilson of Natal", 1990 *J.R.* 35ff.

34 Section 135 of the South Africa Act (9 Edw. 7, c.9) ("Subject to the provisions of this Act, all laws in force in the several colonies at the establishment of the Union shall continue in force in the respective provinces until repealed or amended...") apparently only dealt with statutory law (*Webster v. Ellison* 1911 A.D 73 (99)). However, in all four colonies Roman-Dutch law had previously received statutory recognition as common law. For details, see De Wet, *op. cit.*, n.29, 41f.; De Vos, *op. cit.*, n.29, 255f. They point out that the relevant Free State Ordinance as well as the Charter of Justice of 1832 were subsequently repealed by the South African legislature. Thus, the statutory basis for the application of Roman-Dutch law has, in parts of South Africa, fallen away.

African law into a mixed legal system.[35] This process was, generally speaking, rather unobtrusive, for relatively few English legal institutions "marched [in] openly along the highway of legislative enactment, to the sound of the brass bands of royal commissions and public discussion".[36] Rather, we are dealing here with a kind of *"Juristenrezeption"* along the lines of the reception of Roman law in Europe. The following factors, in my view, were of particular significance: the relatively low standard of the administration of justice during the pre-1806 era; the reception of the English law of procedure and of evidence within a court system remodelled according to the English pattern;[37] the adoption of the doctrine of *stare decisis*; the introduction of English as the official language to be used in court;[38] the jurisdiction of the Privy Council in London as an appeal court against judgements of the Cape Supreme Court; and the admission requirements for advocates at the Cape bar (and hence also of the judges of the Cape Supreme Court): they had to be either members of the English, Scottish[39] or Irish Inns of Court, or graduates of the Universities of Oxford, Cambridge or

---

35   On the reception of English law in the Cape, cf. C.G. Botha, "Early Influence of English Law upon Roman-Dutch Law", in *Collected Works*, vol. 2, 1962, 118ff.; H.D.J. Bodenstein, "English Influences on the Common Law of South Africa", (1915) 32 *S.A.L.J.* 337ff.; Hahlo and Kahn, *Union, op. cit.*, n.29, 17ff.; Heike Jung, *Der Einfluß des englischen Rechts im südafrikanischen Strafrecht*, 1973, 42ff.; Van Zyl, *op. cit.*, n.29, 453ff.; B. Beinart, "The English Legal Contribution in South Africa: The Interaction of Civil and Common Law", 1981 *Acta Juridica* 7ff.; R. Zimmermann, "Die Rechtsprechung des Supreme Court of the Cape of Good Hope am Ende der Sechziger Jahre des 19. Jahrhunderts", in *Huldigingsbundel Paul van Warmelo*, 1984, 286ff.; De Vos, *op. cit.*, n.29, 259ff.; for Natal cf. Spiller, (1985) 48 *T.H.R.H.R.* 170ff.
36   Hahlo and Kahn, *Union, op. cit.*, n.29, at 18.
37   Cf. in particular H.J. Erasmus, "The Interaction of Substantive and Procedural Law: the Southern African Experience in Historical and Comparative Perspective", (1990) 1 *Stellenbosch L.R.* 348ff.; *idem*, "Historical Foundations of the South African Law of Civil Procedure", (1991) 108 *S.A.L.J.* 265ff.
38   Cf. George Denoon, "The Introduction of English as the Official Language at the Cape", (1953) 70 *S.A.L.J.* 90ff.
39   The only Scot appointed in the nineteenth century to the Cape Bench was William Menzies. He remained a member of the Cape Supreme Court from 1828 until his death in 1850 and, with his bias against English law, played a vital role in keeping alive the civilian tradition at the Cape. For details, see C.G. Botha, "The Honourable William Menzies 1795–1850", in *Collected Works*, vol. 2, 1962, 1ff.; Girvin, (1992) 109 *S.A.L.J.* 298ff. and (1992) 109 *S.A.L.J.* 652ff. After Union, another Scot (John Dove Wilson) became Chief Justice of the Natal Provincial Division in 1911 and remained in that post for 19 years; on him, see Girvin, 1990 *J.R.* 35ff. Generally on the historical relation between Scots law and Roman-Dutch law, see T.B. Smith, "Scots Law and Roman-Dutch Law – A Shared Tradition", in *Studies Critical and Comparative*, 1962, 46ff. and the references in Kahn, *op. cit.*, n.27, 225ff. and Feenstra and Zimmermann, *op. cit.*, n.8, 56f.

Dublin.[40] One can easily imagine how awkward advocates and judges, trained in Britain, must have found it to apply a law that was not only, at least initially, completely alien to them but also rather inaccessible. There were no modern textbooks and the authoritative literature of the Roman-Dutch writers was composed in a rather old-fashioned Dutch or in Latin. Thus, it was said about Sir William Hodges, Chief Justice from 1858–1868, that "on his arrival in the Colony his ignorance of Roman-Dutch law was complete. In endeavouring to make himself acquainted with it, his defective scholarship offered an impediment, as he could not read Latin with much facility".[41] Obviously, under these circumstances, judges as well as advocates were continuously tempted to refer to English case law or textbooks for guidance; and this way of proceeding was often justified with the specious argument that the Roman-Dutch authorities were either silent on the point in question or advocated a solution identical to the one in English law. It is hardly surprising that English law managed to slip in on an ever broader front, mainly in the law of procedure, but also increasingly in traditional core areas of private law like agency, delict, contract and succession (as far as executors and trusts were concerned). "It is so much easier to find your law in an English text book or in English reports than to wade through a sea of Latin or to puzzle your head over old Dutch writers and black letter consultations", as Sir John Wessels once put it.[42] In the end, therefore, "[b]y a process of imperceptible accretion, not unlike *alluvio*, aided by legislation with an English bias, a layer of English rules and concepts became superimposed upon the law of Grotius and Voet. Roman-Dutch law was assuming an anglicized look".[43]

---

40 On the judges sent out from Britain in 1827 "...to measure out by a mongrel code a scanty justice to squalid savages", see, most recently, Girvin, (1992) 109 *S.A.L.J.* 295ff.

41 A.W. Cole, *Reminiscences of my Life and of the Cape Bench and Bar*, 1896, at 16. Characteristic also is the following remark uttered by Sir John Wylde, Chief Justice from 1827 to 1855, when the Attorney-General had referred to Roman-Dutch authorities: "Quote what Dutch or Roman books you please – musty or otherwise – and they must be musty if they lay down such doctrines. I belong to a higher court than they refer to – a court not paralyzed by their authority, much less by the maxims of philosophers dozing over their midnight lamp in their solitary chambers. My Queen has sent me here to administer justice under the Royal Charter and the practices of the Courts of Flanders, Batavia or Trinitad are no authority on me"; cf. D.P. Visser, "Daedalus in the Supreme Court – the Common Law Today", (1986) 49 *T.H.R.H.R.* 129. Further on Sir John Wylde cf. Girvin, (1992) 109 *S.A.L.J.* 295ff. and (1992) 109 *S.A.L.J.* 652ff.; Ellison Kahn, *Law, Life and Laughter, Legal Anecdotes and Portraits*, 1991, 353ff.

42 "The Future of Roman-Dutch Law in South Africa", (1929) 37 *S.A.L.J.* 276.

43 Hahlo and Kahn, *System, op. cit.*, n.29, at 578. In order to save Roman-Dutch law, even the idea of a codification was mooted; cf. particularly Wessels, (1920) 37 *S.A.L.J.* 284 ("Without a code, my fears for the Roman-Dutch law are great..."). *Contra*, e.g., R.H. Hahlo, "...And Save Us From Codification", (1960) 77 *S.A.L.J.* 432ff.; Hahlo and Kahn, *System, op. cit.*, n.29, 72ff. Most recently, cf. the

3. At the time of the creation of the Union of South Africa this movement towards English law was, however, beginning to slow down. This can partly be ascribed to the influence of Judges like J.G. Kotzé in the Transvaal[44] and Lord de Villiers, Chief Justice of the Cape of Good Hope, and subsequently of the Union of South Africa, for 41 years.[45] Furthermore, tuition in Roman-Dutch law began to be offered in Cape Town in 1859,[46] the first indigenous academic literature started to appear,[47] and some of the main authorities began to be translated.[48] In 1884 the *Cape Law Journal* was founded, today (under the title *South African Law Journal*) one of the oldest, still existing English-medium law journals in the world.[49] All of this contributed to the consolidation of Roman-Dutch law. Originating in the Afrikaans- medium law schools of Stellenbosch[50] and Pretoria,[51] a strong tendency even began to gain influence which not only wished to preserve the status quo but strove to remove the English "pollution" from the South African *usus modernus pandectarum*.[52] There ensued a sometimes acrimonious academic

"reconsideration" by W.J. Hosten, "*Kodifikasie in Suid-Africa – 'n Heroorweging?*", in *Huldigingsbundel vir W.A. Joubert*, 1988, 59ff.

44 Zimmermann, *op. cit.*, n.29, 22f.; Kahn, *op. cit.*, n.41, 115ff.
45 For details, see E.A. Walker, *Lord de Villiers and His Times*, 1925.
46 D.V. Cowen, "The History of the Faculty of Law, University of Cape Town – A Chapter in the Growth of Roman-Dutch Law in South Africa", 1959 *Acta Juridica* 8ff.; D.H. Sampson, "Legal Education", in *Our Legal Heritage*, ed. The Association of Law Societies of the Republic of South Africa, 1982, 167ff.
47 Cf. e.g. De Vos, *op. cit.*, n.29, at 264; A. van Blerk, "The Growth of South African Legal Literature", 1977 *De Rebus Procuratoriis* 561ff.
48 For example, an English translation of Van der Keessel's *Theses Selectae* was published by C.A. Lorenz in 1868, of Grotius' *Inleiding* by A.F.S. Maasdorp in 1878, of Van der Linden's *Regtsgeleerd Practicaal en Koopmans Handboek* by H. Juta in 1884 and of parts of Voet's *Commentarius ad Pandectas* by J. Buchanan, M. de Villiers and others in the years since 1880.
49 Cf. E. Kahn, (1983) 100 *S.A.L.J.* 1f.; (1983) 100 *S.A.L.J.* 594ff.
50 On its history cf. A.H. van Wyk, "Die Stellenbosse Regsfakulteit 1920–1989", 1989 *Consultus* 42ff.; on its most influential member cf. R. Zimmermann and C. Hugo, "Fortschritte der südafrikanischen Rechtswissenschaft im 20. Jahrhundert: Der Beitrag von J.C. de Wet (1912–1990)" (1992) 60 *T.v.R.* 157ff.
51 The University of Pretoria was established in 1930, as a successor to the Transvaal University College. The *spiritus rector* of the law faculty for many years was Professor Daan Pont (who died in 1991, aged 96). On Pont (who also founded the *Tydskrif vir Hedendaagse Romeins-Hollandse Reg*), D. van Rensburg, (1987) 50 *T.H.R.H.R.* 253ff.; on the history of the Law Faculty of the University of Pretoria in general, see K. van Rooyen, "*Die Regsfakulteit, Universiteit van Pretoria: Meer as Tagtig Jaar Regsonderrig*", 1991 *Consultus* 49ff.
52 On the role of the *Tydskrif vir Hedendaagse Romeins-Hollandse Reg* (which started appearing in 1937) see (1937) 1 *T.H.R.H.R.* 1ff.; D. Pont, (1963) 26 *T.H.R.H.R.* 1ff.; F. Rumpff, (1987) 50 *T.H.R.H.R.* 1f.

battle, a *"bellum juridicum"* about the true sources of South African law.[53] This conflict had strong political overtones resulting, at least partly, from mutual resentment between English- and Afrikaans-speaking South Africans. Return to "our own" pure Roman-Dutch law became an important issue on the agenda of Afrikaaner nationalism. In the fifties and sixties, after the accession to power of the National Party and after the abolition of the right of appeal to the Privy Council, this purist movement, hitherto confined to lecture hall and legal literature, gained a foothold even in the courts. In the wake of the great constitutional crisis of the fifties,[54] L. C. Steyn was appointed Chief Justice, a man who combined, par excellence, "executive-mindedness" and loyalty to the government with a far-reaching programme of "purification" of the private law.[55] The law of delict particularly was reshaped by him in accordance with this programme.[56]

In the meantime the dust of battle has settled. Extreme positions are no longer seriously advocated. It is widely accepted today that South African law has acquired its own identity which is neither purely Roman-Dutch nor purely English. Nobody would resort to English law at all costs;[57] nor does anybody argue for its eradication simply on the ground that it is an alien intruder. A pragmatic approach prevails.[58] South African legislation and precedents are accorded prime authority;

---

53 Cf., as far as contemporary literature is concerned, *Proculus,* "Bellum *Juridicum* – Two Approaches to South African Law", (1951) 68 *S.A.L.J.* 306ff.; G.A. Mulligan, *"Bellum Juridicum* (3): Purists, Pollutionists and Pragmatists", (1952) 69 *S.A.L.J.* 25ff.; P.Q.R. Boberg, "Oak Tree or Acorn? – Conflicting Approaches to our Law of Delict", (1966) 83 *S.A.L.J.* 150ff.; A.S. Mathews and J.R.L. Milton, "An English Backlash", (1965) 82 *S.A.L.J.* 31ff.; *Proculus Redivivus,* "South African Law at the Crossroads or What is Our Common Law?", (1965) 82 *S.A.L.J.* 17ff. For a retrospective assessment cf. A. van Blerk, "The Genesis of the "modernist"–"purist" Debate: A Historical Bird's-eye View", (1984) 47 *T.H.R.H.R.* 255ff.; C.F. Forsyth, *In Danger for Their Talents. A Study of the Appellate Division of the Supreme Court of South Africa from 1950–80,* 1985, 182ff.; R. Zimmermann, *"Usus hodiernus pandectarum",* in R. Schulze, *Europäische Rechts- und Verfassungsgeschichte, Ergebnisse und Perspektiven der Forschung,* 1991, 68ff.

54 On which see, for example, B. Beinart, "The South African Appeal Court and Judicial Review", (1958) 21 *M.L.R.* 587ff.; Hahlo and Kahn, *op. cit.,* n.29, 151ff.; D.H. van Wyk, "Judicial Review in the Republic of South Africa", (1980) 29 *Jahrbuch des öffentlichen Rechts* 677ff.

55 Cf. E. Cameron, "Legal Chauvinism, Executive-mindedness and Justice – L.C. Steyn's Impact on South African Law", (1982) 99 *S.A.L.J.* 38ff.

56 Cf. e.g. Forsyth, *op. cit.,* n.53, 197ff.

57 Cf., as far as J.C. de Wet (usually regarded as the "arch-purist") is concerned, Zimmermann and Hugo, (1992) 60 *T.v.R.* 168f.; cf. also Van Blerk, (1982) 99 *S.A.L.J.* 373ff.

58 Still, however, occasionally in an "antiquarian" disguise: cf. C. Forsyth, "The Juristic Basis of the Testamentary Trust, the Principle of Non-delegation of Will-making Power and the Purism Movement", (1986) 103 *S.A.L.J.* 513ff. (on *Braun* v. *Blann and Botha NN.O. & another* 1984 (2) S.A. 850 (A)).

if one has to venture beyond these formal sources, English and Roman-Dutch law carry about equal weight.[59] Which of these systems one resorts to, depends on whether that specific area of South African law has been mainly shaped by the one or the other.[60] Constitutional law, administrative law, the law of evidence, procedural law,[61] large parts of commercial law (especially those governed by statute; e.g. company law, negotiable instruments and insolvency) and the law relating to the administration of estates and the registration of deeds are largely English. Family law, the law of persons, things and succession, on the other hand, remain mainly Roman-Dutch and have only been anglicised to a limited extent. Notable examples of English imports are the reduction of the age of majority (from twenty-five to twenty-one), perpetual quitrent, leasehold, "attornment" as a mode of delivery, unrestricted freedom of testation (no legitimate portion), the underhand will and many aspects of trust law. The law of obligations is probably that part of the law where the most complex process of blending of the two traditions has occurred.[62]

III.

1. What role does Roman law play in South Africa today? In the first place, we always have to remember that Roman law was not received in its classical or Justinianic form but as mediated by a specific branch of seventeenth century legal science. Secondly, it is inevitable in a legal system based upon a – mitigated – doctrine of *stare decisis*[63] that we concentrate our attention on legal practice. A brief glance, however, at the academic support mechanisms appears to be in order.

Over the last decades, South Africa has witnessed a considerable expansion of tertiary education in law.[64] Until well into the seventies,

---

59   Cf. D.P. Visser, (1986) 49 *T.H.R.H.R.* 127ff., who argues that both Roman-Dutch and English law fulfil the role of "common law" in South Africa.

60   As to what follows, cf. particularly Beinart, 1981 *Acta Juridica* 13ff.; also, as far as the survival of the Roman legal tradition is concerned, *idem*, "Roman Law in a Modern Uncodified Romanistic System", (1970) 10 *Romanitas* 331ff.

61   On the influence of the common law procedural model on the development of South African substantive law cf. Erasmus, (1990) 1 *Stellenbosch L.R.* 348ff.

62   As far as criminal law is concerned (where the choice is between German and English rather than Roman-Dutch and English law), cf. Zimmermann and Hugo, (1992) 60 *T.v.R.* 169ff.

63   Kahn, *op. cit.*, n.27, 254ff.; Zimmermann, *op. cit.*, n.29, 54ff.; cf. also A. van Blerk, "The Irony of Labels", (1982) 99 *S.A.L.J.* 368ff.

64   For details, see Zimmermann, *Gedächtnisschrift Geck, cit. sup.*, n.21, 987ff. On the history of the law faculty of the University of Cape Town, cf. D.V. Cowen, "Taught Law is Tough Law: The Evolution of a South African Law School", (1988) 51 *T.H.R.H.R.* 4ff.; D.P. Visser, "As Durable as the Mountain: The Story of the Cape Town Law School since 1859", 1992 *Consultus* 32ff.

the number of graduates at the university of Cape Town, to mention but one example, did not exceed between twenty and thirty per year; by 1984 it had risen to ninety-one students. Cape Town's Afrikaans-medium sister faculty at Stellenbosch only had three chairs in law until 1973; today, more than four times as many professors are teaching in the same faculty. All in all, there are nineteen law faculties today in eighteen South African universities.[65] Surprisingly, however, at only three of them is there a chair of Roman law.[66] Roman law is still an obligatory course at all South African universities but it is usually taught at an elementary level – too elementary to equip students with a facility for independent historical research.[67] Moreover, the Roman law course tends to be unpopular, on both sides of the lecture desk. Students regard the subject as "dead", its study as "irrelevant", and South African academics, badly paid, tend to specialise in more lucrative, modern subjects rather than waste their time on acquiring the specialised skills of a proper Roman lawyer.[68] As a result, the course in Roman law is often either taught by an expert in modern law, or it is assigned to junior members of staff with little teaching experience. It is a reflection of this state of affairs that the Romanist legal literature produced in South Africa these days largely consists of elementary textbooks.[69]

---

65 Including the universities in the former "homelands" Transkei, Bophutatswana, Venda and Ciskei but excluding the former British protectorates Botswana, Lesotho and Swaziland. Natal has two law faculties (at the Durban and Pietermaritzburg campus respectively). The universities of Fort Hare, the North, Zululand, Western Cape and Durban-Westville were originally founded for the benefit of non-white (i.e. black, "coloured" and "Indian") students. University apartheid began to be abolished with the Universities Amendment Act 83/1983; the English-medium universities started to accept black students in growing numbers. The Afrikaans-medium Universities, too, gave up their exclusivity and abolished race as a criterion for University admission. Cf. *Gedächtnisschrift Geck, cit. sup.*, n.21, 989ff., 1002f.

66 The oldest one is the W.P. Schreiner chair at the University of Cape Town, held from 1924–1948 by John Kerr Wylie (on whom see Cowen, (1988) 51 *T.H.R.H.R.* 20ff.) and from 1950 to 1974 by Ben Beinart (on whom see 1976 *Acta Juridica* xvff.). Today, I think, it can fairly be said that hardly any "Romanist" in the European sense of the word is teaching in South Africa.

67 Cf. also *Erasmus*, (1989) 106 *S.A.L.J.* 673f.

68 Cf. also the comments by F.H. Lawson, "Reflections on Thirty Years' Experience of Teaching Roman Law", 1956 *Butterworth's South African L.R.* 16 and Stoop, (1991) 45 *T.H.R.H.R.* 181.

69 P. van Warmelo, *An Introduction to the Principles of Roman Civil Law*, 1976; D.H. van Zyl, *Geskiedenis en beginsels van die Romeinse privaatreg*, 1977 (an English translation was published in 1983 under the title *History and Principles of Roman Private Law*); J.E. Schiller, *Selected Texts and Cases on the Roman Law of Things*, 1982; P. Spiller, *A Manual of Roman Law*, 1986; Ph.J. Thomas, *Introduction to Roman Law*, 1986.

Latin as a requirement for admission to legal practice appears to be on its way out. Whilst the Admission of Advocates Act[70] used to provide that a prospective advocate had to have passed "not less than one course in the Latin language prescribed or recognized by such university for a *baccalaureus* degree" many students effectively had to pass two courses in Latin; for anyone who had not taken Latin at school first had to go through a preparatory course called "Latin Intensive" in order to qualify for Latin I. But could not Latin Intensive in itself be regarded as the "one course in the Latin language" required by the Act? This interpretation by a growing number of students was indeed endorsed in the early eighties by two provincial divisions of the Supreme Court[71] but ultimately rejected by the Appellate Division.[72] In the meantime the legislature has amended the Admission of Advocates Act;[73] admission depends on successful completion of "Latin in the higher grade required for the matriculation examination" or an equal level of proficiency. Thus, although Latin is still statutorily entrenched,[74] the required standard has been watered down considerably. One may well ask whether a crash course like Latin Intensive on its own makes any sense at all.[75]

This is, from a purely Romanist perspective, a rather disillusioning picture. It is only to a certain extent counterbalanced by the fact that a variety of modern lawyers approach their subject in a historical – perhaps one can say, Pandectist – perspective. Corné van der Merwe's textbook on the law of property provides a good example[76] – as does David Carey Miller's book on the acquisition and protection of

---

70   74/1964, s.3.
71   *Ex parte Barnard* 1982 (2) S.A. 70(N); *Ex parte Friedgut* 1983 (2) S.A. 336(T); on which see Coenraad Visser, "Observations *ex parte Friedgut*: Only Injury Time Left for the Latin Requirement", (1983) 100 *S.A.L.J.* 378ff.
72   *University of Cape Town* v. *Cape Bar Council and Another* 1986 (4) S.A. 903 (A), confirming the decision of the Cape Provincial Division at first instance; on which see L.M. du Plessis, "A Significant Contribution to the Latin Debate" (1986) 103 *S.A.L.J.* 452ff.
73   106/1991, s.3.
74   Most of the universities, consequently, also require matriculation Latin or Latin Intensive for the award of the LL.B. Only at Stellenbosch is Latin I still required. The university of the Witwatersrand, on the other hand, appears to have dropped Latin altogether.
75   The controversy as to the value of Latin continues: cf. R. Zimmermann, "Latin for Lawyers", 1986 *De Rebus* 605ff.; L.J. Boulle, "Latin: the Future of the Past", 1987 *De Rebus* 23ff.; Jo-Marie Claassen, "Latin and Lawyers: a Five-year Dialogue", (1988) 105 *S.A.L.J.* 769ff.; J. Sinclair and E. Mureinik, "Compulsory Latin: a Compelling Case?", (1989) 106 *S.A.L.J.* 158ff.; Erasmus, (1989) 106 *S.A.L.J.* 673f.; D.H. van Zyl, "Is juridiese barbarisme ons voorland?", (1990) 53 *T.H.R.H.R.* 229ff.; C.M.R. Dlamini, "The Law Teacher, the Law Student and Legal Education in South Africa", (1992) 109 *S.A.L.J.* 603f.
76   C.G. van der Merwe, *Sakereg,* 2nd ed., 1989.

property.[77] Not every subject lends itself to this kind of treatment; but
even where it would, we often find what the late Paul Boberg has termed
a "thoroughly modern approach" being adopted. Boberg's textbook on
the law of delict is a prime example. Subscribing to the aphorism of the
earlier polemicist, "Proculus Redivivus", that "a country's law can be
found in the last thirty years of its law reports",[78] he explicitly assigns a
"back seat" to the historical authorities.[79] Not everybody puts it quite so
frankly. Many South African monographs and theses start off with a
lengthy chapter on Roman law. Quite often, however, this is without any
relevance to or consequence for the next chapters. A good example is
provided by the third edition of Caney's authoritative book on
suretyship.[80] Here the section on Roman law has not only been taken
over, substantially unchanged, from the second edition (as if within the
intervening twelve years nothing of relevance had been produced on the
Roman *fideiussio*) but has even been written by a different author from
the rest of the book.[81] This first chapter, therefore, represents nothing
more than a historical introduction: fairly interesting for the cultivated
reader, but without vital importance for what follows. Roman law no
longer appears to be conceived as an integral part of South African law.

2. If we turn our attention now to the South African judiciary, we
may take the statistics compiled by Derek van der Merwe as our starting
point.[82] They are based on all decisions of the Appellate Division of the
Supreme Court of South Africa published between 1970 and 1979. Of
those 782 decisions 24% refer to Anglo-American case law, 14.1% to
Roman-Dutch law in the narrow sense, 6.5% to other authors of the
European *ius commune* and 4.6% to the *Corpus Iuris Civilis* or other
Roman sources. A more recent investigation has been undertaken by
Jacques du Plessis at Regensburg University. Du Plessis has looked at all
the cases reported in the South African Law Reports between January
1990 and December 1991 (a total number of 725 cases). This survey
therefore not only includes decisions of the Appellate Division but

---

77 D.L. Carey Miller, *The Acquisition and Protection of Ownership*, 1986.
    Carey Miller, however, draws a curious line between "recognized authori-
    ties of Roman-Dutch law" (to whom he has "tried mainly to refer") and ref-
    erences to Roman law (which he has "by and large, avoided"). Reason: The
    "Roman-Dutch system should, as far as possible, be taken to represent a
    new starting point in sources. The idea of an intact civilian development
    may be attractive to specialists but there is a danger that the law becomes
    too esoteric" (Preface, at v). The same objection would probably be raised
    by the modern "pragmatist" against referring to Roman-Dutch authorities
    of the seventeenth or eighteenth centuries.
78 (1965) 82 *S.A.L.J.* 24.
79 P.Q.R. Boberg, *The Law of Delict I: Aquilian Liability*, 1984, at v.
80 Caney's *The Law of Suretyship in South Africa*, 3rd ed. by C.F. Forsyth, 1982. The
    matter has been rectified in the 4th ed., 1992, by C.F. Forsyth and J.T. Pretorius.
81 Chapter I *Historical – The Roman Law: Foundations of our Law of
    Sureties* by R.O. Donellan.
82 *Bulletin of the Southern African Society of Legal Historians*, June 1987, 5ff.

those of all local and provincial divisions within the jurisdiction of the
Supreme Court of South Africa, and those from the Supreme Courts of
Zimbabwe, Namibia, Transkei, Bophutatswana, Ciskei and Venda. Of
those 725 cases 44 (i.e. 6.1%) refer to Roman-Dutch authorities *stricto
sensu* (only Holland, i.e. excluding the other Dutch provinces), 32 (i.e.
4.4%) to other authors of the European *ius commune*, and 34 (i.e. 4.7%)
contain references to Roman law.[83] These references to Roman law are
in the form either of general statements or of specific citations of
Roman legal sources. Among the sources quoted, the *Institutes* feature
in 2, the *Digest* in 20, the *Codex* in 5 cases and the *Novellae* in 1 case.
The *Institutes* of Gaius are quoted once. In about half of those 34 cases
reference to Roman law is merely incidental (or ornamental): it is part
of a historical overview which is, strictly speaking, unnecessary
because the issues are settled in modern law; often the references to
Roman law are merely bundled together with those to Roman-Dutch
authorities.[84] As regards the other cases containing references to
Roman law, it is drawn upon mainly with the aim of determining or
extending the validity or contents of existing rules: what exactly is the
ambit of a contractual clause excluding liability for latent defects
(i.e. the aedilitian remedies)?;[85] what is the relevance of the owner's

---

83 These figures must not be cumulated, since we are dealing, as a rule, with
    the same decisions in each of these sections. Any evaluation of these
    figures must take into account that the South African Supreme Court has a
    comprehensive jurisdiction ranging from private and criminal to constitu-
    tional or administrative law. A considerable percentage of decisions is
    therefore devoted to areas of the law where Roman-Dutch law has either
    never applied or where it has been superseded by modern legislation. The
    first survey of this kind was, incidentally, undertaken by Robert Warden
    Lee. He came to the conclusion that "rather less" than 5% of the reported
    decisions of the Appellate Division of the Supreme Court over the period
    from 1910 to 1932 contained references to Roman law ("Roman Law in the
    British Empire, Particularly in the Union of South Africa", in *Atti del con-
    gresso internazionale di diritto romano*, vol. 2, 1935, at 256; the relevant
    decisions are summarised on 265ff.; cf. further *idem*, "*Modernus usus
    juris civilis*", (1947) 22 *Tulane L.R.* 131ff.; *idem*, "The Disappearing Roman
    Law", (1957) 74 *S.A.L.J.* 79ff. Lee's prediction that Roman law in South
    Africa "is dissolving gradually into South African law" has, so far, not been
    substantiated, at least not, if one looks at the quotation practices of the
    Supreme Court (cf. however, the lament echoing Lee by B.C. Stoop,
    "*Hereditas damnosa?* Some Remarks on the Relevance of Roman Law",
    (1991) 45 *T.H.R.H.R.* 178, 180; and see Hosten, *Huldigingsbundel Joubert,
    cit. sup.*, n.43, 65ff.). A further statistical analysis (with rather questionable
    predictions) has been undertaken by J.J. Henning (unpublished LLB. dis-
    sertation): cf. Van Zyl, *op. cit.*, n.29, at 486. It is not available to me. Cf. also
    the studies mentioned by Stoop, (1991) 45 *T.H.R.H.R.* 180.
84 Cf. also the classification of the use of Roman law by Van Warmelo, (1959)
    33 *Tulane L.R.* 570ff. and by Spiller, *op. cit.*, n.69, 246ff.
85 *Van der Merwe* v. *Meades* 1991 (2) S.A. 1 (A); on which see C.-J. Pretorius,
    "Aanspreeklikheid van die verkoper vir verborge gebreke in die koopsaak
    waar die koopkontrak 'n voetstootsbeding bevat", (1992) 55 *T.H.R.H.R.* 325ff.

intentio with regard to *inaedificatio?*;[86] how far does the prohibition of *pacta commissoria* extend?;[87] is the mandator vicariously liable for the conduct of the *mandatarius?*;[88] can gaming or wagering debts be used by way of set-off?;[89] does a court have jurisdiction to try people abducted by agents of the state?;[90] can a person stand surety for his own debt?;[91] when can a spoliation order (*mandament van spolie*) be granted in order to obtain possession of a shipwreck?;[92] does a security firm charged with the protection of cars owe a duty of care towards their owners to avoid damage?;[93] can the *actio Pauliana utilis* be extended to provide for a maintenance order?[94, 95] As far as Roman-Dutch authorities are concerned, Johannes Voet, *Commentarius ad Pandectas*, features particularly prominently (in 36 cases); Hugo Grotius' *Inleidinge* is quoted in 13 cases (*De jure belli ac pacis* only in 2 cases), Van Leeuwen's two most famous works (*Censura forensis* and *Rooms-Hollands Regt*) in 12, Van der Keessel (*Praelectiones ad Grotium*) in 11, Van der Linden (*Koopmans Handboek*) in 10, Groenewegen (*De legibus abrogatis*) in 7, and Vinnius (*Commentaries*

---

86 *Sumatie (Edms.) Bpk.* v. *Venter en 'n ander NN.O.* 1990 (1) S.A. 173 (T); on which see N. Olivier and W. du Plessis, "Vereistes vir eiendomsverkryging by wyse van *accessio* (*inaedificatio*) van roerende sake by onroerende sake" (1990) 53 *T.H.R.H.R.* 106ff.

87 *Hesseling* v. *Meyer* 1991 (1) S.A. 276 (SWA).

88 *Eksteen* v. *Van Schalkwyk en 'n ander* 1991 (2) S.A. 39 (T); on which see W. du Plessis and N. Olivier, "*Mandatum* en middellike aanspreeklikheid", (1991) 45 *T.H.R.H.R.* 818ff.; J.R. Midgley, "Mandate, Agency and Vicarious Liability: Conflicting Principles", (1991) 108 *S.A.L.J.* 419ff.

89 *Nichol* v. *Burger* 1990 (1) S.A. 231 (C).

90 *S.* v. *Ebrahim* 1991 (2) S.A. 553 (A).

91 *Nedbank Ltd.* v. *Van Zyl* 1990 (2) S.A. 469 (A).

92 *Reck* v. *Mills en 'n ander* 1990 (1) S.A. 751 (A); for criticism see H. Booysen, "Die toepassing van die wisselwet om vaderskap te bepaal en van die Romeins-Hollandse reg op berging", (1990) 53 *T.H.R.H.R.* 595ff.

93 *Compass Motors Industries (Pty.) Ltd.* v. *Callguard (Pty.) Ltd.* 1990 (2) S.A. 520 (W).

94 *Reyneke* v. *Reyneke* 1990 (3) S.A. 927 (E).

95 Cf. further *Cotton Marketing Board of Zimbabwe* v. *Zimbabwe National Railways* 1990 (1) S.A. 582 (ZSC) extending the *edictum de nautis, cauponibus et stabulariis* to cover land transport – cf. (1991) 55 *RabelsZ.* 505ff.; *Langley Fox Building Partnership (Pty.) Ltd.* v. *De Valence* 1991 (1) S.A. 1 (A); *Protea International (Pty.) Ltd.* v. *Peat Marwick Mitchell & Co.* 1990 (2) S.A. 566 (A); *Peter* v. *Minister of Law and Order* 1990 (4) S.A. 6 (E); *Raats Röntgen und Vermeulen (Pty.) Ltd.* v. *Administrator, Cape and Others* 1991 (1) S.A. 827 (C); *Commissioner for Inland Revenue* v. *First National Bank Ltd.* 1990 (3) S.A. 641 (A); *Boka Enterprises (Pvt.) Ltd.* v. *Manatse and Another N.O.* 1990 (3) S.A. 626 (ZHC).

ad Institutiones) in 4 cases.[96] Ulrich Huber (11 cases) and Pothier (5 cases) are the most often quoted non-Roman-Dutch authors. As a rule, of course, Roman and Roman-Dutch or Roman, Roman-Dutch and non-Roman-Dutch authorities are referred to in the same decisions: the way back to the *Corpus Iuris*, in other words, nearly inevitably leads through the writers of the *ius commune*. With all due caution, the following observations of a more general nature can perhaps be made.

IV.

1. First of all, it is interesting to note that a large majority of South African judges hardly ever refer to Roman law in their judgements.[97] Of all decisions in 1990 and 1991 where reference to Roman law was not merely incidental, about half are attributable to two judges. On the Appellate Division of the Supreme Court (Dr. C. P.) Joubert, J.A., today appears to be the specialist on old authorities to whom cases requiring this kind of investigation seem to be usually assigned.[98] As a young man, he had studied first at Pretoria, then at Leyden and published a thesis on

---

96   Van der Merwe, *op. cit.*, n.82, provides the following figures: reference to Voet in 14.1% of all cases, Van Leeuwen and Van der Keessel 4.2% each, Grotius 4%, Van der Linden 2.8%, Schorer 1.8%, Groenewegen 1.5%. Among the other authors of the *ius commune*, Huber, Pothier and Glück appear particularly frequently. Both Van der Merwe's and Du Plessis' figures clearly demonstrate the overwhelming importance of Johannes Voet's *Commentarius ad Pandectas* among the "old authorities" for South African courts. For details on Voet cf. Feenstra and Zimmermann, *op. cit.*, n.8, 39ff.

97   One of the reasons may be, as Hosten, *Huldigingsbundel Joubert, cit. sup.*, n.43, at 66, points out, lack of knowledge of Latin.

98   The other Judge on the Appellate Division who used to be renowned for his meticulous probing of Roman and Roman-Dutch sources was Jansen, J.A. He sat on the Appellate Division from 1968 until 1988. For a period of eleven years, Joubert and Jansen were thus colleagues in the same court. Their judgements, however, display a fundamentally different approach towards the old authorities. This comes out particularly clearly in their conflicting views on the role of equity in contract law: cf. the clash of opinion in *Bank of Lisbon and South Africa Ltd.* v. *De Ornelas and another* 1988 (3) S.A. 580 (A) 592ff. and 611ff.; cf. *infra sub* V. 4. For an analysis, cf. C. Lewis, "Towards an Equitable Theory of Contract: The Contribution of Mr. Justice E.L. Jansen to the South African Law of Contract" (1991) 108 *S.A.L.J.* 249ff. Famous decisions by Jansen, J.A., based on extensive research into Roman and Roman-Dutch law are *L.T.A. Engineering Co. Ltd.* v. *Seacat Investments Ltd.* 1974 (1) S.A. 747 (A) (resuscitating a principle found in D.3.3.34 and dealing with the protection of the debtor in cases of cession; cf. Zimmermann, *op. cit.*, n.29, 66ff.), *B.K. Tooling (Edms.) Bpk.* v. *Scope Precision Engineering (Edms.) Bpk.* 1979 (1) S.A. 391 (A) (on which see G.F. Lubbe, C.M. Murray, *Farlam and Hathaway, Contract. Cases, Materials and Commentary*, 3rd ed., 1988, 568ff.) and *Tuckers Land and Development Corporation (Pty.) Ltd.* v. *Hovis* 1980 (1) S.A. 645 (A) (cf. *infra* n.207).

"Die Stigting in die Romeins-Hollandse Reg en in die Suid-Afrikaanse Reg" (1951); after his return from the Netherlands, he lectured for some time at the universities of the Orange Free State and of Pretoria and also commenced practice at the Pretoria bar. He was elevated to the Transvaal Provincial Division in 1974 and to the Appellate Division in 1977. Van Zyl, J., the other of these two judges, also has an academic background; he was professor of *(inter alia)* Roman law at the universities of Bloemfontein and Pretoria before he started a brilliant career as a practitioner which to date has carried him to the Transvaal Provincial Division. He holds four doctorates, three in law and one in classics. This preponderance of two individual judges is not entirely unproblematical, for it confirms a common perception that Roman-Dutch (and Roman) law are matters for the specialist (like company law or water law) rather than the general basis of South African private law.

2. Secondly, there is no specific concern about the position in classical Roman law. "We have received Roman law as corrupted by the Byzantines": this statement by Van den Heever, J.A.,[99] still represents the prevailing opinion.[100] The sources from the *Corpus Iuris* tend to be accepted at face value, without the kind of textual criticism familiar to the modern European Roman lawyer. Modern Roman law textbooks are very rarely referred to; thus, for instance, references occur in only four of the above-mentioned decisions reported in 1990 and 1991 (to Buckland/Stein, Van Zyl and Kaser on *Römisches Zivilprozeßrecht*).[101] The more conservative attitude towards textual criticism prevailing today in Europe, of course, renders the difference between classical Roman law and the law of Justinian in any case rather less dramatic than was once thought. What South African courts accept as Roman law therefore usually broadly coincides with the picture presented by Kaser and others. Thus, the obvious reluctance to use this kind of literature appears rather odd.[102]

---

99 *Pahad* v. *Director of Food Supplies and Distribution* 1949 (3) S.A. 695 (A) 710; cf. also the inaugural lecture of B. Beinart, *Roman Law in South African Practice,* 1952, 8ff.

100 Stoop, (1991) 54 *T.H.R.H.R.* 181 observes "an increasing tendency by the courts to disregard Roman law altogether".

101 Cf. also D.H. van Zyl, *"Die regshistoriese metode",* (1972) 35 *T.H.R.H.R.* 23 specifically rejecting the proposition that attention should be paid to the research produced in the neo-humanistic spirit of the past eighty years.

102 On the value of classical Roman law for South African jurisprudence cf. M. Kaser, "Das römische Recht in Südafrika", (1964) 81 *Z.S.S. (RA)* 20ff. (using the decision of *Van der Westhuizen* v. *Yskor Werknemers se Onderlinge Bystandsvereniging* 1960 (4) S.A. 803 (T) as an example). Cf. also already, in a similar vein, Beinart, *op. cit.,* n.99, 18ff.; P. van Warmelo, "The Function of Roman Law in South African Law", (1959) 33 *Tulane L.R.* 574ff.; *idem,* "Roman Law and the Old Authorities on Roman-Dutch Law", 1961 *Acta Juridica* 56ff. *Contra,* very pointedly, J. Kerr Wylie, "The Present Crisis of Roman Law and its Bearing on the Legal Situation in South Africa", (1939) 56 *S.A.L.J.* 210ff. ("...for the immediate purposes of legal practice in South Africa, Roman law no longer possesses any real value and should be eliminated").

3. The main reason why South African courts do not venture back beyond Justinian is, of course, that the Roman-Dutch writers had not done so either. Roman law, in other words, tends to be seen through the eyes of seventeenth and eighteenth century Roman-Dutch authorities; and they did not, for instance, have the *Gaius Veronensis* available.[103] This has further implications. The Dutch writers reinvigorated the *mos italicus* on the level of the humanistic learning provided by the *mos gallicus*. They thus brought about a modernisation of Roman law which, for the time being, ensured its survival. Most important for the emergence of this kind of *usus modernus pandectarum* was the integration of the "*mores hodierni*" into the learned law.[104] Thus, there is always the possibility of a conflict between (Justinianic) Roman and Roman-Dutch law. This kind of conflict is nearly always resolved in favour of the Roman-Dutch position by the South African courts: "...this Court administers the Roman-Dutch law, and not the Roman law of Justinian. If the courts of Holland have placed a certain interpretation upon a *lex* of the Digest,...then this Court should follow the interpretation of the Dutch courts", as Wessels, J., put the matter nearly ninety years ago.[105] If Roman law is therefore still usually

---

103 Occasionally, however, the Roman-Dutch authors specifically rejected Justinianic changes to the classical law. Thus, for instance, according to classical Roman law arrears of interest could not be charged to the extent that they exceeded the amount of the capital that had been borrowed: Ulp. D.12.6.26.1; C.4.32.10 (Antoninus); Laura Solidoro, "*Ultra sortis summam usurae non exiguntur*" (1982) 28 *Labeo* 164ff. In post-classical times the accrual of interest also ceased, rather strangely, when the amount of interest *paid* had reached the amount of the capital sum: Nov. 121, 2; 138; 160pr. Cf. Max Kaser, *Das römische Privatrecht*, Zweiter Abschnitt, 2nd ed., 1975, at 342. The Roman-Dutch writers recognised the rule of classical law; they did not receive Nov. 121, 2; 138 and 160pr.; cf. e.g. S. van Groenewegen van der Made, *Tractatus de legibus abrogatis et inusitatis in Hollandia vicinisque regionibus*, Amstelaedami, 1669, Cod., Lib. IV, Tit. XXXII, l. 27. In this situation South African courts, of course, follow Roman-Dutch, and through it classical Roman, rather than Justinianic law. Cf. now *L.T.A. Construction Bpk.* v. *Administrateur, Transvaal* 1992 (1) S.A. 473 (A) (on which see J. M. Otto, "Die gemeenregtelike verbod teen die oploop van rente", (1992) 55 *T.H.R.H.R.* 472ff.); also already G.F. Lubbe, "Die verbod op die oploop van rente *ultra duplum* – 'n konkretisering van die norm van *bona fides*?", (1990) 53 *T.H.R.H.R.* 190ff.
104 Cf. *supra* n.8.
105 (1907) T.S. 925, at 928f.; cf. also, e.g., *Bisschop* v. *Stafford* 1974 (3) S.A. 1 (A) 7: "In determining the common law requirements indiscriminate reference to the Roman law is to be guarded against" (per Jansen, J.A.); *L.T.A. Engineering Co. Ltd.* v. *Seacat Investments Ltd.* 1974 (1) S.A. 747 (A) 769: "Sande is, however, not to be read or explained in the light of classical Roman law. What was received in Europe was not the law as it was during the second and third centuries, but the law as understood and developed by the much later Glossators, Commentators and subsequent writers" (per Jansen, J.A.). For further comment, see Kaser, (1964) 81 *Z.S.S. (RA)* 16ff.; Erasmus, (1989) 106 *S.A.L.J.* 667ff.

regarded as "*ius in subsidio*" even today[106] this means that it may be referred to where "our commentators do not deal directly with any point on the subject or are rather laconic in their treatment of it".[107] One can, however, hardly imagine an issue on which the Roman-Dutch authorities should have been silent regarding a matter discussed in the Roman sources available to them[108] – unless, that is, where those sources had been abrogated by disuse or were for any other reason regarded as obsolete. Generally, therefore, South African courts refer to Roman law either as part of a general historical overview or they use it to elucidate the significance of what the Roman-Dutch authors (who may be vague or contradictory at places) are saying.[109]

4. Only very rarely does it happen that a rule recognised in Roman-Dutch but not in Roman law is thrown overboard, and that consequently the position in Roman law is restored. *Goldberg* v. *Buytendag Boerderye Beleggings*[110] is such an exceptional case.[111] The view was held very widely by the writers of the *ius commune* (on the basis of D.19.2.54.1 and 56) that a lessor, in the absence of a *lex commissoria*, has no right to cancel the lease and to withdraw therefrom unless the lessee is two years in arrears with the payment of his rent. However, according to Joubert, J.A., this rule "has really become a superfluous historical legal anachronism which can no longer fulfil any useful function in our law and should therefore no longer be applied".[112] Historically, this proposition is supported by a comprehensive analysis of Roman law which, according to Joubert, J.A., never in fact recognised a fixed rule of this kind.[113] In other cases, certain enactments by Justinian have

---

106 For clarification on this point, cf. De Vos, *op. cit.*, n.29, at 161.
107 *Lammers and Lammers* v. *Giovannoni* 1955 (3) S.A. 385 (A) 396; Dale Hutchison, in *Wille's Principles of South African Law*, 8th ed., 1991, at 21 ("A rule of Roman law that has not been abrogated by custom, legislation or judicial decision remains in force in South Africa today, provided that it was originally received into the law of Holland") and 35ff. (listing Roman law, after legislation, customs, judicial decisions and treatises of Roman-Dutch jurists, among the "authoritative sources" of South African law).
108 This allows Carey Miller in his book on acquisition and protection of property to avoid references to Roman law and to take Roman-Dutch law as "a new starting point in sources" (cf. *supra*, n.77).
109 In similar vein, cf. Van Warmelo, (1959) 33 *Tulane L.R.* 570ff.
110 1980 (4) S.A. 775 (A).
111 Cf. also *Tjollo Ateljees (Eins.) Bpk.* v. *Small* 1949 (1) S.A. 856 (A) 868ff. (per Van den Heever, J.A.), concerning *laesio enormis* (eventually abolished by 25 General Law Amendment Act 32/1952).
112 1980 (4) S.A. 775 (A) 776.
113 As far as modern Romanistic opinion on this point is concerned, cf., however, T. Mayer-Maly, "*Das biennium von* c. 3, X, 3, 18" (1955) 41 *Z.S.S. (KA)* 412ff.; M. Kaser, *Das römische Privatrecht*, Erster Abschnitt, 2nd ed., 1971, at 568, n.48 (Byzantine rule); but cf. also M. Kaser, *op. cit.*, n.103, at 406, n.42 (rule was probably classical). The question turns around the interpretation of D.19.2.54.1 and 56.

been taken to have been abrogated by disuse in South Africa, even though they had still been accepted by the Roman-Dutch authorities. Such was the fate, for instance, of the arbitrary and purely mechanical limit to the extent of the defendant's liability for damages, as introduced in C.7.47.1 (*"quantitas dupli"*).[114]

Much more characteristic is a decision like *Clifford* v. *Farinha*.[115] According to Roman law, only the owner of the object stolen could bring the *condictio ex causa furtiva*.[116] But that, in the words of Groenewegen, was one of those *subtilitates iuris civilis* that Roman-Dutch law had outgrown:

> *Caeterum cum hodie actionum nomina libellis inseri non soleat, ideo explosa hac Romanorum anxia scrupulositate, nostris et aliorum moribus dominus et caeteri quorum interest indistincte admittuntur ad repetendum quicquid furto sibi ablatum dixerint* (Since today it is no longer usual for the names of actions to be mentioned with the result that the over-refinement of the Romans has been discarded, by our customs and those of others, the owner and those whose interest is similar are equally able to reclaim whatever they allege has been removed from them by theft).[117]

It is this more recent and more liberal view that is followed by the learned judge.[118]

5. Roman and Roman-Dutch law are inextricably interwoven. Access to Roman law leads via Roman-Dutch law; yet, at the same time, Roman law is the basis on which Roman-Dutch law can often only be properly understood. But what exactly does Roman-Dutch law, generally regarded in South Africa as the common law of the country,[119] mean? Two main views are propounded today. On the one hand, it is argued that an authoritative status can only be attributed to Dutch legislation, decisions and (particularly) writers in the narrow sense: "Since we observe the law of Holland we must exclude the Romanists of other

---

114 Cf. H.J. Erasmus, "'n Regshistoriese Beskouing van Codex 7, 47", (1968) 31 *T.H.R.H.R.* 237ff.; Zimmermann, *Obligations,* 828ff. As far as *laesio enormis* is concerned, South African courts, though very critical, were not prepared to go quite so far; cf. *supra,* n.111.

115 1988 (4) S.A. 315 (W).

116 Kaser, *op. cit.*, n.113, at 618; *Obligations,* 941f.

117 *Tractatus de legibus abrogatis et inusitatis in Hollandia vicinisque regionibus, Lugduni-Batavorum,* 1649, Dig., Lib. XIII, Tit. I, l. 1.

118 *Clifford* v. *Farinha* 1988 (4) S.A. 315 (W) 321ff.; cf. also Erasmus, (1989) 106 *S.A.L.J.* 668; A.J. van der Walt, "Die *condictio furtiva* en die besitaksie" (1990) 53 *T.H.R.H.R.* 238ff.; *Obligations,* 951ff. And see already P. Pauw, "Historical Notes on the Nature of the *condictio furtiva*", (1976) 93 *S.A.L.J.* 395ff.

119 Hutchison, in *Wille, op. cit.*, n.107, 1, 36; Hahlo and Kahn, *System, op. cit.*, n.29, at 578; De Vos, *op. cit.*, n.29, 3ff.; but cf. also Visser, (1986) 49 *T.H.R.H.R.* 127ff.; Dlamini, (1992) 109 *S.A.L.J.* 608 ("[Ons moet] begin wegbeweeg van die paradigma van Romeins-Hollandse reg as die gemenereg van Suid-Afrika").

countries as well as the pragmatists from neighbouring regions".[120] Thus, it is writers like Voet and Grotius, Van Leeuwen and Groenewegen, Vinnius and Van der Keessel who carry specific weight. If they agree on a particular question, their view is binding for a modern South African court. Even writers from Frisia (like Sande and Huber) or Utrecht (like Antonius Matthaeus II) can only be used with circumspection. This view can be regarded as the "official" position of the South African courts (particularly the Appellate Division of the Supreme Court) and has fairly recently, once again, been forcefully endorsed.[121] On the other hand, however, there are those who argue that Roman-Dutch law was part and parcel of the Roman-Canon *ius commune* – a common law and a common legal science prevailing in the countries of Western and Central Europe from the late Middle Ages until the time of the French Revolution.[122] If Roman-Dutch law belonged to this tradition, and if that is what was transplanted to the Cape of Good Hope in 1652, it follows that the supra- or pre-national approach should live on in South Africa as well.[123] Strictly speaking, therefore, the South African lawyer is not indulging in a comparative study when he ranges, as Ben Beinart once put it, "into the depths of Germany, and through the breadth of France even into the heart of Spain".[124] Any parochial narrowness would have been alien to the Roman-Dutch writers themselves. They, obviously, did not regard law as a system of rules enacted for, and exclusively applicable in, a specific territory; instead, they took it for granted that the whole treasure house

---

120 *Tjollo Ateljees (Eins.) Bpk.* v. *Small* 1949 (1) S.A. 856 (A) 865 (concerning the doctrine of *laesio enormis*); cf. further, e.g., *Trust Bank van Afrika, Bpk.* v. *Eksteen* 1964 (3) S.A. 402 (A) 410f.; *Johaadien* v. *Stanley Porter (Paarl) Pty. Ltd.* 1970 (1) S.A. 394 (A); *Magna Alloys and Research (SA) (Pty.) Ltd.* v. *Ellis* 1984 (4) S.A. 874 (A) 890f. (cf. also the criticism by J.T. Schoombee, "Agreements in Restraint of Trade. The Appellate Division Confirms New Principles", (1985) 48 *T.H.R.H.R.* 127ff.); Van Warmelo, (1959) 33 *Tulane L.R.* 565ff.

121 *Du Plessis N.O.* v. *Strauss* 1988 (2) S.A. 105 (A) 133, 150; *Bank of Lisbon and South Africa Ltd.* v. *De Ornelas and another* 1988 (3) A.D. 580 (A) 604.

122 H. Coing, *Die ursprüngliche Einheit der europäischen Rechtswissenschaft*, 1968; *idem, Europäisches Privatrecht*, Band I, 1985; *idem,* "The Sources and Characteristics of the *ius commune*", (1986) 19 *C.I.L.S.A.* 483ff.; R. Zimmermann, "Das römisch-kanonische *ius commune* als Grundlage europäischer Rechtseinheit", (1992) *Juristenzeitung* 10ff.

123 D.H. van Zyl, *op. cit.*, n.69, 489f.; P. Pauw, "Die Romeins-Hollandse Reg in Oënskou", (1980) *Tydskrif vir die Suid-Afrikaanse Reg* 32ff.; R. Zimmermann, "Synthesis in South African Private Law: Civil Law, Common Law and *Usus Hodiernus Pandectarum*", (1986) 103 *S.A.L.J.* 259ff.; Erasmus, (1989) 106 *S.A.L.J.* 676. Cf. also F.P. van den Heever, *The Partiarian Agricultural Lease in South Africa*, 1943, at 4, describing Roman-Dutch law as a "misnomer".

124 *Roman Law in South African Practice*, 1952, at 16.

of the civilian tradition was at their disposal. The most influential
adherent of this approach today is Van Zyl, J., who thus, occasionally,
refers to Roman-European rather than Roman-Dutch law.[125]
Interestingly, the "official" approach is not always applied in practice – not even by the Appellate Division. Joubert, J.A., in particular, is
renowned for his very broadly based, *ius commune*–oriented investigations into the historical sources; for details of the duty of disclosure in
contracts of marine insurance, for instance, he referred to two treatises
by Petrus de Santerna and by Benevenutus Straccha (entitled *De
Assecurationibus et Sponsionibus* and *De Assecurationibus*);[126] both
were specifically designated "Roman-Dutch authorities".[127, 128] The
influence of the French jurist Pothier on the development of South
African law provides another prominent example. Van den Heever, J.A.,
said of him that he was "a great authority on the Civil law, but his
authority is merely suasive...[It] cannot prevail against the opinions of
the accepted Dutch authorities".[129] In a very similar vein, Steyn, J., had
previously indicated that he "would hesitate to prefer [Pothier's opin-
ion] to that of Sande and to Voet's statement of the law, unless it
appears that it was adopted by other Roman-Dutch authorities".[130]
These statements are in line with the "official" view. And yet, it is not
difficult to pinpoint instances where Pothier's views did in fact prevail
even where they had neither been anticipated nor received by Roman-
Dutch authors *stricto sensu*.[131]

6. English law, where it has taken root, tends to be accepted as
forming part of the specific South African *usus modernus pandectarum* today. The days of a relentless purification of Roman-Dutch law
are gone. Characteristically, even in 1972 the Appellate Division was
prepared to acquiesce in the retention of the doctrine of the undis-
closed principal, although it was specifically criticised as being out of

---

125 Cf., e.g., *Blesbok Eiendomsagentskap* v. *Cantamessa* 1991 (2) S.A. 712 (T)
716.
126 *Mutual and Federal Insurance Co. Ltd.* v. *Oudtshoorn Municipality* 1985
(1) S.A. 419 (A) 427; on which, see S. van der Merwe, "Insurance and Good
Faith: Exit *uberrima fides* – Enter What?", (1985) 48 *T.H.R.H.R.* 456ff.
127 1985 (1) S.A. 419 (A) 432.
128 In the *Bank of Lisbon* case (*supra* n.165), too, Joubert, J.A., on the one
hand stresses that the "law of the Province of Holland constitutes the
common law of South Africa" but, on the other hand, refers, *inter alios*, to
authors like Cujacius, Donellus, Brunnemann, Zoesius and Huber. Cf. in
this context also the discussion on the meaning of the term Roman-Dutch
authority by Visser, (1986) 49 *T.H.R.H.R.* 135f. (referring to the interesting
decision in *Rooth* v. *The State* (1888) 2 S.A.R. 259ff.); Visser and Hutchison,
(1988) 106 *S.A.L.J.* 629; and Erasmus, (1989) 106 *S.A.L.J.* 675f.
129 *Gerber* v. *Wolson* 1955 (1) S.A. 158 (A) 170f.
130 *Wolson* v. *Gerber* 1954 (3) S.A. 94 (T).
131 For details, see R. Zimmermann, "Der Einfluß Pothiers auf das römisch-holländische Recht in Südafrika" (1985) 102 *Z.S.S. (GA)* 176ff. Interestingly,
the reception of Pothier came about, usually, via English law.

tune with basic principles "of our law".[132] Among the decisions published in 1990 and 1991 we find two in which a similar attitude is
adopted. In *Raats Röntgen and Vermeulen (Pty.) Ltd.* v. *Administrator,
Cape, and others*,[133] the Cape Provincial Division of the Supreme Court
had to deal with the presumption that the State is not bound by its own
enactments, except by express words or by necessary implication. The
Court was highly critical of this judge-made rule of construction and
pointed out that it has no foundation in either Roman or Roman-Dutch
law. Deriving solely from English law, it had been consistently applied
in South Africa for many years and could not now be overruled – not, at
any rate, by a Provincial Division of the Supreme Court. In
Commissioner for Inland Revenue v. *First National Industrial Bank
Ltd.*[134] the question was briefly raised whether the *condictio indebiti* is
confined to the recovery of an *indebitum* that had been paid *per
errorem*; or whether it is also available when the payment, although
deliberate, was nevertheless involuntary because it was effected under
pressure and protest. "Whatever may have been the position in Roman-
Dutch law", opined Nienaber, A.J.A., "our present law appears to have
assimilated the basic notion of English law with regard to 'payments
made under duress of goods'".[135] Yet, on the other hand, we also have
the remarkable judgement of Van Zyl, J., in *Sumatie* v. *Venter*[136] on the
requirement of *inaedificatio*.[137] Contrary to long-established South

---

132 *Cullinan* v. *Noordkaaplandse Aartappelkernmoerkwekers Bpk.* 1972 (1)
     S.A. 761 (A) 767; cf. *Obligations*, at 47 for further literature. For another
     example, see *Pakendorf* v. *De Flamingh* 1982 (3) S.A. 146 (A) (strict liabil-
     ity of the press for defamation); for further comment, see J.M. Burchell,
     The Law of Defamation in South Africa, 1985, 181ff.
133 1991 (1) S.A. 827 (C).
134 1990 (3) S.A. 641 (A).
135 1990 (3) S.A. 641 (A) 646. One of the most disputed questions relating to
     the *condictio indebiti* is whether an *error iuris* precludes recovery; cf.
     Visser, (1986) 49 *T.H.R.H.R.* 135ff.; *Obligations*, 868ff.; and, most recently,
     Willis Faber Enthoven (Pty.) Ltd. v. *The Receiver of Revenue* 1992 (4) S.A.
     202 (A); on which see D.P. Visser, "Error of Law and Mistaken Payments: A
     Milestone", (1992) 109 *S.A.L.J.* 177ff.
136 1990 (1) S.A. 173 (T).
137 Or, see *Magna Alloys and Research (SA) (Pty.) Ltd.* v. *Ellis* 1984 (4) S.A. 874
     (A) (per Rabie, C.J.) reversing the traditional rule received from English
     law that agreements in restraint of trade are *prima facie* invalid (for com-
     ment, see Schoombee, (1985) 48 *T.H.R.H.R.* 127ff.; A.J. Kerr, "Restraint of
     Trade After *Magna Alloys*", in *Essays in Honour of Ellison Kahn*, 1989,
     186ff.); or *Mutual and Federal Insurance Co. Ltd.* v. *Oudtshoorn
     Municipality* 1985 (1) S.A. 419 (A) (per Joubert, J.A.), jettisoning the con-
     cept of *uberrima fides* in the law of insurance that had been taken over
     from English law: cf. *Fine* v. *The General Accident Fire and City Assurance
     Corporation Ltd.* (1915) A.D. 213 (218), E. Spiro, "*Uberrima fides*", (1961)
     24 *T.H.R.H.R.* 196ff. (for comment, see S. van der Merwe, (1985) 48
     T.H.R.H.R. 456f. and Van Zyl, J., in *Trust Bank van Afrika Bpk.* v. *President
     Versekeringsmaatskappy Bpk.* 1988 (1) S.A. 546 (W) 552f.).

African practice[138] (which in turn appears to have been inspired by English law) the annexor's intention is no longer to be regarded as the decisive touchstone for determining whether annexation has taken place.[139] An elaborate analysis of Roman and Roman-Dutch sources provides, instead, the basis for the proposition that primarily the purpose (*causa*) of the attachment has to be established and that this purpose may be determined from a variety of factors, such as the nature and function of the attached object, the manner of the attachment, or conduct and subjective intention of the owner of the attachment.[140] However, decisions such as these no longer display a specifically anti-English bias.[141]

V.

1. It is very difficult, if not impossible, to provide a general assessment of the role of the historical civilian sources in a mixed jurisdiction like South Africa. Like all other sources of law, they can be put to good and to bad use and they can be competently or incompetently handled. Still, however, one more general observation can possibly be made. As may already have become obvious, the exact status and hierarchy of the sources of South African law is by no means clear.[142] The scope for uncertainty is considerable. Does South Africa have one, or perhaps even two, common laws?[143] And if Roman-Dutch law is the common law, what exactly does that mean? How can even the law of Holland be regarded as a formal source of law,[144] if it has to be gauged, mainly, from the books of seventeenth and eighteenth century legal writers? Neither the Roman-Dutch

---

138 Cf. e.g. *Standard-Vacuum Refining Co. of South Africa (Pty.) Ltd.* v. *Durban City Council* 1961 (2) S.A. 669 (A) 677f.; *Trust Bank van Afrika* v. *Western Bank* 1978 (4) S.A. 281 (A) 295.

139 For criticism cf. already Van der Merwe, *op. cit.*, n.76, 256ff.; and see the discussion of the matter by Carey Miller, *op. cit.*, n.77, 22ff.

140 *Sumatie (Edms.) Bpk.* v. *Venter en 'n ander NN.O.* 1990 (1) S.A. 173 (A) 178ff.

141 Cf., as far as van Zyl, J., is concerned e.g. *Trust Bank van Afrika Bpk. v. President Versekeringsmaatskappy Bpk. en 'n ander* 1988 (1) S.A. 546 (552).

142 Cf. also R.W. Lee, "Roman-Dutch Law in South Africa", (1924) 41 *S.A.L.J.* 303 describing South African law as a system of law "untrammelled by authority" and "unrestricted in the sources upon which it draws"; Visser, (1986) 49 *T.H.R.H.R.* 128 ("intricate and delicately balanced structure..."; "...our private law is at the same time both a work of art and a trap for the unwary").

143 Cf. *supra*, n.59. Cf. also *Mutual and Federal Insurance Co. Ltd.* v. *Oudtshoorn Municipality* 1985 (1) S.A. 419 (A) 430 ("...the South African law of insurance is governed *mainly* by Roman-Dutch law as our common law"; emphasis added).

144 Hutchison, in *Wille, op. cit.*, n.107, at 36; D.P. Visser and D.B. Hutchison, "Legislation from the Elysian Fields: The Roman-Dutch Authorities Settle an Old Dispute", (1988) 105 *S.A.L.J.* 627ff.

nor the – subsidiary – Roman sources are particularly easy to handle. Obviously, under those circumstances, there is a much greater danger of unclarity and confusion than in a modern codified legal system.[145] On the other hand, however, the very open-ended texture of South African law and the infinite variety of potentially relevant sources[146] are able to engender a richness and flexibility hardly conceivable under a codification. In a way, therefore, the potential for both chaos and perfection is particularly pronounced. I want to conclude this paper by providing some examples illustrating this assertion.

2. The potential for chaos has clearly materialised with regard to the accrual presumptions.[147] Every student of the South African law of succession must, I think, have wondered why, according to firmly established practice,[148] accrual is to be presumed if a will reads "Titius and Maevius shall be my heirs", while for a will of the type "Titius and Maevius shall be my heirs in equal shares" a presumption against accrual is held to apply. Thus, if for instance Titius has predeceased the testator, his share, in the first case, accrues to Maevius, whilst in the second example, *ceteris paribus*, Maevius will get only half of the estate. This absurd and artificial distinction goes back, as far as South African law is concerned, to a decision of 1893[149] by Lord de Villiers, who in turn based his analysis of Roman-Dutch law solely on the authority of Voet.[150] Voet, in turn, had correctly preserved the distinctions between *coniuncti re et verbis*, *re tantum* and *verbis tantum*, as they are apparent from the Roman sources, without, however, taking into account that the conceptual background had changed. No longer did one apply the "*nemo pro parte testatus pro parte intestatus decedere potest*" rule;[151] no longer therefore did one have a system of necessary accrual. In view of this, the Roman accrual presumptions no longer made sense – a fact fully recognised by other Roman-Dutch authors. The confusion in this particular case, incidentally, has been compounded by virtue of the fact that the South African courts today have inadvertently changed the meaning of the term "*coniunctio verbis tantum*" and no longer use it in the same sense as the Roman-Dutch

---

145 Cf. also the considerations by Hosten, *Huldigingsbundel Joubert, cit. sup.*, n.43, 63ff.

146 Stressed also, for instance, by Sir John Wessels, "The Future of Roman-Dutch Law in South Africa", (1920) 37 *S.A.L.J.* 267f.

147 For details as to what follows, see R. Zimmermann, "'*Coniunctio verbis tantum*'. Accrual, the Methods of Joinder in a Will and the Rule Against Partial Intestacy in Roman-Dutch and Roman Law", (1984) 101 *Z.S.S. (RA)* 234ff.

148 See, for example, *Ex parte Knight: In re Estate Gardner* 1955 (3) S.A. 577 (C) 587; H.J. Erasmus, in Lee and Honoré, *Family, Things and Succession*, 2nd ed., 1983, n.726.

149 (1893) 10 S.C. 56.

150 *Commentarius ad Pandectas*, Parisiis, 1827, 1829, Lib. XXX – XXXII, 61.

151 Cf. for example, Groenewegen, *op. cit.*, n.103, Inst., Lib. II, Tit. XIV, 9.

lawyers.[152] When, from time to time, they expressed their dissatisfaction with these "cumbersome and unnatural"[153] distinctions, they questioned whether a clause of the type "Titius and Maevius shall be my heirs in equal shares" should be regarded as a (mere) *coniunctio verbis tantum*. They did not realise, however, that according to Roman-Dutch law a bequest in equal shares leads to accrual because it is, not because it is not, a bequest *verbis tantum*. Obviously, this kind of muddle can, and ought to, be cleared up by a proper historical analysis of the development; an analysis, incidentally, which should also take into account the later history of the accrual presumptions in the European *ius commune*.[154] Here we see a development towards a general presumption in favour of accrual, if one or several of the co-heirs could not or did not want to be heir. There is absolutely no reason why the South African courts should not take up and develop this line of thought. It would be quite wrong to say that they are bound by the majority opinion of writers in the seventeenth and eighteenth centuries.[155] These Roman-Dutch writers themselves would never have encouraged such a stale and antiquarian attitude and would not have hesitated to adapt the law to the changing needs of the time.

3. What is the position if a South African court suddenly discovers the discrepancy between what the Roman-Dutch authors actually said and what they were, for many years, wrongly taken to have said? This was the problem addressed relatively recently by the Appellate Division in *Du Plessis N.O.* v. *Strauss*.[156] The issue at stake was the correct interpretation of a "*si sine liberis decesserit*" clause in a will; of a provision, that is, in which the testator directs his property to pass to A; but should A die without having issue, to B. If A dies leaving children, the condition under which B has been instituted, is not fulfilled. Does the property now go to A's children? Essentially, this boils down to the question whether a "*si sine liberis*" condition attached to a testamentary disposition in itself gives rise to a presumption that the testator intended to create a *fideicommissum* in favour of the *liberi*. Ever since a decision of the Cape Supreme Court in 1908[157] it has been held that this is not the case. In *Du Plessis, N.O.* v. *Strauss*, Van Heerden, J.A. has now, however, demonstrated that their view was based on an incorrect and superficial reading of the Roman-Dutch authorities; such a clause did in fact give rise to a presumption that the testator intended to

---

152 Cf., for example, *Winstanley & others* v. *Barrow & others* (1937) A.D. 75.
153 *Administrator of Estate O'Meara* v. *O'Meara & others* (1943) N.P.D. 144 (149).
154 (1984) 101 *Z.S.S. (RA)* 268ff.
155 "The original sources of Roman-Dutch law are important, but the exclusive preoccupation with them is like trying to return an oak tree to its acorn": *Ex parte De Winnaar* 1959 (1) S.A. 837 (N) 839.
156 1988 (2) S.A. 105 (A).
157 *Steenkamp* v. *Marais N.O. & others* (1908) 25 S.C. 483; Erasmus, in Lee and Honoré, *op. cit.*, n.148, n.647.

create a tacit *fideicommissum* in favour of A's children, provided they are descendants of the testator and there are no contrary indications in the will.[158] Van Heerden, J.A. appears to have regarded that as reason enough to overrule the series of cases to the contrary and to return to the position adopted in the law of Holland in the seventeenth and eighteenth centuries.[159] Corbett, J.A., delivering the minority judgement, ultimately came to the same conclusion. Interestingly, he would have preferred the alternative view. "With some reluctance, therefore", he concluded,[160] "I accept the law of Holland as propounded by my Brother Van Heerden. And I agree that the South African case law should not be permitted to override the law of Holland". Of course, such a dramatic reversal of judicial opinion is not an everyday occurrence.[161] In the same issue of the South African Law Reports, in fact, the Appellate Division declined to reconsider the correctness of another rule relating to the construction of wills – that had been consistently applied by South African courts[162] – "despite the temptation to correct a possibly false perception of the Roman-Dutch law".[163] But since the law of Holland of some two hundred years ago is regarded as the common law, and since the relationship between the old sources and modern precedent has never been precisely defined, this kind of antiquarian turnabout is always possible. Yet, even where the rule at issue can be regarded as a beneficial one, the fact "that its resurrection is justified solely...by its having been adopted in seventeenth and eighteenth century Holland will have an effect opposite to the intended one".[164] It is not likely to enhance respect for the remoter layers of the South African legal system.

4. (a) Closely related is another problem highlighted in a recent *cause célèbre* of much greater significance. I am thinking of the majority opinion, delivered by Joubert, J.A., in the *Bank of Lisbon* case on the fate of the *exceptio doli generalis* in South African law.[165] In the first

---

158 1988 (2) S.A. 105 (A) 132ff.; and see Visser and Hutchison, (1989) 105 *S.A.L.J.* 619ff.
159 Cf. the criticism by Visser and Hutchison, (1988) 105 *S.A.L.J.* 632ff.
160 1988 (2) S.A. 105 (A) 150.
161 But cf. also *Sumatie (Edms.) Bpk.* v. *Venter en 'n ander NN.O.* 1990 (1) S.A. 173 (T) (cf. *supra*, n.86).
162 *Galliers & others* v. *Rycroft* (1900) 17 S.C. 569.
163 *Horowitz* v. *Brock & others* 1988 (2) S.A. 160 (A) 187; pointed out by Visser and Hutchison, (1989) 105 *S.A.L.J.* 633f.; cf. also D.S.P. Cronjé, "Wysiging van verkeerde reg" (1989) 52 *T.H.R.H.R.* 121ff.
164 Visser and Hutchison, (1989) 105 *S.A.L.J.* 635.
165 *Bank of Lisbon & South Africa Ltd.* v. *De Ornelas* 1988 (3) S.A. 580 (A). The issue had been disputed for some time. Some judges expressed great scepticism as to the survival of the *exceptio doli* (*Novick* v. *Comair Holdings Ltd.* 1979 (2) S.A. 116 (W) 156f.), others merely assumed its existence (*Zuurbekom Ltd.* v. *Union Corporation Ltd.* 1947 (1) S.A. 514 (A) 535ff.) while still others came out strongly and unambiguously in favour of it (*Sonday* v. *Surrey Estate Modern Meat Market (Pty.) Ltd.* 1983 (2) S.A.

place, a remark by Judge Rubin,[166] aimed at the American judiciary, appears to me to apply to this kind of judgement:

> Let me mention one other time-consuming task of judges that appears to me to be an obsessive preoccupation. It is our concern, particularly at the appellate level, with trying to write the kind of opinion that we think law school teachers will consider scholarly.

Many pages of the *Bank of Lisbon* case read like a legal article, not like a judgement of a court. Thus, for example, more than a hundred lines of the reported judgement are devoted to the discussion (or perhaps rather: the plucking to pieces)[167] of the unpublished thesis of an academic of the University of the Orange Free State. The robust discussion of fine academic points has, unquestionably, a long tradition, particularly among proponents of the humanistic (or antiquarian) school of thought.[168] But South African jurisprudence is firmly rooted in the Bartolist, not the Cujacian way of thinking. A modern practical lawyer simply does not expect to find a critical evaluation of a learned treatise in a judgement of a court of justice; nor does he want to be instructed about details of Roman civil procedure which can conveniently be studied in the relevant modern literature.[169]

------

521 (C) 530; cf. also e.g. J.C. de Wet, *"Estoppel by Representation" in die Suid-Afrikaanse Reg*, 1939, 83ff. (taking a sharply negative attitude); A.J. Kerr, The *Principles of the Law of Contract*, 3rd ed., 1980, at 137 ("an outstanding example of equity at work"); C.F.C. van der Walt, "Die huidige posisie in die Suid-Afrikaanse reg met betoekking tot onbillike kontraksbedinge", (1986) 103 *S.A.L.J.* 646ff.).

166 "Bureaucratization of the Federal Courts. The Tension between Justice and Efficiency", (1979–1980) 55 *Notre Dame Lawyer* 655. For a comparative analysis of citation practices by appellate courts, see H. Kötz, (1988) 52 *RabelsZ.* 644ff. (where a fuller extract from the article of Rubin, J., appears at 657).

167 "These views of Botha are untenable and must be rejected..." (604); "They would seem to be pure speculation on his part" (605); "He also overlooked the fact that..." (605). Jansen, J.A., who delivered the minority opinion, is also severely censured by Joubert, J.A. ("His explanation...is, with respect, entirely unacceptable. It fails to take cognizance of the fact... There is not a scintilla of evidence...not supported by any authoritative Roman-Dutch legal sources...He also, with respect, overlooks the fact..." (609f.).

168 Cf. the amusing examples discussed by G.C.J.J. van den Bergh, *The Life and Work of Gerard Noodt*, 1988, 207ff., 300ff.; O.W. Star Numan, *C. van Bynkershoek, Zijn leven en zijne geschriften*, 1869, 198ff.

169 I am not, of course, suggesting that judges should not take account of and refer to the relevant (modern) legal literature (for criticism in this regard see Susan Scott, "To Burden, or not to Burden?" (1991) 54 *T.H.R.H.R.* 264ff.; by and large, however, South African courts have traditionally given "a place of honor to the legal scholar" (A. Watson, *The Making of the Civil Law*, 1981, at 41; on the role of legal literature cf. also Kahn, *op. cit.*, n.27, 245ff.; Zimmermann, *op. cit.*, n.29, 70ff.; Hosten, *Huldigingsbundel Joubert, cit. sup.*, n.43, 67f. and – on the influence of one particularly prominent scholar on the course of legal development – Zimmermann and Hugo, (1992) 60 *T.v.R.* 157ff.)). But a court decision should not provide a substitute for a legal article or textbook.

This kind of approach is bound to conjure up the image of a rather dry and pedantic school-room jurisprudence rather than that of the *ius commune* as a dynamic judicial law, as *jurisprudentia forensis*:[170] a law in action.

(b) Secondly, and more importantly, however, not only the style but also the substantive approach adopted by the majority in the *Bank of Lisbon* case appears to be out of tune with the spirit of the *ius commune*. More particularly, its ongoing,[171] dynamic and developing character[172] is disregarded; and it is to be feared that findings like the one in the *Bank of Lisbon* case may in fact be counterproductive as far as the general appreciation of the practical value of studies in legal history is concerned. For the finding of the court is an entirely negative one. "The *raison d'être* of the *exceptio doli generalis*", so the argument of Joubert, J.A., runs,[173] "ha[s] disappeared in the law of contract at the end of the Middle Ages...[and therefore a]ll things considered, the time has now arrived, in my judgement, once and for all, to bury the *exceptio doli generalis* as a superfluous, defunct anachronism". And he adds, for good measure: "*Requiescat in pace*".

From a purely technical point of view, of course, this view cannot be faulted. The *exceptio doli*, to put it very simply, was a specific standard clause, inserted at the request of the defender into the formula of *iudicia stricti iuris* such as the one applicable to stipulations. It allowed the judge to take account of whether at any stage since the commencement of negotiations between the parties the pursuer had acted in contravention of the precepts of good faith; in other words: it gave the judge an equitable discretion to decide the case before him in accordance with what appeared to be fair and reasonable.[174] If our modern law of contract had derived from the Roman stipulation (as well it might have), we might still need the *exceptio doli* as a procedural device. In the Middle Ages, however, the stipulation was usually incorporated into a written document for which specific words and clauses had to be used; and thus, it was ultimately turned into an *arcanum* of notarial practice. As such it had lost its appeal as a suitable cornerstone of contractual theory. And with the demise of the stipulation in the

---

170 Cf. e.g. G. Gorla, "La '*Communis opinio totius orbis*' et la Réception Jurisprudentielle du Droit au cours des XVIᵉ, XVIIᵉ et XVIIIᵉ Siècles dans la "Civil Law" et la "Common Law"", in *New Perspectives for a Common Law of Europe*, ed. M. Cappelletti, 1978, 54ff.; G. Gorla and L. Moccia, "A 'Revisiting' of the Comparison between 'Continental Law' und 'English Law' (16th – 19th Century)", (1981) 2 *Jour. Leg. Hist.* 143ff.; Stein, *op. cit.*, n.5, 115ff.; and the contributions in J. H. Baker (ed.), *Judicial Records, Law Reports and the Growth of Case Law*, 1989.

171 On the "ongoingness" of the Western legal tradition, see Berman, *op. cit.*, n.11, at 9.

172 Cf. (1992) *Juristenzeitung* 11f.

173 *Bank of Lisbon & South Africa Ltd.* v. *De Ornelas* 1988 (3) S.A. 580 (A) 605, 607.

174 For details, see *Obligations*, 662ff.

Middle Ages,[175] the *exceptio doli*, too, was bound to fall into oblivion. This, however, did not mean that the equitable discretion in the evaluation of contractual rights and duties (which the Roman judge had been granted as a result of the *exceptio doli*) had also been abandoned. The modern theory of contract descends in direct line from the consensual contracts of Roman law,[176] and these were governed by the principle of *bona fides*. A specific procedural device in the form of an *exceptio doli* was not necessary here in order to check the improper exercise of contractual rights: the judge had this discretion anyway.[177] The substantive content of the *exceptio doli*, in other words, had been absorbed into the requirement of *bona fides*; and if the term *exceptio doli* continued to be used, it was tantamount to a recourse to the principle of good faith inherent in the modern concept of contract.

Strangely, however, the majority in the *Bank of Lisbon* case, while recognising that all contracts in modern law are *bonae fidei*,[178] not only reject the *exceptio doli* but also deny that *bona fides* has developed to fulfil its function.[179] Good faith, the court appears to say, was the fountainhead of a whole variety of rules of substantive law and it has rendered Roman-Dutch law an "inherently...equitable"[180] system. But even in Roman-Dutch law it was no longer conceived as conferring wide powers on the court either to complement or to restrict the duties of the parties or to imply terms in accordance with the requirements of justice, reasonableness and fairness.[181] All the less, therefore, it

---

175 Cf. e.g. K.-P. Nanz, *Die Entstehung des allgemeinen Vertragsbegriffs im 16. bis 18. Jahrhundert*, 1985, 36ff. and passim.

176 For details of the development see *Obligations*, 537ff.

177 Cf. e.g. D.30.84.5: "...*quia hoc iudicium fidei bonae est et continet in se doli mali exceptionem*"; B. Windscheid, *Lehrbuch des Pandektenrechts*, 9th ed. by T. Kipp, 1906, 47, n.7.

178 Cf. also, e.g., *Mutual and Federal Insurance Co. Ltd.* v. *Oudtshoorn Municipality* 1985 (1) S.A. 419 (A) 433 (*per* Joubert, J.A.): "By our law all contracts are *bonae fidei*" (basing this assertion on Ludovicus Molina, *Disputationes de contractibus*); *L.T.A. Construction Bpk.* v. *Administrateur, Transvaal* 1992 (1) S.A. 473 (A) 480 (*per* Joubert, J.A.).

179 Cf. particularly 1988 (3) S.A. 580 (A) 605, 609f.; cf. also Jansen, J.A., in his minority opinion (616) who for this very reason asserts that the *exceptio doli* has not yet become redundant as a specific mechanism of equity.

180 1988 (3) S.A. 580 (A) 606; on this "cryptic" assertion cf. Lubbe and Murray, *op. cit.*, n.98, at 391. For further comment, see Michael A. Lambiris, "The *exceptio doli generalis*: an Obituary", (1988) 105 *S.A.L.J.* 648f.; A.J. Kerr, *The Principles of the Law of Contract*, 4th ed., 1989, 479ff., 483ff.; C. Lewis, "The Demise of the *exceptio doli*: Is There Another Route to Contractual Equity?", (1990) 107 *S.A.L.J.* 26ff.

181 Cf. the words used by Jansen, J.A., in *Tuckers Land and Development Corporation (Pty.) Ltd.* v. *Hovis* 1980 (1) S.A. 645 (A) 651ff. and D.L. Carey Miller, "*Judicia bonae fidei*: A new Development in Contract?", (1980) 97 *S.A.L.J.* 532f. On the significance of the concept of "equity" in South African law cf. D.H. van Zyl, (1988) 105 *S.A.L.J.* 278, 289.

can be used today to subvert established rules of contract law.[182]

It is, however, doubtful whether the productive force[183] of the *exceptio doli* (as well as the creative role of Roman law!)[184] can be quelled that easily; in fact there are already indications that it has started haunting courts and legal writers from its grave.[185] Moreover, the development of the *ius commune* was never simply a matter of "formalistic and clinical"[186] conclusions like the ones advanced by the majority in *Bank of Lisbon*. A historico-doctrinal investigation alone does not appear to be sufficient to settle the issue of an equitable discretion in modern contract law.[187] On the contrary: the civilian tradition, generally speaking, has in the past displayed sufficient flexibility[188] to react to new challenges and to accommodate new problems; it was intimately linked to, determined by and open for considerations of policy.[189] The removal of this kind of flexibility from the centre of contract law would sadly stifle this tradition.[190] Or, as Rumpff, J.A., once asked rhetorically, when

---

182 It is in line with this approach that the Appellate Division of the Supreme Court (*per* Joubert, J.A.) has recently confirmed the prohibition on interest *in duplum* (as taken over from classical Roman through Roman-Dutch law; cf. *supra*, n.103) – *L.T.A. Construction Bpk.* v. *Administrateur, Transvaal* 1992 (1) S.A. 473 (A)) – without considering the suggestion by Lubbe, (1990) 53 *T.H.R.H.R.* 190ff., of relating this rule to the operation of the norm of *bona fides*.

183 H. Dernburg, *Pandekten*, 6th ed., 1900, 138, 4 *in fine*.

184 Erasmus, (1989) 106 *S.A.L.J.* 676.

185 Cf. *Van der Merwe* v. *Meades* 1991 (2) S.A. 1 (A) confirming the existence of the *replicatio doli*; see A.J. Kerr, "The *replicatio doli* Reaffirmed. The *exceptio doli* Available in our Law", (1991) 108 *S.A.L.J.* 583ff. Cf. also, in this context, the "rather cursory and unelaborated" reference of the Appellate Division to the notion of unconscionability in *Sasfin (Pty.) Ltd.* v. *Beukes* 1989 (1) S.A. 1 (A) and the criticism by Gerhard Lubbe, "*Bona fides,* billikheid en die openbare belang in die Suid-Afrikaanse kontraktereg", (1990) 1 *Stellenbosch L.R.* 7ff.; S. van der Merwe and G. Lubbe, "*Bona fides* and Public Policy in Contract", (1991) 2 *Stellenbosch L.R.* 91ff.

186 S.W.J. van der Merwe, G.F. Lubbe and L.F. van Huyssteen, "The *exceptio doli generalis: requiescat in pace – vivat aequitas*", (1989) 106 *S.A.L.J.* 239.

187 Cf. also Lewis, (1990) 107 *S.A.L.J.* 29: "...I do not believe that a close examination of the Roman or Roman-Dutch authorities serves much purpose in this context"; similarly, in a different context, Forsyth, (1986) 103 *S.A.L.J.* 521.

188 This point was also emphasised by Beinart in his famous inaugural lecture, *cit. sup.*, n.99, at 25; cf. also *idem, Acta Juridica* 140.

189 Cf., as far as modern South African common law is concerned, M.M. Corbett, "Aspects of the Role of Policy in the Evolution of Our Common Law", (1987) 104 *S.A.L.J.* 52ff.

190 Cf. also the criticism by Jansen, J.A., delivering the minority opinion in the *Bank of Lisbon* case, 1988 (3) S.A. 580 (A) 611ff.; Erasmus, (1989) 106 *S.A.L.J.* 676f.; Van der Merwe, Lubbe and Van Huyssteen, (1989) 106 *S.A.L.J.* 235ff.; Kerr, *op. cit.*, n.180, (4th ed.), 483ff., 488ff.; Lubbe and Murray, *op. cit.*, n.98, at 391; Lewis, (1991) 108 *S.A.L.J.* 262ff.

faced with a similar issue in the law of unjustified enrichment:[191]
"Should the description of Roman-Dutch law as a strong and vibrant
legal system with a powerful inherent capacity for growth, be pure
hypocrisy? Should the Roman-Dutch law perhaps have started to suffer
from the modern disease of sclerosis?".[192]

5. Another problematic aspect of South African decisions referring to
Roman or Roman-Dutch sources is that the historical discussion is not infrequently without any relevance for the outcome of the case in question. In
about half of all cases in which Roman law is referred to, such references
are merely incidental, often constituting part of a historical overview of
issues that are already settled.[193] This tends to confirm the widely held view
that the pursuit of Roman law may be elegant but tends to be irrelevant. A
good example of a discussion of the old authorities in the grand style that
displays a dazzling erudition but is still, strictly speaking, only *obiter,* is provided by another decision of the Appellate Division by Joubert, J.A..[194]
According to South African law, a testator may not normally leave the determination of a beneficiary under his will to another person.[195] There are

---

191 On which, see *Obligations,* 885ff. and the contributions in *Unjustified
      Enrichment, Essays in Honour of Wouter de Vos,* 1992, 115ff., 175ff., 203ff.
192 *Nortje en 'n ander* v. *Pool N.O.* 1966 (3) S.A. 96 (A) 113 (translated from
      the Afrikaans original). Ultimately, in this decision, Rumpff, J.A.'s view did
      not prevail and the Appellate Division refused to recognise a general
      enrichment action; as a result, a principle "vibrant with life and struggling
      for growth [has been] locked...in tight compartments, a prisoner of the
      past" (Weeramantry, J., in *Da Costa* v. *Bank of Ceylon* (1970) 72 New Law
      Reports (Ceylon) 457 (544ff). The law of unjustified enrichment is thus
      still based, essentially, on the Roman *condictiones.* This approach has
      recently been challenged; cf. *Blesbok Eiendomsagentskap* v. *Cantamessa*
      1991 (2) S.A. 712 (T) per Van Zyl, J.; D.H. van Zyl, "The General Enrichment
      Action is Alive and Well", in *Unjustified Enrichment, Essays in Honour of
      Wouter de Vos,* 1992, 115ff.; G.T.S. Eiselen, "Herlewing van die algemene
      verrykingsaksie", (1992) 55 *T.H.R.H.R.* 124ff.; J.C. Sonnekus, "Algemene
      vordering gebaseer op ongeregverdigde verryking in heroorweging",
      (1992) 55 *T.H.R.H.R.* 301ff.
193 Cf. *supra,* text before n.84.
194 *Braun* v. *Blann and Botha, NN.O. & another* 1984 (2) S.A. 850 (A); on
      which see Forsyth, (1986) 103 *S.A.L.J.* 513ff. A similar criticism can be lev-
      elled against *Mutual and Federal Insurance Co. Ltd.* v. *Oudtshoorn
      Municipality* (1985) 1 S.A. 419 (A) (on which see *supra,* n.137). The court
      rejected the concept of *uberrima fides* as "alien, vague [and] useless" but
      still came down in favour of the defendant since the plaintiff had failed to
      comply with a duty of disclosure flowing from the insurance contract.
195 Cf. *Estate Watkins-Pitchford & others* v. *C.I.R.* 1955 (2) S.A. 437 (A) 458;
      Estate Orpen v. *Estate Atkinson & others* 1966 (4) S.A. 589 (A) 596; *Braun*
      v. *Blann & another NN.O.* 1982 (4) S.A. 166 (W); Johannes Voet,
      Commentarius ad Pandectas, Parisiis, 1827, 1829, Lib. XXVIII, Tit. V, 29;
      Arnoldus Vinnius, *In Quatuor Libros Institutionum Imperialium
      Commentarius,* Lugduni, 1761, Lib. II, Tit. XIV, 9 pr. For a general discus-
      sion, see R. Zimmermann, *"Quos Titius voluerit" – Höchstpersönliche
      Willensentscheidung des Erblassers oder "power of appointment"?,* 1991.

certain exceptions to this no-delegation rule, most notably the one relating to testamentary *fideicommissa:* here the fiduciary may be granted the power to appoint the fideicommissary or fideicommissaries. Can a similar power of appointment be conferred upon a trustee? This was the question decided in *Braun* v. *Blann and Botha.* The answer would have to be in the affirmative if according to South African law a testamentary trust could be regarded as a *fideicommissum.* This, in turn, would appear to be a rather far-fetched equation,[196] if South African and English trust law were identical. But they are not.[197] A South African trustee, for instance, is regarded as the owner of the trust property; vis-à-vis the beneficiary he is simply under a personal obligation. The distinction between legal ownership and equitable ownership is thus unknown in South Africa. Dogmatically, this kind of "trust" has indeed for many years been considered to constitute a special kind of *fideicommissum:* "...a testamentary trust", in the often-quoted words of Innes, C.J.,[198] "is in the phraseology of our law a *fideicommissum* and a testamentary trustee may be regarded as covered by the term fiduciary". In *Braun* v. *Blann and Botha* this way of looking at things has now been rejected.[199] The discussion focuses on Papinian D.36.2.26.1 and the learned commentaries and interpretations of this fragment by the authors of the *ius commune* from Bartolus via Cuiacius down to Simon van Leeuwen. Rather surprisingly, in view of these elaborate historical investigations aimed at keeping trust and *fideicommissum* apart, the learned judge ultimately declared the power of appointment in the case at hand to be valid: "To recognize the validity of [such a disposition] would be a salutary development of our law of trusts and would not be in conflict with the principles of our

---

196   But see the most recent monograph on the Roman law of *fideicommissa* by David Johnston that appeared under the title *The Roman Law of Trusts,* 1988. On Roman-Dutch law, cf. L.I. Coertze, *Die Trust in die Romeins-Hollandse Reg,* LL.D. thesis, Stellenbosch, 1948. The trust is usually regarded as one of the "most original creation[s] of English law" (W.W. Buckland and A.D. McNair, *Roman Law and Common Law,* 3rd ed. by F.H. Lawson, 1952, at 176; cf. also e.g. K. Zweigert and H. Kötz, *Einführung in die Rechtsvergleichung auf dem Gebiete des Privatrechts,* 1st ed., 1971, vol. 1, 328ff.). In reality, however, it was the English version of a common European idea. Cf., for details, H. Patrick Glenn, *"Le trust et le jus commune",* in P. Legrand jr., *Common law d'un siècle à l'autre,* 1992, 91ff. (pointing out that the trust, consequently, is not alien to the continental *ius commune*).

197   Cf., in particular, T. Honoré and E. Cameron, *The South African Law of Trusts,* 4th ed., 1992, e.g. 15ff.

198   (1915) A.D. 491 (499) (per Innes, C.J.); cf. further B. Beinart, *"Fideicommissum* and *modus",* 1968 *Acta Juridica* 157ff., 194ff.; *idem,* "Trusts in Roman and Roman-Dutch Law" (1980) 1 *Jour. Leg. Hist.* 6ff.; Honoré and Cameron, *op. cit.,* n.197, 40ff.

199   1984 (2) S.A. 850 (A) 866 (*per* Joubert, J.A.).

law".[200] And whilst this decision can certainly not be criticised for not keeping "pace with the requirements of changing conditions in our society",[201] one wonders what lesson the reader will draw from it as to the advantages, or otherwise, of such a multi-layered legal system.[202]

6. We have, so far, been focusing on certain problems arising from the use of old authorities in a mixed legal system. It appears to be hardly necessary, before a Scottish audience, to emphasise the rich potential for refinement inherent in this kind of tradition. South African private law can still to a large degree be regarded as a testimony to the characteristic vitality of the civilian tradition in its original, uncodified form.[203] It combines maturity with an undogmatic openness towards challenging new departures. Examples abound. A German observer, for instance, who is appalled at the eccentricity of results flowing from an excessively technical application of the modern codified version of the *"in pari turpitudine"* rule (§817, 2 B.G.B.), is bound to admire the cautiously flexible way in which South African courts tend to apply this rule – guided always by public policy and taking account of, *inter alia*, the relative degree of turpitude displayed by pursuer and defender and the extent to which the contract has been executed.[204] This attitude is very much in tune with the spirit in which the *in pari turpitudine* rule was once devised by the Roman lawyers;[205] much more so, in any event, than an approach which, as the German Federal Supreme Court once put it, intentionally disregards the precepts of justice.[206] Or take a decision

---

200 1984 (2) S.A. 850 (A) 866f.
201 *Blower* v. *Van Noorden* (1909) T.S. 890 at 905 *per* Innes, C.J. Cf. also *Nortje en 'n ander* v. *Pool N.O.* 1966 (3) S.A. 96 (A) 113 (*per* Rumpff, J.A.).
202 Cf., e.g., Forsyth, (1986) 103 *S.A.L.J.* 521, criticising the "obsession with the detail of the [ancient] texts".
203 Cf. also Lord Tomlin, in *Pearl Assurance Co.* v. *Union Government* (1934) A.D. 560 (PC) 563: "Roman-Dutch law...is a virile living system of law, ever seeking, as every such system must, to adapt itself consistently with its inherent basic principles to deal effectively with the increasing complexities of modern organized society". Or, see the approach adopted by Jansen, J.A., in the *Bank of Lisbon* case (supra n.190), 611ff. or in *B.K. Tooling (Edms.) Bpk.* v. *Scope Precision Engineering (Edms.) Bpk.* 1979 (1) S.A. 391 (A).
204 *Jajbhay* v. *Cassim* (1939) A.D. 537; L.E. Trakman, "The Effect of Illegality in South African Law", (1977) 94 *S.A.L.J.* 468ff.; W. de Vos, *Verrykingsaanspreeklikheid in die Suid-Afrikaanse Reg*, 3rd ed., 1987, 160ff. In favour of a great degree of flexibility also, as far as German law is concerned, D. König, *Ungerechtfertigte Bereicherung, Tatbestände und Ordnungsprobleme in rechtsvergleichender Sicht*, 1985, 126ff.; and, *de lege ferenda, idem,* in *Gutachten und Vorschläge zur Überarbeitung des Schuldrechts*, 1981, vol. 2, 1531ff.
205 H.H. Seiler, "§817 S.2 B.G.B. und das römische Recht", in *Festschrift für Wilhelm Felgentraeger*, 1969, 381ff.; *Obligations*, 846f., 865f.
206 B.G.H.Z. 8, 348 (373).

like *Tuckers Land and Development Corporation (Pty.) Ltd.* v. *Hovis*:[207]

> It could be said that it is now, and has been for some time, felt in our domain,...that in all fairness there should be a duty upon a promisor not to commit an anticipatory breach of contract, and such a duty has in fact often been enforced by our Courts. It would be consonant with the history of our law, and also legal principle, to construe this as an application of the wide jurisdiction to imply terms conferred upon a court by the Roman law in respect of *judicia bonae fidei*. It would not then be inapt to say, elliptically, that the duty flows from the requirement of *bona fides* to which our contracts are subject, and that such duty is implied in law.[208]

Here we have a doctrine (repudiation as a form of breach of contract *in anticipando*) that has been taken over from English law,[209] although it had no antecedents in Roman-Dutch law.[210] But the equitable discretion in the evaluation of contractual rights and duties deriving, originally, from the *ex bona fide clause* in the *formulae* of consensual contracts, allowed South African jurisprudence harmoniously to graft it upon the Roman-Dutch law relating to breach of contract (which, incidentally, has never been fettered by Friedrich Mommsen's impossibility-doctrine).[211] As a result, therefore, repudiation is today recognised as a special type of breach of contract even by Roman-Dutch "purists" like J.C. De Wet.[212] This shows how, in the pre-*Bank of Lisbon* days, *bona fides* could be used as an agent of organic change;[213] and how sadly the anti-quarianism advocated in that case would curtail the creative potential of Roman law.

Tuckers v. *Hovis* thus leads us into what I consider the most stimulating feature of modern South African private law. If we analyse, *sine ira et studio*, i.e. without adopting a "purist" or "pollutionist" perspective, its development over the past two hundred years, we can detect a whole variety of areas in which a synthesis has actually been brought about between what are usually regarded as the two main traditions of European private law; areas, in other words, where the South African

---

207 1980 (1) S.A. 645 (A) (*per* Jansen, J.A.); on which see Carey Miller, (1980) 97 *S.A.L.J.* 531ff.; Lewis, (1991) 108 *S.A.L.J.* 249ff.

208 1980 (1) S.A. 645 (A) 652.

209 *Hochster* v. *De la Tour* (1853) 2 El. & Bl. 678, 118 E.R. 922.

210 Cf. the literature referred to in *Obligations*, at 816, n.228.

211 *Obligations*, 809ff.

212 De Wet en Van Wyk, *Die Suid-Afrikaanse Kontraktereg en Handelsreg*, 5th ed. by G.F. Lubbe, 1992, 168ff.

213 Another example is provided by the gradual extension of aedilitian relief; cf. e.g. *Hall* v. *Milner* 1959 (2) S.A. 304 (O) 310; *Phame (Pty.) Ltd.* v. *Paizes* 1973 (2) S.A. 397 (A) (cf. *Obligations*, 328ff.). But see now *Mountbatten Investments (Pty.) Ltd.* v. *Mahomed* 1989 (1) S.A. 172 (D) (*per* Bristowe, J.) refusing to extend the *actio quanti minoris* to cover trade-in agreements; for a critical discussion, see L. Hawthorne, "The Nature of Trade-in Agreements", (1990) *T.H.R.H.R.* 116ff.; Stoop, (1991) 54 *T.H.R.H.R.* 184ff.

4

usus modernus has proved flexible enough to accommodate, integrate and productively assimilate certain rules and institutions from the English Common law. True it is that mixed systems can be muddled systems; the story of the attempted reception of the English consideration doctrine and its fusion with the continental *causa* requirement around the turn of the century provides a somewhat unfortunate example.[214] The story of the South African law of trusts[215] or of the *usus modernus* of the *actio iniuriarum*,[216] on the other hand, are instances which substantiate my thesis: in both cases, English doctrines have been adapted ingeniously to a Civil law environment. The usefulness of these experiences for the great task ahead of European jurisprudence, namely the creation of a new *ius commune Europaeum*,[217] is obvious.

VI.

All in all, I should think that devotion and faithfulness to our civilian heritage cannot be counted by the number of judgements which abound with learned disquisitions on the Roman sources or with elaborate analyses of Bartolus, Donellus, Voet or Stair. Much as we may admire them, such judicial pronouncements must appear somewhat odd in our modern world. Maitland once put his uneasiness into the following words:

> It is pleasant, and I even believe that it is profitable, to trace the origin of legal rules in the social and economic condition of a bygone age. But any one who really possesses what has been called the historic sense must, so it seems to me, dislike to see a rule or an idea unfitly surviving in a changed environment. An anachronism should offend not only his reason, but his taste. Roman law was all very well at Rome; medieval law in the Middle Ages. But the modern man in a toga, or a coat of mail, or a chasuble, is not only uncomfortable but unlovely.[218]

It is when they turn against the purely antiquarian allure, when they perpetuate the spirit and not necessarily the letter of the civilian tradition, when they use Roman law in order to venture beyond it, that South African lawyers can be said to emulate their masters of the past.[219]

---

214 *Obligations*, 556ff.
215 Cf. generally, *supra,* nn.197f. For an analysis of the "*cy-près*" doctrine and its development see, in this context, R. Zimmermann, "Cy-près" in *Iuris Professio. Festgabe für Max Kaser*, 1986, 396ff.
216 Cf. the evaluation by P.Q.R. Boberg, "Defamation South African Style - The Odyssey of *animus iniuriandi*", in *Essays in Honour of Ellison Kahn*, 1989, 35ff.; and see *Obligations*, 1078ff.
217 For a programmatic statement, cf. (1992) *Juristenzeitung* 8ff. as well as the first editorial of the new *Zeitschrift für Europäisches Privatrecht*, 1993 *Z.Eu.P.* 1ff.
218 "The Making of the German Civil Code" in *The Collected Papers of F.W. Maitland*, ed. H.A.L. Fisher, 1911, vol. 3, at 486.
219 This essay reflects South African law as of the end of 1991.

Section Two

4. THE FOUNDATION OF LEGAL RATIONALITY IN SCOTLAND

By PETER BIRKS

Introduction

Scots law looks back with pride on its civilian tradition – that is to say, on its belonging to the family of modern jurisdictions which based themselves on the Roman law library as compacted by Justinian in the sixth century and later expounded, and expanded, by generations of European jurists from the twelfth. The second life of Roman law, in which it entered into the foundations of modern European law, is usually dated from the life and work of Irnerius in the University of Bologna. Irnerius died in about 1125. Through his work and that of his successors the *ius civile* of Rome – the law pertaining to the state and citizens of Rome[1] – thus became the *ius commune*, the common law of Europe. And Scotland attached itself to that tradition. It is at the same time undeniable that Scots law has long been and continues to be heavily influenced by the methods and substance of that other common law, the Common law of England. The law of Scotland is thus an example of a mixed system, with intellectual ascendants in both the principal legal families of the Western European tradition.

The theme of this paper is that the most important item in Scots law's inheritance on its Roman side is its capacity for orderly overview, both of the law as a whole and of the large subdivisions within it – the continents and countries, so to say, which make up the map of the legal world. A sub-theme, less optimistic, is the failure of the modern literature, and the law schools, to emphasise this element of the tradition and thus to ensure that full advantage is taken of it. Towards the end we will notice a number of factors which combine to make Scots law look more English. Lip service to the civilian tradition and to the superior rationality which purportedly comes with it is worth precisely nothing if insufficient intellectual energy is actually devoted to preserving the structural framework on which that rationality depends. Nor is it merely a matter of preservation. Respect for the tradition equally importantly implies modification, improvement and renewal, which require in their turn that the inherited framework be subjected in the law schools to the pressures of criticism and independent thought. It is sadly true that that is no longer being done, certainly not in any

---

1   As "the poet" was to the Greeks Homer, to the Romans Virgil, so the *ius civile*, with no *civitas* named, was the law of the Roman citizenship: *Inst.* 1.2.2. 'Civilian' merely adapts '*civile*'.

sustained and regular fashion. The effect is to imperil Scots law's principal asset, and to mimic English law's principal defect. In England there has been almost no tradition of orderly overview.

I Sentiment and Intellect

Feelings which cannot be shown to have rational value have no place in legal science. A gut-reaction may make sense, but until it does so it must be presumed unsafe. Among alien sentiments, it is important to say at the outset that blood, or parentage, has no rational value, no more with law than people. Except as a matter of history, which if known may indeed bring deeper understanding, it is neither significant nor even very interesting that a concept, rule or practice has a Roman origin or that a proposition was first propounded by English judges.

If, for example, there is a question whether relief should be accorded more cautiously for mistakes of law than for mistakes of fact,[2] nothing whatever is gained by asking whether it was in his capacity as an English lawyer that a Scottish Lord Chancellor foisted a yes on a legal system strongly disposed to answer no.[3] What matters is obviously the reason of the thing. Are there or are there not special grounds for caution in respect of mistakes of law? Lord Chancellor Brougham, whether we think of him as Scottish or English, certainly conceived himself to be about that rational business.[4]

Just as there is no place in legal science for any argument that a rule is good or bad because it has or has not a Roman grandparent, so there is no intrinsic merit in the survival or preservation of externalities of civilian origins. Membership of the civilian legal family has no value if all it means is occasional curious monuments to the past and a graveyard of indecipherable inscriptions. Latin terms and maxims, and latinate language which cannot be properly understood without the subjacent original, are an impediment to rationality. It should not be forgotten just how far the knowledge of Latin has declined. Tags which used to be useful have become dangerous. Even relatively simple and basic terms, such as *vindicatio* and *condictio*, will have to be replaced.

---

2   A subject now once again hotly debated in many jurisdictions: Scottish Law Commission, *Recovery of Benefits*; *Morgan Guaranty Trust Co.* v. *Lothian Regional Council* 1995 S.L.T. 299. Cf. *David Securities Pty. Ltd.* v. *Commonwealth Bank of Australia* (1992) 175 C.L.R. 353; *Air Canada* v. *British Columbia* (1989) 59 D.L.R. (4th) 161, to be read with *Canadian Pacific* v. *British Columbia* (1989) 59 D.L.R. (4th) 218; *Willis Faber Enthoven (Pty.) Ltd.* v. *Receiver of Revenue* 1992 (4) S.A. 202 (A).

3   Cf. the surprising tone of the discussion of Lord Brougham L.C.'s speeches in *Wilson and McLellan* v. *Sinclair* (1830) 4 W. & S. 398 and *Dixon* v. *Monklands Canal Co.* (1831) 5 W. & S. 445 in T.B. Smith, *A Short Commentary on the Law of Scotland* (Edinburgh, 1962), 825.

4   It is evident on the face of his speech in *Wilson and McLellan* v. *Sinclair* (1830) 4 W. & S. 398 that he was not set on imposing English law on Scots law, or vice versa, but simply looking to the best of his ability for the most rational rule.

They survive through an alliance of two unworthy habits of mind and one timid one. It is timid to cling on to worn-out terminology, for want of the confidence in any modern substitute, and it is unworthy in a lawyer to dignify himself with mystifying language and his system with empty Roman allusion. Harmless, even beautiful, in gardens and buildings, in the law such decorations obstruct doors through which law student and judge alike should pass easily and without distraction.

II An Inferiority of English Law

English law has not attended to the need for systematic overview. The law used to be kept stable by the forms of action. Thus the action of debt was a package of law focused on the writ of debt and the counts countable under it. The words of those texts, illustrated by cases, formed a single package of law. The action of *assumpsit* (he promised) formed another such package. Every now and again there were shifts of matter from one package to another, as *Slade* v. *Morley*[5] took many causes of indebtedness from debt to *assumpsit* and, in the twilight of the forms of action, *Williams* v. *Holland*[6] finally transferred many claims for personal injury and damage from trespass *vi et armis* to the action on the case for negligent harm. The actional packages could exist each in its own isolated space, and within each one nothing prevented the development of a relatively advanced, sophisticated and detailed body of substantive law. So far as the words of the action themselves created obstructions, fictions could be and were resorted to, deeming some allegations which could not be dropped to be satisfied without evidence. It was more difficult to ensure coherence as between one actional package and another. The only way of overcoming their isolation one from another was to know all the law inside out and backwards, but even then it was difficult to compare like with like. For convenience the actions were bound together by that most basic of all systems of classification, alphabetical order. From the old abridgments to the indispensable *Halsbury*,[7] the Common law has been, and remains, dependent on the alphabet.

Until relatively recently, there was at least one more thing to be said. Most Common lawyers had been introduced directly or indirectly to the Roman scheme of things as represented in Justinian's *Institutes*. In the eighteenth century Lord Mansfield is known to have recommended that a beginner in the law should start by getting to grips with that small book.[8] And so the *Institutes* served common lawyers as a conceptual map, performing the same function for them as it had for the

---

5 (1602) 4 Co. Rep. 92, 76 E.R. 1074, but now best reported in J.H. Baker and S.F.C. Milsom, *Sources of English Legal History* (London, 1986), 420–41.

6 (1833) 10 Bing. 112, 131 E.R. 848.

7 *Halsbury's Laws of England*, now in its fourth edition, ed. Lord Hailsham (London, 1973, continuing).

8 C.H.S. Fifoot, *Lord Mansfield* (London, 1936), 29.

Romans themselves, whose primary materials no less resembled what
Wood called "a heap of good learning".[9] Moreover, when the forms of
action were abolished in the nineteenth century and the need for university legal education began to be felt in England, to order and make
sense of the mountainous and ever-enlarging heap of primary
materials,[10] the university jurists who rose to the challenge knew the
Roman map and, in their writing, consciously adhered to it or, like
Austin, wrestled to improve upon it.[11]

Sir Frederick Pollock, for example, in writing on contract and on
tort,[12] not only used those institutional categories but took it for granted
that they would be perceived as belonging together as part of the larger
Roman category of obligations. *Pollock on Torts*[13] was dedicated to the
memory of Willes, J., "a man of profound learning in the law, joined with
extraordinary and varied knowledge of other kinds". Expanding on the
dedication, Pollock went out of his way to recall of Willes that "once and
again he spoke or wrote to me to the effect of desiring to see the Law of
Obligations treated in English". Pollock thought of his book as a contribution of materials towards that end: "of materials only, for a book on Torts
added to a book on Contracts does not make a treatise on Obligations".

The consciousness of how the pieces of the jigsaw fit together is
now being lost. The reason is obvious. The number of lawyers familiar
with the Roman map is diminishing, and the law schools have not taken
any interest in perpetuating the lessons which were learned through a
basic study of the elementary Roman texts. The result is that the only
overview that most common lawyers have is the list of courses which

---

9   Thomas Wood, *Institute of the the Laws of England* (London, 1720), pref-
     ace, at ii.
10   This development is neatly caught by A.V. Dicey's inaugural lecture in
     Oxford, 21st April, 1883: *Can English Law be Taught at the Universities?*
     (London, 1883), discussed by D. Sugarman, "Legal Theory, the Common
     Law Mind and the Making of the Textbook Tradition" in *Legal Theory and
     Common Law*, ed. W. Twining (Oxford, 1986), 26, and Birks in P.B.H. Birks
     (ed.), *Reviewing Legal Education* (Oxford, 1994).
11   John Austin, first professor of jurisprudence, at University College,
     London, 1826–1832, is nowadays read as though his chair of jurisprudence
     was a chair of legal philosophy; but it was a chair of law, and his reputation
     as a legal philosopher is in truth only a by-product of his determination to
     make sense of English law and to present it in an orderly fashion. His
     famous *Province of Jurisprudence Determined* (London, 1832) was
     intended only as the basis upon which he could build that systematising
     work, published posthumously by his wife as *Lectures on the Philosophy
     of Positive Law* (London, 1863). For an account of the unhappiness of
     being ahead of his time: L. and J. Hamburger, *Troubled Lives: John and
     Sarah Austin* (Toronto, 1985), esp. 54ff.
12   For tort, see the following note. The first edition of *Contract* came out six
     years earlier: *Principles of the Law of Contract at Law and in Equity*
     (London, 1876).
13   In full: *The Law of Torts: A Treatise on the Principles of Obligations
     Arising from Civil Wrongs in the Common Law* (London, 1887).

they encountered as law students in their faculty prospectus. They recall the courses which were obligatory; beyond them the courses which were optional but which they themselves did take; beyond them there are the options which their friends took, and, in the outermost circle and shading off into the unknown, the options which were available but which no acquaintance ever visited and, yet more hazily, those lost in the distance of postgraduate study or other law schools.

The courses in the curriculum are perceived as islands and from sea level, an archipelago to be visited in an order determined by chance. Almost no work is done on the interrelation of legal categories or on the long history of legal taxonomy. The suggestion, elementary to Pollock, that contract and tort belong together as parts of the law of obligations, when obligations are divided by the events which bring them into being, is presented, some eighteen hundred years too late, as an innovation.[14] On the sidelines the Law Society of England and Wales, which devotes great energy to defending the right of aspiring lawyers to visit the fewest possible islands and stay for the shortest possible time, inveighs against all categories and the very notion of categorisation, a nostrum for returning English legal science to the stone age.

There were once the makings of a tradition of classification and systematic overview. Blackstone thought that the business of a university jurist was precisely to map out the main areas of the law so as to show their relation one with another and the principal features of each one.[15] His *Commentaries*, though they do have predecessors[16] and successors,[17]

---

14   The preface to the first edition of *Cooke and Oughton*, which at no point looked back at the history of the relevant classifications, appeared to suggest that the need for a book on obligations arose from the discoveries of "recent scholarship": P.J. Cooke and D.W. Oughton, *The Common Law of Obligations* (London, 1989). Note also the error at 1, where it is asserted that beyond contract and tort lies only unjust enrichment, short shrift for all the problems of the miscellany.

15   "[An academical expounder of the law] should consider his course as a general map of the law, marking out the shape of the country, its connexions and boundaries, its greater divisions and principal cities: it is not his business to describe minutely the subordinate limits, or to fix the longitude and latitude of every inconsiderable hamlet" – W. Blackstone, *Commentaries*, 1.35. On Blackstone's place in the history of "institutional" literature, see J.W. Cairns, "Blackstone, an English Institutist: Legal Literature and the Rise of the Nation State", (1984) 4 *Oxford J.L.S.* 318.

16   Notably, Sir Henry Finch, *Nomotechnia – Law, or a Discourse Thereof in Four Books* (1613); Sir Matthew Hale, *An Analysis of the Civil Part of the Law* (1713 – after his death); Thomas Wood, *An Institute of the Laws of England* (1720). For a general account see, P.B.H. Birks and G. McLeod, *Justinian's Institutes* (London, 1987), 23–26.

17   Not only H.J. Stephen's *Commentaries*, which were directly evolved from Blackstone, but also smaller works such as Sir W. Markby, *Elements of Law* (Oxford, 1871); W. Geldhart, *Elements of English Law* (Oxford, 1911). Most successful was P.S. James, *Introduction to English Law* (London, 1950), which has enjoyed many editions.

really mark the lonely highpoint of this kind of work in English law. The alphabet reasserted itself. Such systematic overview literature as has survived exists in the nether reaches of legal education, below the notice of those who teach and learn in a university law school, although at least one of the books condemned to that half-light started life with loftier ambitions.[18]

III The Superiority of Roman Law and Scots Law

Though it has in recent times failed to value its own achievement, Scots law could not be more different from English law in this matter. It has a strong tradition of rationality founded ultimately on careful and sustained attention to the coherence of its view of the whole law. Its overview of the law was taken directly from Roman law in the seventeenth century but, unlike most civilian jurisdictions, it has been maintained through successive generations of interpretative juristic literature and has not been ossified by legislative intervention in the form of a code. In this section, we will first consider why a systematic structure matters, then outline the Roman scheme and its reception in Scotland and finally notice the transformation of other similar systems by the process of codification. In the next section we will revert briefly to the curious indifference of Scots law in the twentieth century to this crucial aspect of its Roman inheritance.

Why a systematic structure matters

The almost complete neglect in England of the business of systematic overview is bad and dangerous for two related reasons. The first is that the most elementary principle of justice is that like cases should be treated alike, which supposes a stable basis of differentiation. The second is that the human brain cannot function in any field, or not in a predictable fashion, without some taxonomy of the relevant data. A defective taxonomy will produce actions and decisions which are open to rational criticism, but in the absence of a taxonomy decisions can only be intuitive and either good or bad according to the whims of the decider.

Law which has no systematic overview can neither produce predictably similar resolutions of similar disputes nor fulfil the duty of the law to restrain arbitrary power, whether political or judicial. English law not infrequently falls into these dangers, because neither the alphabet nor the declining influence of the institutional scheme can provide any assurance that, in an unusual case, the right authorities will be presented to the court. How such a case will be analysed is a matter of chance, influenced by the intellectual habits and background of counsel. Chambers in Lincoln's Inn will produce one analysis and one set of

---

18 James, cited n.17 above, was expressly intended as an English *Institutes*: see the preface to the first edition.

authorities, when other chambers in Middle Temple would have advanced another family of cases and a quite different answer. The law thus becomes a guessing game played by amateurs with groups of cases selected as randomly as a beginning ornithologist might assign names to the innumerable varieties of small brown bird. Nor, finally, is there any way in which a category in trouble can be sure to reveal its difficulties. Hardly any work is done in the law schools on personal property.[19] If we shared a systematic overview we would certainly notice a hole appearing in the landscape, but the alphabet rings no alarm bells.

Roman Law: The Institutional Scheme

In Roman law the need for a stable overview was provided by the *Institutes*. That book and, ultimately, the system of legal education,[20] ensured that the lawyer knew how to review the whole law. Contrary to widespread belief, the advanced materials of Roman law were not well ordered. The great edictal commentaries, for example, just followed word by word the text of the praetor's edict; and the edict itself, even after the revision by Salvius Julianus in the reign of Hadrian, was not arranged according to an intelligible scheme but remained in large measure merely historically determined. It had grown up over the years; it was not elegant and rational like the *Institutes*. Even Justinian's commissioners in the sixth century did not re-arrange the material systematically. Neither the *Digest* nor the *Codex,* between them a compacted law library between two and three times the length of the Bible, has the conceptual coherence aimed at by the relatively tiny *Institutes*. A common lawyer could come and rearrange the *Digest*'s four hundred and thirty-two titles in alphabetical order. It would make no difference.

The *Institutes* was a kind of map of the law for beginners, the cradle of the law in more than one sense.[21] If you opened a page at random in any of the other books – conceptually disordered as they were albeit intensely exact at the highest level of magnification – you would quickly know where the subject-matter belonged on the institutional conceptual map – that is to say, where it would have been treated in the *Institutes* if the *Institutes* went into any kind of detail. In other

---

19   The beginning of an improvement can be seen in the books produced by Bell and Bridge: A.P. Bell, *The Modern Law of Personal Property in England and Ireland* (Dublin, 1989); M. Bridge, *Personal Property Law* (London, 1993); also the very useful multiauthored book, N.E. Palmer and E. McKendrick (edd.), *Interests in Goods* (London, 1993).

20   Justinian made the *Institutes* the foundation first-year course: see the *Constitutio Omnem* (The Imperial Pronounce-ment "That the whole body of the law") prefaced to the *Digest: Pennsylvania Digest*, ed. A. Watson. 4 vols. (Philadelphia, 1985), vol. 1, 1–liv.

21   *"Cunabula legum": Constitutio Imperatoriam* (The Imperial Pronouncement "Imperial Majesty") 3. This pronouncement promulgated the *Institutes* on 21 November 533. See Birks and McLeod, cited n.16 above, at 33.

words the Roman lawyer was supplied with a map of the law, separately from the heap of primary material which was itself no more orderly interrelated than the common law.

Roman law and the Common law developed on a similar pattern and with a similar character. A Common lawyer would be perfectly happy if he woke up to find himself having to work with the Roman materials. Roman law before the time of Gaius in the second century A.D. was much the same as English law before Blackstone, with the difference that in the subsequent periods Blackstone's organising gifts never bore fruit to the same extent as those of Gaius. The pre-Gaian law was dominated by forms of action; within each of the actional packages there was an abundant and detailed casuistic literature; and there was no conceptual map to organise the mass of detail.

Then came Gaius' *Institutes,* a short but brilliant exposition of the law which demonstrated that it could be presented as a coherent whole, rather than a list of actions each with its own commentary and case-law illustration. In the end it would be Justinian's *Institutes,* compiled more than three hundred years later, which would be taken into European law to provide the legal map for almost every jurisdiction, but, unless he had forbears now unknown to us, it was Gaius who made the decisive breakthrough. Despite the long interval between the two, the modern analogy is with successive editions. Though it drew also on other works and made some input of its own, Justinian's *Institutes* is really no more than a second edition of Gaius's uniquely important book.

The key to Gaius' achievement lay in his recognition of the fact that the substantive law tied to the forms of action could not only be discussed independently of the actions themselves but could be rearranged in new relationships, different from those to which the list in the praetor's edict had accustomed lawyers. In some cases that even meant that an actional package would have to be broken up and distributed to different places in the new conceptual arrangement. The difficulty and creativity of this intellectual breakthrough is nowadays not easy to recreate. Like many great advances, it seems simple and obvious in retrospect. Even the basic nature of what Gaius had to do remains elusive so long as it is decribed in the abstract. It is necessary therefore to spend a few lines on a specific example, namely the law of debt.

Before Gaius' conceptual map was drawn the law was simply a list of actions, models of which were set out in the praetor's edict. Legal learning consisted largely in knowing the list and knowing the scope of each individual action in the list. Thus, the whole law relating to debt existed within the actional package formed by the *condictio,* the Roman equivalent to the action of debt. The *condictio* took its name from the fact that in its original form it required the pursuer to give notice to the defender (*condicere*) to accept a judge in the matter of the sum or thing owed.

It has to be remembered that an action was above all a set of words, a winning proposition which the pursuer (Aulus Agerius, the person doing the *agere,* the claiming or pleading) undertook to substantiate at a trial before a judge. The key allegation of the *condictio* was that the defender ought to give a sum of money, a quantity of goods or a specific thing to the pursuer. Long before the time of Gaius, the formulary system of pleading had reduced that to a conditional clause qualifying a command to the judge to condemn: "If it appears that NN ought to give AA 1000 sesterces, judge condemn NN to AA for 1000 sesterces; if it does not appear, absolve".

The law of debt was the law of what the pursuer had to prove to substantiate that proposition and what answers the defender might plead to negative a seemingly successful substantiation. There was learning on who could be a creditor and who a debtor, but the core of the matter was the list of facts which gave rise to indebtedness – formal promises, loans, mistaken payments, and so on. Viewed as a legal category, the *condictio* (the law of debt depending from the action of debt) took its unity, not from a causative event, but from a kind of claim triggered by many causative events; it was the category of all claims, "You ought to give me x". In this it differed markedly from many other actional categories. The action on sale, for example, focused on the causative event, sale. Sale could not be aligned with debt any more than carnivores can be aligned with mammals. If anything was alignable in the two categories it was sale and one or two of the factual causes of indebtedness, those in which it could be said that debt had a consensual origin. A formal promise could be aligned with sale within a new category of "contract" but a mistaken payment could not be included. To achieve that alignment, the actional category of debt, the *condictio* would have to be broken up.

Mismatched categories, whether they are actional categories or not, are impossible to rationalise, are indeed the greatest enemies of rationality. That is why interrelationship of categories has to be kept continually under review. On the other hand, the law hates to be disturbed. A jurist who seeks to persuade his colleagues to think in new categories has to be very bold, very persuasive and very very right. In the nineteenth century John Austin tried to make English lawyers rethink their categories. His lecture hall emptied. He had to abandon his chair and join the many great minds whose only glory has been posthumous.[22] We do not really know what success Gaius had in his own lifetime. Even for him glory may have been long delayed.

Although even after its revision by Julian under the Emperor Hadrian the list of actions which had grown up over time still consisted of mismatched categories in no very discernible order, Gaius was able to make out in the accretion of commentary and illustration two recurrent types of question. One concerned the persons able to make the

---

22   Cf. n.11 above.

claims and to defend them, and the other the factual conditions on which a claimant could have the thing which he claimed. If one dealt with those matters separately, withdrawing all the substantive meat from the actional shells, it was nonetheless obvious that there would still remain to be considered the actual business of pleading in court. The eviscerated actions would not disappear. And so he advanced and acted upon a proposition of extreme simplicity and revolutionary impact which has dominated Western legal thinking ever since: the whole law can be divided according as it deals with persons, things and actions.[23]

In a society which recognised slavery and concentrated entitlements in the head of each agnatic family, there was much to say about the different capacities of persons, the acquisition of one or another status and transition from one status to another. The crucial distinction was between freedom and slavery, but, hardly less important, free people were either independent or still dependent on the exercise of authority by the head of the agnatic family, the *paterfamilias.*

However, the largest and most difficult category was *res* – things demandable or assets. Here the most important of Gaius's insights was his perception of the possibility of dividing things between those which were corporeal, like land, a horse or silver cup, and those which were incorporeal, mere abstractions or ideas, such as a deceased's estate (full of corporeal things but as a single entity incorporeal), a right to cross another's land, or a right to insist on another person's making some performance.

The most brilliant achievement of his taxonomic genius was the perception that the common substance of the innumerable actions in which in one form or another the pursuer claimed that the defender ought to do something could be rendered as the incorporeal thing *obligatio.* The "thing" which they were about and which the pursuer was claiming was the "obligation" of the defender to make a performance. In that way he both created from those scattered actions the unity of the law of obligations and achieved an alignment between obligations, incorporeal things, and those other more obvious assets, the corporeal things such as land, horses and silver cups.

His subdivision of obligations was no less important. Gaius intended that the law of things or assets should reflect the long-standing reality of actions and the learning on actions in putting in the foreground the facts creative of the various entitlements: on what facts do you own a horse, and on what facts is it true that another person ought to make some performance in your favour? The various levels of the

---

23 Gaius, 1.8: *Omne autem ius quo utimur vel ad personas pertinet, vel ad res, vel ad actiones. Sed prius videamus de personis* (All our law is about persons, things or actions. We turn to persons first). Text and translation in W.M. Gordon and O.F. Robinson, The *Institutes of Gaius* (London, 1988).

subdivision of obligations answer the latter question. Obligations are born of contracts and wrongs and – here a quagmire of legal classification still difficult to traverse – other miscellaneous events.[24] And below that the now familiar speciation of contracts and wrongs.

A short account makes the Gaian overview seem smoother and more free of bumps and discontinuities than it really is, but, with all its puzzles, it was a brilliant advance, as wonderful and as important in the law as Darwin's *Origin of Species* in the understanding of the natural world. From pockets of logic-chopping it discovered the rationality of the seamless web. A simple event such as a punch in the face and a broken nose could be handled soundly enough by a lawyer who knew that that was matter for the *actio iniuriarum*, but the law on that and surrounding matters would be perceived differently and developed more coherently by lawyers who could find its place on a map which told them what its true neighbours were and how, with them, it related to larger divisions: a slap was a species of the civil wrong *iniuria*, of which there were others; the category of wrongs was, with contract and other events, a source of obligation; obligations were incorporeal things within the law of things; and the law of things was, alongside persons and actions, one of the three great divisions of the whole law.

Widespread in the ancient world, Gaius' *Institutes* never entered the second life of Roman law. Displaced by Justinian's *Institutes*, Gaius's book was lost until wonderfully rediscovered in 1816.[25] The Gaian scheme was transmitted to the Western world in Justinian's version. The structure remained fundamentally unchanged. Ahead of the threefold division, Gaius had included a section which combined constitutional matters relevant to the making of law with some jurisprudential generalities. Justinian's commissioners slightly expanded that prefix, and he added on at the end by way of suffix the shortest possible sketch of criminal law. The three heads – persons, things and actions – therefore became five: sources-with-jurisprudence, persons, things, actions, crime. He also slotted in ahead of the central trichotomy the important observation that an anterior division must distinguish public and private law. Public law was represented only by the extremely short top and tail on law-making and crime. The real business of the book was not all law but just private law.[26]

There were other changes at lower levels. Rather as English lawyers often ignore or fail to integrate equity, so that, for example, the law of tort tends not to take account of equitable wrongs, so Gaius had excluded much law rooted only in the praetor's jurisdiction, the *ius*

---

24 Gaius, 3.88-91, especially the problem encountered in 3.91, is to be compared with D.44.7.1*pr.*, where Gaius achieves the threefold categorisation given in the text.
25 A text was discovered, overwritten, by Niebuhr the year after the battle of Waterloo, 1816. See Gordon and Robinson, cited n.23, at 1, 11-12.
26 *Inst.* 1.1.3.

honorarium. Under obligations, Justinian inserted a division designed to retrieve the praetorian equivalents: obligation are either civil (based on the *ius civile*) or praetorian.[27] And on the next level down he purported to resolve the problems of the miscellany of causative events beyond contract and tort by a stratagem whose symmetrical beauty long concealed its dangerous futility: obligations arise from contract or *quasi* from contract, from delict or *quasi* from delict.[28]

The Institutional Scheme in Scotland

If one studies the structure of T.B. Smith's *Short Commentary*, published as recently as 1962,[29] a book of nearly a thousand pages and as such six or seven times longer than Justinian's *Institutes,* one can immediately see in it the survival of the scheme, as modified by Justinian, which Gaius devised in A.D.161, almost exactly eighteen hundred years earlier. It is an astonishing tribute to Gaius' genius, and one which is repeated in almost every European civil code.

Part One, called "Background and Sources", and Part Two, called "Public Law", are together equivalent to the prefix to the *Institutes,* except that "Public Law" includes crime and criminal procedure. Justinian, it will be recalled, made crime a suffix, thus creating an outer shell of public law, with constitutional matters touching law-making at the front and crime at the back. In T.B. Smith's treatment, all that has been consolidated and, instead of being treated in barest outline even by the standards of the *Institutes,* is allowed some two hundred and forty pages.

The whole of the rest of the book is Part Three, called "Private Law". Following the model of the *Institutes* we would expect it to begin with the law relating to persons; and, after a brief introduction about general concepts and themes, that is what it does. Almost a hundred pages are devoted to family law. There then follow, out of their institutional order, some fifty pages on the law of succession, associated as in the German code with the law of persons. In the Roman institutional scheme a very extensive discussion of succession comes in the law of things, between what we would think of as property and obligations.[30]

Succession having been brought forward, about one hundred and fifty pages are devoted to property, both corporeal things and rights over other people's things, such as rights of way. The law of trusts then

---

27 *Inst.* 3.13.1.
28 *Inst.* 3.13.2.
29 T.B. (later Sir Thomas) Smith, *A Short Commentary on the Law of Scotland* (Edinburgh, 1962).
30 Modern law draws a strong line between rights *in rem,* (property interests) and rights *in personam* (personal rights or, from the other end, obligations). That does not correspond with the line within the Roman law of things between corporeal and incorporeal things. A praedial servitude, for example, is incorporeal, in that resembling an obligation, but it is a right *in rem,* a property interest.

stands where the whole law of succession would have stood.[31] Pages 615 to 868 then deal with obligations, the order of the treatment being inverted, so that the miscellaneous category is dealt with first, followed by delict, followed by a long treatment of contract. The law of actions is not considered.

There are therefore all sorts of minor changes, and a number of emphatic breaks are introduced which in the original would have been less marked. The amount of detailed information is greatly increased. Crime is moved forward; succession is moved forward; trusts is inserted in the slot vacated by succession; the order of the sub-categories of obligations is inverted. Nevertheless the preponderant and very remarkable truth is that the divisions and sub-divisions of the law worked out by Gaius eighteen hundred years before still provide the organising structure of the *Short Commentary.*

In this T.B. Smith was and knew himself to be the beneficiary of a long tradition which in Scotland stretched back to the middle of the seventeeth century and, in particular, to two similarly titled but very different books. Both of these belonged in a wide European movement, lucidly described by Luig,[32] which brought it about that in one jurisdiction after another Justinian's *Institutes* were used to provide the structure to control and organise treatments of national law, usually presented in the vernacular and drawing on the substance of Roman law only to fill lacunae. The paradigm was Grotius' *Inleiding tot de Hollandsche Rechtsgeleertheyd* (*Introduction to the Jurisprudence of Holland*), written during his imprisonment for the instruction of his sons and published in 1631, ten years after his dramatic escape.

Of the two crucial Scottish books, one, very short, was Sir George Mackenzie's *Institutions of the Law of Scotland,* published in 1684. The other, very long, was Viscount Stair's *Institutions of the Law of Scotland* which came out first in 1681 and was expanded in 1693.[33] Leaving aside the hugely different scale of these two works, they belong to different intellectual traditions in the history of the Gaian institutional scheme. Mackenzie accepted that scheme in its Justinianic form more or less uncritically, seeking only to make its structure stand out even more simply and clearly; Stair, by contrast, was a revisionist, forceful and independent

---

31 A slender justification might be found for this in the two titles on *fideicommissa, Inst.* 2.23 and 2.24. However, the truth is that trusts as derived from English law are best regarded as without any institutional forerunner. It is arguably right to annexe them to the law of property.

32 K. Luig, "*Institutes* of National Law in the Seventeenth and Eighteenth Centuries" 1972 *J.R.* 193. Cf. A. Watson, *The Making of the Civil Law* (Cambridge Mass., 1981), 62ff. and "Justinian's *Institutes* and Some English Counterparts", in *Studies in Justinian's Institutes* (London, 1983), edd. P.G. Stein and A. Lewis, 181. Further: J. W. Cairns, "Institutional Writings in Scotland Reconsidered", in *New Perspectives in Scottish Legal History*, edd. A. Kiralfy and H.L. Macqueen (London, 1984), 76.

33 Tercentenary edition: D. M. Walker (ed.), James Dalrymple, Viscount Stair, *The Institutions of the Law of Scotland* (Edinburgh and Glasgow, 1981).

in his attempt to modify and improve the overview inherited from the past.[34] Although some readers now find his language difficult, all who get on terms with it recognise an intellect far ahead of its time in its power and, even more remarkable, its freedom. His mind was not daunted by authority. An important example, going to the structure of his book is this:

> The Roman law taketh for its object Persons, Things and Actions, and according to these, orders itself, but these are only the extrinsic object and matter, about which the law and right are versant. But the proper object is the right itself, whether it concerns persons, things, or actions: and, according to the several rights and their natural order, the order of jurisprudence may be taken up in a threefold consideration, First, in the constitution and nature of rights; Secondly, in their conveyance, or translation from one person to another, whether it be among the living or from the dead; Thirdly, in their cognition, which comprehends the trial, decision, and execution of every man's right by the legal remeids.[35]

So far as concerns the main building blocks of the Gaian scheme, the principal consequence of Stair's revisionist approach was the elimination of an independent law of persons and projection of the law of obligations to the front of the book. However, his division of the law of obligations between those imposed (obediential) and those accepted (conventional) allowed him to begin with obligations imposed on persons by reason of their status, thus in effect achieving a continuity with the orthodox institutional scheme: though the analysis was different, the same matter finally appeared at the beginning of the substantive discussion. His division of obediential obligations also boldly and rightly rejected the unhelpful "*quasi*" categories by which Justinian had pretended to resolve the miscellaneous category which Gaius had discerned beyond contract and wrongs.[36] However, Stair's attempt to twist the basis of classification round from the causative events to the content of the obligation – obligations to make reparation, restitution, repetition, recompense[37] has itself created enduring problems.[38]

---

34 Compare the work of Jean Domat (1625–1696) in *Les lois civiles dans leur ordre naturel* (1689–94), translated by W. Strahan as *The Civil Laws in the Natural Order* (1722).

35 Stair, *Inst.,* 1,1,23.

36 Cf. text to n.24 above.

37 Stair, *Inst.,* 1,7–9.

38 See the discussion by N. R. Whitty, "Some Trends and Issues in Scots Unjust Enrichment Law" 1994 *J.R.* 127. The author there manifests a preference for the German way of organising the law of unjust enrichment, as being civilian and therefore not alien, as is the Common law of England. However, there is no single civilian tradition in this matter. For example, the Dutch law, with which Scots law might claim a closer affinity, differs markedly from the German: contrast (conveniently in the same issue of the *Restitution Law Review*, E. Schrage, "Restitution in the New Dutch Civil Code" 1994 *Restitution L.R.* 208 (see the provisions of the Code at 202-7), with R. Zimmermann and J. du Plessis, "Basic Features of the German Law of Unjust Enrichment" 1994 *Restitution L.R.* 14.

Revisionism, however admirable in the attempt, has by and large not proved very successful, and, subject to the persistence of Stair's internal classification of obligations, in Scotland it was Mackenzie and the unimproved institutional structure which prevailed. In the eighteenth century Lord Bankton (Andrew McDouall), in the three large volumes of his *Institute of the Laws of Scotland*,[39] elected to follow the system used by Stair, although even he took a small step towards the other camp by reintroducing a substantial early chapter on "The State and Condition of Persons".[40]

However, the future turned out to belong more to Bankton's contemporary, John Erskine of Carnock, the second holder of the chair of Scots law in the University of Edinburgh. His *Principles of the Law of Scotland* of 1754 and his massive, posthumously published *Institute of the Law of Scotland* of 1773 both adhered closely to the system of Justinian's *Institutes,* albeit with succession addressed after obligations. As with Stair's and Bankton's works, the scale of Erskine's books, especially the *Institute,* was much larger, more like Justinian's *Digest* than the tiny *Institutes,* but the system, cleverly adapted to new circumstances,[41] differed only in relatively minor details from that which Gaius had invented in the second century. One such detail was the attempt, not very successful in retrospect, to integrate into the traditional scheme that part of Stair's division of obligations which served to eliminate the *"quasi"* categories used by Justinian.[42]

Erskine's success was due in large measure to his smaller book. His *Principles of the Law of Scotland* (1754) went through many editions and became the standard university book on Scots law, in a world in which, in a small market, there were not many to choose from. The *Principles* maintained its position right into the twentieth century. The twenty-first and last edition, by Sir John Rankine, was published in 1911. Evidences were by then appearing of the tendency of modern Scots lawyers to neglect the systematic handed down by the great institutional writers.

---

39   Published 1751–53; reprinted by the Stair Society (1993–95). The work is notable *inter alia* for its methodical comparisons with the law of England.

40   *Ibid.,* 1,2. This title essentially reintroduces the law of persons, which Stair had rejected.

41   Erskine deals with the church in the law of persons, under the heading "ecclesiastical persons" (*Inst.,* 1,5) and, slavery having lost its place in the same book, he deals with the relations of master and servant (*Inst.,* 1,7,60–62). On the latter preference on the part of institutists, see J.W. Cairns, "Blackstone, Kahn-Freund and the Contract of Employment", (1989) 105 *L.Q.R.* 300.

42   Erskine, *Inst.,* 3,1,9–15, in the light of which the later reader can only have been very puzzled by the tension in Erskine, *Prin.,* between 3,1,4–5 (obediential obligations) and 3,3,16–17 (quasi-contract). There is a failure to make a clear choice between revisionist and conservative precedents.

By way of example, delict – tort, in the French which English law prefers – held little interest for Erskine. He dealt with it perfunctorily.[43] It is difficult for us now to recreate even in imagination the conditions under which a legal system can have taken so little interest in the law of civil wrongs. However, as that subject began to acquire its modern importance the needs of the law students meant that the *Principles* had to be made to receive it. The discussion was not inserted under obligations but spatchcocked into the end of the law of persons, on the feeble pretext of being about "personal wrongs".[44]

This same weakening of intellectual commitment to the task of classification can be detected in the book's successor, Gloag and Henderson's *Introduction to the Law of Scotland*,[45] in which it takes a practised eye to detect the continuing influence of the institutional tradition. Part of the trouble lies precisely in the continued existence of two versions of that tradition, Stair's revisionist model and Mackenzie's conservativism. Halfhearted borrowings from one to the other, such as is found in relation to the classification of obligations, are bound to misfire. If Scots law was to capitalise on its original advantage in this matter, it needed minds as powerful as Stair's own to continue the dialogue and to ensure the evolution of the single taxonomy best fitted to the modern law.

Codification

It is all the sadder that the tradition should show signs of succumbing to indifference in Scotland when in nearly all other countries it was abruptly interrupted by codification. The great advantage of an overview tradition which rests on literature rather than legislation is that the deficiencies of the systematic which is advanced remain, however ancient and revered, open to debate and revision. This is also one great argument for still letting the original texts of Roman law do the work of overview: being outside the living system, they can provide the necessary breadth of legal vision without, where they may be wrong, stultifying attempts to escape their errors. It is easy to say that the scheme of a certain writer is at a certain point unhelpful and, though things were long otherwise, there is no need at the end of the twentieth century to be caught like a rabbit in the headlights of the *Institutes*. By contrast, from an error or supervening inconvenience in the structure of a code there is little hope of escape.

Nevertheless, among those jurisdictions which based their law on the structure of the *Institutes* Scots law is now almost unique in having resisted the ossifying decision to move from a literary overview to a

---

43   Erskine, *Inst.*, 3,1,13–15; *Prin.*, 3,1,4, where there is merely a mention *en passant.*

44   Erskine, *Prin.*, 1,7A.

45   W.M. Gloag and R.C. Henderson, *Introduction to the Law of Scotland* (1st ed., Edinburgh, 1927).

code. It shares that honour with the Roman-Dutch law of South Africa. We noticed above that Scots institutional literature included fine examples of both revisionist and conservative scholarship, Stair being the notable revisionist. Among the many civil codes the same division can be seen. Somewhat surprisingly, since it was enacted so soon after the heyday of revisionism when every dimension of human life was reassessed in the light of reason, the French Code Civil adheres very closely to the sequence of Justinian's *Institutes,* omitting the law of actions.[46] The German code by contrast is revisionist. The influence of the institutional scheme is instantly recognisable, but the ordering of the parts is substantially changed, and "the general part" which is the code's most distinctive feature is the product of advanced theoretical jurisprudence and has no predecessor in the Roman materials.[47]

Sadly, revisionism even of the highest quality offers no guarantee against the endemic tendency of a legislated overview to inconvenience later generations.[48]

IV A More English Future?

Sooner or later English law will realise that it cannot continue to neglect the relationship between the many islands in the archipelago with which it is currently content. Its thin rationality will otherwise seem threadbare under the now closer gaze of continental neighbours. In short English law will have to become more Scottish. But in the short term many facts now conspire to make Scots law look ever more English. To the onset of indifference which we have noticed must be added changes in the form of legal literature and the nature of the market in legal books. More dangerous is the weakening commitment to Roman law, and more elusive but equally subversive is a certain failure to sort out which differences from English law really matter and which do not and, on the whole, the tendency to defend the wrong ones.

The one invaluable inheritance which Scots law took from the Roman past was its gift for systematic overview and the aspiration to principled rationality which went with it, making precedent the handmaid to reason rather than, as some would say of English law, reason the slave of precedent. The hyperbole served and still serves to express

---

46 K. Zweigert and H. Kötz, *An Introduction to Comparative Law,* tr. T. Weir (2nd ed., Oxford, 1987), vol. 1, 87–99; A.-J. Arnaud, *Les origines doctrinales du code civil français* (Paris, 1969). Further background: C. Chêne, *L'enseignement du droit français en pays de droit écrit* (Geneva, 1982).

47 K. Zweigert and H. Kötz, cited n.46 above, 149, esp. 152–3; F. Wieacker, *Privatrechtsgeschichte der Neuzeit* (2nd ed., Munich, 1967), 486.

48 See Zimmermann's discussion of the decisions allowing damages for non-pecuniary harm arising from violations of the personality, a course of jurisprudence which he describes as "blatantly *contra legem*": Zimmermann, Obligations, 1092–94.

and strengthen the self-image. And self-image does to some extent control behaviour. Yet if truth were told it would not be easy to prove from the cases and literature of the half-century since the war that it is great Scottish lawyers who have consistently taken the palm for creative rationality. Both systems were blessed in Lord Reid, but, abstaining from names still on the bench, Lord Devlin and Lord Wilberforce were English judges.

However the spirit may have faltered, it nonetheless remains a historical truth, going back to the seventeenth century, that it was the enlightened belief in the ordered rationality of the law, realised in the Gaian systematic of the great institutional writers, that constituted the one distinction which really mattered between Scots law and the English law. Notwithstanding Blackstone, English law never escaped from its dependence on the alphabet.

Books and the Book Market

Over the centuries the systematic overview was protected to some extent by the size of the market and the relatively few reported cases. The law could be kept within the covers of a large volume or a short series of volumes, and there was not much incentive to the fragmentation which comes when publishers bring out isolated monographs on every conceivable topic. Computerised technology has put an end to that. No case is nowadays committed to oblivion by the benevolent censorship of a reporter, and a market of a few hundred will now repay the costs of producing a short book. The increase in the quantum of primary materials is thus matched by many more books and rapid fragmentation. The Scots curriculum begins to look very like the English archipelago.

Then there is the great project, the care successively of T.B. Smith and Professor Robert Black, of a new and vast encyclopaedia of Scots Law, the *Stair Encyclopaedia*, now in course of publication. Similar projects are currently absorbing the energy of almost every thinking lawyer in Australia, and one suspects that the ultimate reason for the flowering of this useful but unlovely form of legal literature is that it is the huge and seemingly indispensable *Halsbury* and its imitators that earn the publishers their richest profits. However, the most obvious feature of all such works is that they are organised in the English manner, alphabetically. The *Stair Encyclopaedia* is set to dominate the research of Scottish practitioners and judges for years to come. Superb as some of its volumes are, it will not be a friend of the characteristic Roman superiority of the Scottish legal mind.

Roman Law and Legal Education

However, Roman law itself shows that the map can survive even if the bulk of the literature is arranged on some quite different basis. Justinian's commissioners did not attempt to arrange the *Digest* or *Codex* in the order of the *Institutes*. Hence the responsibility has to move from literature occupying a central and dominant position to legal education and to specialist books concerned precisely with maintaining and renewing the structure of the law.

In the system of legal education the one course routinely able to maintain the knowledge of the institutional overview, and review its application to modern conditions, has been the compulsory first year course in Roman Law, based on the *Institutes*. The decline of Latin in the schools raises a question mark over the future of that course. In England the professions and nearly all the universities have given in, so that the old compulsory institutional course is almost dead. In Scotland things are less different than one would expect. The Law Society of Scotland no longer insists on the course. The Faculty of Advocates still does and therefore stands between the body of Scottish lawyers and a critical species of amnesia. Since it remains true that the *Institutes* remains the best way into European private law, the hope will be that the new European orientation of the United Kingdom, and of Scotland in particular, will strengthen the hand of those who know and value the several practical responsibilities discharged by the first-year Roman law course.

Outside the course in Roman law the only hope of maintaining the traditional virtue of Scots law would be a modern version, a Scots law version, of the very course which Justinian intended the *Institutes* to support in sixth century Constantinople and Beirut. His notion of legal education was that that first year course should give a bird's eye view of the whole terrain and, having thus ensured that the students were armed with the means of finding their way about, to lead them only later into darker places where the wood was difficult to see for the denseness of the trees. Such a course would require a new *Inleiding* for Scotland, perhaps a slimmed down and more reflective *Gloag and Henderson*.

5. *SPECIFICATIO* IN SCOTS LAW

By DOUGLAS J. OSLER

I Roman Law: The Principle of Reducibility

In civilian legal systems the effect on the ownership of property used without the consent of the owner in the manufacture of a new artifact is treated under the heading of *specificatio*. This classification is derived from Roman law, although the word itself is a neologism; the Roman texts themselves speak of *speciem facere*. It is treated as a means of acquisition of ownership, being located in the title of Justinian's *Digest* "On the acquisition of ownership".[1] In the mature system of classification of the civilians it is treated as one of three main species of industrial accession, the other two being *adiunctio* or joining (sometimes called by the synonym *accessio*) and *commixtio/confusio*, mixture of solids and liquids respectively.

The rule applied in cases of *specificatio* as outlined in the basic *Digest* text, (complemented by a closely parallel text in the *Institutes*),[2] is surely one of the most famous in Roman law. "No-one is unaware that there was a controversy on this subject between the Proculians and Sabinians", thought the eminent Dutch elegant jurist Gerardus Noodt (1647–1725).[3] No less renowned is the solution to this controversy adopted in Justinian's texts. Since modern Scots law is based ultimately on this text, it is worth quoting in full:[4]

---

1   D.41.1 *De acquirendo rerum dominio*; cf. *Inst.*2.1 *De rerum divisione*.
2   D.41.1.7.7; cf. *Inst.*2.1.25.
3   *Commentarius in Digesta* 10.4: *Nemo ignorat de ea fuisse litem inter Proculianos et Sabinianos*.
4   D.41.1.7.7 *Cum quis ex aliena materia speciem aliquam suo nomine fecerit, Nerva et Proculus putant hunc dominum esse qui fecerit, quia quod factum est, antea nullius fuerat. Sabinus et Cassius magis naturalem rationem efficere putant, ut qui materiae dominus fuerit, idem eius quoque, quod ex eadem materia factum sit, dominus esset, quia sine materia nulla species effici possit, veluti si ex auro vel argento vel aere [tuo] vas aliquod fecero, vel ex tabulis tuis navem aut armarium aut subsellia fecero, vel ex lana tua vestimentum, vel ex vino et melle tuo mulsum, vel ex medicamentis tuis emplastrum aut collyrium, vel ex uvis aut olivis aut spicis tuis vinum vel oleum vel frumentum. Est tamen etiam media sententia recte existimantium, si species ad materiam reverti possit, verius esse quod et Sabinus et Cassius senserunt, si non possit reverti, verius esse quod Nervae et Proculo placuit, ut ecce vas conflatum ad rudem massam auri vel argenti vel aeris reverti potest, vinum vero vel oleum vel frumentum ad uvas et olivas et spicas reverti*

D.41.1.7.7 *(Gaius, Res cottidianae sive Aurea*, Book 2): When some-one has made a new thing on his own behalf from material belong-ing to another, Nerva and Proculus hold that he who made the new thing is the owner, since what was made previously belonged to no-one. Sabinus and Cassius hold that natural reason demands that he who was owner of the material is also owner of that which was made from it, since without material no thing can exist; as for example if I have made some vase from [your] gold or silver or bronze, or I have made a ship or cupboard or chairs from your planks, or a garment from your wool, or mead from your wine and honey, or a plaster or ointment from your drugs, or wine or oil or corn from your grapes or olives or ears of corn. There is, however, also a middle opinion held by those who correctly maintain that if the thing can revert to the material, it is more correct what Sabinus and Cassius believed, but if it cannot revert, the better opinion is that of Nerva and Proculus. For example, a vase can revert to the crude mass of gold or silver or bronze, whereas wine or oil or corn cannot return to the grapes or olives or ears of corn, and mead cannot revert to wine and honey, and a plaster and ointment cannot revert to the drugs.[5]

As is stated by Justinian himself in his preface to the *Digest*, some major doctrines of Roman law which had suffered change over the centuries were necessarily altered by the compilers of the *Digest* in order to bring the law up to date. These cases aside, it is clear that the main thrust of the compilers' activity was devoted to abbreviating the classical texts and necessarily shortening the discussion of divergent views which they exhibited. The text on *specificatio* is thus particularly interesting since this extended discussion has been left to stand, giving us a glimpse of conflicting opinions among different jurists, and also of the development in the legal doctrine itself.

---

    non potest, ac ne mulsum quidem ad mel et vinum vel emplastrum aut collyria ad medicamenta reverti possunt.

5   The parallels with *Inst.*2.1.25 will be clear: When some object has been made by someone out of material belonging to another, it is to be asked which of them is owner by natural reason, whether he who made it or rather he who was owner of the material, as for example if someone has made wine or oil or corn out of someone else's grapes or olives or ears of corn, or has made some vase out of someone else's gold or silver or bronze, or has mixed mead out of someone else's wine and honey, or has made a plaster or ointment out of someone else's drugs, or has made a gar-ment out of someone else's wool, or a ship or cupboard or chair out of someone else's planks. And after many ambiguities on the part of the Sabinians and Proculians, the middle opinion was approved of those who hold that if the object can be reduced to the previous material, he would seem to be owner who had been owner of the material, but if it cannot be reduced, rather he would be understood as owner who had made it, as for example a vase can be reduced to the raw mass of copper or silver or gold, whereas wine or oil or corn cannot revert to grapes or olives or ears of corn, and mead too cannot be returned to wine and honey.

It was the Humanist jurists of the Renaissance who for the first
time began to investigate the historical development of Roman law
which lay hidden behind the uniform façade of Justinian's compilation.
Clearly, the doctrine of *specificatio*, even as presented in dogmatic form
in the *Digest*, actively demands some analysis of its development. The
basic *Digest* passage on *specificatio* quoted above, is excerpted from a
work of the jurist Gaius (fl. A.D.160) bearing the title *Res cottidianae*.
This text reports the two school views together with the *media sententia*.[6] It is noticeable, then, that in the same jurist's treatment of
specificatio in a separate work, the *Institutiones*, which is one of the
few works of Roman law which has been handed down to us independently from Justinian's *Digest*, only the two school opinions are mentioned, and no hint is given of a third, intermediate opinion. This
discrepancy has led to speculation about whether the *media sententia*
was really known to Gaius himself, or whether it might in fact be a later
development, appended to Gaius' work by a subsequent editor, if not
indeed by Justinian's compilers. This apparent difficulty did not pass
unnoticed by the Humanists. For although the full text of the
Institutiones was only discovered in 1816, an epitome of the work survived in a separate tradition, and this was already published in 1517. The
epitome differs from the complete work in that it states the law simply
according to the view of the school to which Gaius belonged, namely
the Sabinians.[7] However, the significant point is that in both epitome
and full text, the *media sententia* is conspicuously absent. This led the
French Humanist, Emundus Merillius (1579–1647), to suggest that the
Digest text purporting to be drawn from Gaius' *Res cottidianae* had in
fact been tampered with by Tribonian and the other *Digest* compilers
in order to take account of a doctrine which was in reality developed
after Gaius' time. Merillius suggests that the true originator of the
media sententia was not Gaius but the later jurist Paul:[8]

> Among the two sects of jurists some chose a middle opinion.
> Justinian states that after much dubiety between the Sabinians and

---

6   D.41.1.7.7.
7   *Gai Epitome* 2.1.5, in *Fontes iuris Romani Antejustiniani. Pars altera.
     Auctores. Edidit notisque illustravit Johannes Baviera.* (Florentiae, 1968)
     at 242: But if someone has made wine from my grapes, or corn from my
     corn ears, or oil from my olives, the wine, corn or oil belong to him who
     was the owner of the corn ears, grapes, or olives. Or again, if someone has
     made a ship, or a chest, or any other object for use out of planks belonging
     to another, by the same reasoning those things which have been made will
     belong to him from whose wood they are proved to have been made.
     Similarly, too, if he has made garments from wool or linen belonging to
     another, the garments will belong to him to whom the wool or linen is
     proved to have belonged.
8   *Observationes libri III*, (Lutetiae Parisiorum, 1618), 4°, Book I. 6. *Inter
     duas iurisconsultorum sectas quidam mediam sententiam elegerunt.
     Iustinianus refert, post multam Sabinianorum et Proculeianorum ambi-
     guitatem, mediam sententiam placuisse, ſ. Cum ex aliena. 25. Instit. de*

Proculians, a middle opinion was approved (*Inst.*2.1.25), which Gaius supports (D.41.1.7). I fear, however, that Gaius thought otherwise, and that Tribonian has interpolated that text. For in those fragments of the *Institutes* which are attributed to Gaius, Gaius approves the opinion of the Sabinians ... The middle opinion was that of Paul, who held that the owner of the material remained owner if the material was able to revert to the original form (D.41.1.24; D.32.88).

Whatever the validity of this historical excursus, it is certainly true that the doctrine of the *media sententia* is discussed in a *Digest* text of one of the leading jurists who flourished under the Severan Emperors at the beginning of the third century, Julius Paulus.[9]

The relevant text of Paul demanded the application of the other main innovation of the Humanists, philological analysis. The text reads:[10]

In all cases which *cannot* revert to the same form, it should be said that if the material remains the same and only the form has been substantially changed, as for example if you have made a statue from my bronze, or a goblet from my silver, then I remain owner of these things ... But if you have made a ship from my planks, the ship belongs to you, since it does not remain cypress wood, just as is true of wool when a garment is made, but it becomes an object made out of cypress or out of wool.

There is a textual problem in the opening phrase. The above reading, "which cannot revert", (*reverti non possunt*) is that of our oldest manuscript, the Florentine, dating from the time of Justinian himself. Yet the logic of the sentence would seem to be, on the contrary, that I remain owner in those cases where the object *can* revert to its previous form, as in the case of a statue which can be melted down to the original bronze, or a goblet to the original silver. The Humanists, turning to an examination of the integrity of the Latin text itself, found that the manuscripts from the vulgate tradition, dating from the revival of Roman law in the twelfth century, had the opposite reading "*reverti possunt*" ("which *can* revert"). Iacobus Cuiacius (1522–90) in particular

---

rer. divis. quam probat Caius L. 7. D. de acquir. rer. domin. Vereor tamen, ne non aliter Caius senserit, eumque locum Tribonianus interpolaverit: nam in fragmentis illis Institutionum, quae Caio tribuuntur, Caius sententiam Sabinianorum probavit, tit. de rer. divis. ... media illa sententia fuit Pauli, qui putabat, materiae dominum manere, si ad eandem speciem reverti posset, L.24. D. de acquir. rer. domin., L. lana 88. D. de legat. 3 ...

9   D.41.1.24 and 26*pr.*: Paulus, *ad Sabinum*, Lib. 14.

10 Paulus, *ad Sabinum*, Lib. 14: *In omnibus, quae ad eandem speciem reverti non possunt, dicendum est, si materia manente species dumtaxat forte mutata sit, veluti si meo aere statuam aut argento scyphum fecisses, me eorum dominum manere ... Sed si meis tabulis navem fecisses, tuam navem esse, quia cupressus non maneret, sicuti nec lana vestimento facto, sed cupresseum aut laneum corpus fieret.*

was to emphasise the validity of the vulgate readings against those of the Florentine, while he very often emended texts by noting that the omission or addition of a "*non*" is one of the simplest and commonest of scribal errors in a Latin text.[11] At any rate it was the vulgate reading which received general acceptance. Indeed, when the Humanist Laelius Taurellus (1489–1576) produced his monumental facsimile edition of the Florentine manuscript in 1553, in which he sought to make an exact reproduction of the manuscript in print, the negative in the manuscript in this text was one of the very few readings which he bracketed as being indubitably in error and requiring to be deleted.[12]

Whatever may have been the historical development of the Roman law, the variety of opinions held by different jurists, or the correct solution to textual conundrums, the principle of the Roman law endorsed by Justinian and thus handed down to later times was clear: where the new thing can be reduced to its previous form, it belongs to the original owner of the material; where it cannot be so reduced, it belongs to the maker.

II   Franciscus Connanus: The Principle of Relative Value

This reducibility test has not been spared juristic criticism. Under the influence of natural law theories, the individual rules of Roman law came to be subjected to criticism on the basis of what was regarded as their innate rationality. In the case of *specificatio* it was in fact a Humanist, Franciscus Connanus (1508–51), who first voiced criticism of the Roman doctrine. Yet, as we shall see, even in this case the solution proposed is expressly stated to emerge from the *ius naturale*. Thus Connanus' first liberates himself from the authority of the Roman law:[13]

---

11   Thus, treating of a different *Digest* text, he writes in the opening chapter of his masterwork, the *Observationes et Emendationes*:

Certainly, the negative is missing from the Florentine manuscript, the extent of the authority of which for everyone is not unknown to me. But I myself attribute more to the logic of the law than to any manuscript, than which nothing can more easily be corrupted. Nevertheless I too do not lack the authority of manuscripts.

12   *Digestorum seu Pandectarum libri quinquaginta, ex Florentinis Pandectis repraesentati*, (Florentiae, in officina Laurentii Torrentini, 1553), fol., at 1219. Mommsen, however, in his *Editio maior*, vol. 2, 494, line 9, has the following cryptic note: non possunt] *F recte, nam res ad materiam reuerti potest (l.7 ʃ7 h.t.), ad speciem non potest, possunt XYMOC*. The present writer finds Taurellus' understanding of the text more comprehensible.

13   *Commentariorum iuris civilis tomus prior (-posterior)...* (Lutetiae Parisiorum, ex officina typographica Michaelis Vascosani, 1553), fol., Book 3.6.4: *Aequi lectores iudicabunt, neque me temeritatis aut arrogantiae insimulent, quod a veterum iurisconsultorum scitis recedam, quorum ego authoritatem tantisper sequi decreui dum doctrinae suae rationem afferant. Illos enim mihi semper et doctores et magistros esse duxi, qui mihi persuaderent, reges aut tyrannos qui mihi possent imperare nunquam existimavi.*

Fair readers will judge, and not accuse me of temerity or arrogance, because I depart from the decisions of the ancient jurists, whose authority I have determined to follow when they provide a rationale for their doctrine. I have always considered them as doctors or masters who might persuade me; I have never considered them to be kings or tyrants who might give me orders.

Connanus was not persuaded by the rationality of the Roman doctrine of *specificatio*. His theory was that the test which should be applied was that of relative value; whichever was more valuable, the material or the workmanship, should determine the question of ownership:[14]

> I think we should hold that the opinion of Sabinus is the better, namely that the owner of the material acquires ownership of the whole article, except when there is more value in the workmanship than in the material. Thus if from my gold, silver or bronze, or any other material, you manufacture a vase which is of low quality, and of no great workmanship, I am owner of the vase; but if the vase is of elaborate workmanship, and outweighs the material, then the material cedes to the workmanship ... By this reasoning wine or oil pressed from my grapes or olives will be mine, as also cheese or butter manufactured from my milk; for what do such things have in the way of workmanship?

Connanus' examples are unfortunately disconcerting for the modern reader, whose natural expectation is that raw materials will generally represent only a small proportion of the value of the manufactured object: unlike Connanus, we would tend to think of wine as being of considerably more value than the grapes from which it is pressed; for us, then, wine would serve as a prime example of the manufacturer acquiring ownership. Nevertheless, the principle is absolutely clear: the question of ownership is determined by the relative value of material and workmanship in the article manufactured. In the case that material is worth 100 Ecus, if the workmanship is worth 99 Ecus, the owner of the material becomes owner of the new thing (worth 199 Ecus); if the workmanship is worth 101 Ecus the manufacturer becomes owner of the new thing (worth 201 Ecus).

Given the importance of the principle of relative value in later times, it is worth noting Connanus' formulation. The view of Sabinus, that the owner of the material becomes owner of the new thing, is presented as the normal result, whereas the material ceding to the workmanship is

---

14 *Commentaria iuris civilis*, 3.6.2: *Dicendum arbitror Sabini veriorem esse sententiam, ut materiae dominus sibi habeat totius speciei dominium, nisi cum plus est in opere pretii quam in materia, ut si ex auro, argento, aut aere meo, vel alia qualibet materia, vas feceris, quod sit vulgaris, neque valde magni artificii, ego sim illius dominus; at si quod est elaborati operis superetque materiam, tum cedat materia artificio... Qua ratione ex uvis aut oleis meis expressum vinum, aut oleum, meum erit; similiter ex lacte meo formatus caseus aut coactum butyrum; quid enim habent ista artis?*

presented as the exception. Yet the identical result is achieved by the formulation that the opinion of Proculus is better, except where the value of the material exceeds that of the workmanship. Further evidence of the Roman law background to Connanus' thinking is found in a second passage where he again enunciates the principle of relative value. Here he considers the manufactured articles under two heads: those that cannot, and those that can be restored to their former materials. Yet under both heads the test applied is that of relative value, so that the distinction is revealed to be wholly redundant. He writes:[15]

> I think we should hold as follows. Those things which cannot be restored to their former material remain the property of the owner of the material when they consist more in nature and material than in workmanship, such as wine, oil, mead, perfume, cheese, butter and things of this sort. But if they encompass a great deal of workmanship, so that they consist more of workmanship than of material, then they become the property of the manufacturer since he would appear to have contributed more of his own than has remained of the first material, such as a bed, a ship, a garment and some things made of wood or stone or other non-liquifiable material; for all these things are objects of workmanship and, as the scientists say, of form, not of substance or material; rightly in such cases the workmanship vindicates its right. But if they can be reduced to their previous form and material, such as anything made out of gold, silver, bronze, lead and similar metals, then it should be enquired whether there is more value in the workmanship than in the material; whichever is of less value cedes to the more valuable.

The distinction between reducible and irreducible new species is simply confusing here. In both cases the test suggested by Connanus is that of relative value. The examples given were for Connanus simply good illustrations of cases where there was clear disparity between these relative values. But in every instance the rule applied is that of the closing words of the passage: whichever is of less value cedes to the more valuable.

Value as a test of ownership is always lurking close to the surface of the Roman texts in the analogous cases of *accessio*, even if it is only

---

15 *Commentaria iuris civilis* 3.6.3: *Sic autem dicendum arbitrarer, ut quae species priori materiae reddi nequeunt, maneant eius cuius est materia, cum plus habent naturae et materiae quam artis, ut sunt vinum, oleum, mulsum, unguentum, caseus, butyrum, et quae sunt eius generis; parum enim et fere nihil differunt a prima sua natura. Si vero multum habent artis, ut ipsa per se artificii sint magis quam materiae, tum fiant eius qui fecit, quia plus hic videtur de suo contulisse quam de prima materia manserit, ut lectus, navis, vestis, et quaecunque species ligneae aut lapideae et similis non fusilis materiae; nam ista omnia sunt artis et, ut loquuntur physici, qualitatis, non substantiae aut materiae nomina; merito in his praecipuum sibi ius ars vendicat. Quod si restitui possunt priori naturae et materiae, ut quaecunque ex auro, argento, aere, plumbo et similibus metallis, tum attendatur an plus sit in arte quam in materia, quodque minus erit cedat maiori.*

to emphasise that this was not the test to be applied. Thus it was a famous rule that writing acceded to the paper, even though the letters were of gold.[16] Similarly, purple cloth accedes to a garment into which it has been woven, even though the purple is more valuable.[17] The very fact that it was necessary to stress the point indicates that the natural assumption would be that something much more valuable should be considered the principal, and the less valuable the accessory. In truth, this common sense approach did assert itself against strict legal principle in the famous case of painting on another's canvas. In principle the painting, like the letters of gold, ought to accede to the canvas.[18] But this was too much for some of the Roman jurists. As we read in Justinian's *Institutes*, the canvas accedes to the painting, for it would be absurd that a masterpiece should be considered the accessory of a cheap piece of canvas.[19] Even when trying to liberate himself from its individual rules, then, Connanus still remains firmly anchored in the civilian tradition.

III   Hugo Grotius: The Principle of Common Ownership

In his willingness to attack what he considered anomalous or irrational doctrines of Roman law, Connanus anticipates the school of natural law which was to flourish in the seventeenth and eighteenth centuries. It is noticeable that Connanus summed up the benefit, as he saw it, of his theory with the words:[20]

> ... thus it will come about that the law of nature *(naturae ius)* will be preserved, and the least damage done to both, namely the owner of the material and the workman.

The second main doctrine of natural law is propounded by the famous Dutch jurist, Hugo Grotius (1583–1645). Treating the matter in his *De iure belli ac pacis*, Grotius first claimed that this was one of the most unsatisfactory areas of Roman law:[21]

> There is scarcely any area of law in which there are so many conflicting opinions of the jurists, and so many errors.

In seeking an alternative solution, he rejected the suggestion of Connanus, and proposed that the result in all cases of *specificatio* should be common ownership:[22]

---

16   D.41.1.9.1; Gaius, *Inst.*2.77.
17   *Inst.*2.1.26.
18   D.6.1.23.3.
19   *Inst.*2.1.34; D.41.1.9.2; Gaius, *Inst.*2.78
20   *Commentaria iuris civilis* 3.6.3: *Sic fiet ut naturae ius conservetur, et minore utriusque damno utrique, materiae domino scilicet et artifici.*
21   *De iure belli ac pacis,* 2.8.21: *Vix autem ulla est tractatio iuris in qua tot discrepantes sunt iurisconsultorum sententiae et errores.*
22   *De iure belli ac pacis,* 2.8.18: *At si naturalem veritatem respicimus, sicut confusis materiis communionem induci pro rata eius quod quisque habeat, Romanis quoque iurisconsultis placuit, quia res alium exitum*

But if we look to natural truth, then just as the Roman jurists
approved the rule that when liquids were mixed together the result
was common ownership according to the shares of each, since the
matter was unable naturally to find another solution, so too it follows, that since a thing consists of material and form as if its parts,
if the material belongs to one person and the form to another, it follows naturally that there is common ownership according to the
value of the shares of each.

IV The Usus Modernus Pandectarum

Thus from early in the seventeenth century three distinct doctrines of
specificatio were competing for precedence: the reducibility test of the
media sententia of the mature Roman law; the test of relative value of
Franciscus Connanus; and the solution of common ownership in all
cases proposed by Hugo Grotius. The innovations of Connanus and
Grotius were subject to the criticism of two of the greatest names of the
Dutch Elegant Jurisprudence. In his commentary on the *Institutes*, one
of the most influential juridical works of the seventeenth to eighteenth
centuries, Arnoldus Vinnius (1588–1657) considered both opinions and
rejected them in favour of the traditional Roman rule. He writes:[23]

> I am of course aware that Connanus criticises the authors of this
> opinion, and that in this topic they would look only to the question
> whether the workmanship or the material was of more value; and
> also that Grotius believes that the new thing should be held in
> common, just as common ownership in *pro rata* shares results in
> the case of the mixing of liquids. I, on the other hand, do not depart
> from that distinction of the old jurists, and consider it more natural
> that in the question at issue we should examine whether the thing
> which previously existed has been extinguished or not, than that a
> question of ownership should be determined according to the
> value of the material or workmanship, or alternatively that without
> any necessity discordant common ownership should be brought
> into existence; and this is the law which even now is in force.

---

*naturaliter reperire non poterat, ita cum res constent materia et specie
tanquam suis partibus, si alterius sit materia, alterius species, sequitur
naturaliter rem communem fieri pro rata eius quanti unumquodque est.*
23 *Commentarius locupletissimus, academicus & forensis, in quatuor libros
Institutionum imperialium...* (Lugduni Batavorum, ex officina Ioannis
Maire, 1642), 4°, Book 2.1.25 §4: *Scio equidem dominum Connanum auctores huius sententiae reprehendere atque hoc solum hic spectare velle,
plusne pretii sit in opere an in materia; dominum quoque Grotium
censere speciem communicandam, sicut confusis materiis communio
inducitur pro rata eius quod quisque habuit. Ego tamen a veterum illa
distinctione non recedo, magisque naturale esse arbitror ut in quaestione
proposita inspiciatur utrum res quae prius fuerat extincta sit necne,
quam ut vel ex pretio rei operisve de iure dominii statuatur, aut citra
necessitatem inducatur discordiosa communio; eoque iure etiam nunc
utimur.*

Ulrich Huber (1636–94) also took up the cudgels on behalf of the traditional doctrine in his *Eunomia Romana*, a work written indeed to demonstrate the justice of the solutions of the Roman law against the criticism of the natural lawyers. *Specificatio* was a case in point. First, the solution of Connanus is rejected:[24]

> Jurists, however, look to the actual nature of objects, and do not pay attention to their value ... I would approve either opinion of the ancients, since the constitution of objects is natural and fixed in itself; value and price depends on the opinion and variable estimation of men; one may value the workmanship highly, while another dismisses the worth of the work; finally, it is irrational that the question of ownership should be decided by a factor such as value, which is extrinsic, rather than by the actual constitution of the thing itself.

Grotius' solution he rejects even more firmly:[25]

> I consider the opinion of the jurists to be not a little more doctrinally sound than this Grotian one, according to which there is immediately brought about that which jurists think should be avoided above all else, namely common ownership, which they are always opposed to as the mother of discord, according to the principle of natural law itself, that harmony is ever to be sought.

V Natural Law Developments

Undeterred by these criticisms, jurists working in the tradition of natural law continued to develop the new principles. From the beginning preference was shown for the doctrine of Connanus. The important innovation in these subsequent writings was the insistence on a "considerable" or "substantial" difference between the value of material and workmanship. Then of course it becomes important to determine which party is being favoured. Divergent formulations may cause

24 *Eunomia Romana, sive censura censurae juris Justinianaei, continens examen praecipuorum juris locorum secundum Pandectas & Institutiones uberrimum indicem adjecit, una cum oratione funebri habita in memoriam auctoris, Zacharias Huber Ulr. fil.* (Franequerae, apud Leonardum Strickium, 1700) 4°, Book 6.1 §2: *Iurisconsulti vero naturam ipsam rerum, non aestimationem pretii spectant... Nobis utravis antiquorum sententia magis placet, quia constitutio rerum naturalis et stabilis est in se; valor et pretium ab hominum arbitrio et variabili aestimatione pendet, dum alius artificium plurimi facit, alius operam manusque pretium contemnit. denique rationem dominii ab eo quod extrinsecus accedit, ut est pretium, potius quam ab ipsius rei constitutione petere, non habet rationem.*

25 *Eunomia Romana,* 6. 1. §3: *Existimo iurisconsultorum sententiam non paulo civiliorem et solidiorem esse quam haec Grotiana, per quam primo fit hoc quod iurisconsulti summopere evitandum putarunt ut communio introducatur, quam illi ut matrem discordiarum, secundum ipsam rationem naturalem de pace quaerenda, semper aversati sunt.*

confusion. The point to look for is not whether the owner or the maker is presented as acquiring as the general principle. The test is rather, which has to exceed considerably the other in value: the workmanship (=favouring the owner), or the material (=favouring the workman). This distinction will emerge from the following pairs of formulations:

In Favour of the Owner

A.   Where a workman makes a new thing out of someone else's material, the owner of the material becomes owner of the new thing, unless the value of the workmanship greatly exceeds that of the material.

B.   Where a workman makes a new thing out of someone else's material, the workman becomes owner of the new thing, provided that the value of the workmanship greatly exceeds that of the material.

Both the above formulations lead to the identical factual result. The reader must not be deceived by the opening words, "the owner of the material becomes owner", or "the workman becomes owner"; everything depends on the condition which immediately follows. In a concrete example, let us assume that a court defines the words "greatly exceeds" to mean at least twice the value. Thus if the material is worth 100 Ecus, then the workman will only acquire if the workmanship is worth at least 200 Ecus, the new object having a value of 300 Ecus. Under Connanus' principle of simple relative value the workman would have acquired as soon as the workmanship had a value of 101 Ecus.

Let us turn to the opposite formulation which favours the workman:

In Favour of the Workman

A.   Where a workman makes a new thing out of someone else's material, the workman becomes owner of the new thing, provided that the value of the material does not greatly exceed that of the workmanship.

B.   Where a workman makes a new thing out of someone else's material, the owner of the material becomes owner of the new thing, provided that the value of the material greatly exceeds that of the workmanship.

Here, according to our example, the workman acquires where the material is worth 100 Ecus and the workmanship only 50 Ecus (assuming the same definition of "considerable excess" applies). Clearly, the variation introduced into Connanus' principle by the insistence on a significant or considerable disparity between the relative values of material and workmanship lends considerable importance to the particular formulation adopted.

The second great name in the natural law tradition, Samuel Pufendorf (1632–94), overwhelmingly favours the original owner in cases of *specificatio*. In his *Elementa iuris universalis* he lays down that the owner should have the option to choose whether to keep the new thing, compensating the workman for his workmanship, or to cede the object in return for the value of the material:[26]

> For it would be absurd that the error of someone else could, against my will, generate a right in my property, in which my right preponderates, in particular when the workmanship does not exceed the value of the material. For why should anyone who by error has made oil or wine or loaves out of my olives or grapes or corn have a stronger right to them than I? Or why should he rather than I have the right of choosing? ... On the other hand, where the value of the material bears almost no proportion to the form, as is the case of painting on someone else's canvas ... equity altogether demands that the owner of the material accept the value of the material and cede the object to the workman.

Thus Pufendorf accords the principle of relative value a decisive role, but insists on more than a bare excess in value. Attending to the question of ownership, we may formulate Pufendorf's principle as follows: where someone makes a new object out of someone else's materials, the original owner becomes owner of the new thing, except where the value of the workmanship is out of all proportion to/greatly exceeds the value of the material.[27]

The opposite direction is followed by Ioannes Gottlieb Heineccius (1681–1741). In his elementary student handbooks he simply sets out the *media sententia* applicable in contemporary legal systems.[28] However, in his *Elementa iuris naturae et gentium* he is in a position to set out his criticism of this doctrine. He holds, once again, that value should be the determining factor. Why, he demands, should something in which the workmanship is one hundred times more valuable than the material be accorded to the owner of the material merely because the thing is reducible to its original form? This example is in accord with his general principle, which markedly favours the workman:[29]

---

26 *Elementorum jurisprudentiae universalis libri duo*, 1.5.22: *Nam absurdum foret, errorem alterius in rem meam invito me ius posse generare, quod iuri meo praeponderet, praeprimis ubi opera ipsius materiae pretium non excedit. Sic cur is qui ex olivis, uvis aut frumento meo per errorem velut ex suis oleum, vinum, aut panes presserit vel coxerit, validius quam ego ius habeat? Aut cur illi potius quam mihi optandi sit praerogativa?... At vero ubi materiae pretium ad formam nullam fere proportionem habet, uti fit in tabulis pictis ... omnino aequitas postulat ut accepto pretio materiae dominus rem artifici cedat.*

27 Pufendorf treats the matter quite differently in his most important work, the *De iure naturae*, Book 4.7.10.

28 *Elementa iuris civilis secundum ordinem Institutionum* (Amsterdam, 1725) §368, *Elementa iuris civilis secundum ordinem Pandectarum* (Amsterdam, 1727) §187.

29 §*Elementa iuris naturae et gentium*, §259: *Cum enim plerumque in materiam nulla cadat adfectio, in formam ob artificium vel maxime cadat, nova species merito addicenda fuerit specificanti... quamvis ex eadem ratione, omnino praeferendus materiae dominus, si haec rarior et*

> Since as a rule no special worth attaches to material, but a great deal attaches to the form, because of the workmanship, the new thing ought to be accorded to the maker ... whereas by the same reasoning, the owner of the material is altogether to be preferred if the material is rare and has more value than the form which has been added through the work of the other, as for example if someone has made a seal or a vase out of someone else's electrum or Corinthian bronze.

It is not quite explicit, of course, but from the examples given Heineccius is clearly considering the case where the material is worth very much more than the workmanship. He is thus moving clearly in the opposite direction from Pufendorf towards the rule that in cases of *specificatio* the workman acquires except where the value of the material greatly exceeds that of the workmanship.

VI The European Codification Movement

Over the centuries the Roman law principle of the *media sententia* continued to be applied in the various legal systems of Europe – *eoque iure etiam nunc utimur,* as Vinnius had said – while the competing principles of Connanus and Grotius continued to be debated and refined by the jurists. The coming of the era of codification was to see the triumph of natural law theories. As a result, in their treatment of *specificatio* the major European codes embody pure natural law, and within that tradition the principle that derives from Connanus is generally favoured. The principle is found in its purest form in the Swiss civil code:[30]

> When a person has worked upon or transformed material which did not belong to him, the new thing is acquired by the workman if the workmanship is more valuable than the material, if not by the owner of the material.

In this case the bare excess of value of material or workmanship determines ownership.[31] The same principle is enunciated in the Spanish *Codigo Civil* of 1889, albeit the formulation is slightly more opaque:[32]

---

   pluris sit quam forma. quae alterius opera accessit, e.g. si quis ex alterius electro vel aere Corinthiaco signum vel vas confecerit.

30   Art. 726. 1. Lorsqu'une personne a travaillé ou transformé une matière qui ne lui appartenait pas, la chose nouvelle est acquise à l'ouvrier, si l'industrie est plus précieuse que la matière, sinon, au propriétaire de celle-ci.

31   Notice that precisely the same result would ensue from the formulation: the new thing is acquired by the owner of the material if the material is more valuable than the workmanship, if not, by the workman.

32   Art. 383. El que de buena fe empleó materia ajena en todo o en parte para formar una obra de nueva especie, hará suya la obra, indemnizando el valor de la materia al dueño de ésta. Si ésta es más preciosa que la obra en que se empleó o superior en valor, el dueño de ella podrá, a su elección, quedarse con la nueva especie, previa indemnización del valor de la obra, o pedir indemnización de la materia.

> He who has employed in good faith material belonging to another, either in whole or in part, to make a thing of a new kind, will acquire ownership of the thing, indemnifying the owner for the value of the material. If the material is more precious, or of greater value, than the work in which it was employed, the owner has the option whether to keep the new thing, paying compensation for the value of the work, or to accept compensation for the material.

This rule would seem to leave the question of ownership in suspense in the case that the value of the material exceeds that of the workmanship; but the principle of simple excess of value of material or workmanship clearly lies behind the provision.

In most European codes, however, the basic principle of Connanus has been modified by the requirement that either workmanship or material should considerably exceed the other in value, a modification we have already seen formulated in the natural law writings of Pufendorf and Heineccius. Attention therefore has to be paid to the formulation to see which party is being favoured. The French *Code Civil* favours the original owner:[33]

> Art.570. If a workman or anyone else has worked upon material which did not belong to him in order to make a thing of a new kind, whether or not the material is able to retake its previous form, he who was the proprietor of the material has the right to claim the thing which has been made ...

> Art.571. If, however, the workmanship was so important that it greatly surpassed the value of the material employed, the workmanship will be considered the principal part, and the workman will have the right to retain the thing worked upon ...

First of all we may note in passing that the incidental detail in Article 570, *whether or not the material is able to retake its previous form*, is entirely superfluous to the test of relative value being enunciated; it adds no more than if one had written, for example, *whether or not the material was made of gold*. This is in fact merely a reminisence of the reducibility test of the *media sententia* of the Roman law.

It is clear that we are here dealing with the variation on the theme of Connanus' principle of relative value first propounded by Pufendorf. At the same time it is important to penetrate behind the rhetoric of the formulation here to perceive the reality. On a superficial reading, Art.

---

33   Art. 570. Si un artisan ou une personne quelconque a employé une matière qui ne lui appartenait pas à former une chose d'une nouvelle espèce, soit que la matière puisse ou non reprendre sa première forme, celui qui en était le propriétaire a le droit de réclamer la chose qui en a été formée en remboursant le prix de la main-d'oeuvre estimée à la date du remboursement. Art. 571. Si, cependant la main-d'oeuvre était tellement importante qu'elle surpassât de beaucoup la valeur de la matière employée, l'industrie serait alors réputée la partie principale, et l'ouvrier aurait le droit de retenir la chose travaillé, en remboursant au propriétaire le prix de la matière, estimé à la date du remboursement.

570 of the *Code Civil* would seem to present a pure Sabinian view: in cases of *specificatio* the owner of the material becomes owner of the new thing. Only in the following article is this modified. Rhetorically then, the principle that the owner of the material becomes owner of the new thing is presented as the general rule, with an article to itself; the case where the workman acquires is then presented as merely an exception to the general rule. It should be clearly seen, however, that precisely the same legal rule could be formulated as follows:

> Where a workman makes a new thing out of someone else's material, the workman becomes owner of the new thing, provided that the value of the workmanship greatly exceeds that of the material.

The crucial point behind both these formulations is that the balance in Connanus' test has here been tipped in favour of the original owner, as proposed by Pufendorf; it is not enough that the workmanship simply outweighs the value of the material, it must greatly surpass it in value (the definition of which being left to be worked out in the actual practice of case law).

The German *Bürgerliches Gesetzbuch* follows the alternative approach, favouring the workman. Thus ownership is awarded to the workman except where the workmanship is considerably less valuable than the material:[34]

> §950. 1. He who creates a new moveable thing through the working upon or alteration of one or more materials acquires ownership in the new thing in so far as the value of the workmanship or alteration is not significantly less than the value of the material.

Again the formulation is somewhat confusing, since now the question is posed not which element is worth more, but which is worth less. In fact, however, there is no practical difference between the two following formulations:

A.   provided that the value of the workmanship is not considerably less.
B.   provided that the value of the material is not considerably more.

If one imagines that the workmanship is worth 95 Ecus and the material 100 Ecus, it will be seen that both formulations have the identical result: the workman acquires the new thing he has made. The German code thus adopts the position favoured by Heineccius.

According to the ideologies prevailing at the time in question, the Italian *Codice Civile* of 1865 translates the *Code Civil*[35] that of 1942

---

34   §950. 1. Wer durch Verarbeitung oder Umbildung eines oder mehrerer Stoffe eine neue bewegliche Sache herstellt, erwirbt das Eigentum an der neuen Sache, sofern nicht der Wert der Verarbeitung oder der Umbildung erheblich geringer ist als der Wert des Stoffes.

35   Art. 468: Se un artefice o altra persona abbia adoperata una materia che non gli apparteneva, per formare una cosa di nuova specie, possa o non possa questa materia riprendere la sua prima forma, il proprietario di essa ha diritto alla proprietà della cosa che se n'è formata... Art. 470: Quando

follows the *BGB*.[36] Indeed, the influence of the French and German codes will be found to have carried one of the above formulations into most of the codified systems in the civil law world. One interesting exception is the Austrian civil code of 1811. In this case the provisions on *specificatio* represent a unique amalgam of the *media sententia* and the common ownership doctrine of Grotius:[37]

> §415. If the materials which have been worked upon can be brought back into their previous condition ... then his own property will be given back to each owner, and compensation given to each. If the return to the previous state ... is impossible, then the new thing will belong to the contributors in common.

Finally, as a reminder of the timeless, or relatively timeless, character of juridical principles which have been applied over centuries in widely divergent social and economic circumstances from ancient Rome to the present day, we may consider the new Dutch civil code of 1992, which unsurprisingly offers yet another slight variation on the principle enunciated by Connanus in the mid-sixteenth century:[38]

> If someone has on his own account made a new thing out of, or partly out of, one or more moveable things which did not belong to him, he will acquire ownership of the new thing, unless the cost of the workmanship is so negligible that it does not justify this.

VII Scots Law in Europe

Since Scots law bypassed the European codification movement, Vinnius' comment on the *media sententia, eoque iure etiam nunc utimur*, remains valid to this day. The *media sententia* is generally set out without further comment by the institutional writers as an

---

però la mano d'opera fosse tanto pregevole da sorpassare di molto il valore della materia adoperata, la mano d'opera è considerata come principale, e l'artefice ha diritto di ritenere la cosa lavorata...

36   Art. 940: (Specificazione). – Se taluno ha adoperato una materia che non gli apparteneva per formare una nuova cosa, possa o non possa la materia riprendere la sua prima forma, ne acquista la proprietà pagando al proprietario il prezzo della materia, salvo che il valore della materia sorpassi notevolmente quello della mano d'opera. In quest' ultimo caso la cosa spetta al proprietario della materia, il quale deve pagare il prezzo della mano d'opera.

37   §415. Können dergleichen verarbeitete Sachen in ihren vorigen Stand zurückgebracht,...so wird einem jeden Eigentümer das Seinige zurückgestellt, und demjenigen Schadloshaltung geleistet, dem sie gebührt. Ist die Zurücksetzung in den vorigen Stand ... nicht möglich, so wird die Sache den Teilnehmern gemein.

38   Boek 5, Art. 16.2: Indien iemand voor zichzelf een zaak vormt of doet vormen uit of mede uit een of meer hem niet toebehorende roerende zaken, wordt hij eigenaar van de nieuwe zaak, tenzij de kosten van de vorming dit wegens hun geringe omvang niet rechtvaardigen.

unchallenged doctrine of Scots law.[39] However, Andrew McDouall, Lord
Bankton (c. 1685–1760), does state explicitly that it is the Roman principle of the *media sententia* which has been adopted in modern Scots
law:[40]

> Specification, (from *"speciem facere"*) is, "where one makes a
> species or piece of workmanship out of another's materials". The
> rule in the civil law, followed by us, is, that, if the subject can be
> reduced to its first state, it belongs to the owner of the matter, as in
> things made of gold, silver, and other metals, but, if it cannot be
> brought to its first form, as when a statue or table is made of
> another's wood, it belongs to the artificer.

A modern Scottish case provides an interesting practical example
of the application, in a modern industrial society, of the traditional
Roman rule of the *media sententia*. In *International Banking
Corporation and others* v. *Ferguson, Shaw and Sons*, decided by the
Court of Session on 3 December 1909,[41] the essential facts were as follows. A firm of oil merchants, Ferguson, Shaw and Sons, had made use
of refined cotton seed oil which had been sold to them by a party lacking title to do so due to a preceding security right over the oil. The oil
merchants mixed this oil with their own suet to produce a new species,
namely a lard compound. Lord Low held:[42]

> In this case I think that the lard compound, of which the pursuers'
> oil was one of the ingredients, became wholly the property of the
> defenders ... My reason for saying that the lard became wholly the
> property of the defenders is that after it was compounded it was
> plainly impossible again to separate the oil from the other sub-
> stances of which it was composed.

As authorities he cites the relevant passages of Erskine and Bell on
specificatio.[43] But it is the judgment of Lord Dundas which deals at
length with the rules of *specificatio*. He held as follows:[44]

---

39   *Specificatio* is treated in the following institutional works: Stair, 2,1,41;
     Mackenzie, 2,1,7; Bankton, 2,1,13; Erskine, *Inst.*, 2,1,16, *Prin.*, 2,1,8; Bell,
     Comm., (7th ed.), i,294ff; *Prin.*, s. 1298.1. The particular views of Stair and
     Bell will be discussed in more detail below.
40   Bankton, 2,1,13.
41   1910 S.C. 182.
42   at 192.
43   Erskine, *Inst.*, 2,1,17; Bell, *Prin.*, s. 1298. Both texts consider the point of
     intersection between *specificatio* and *confusio*. *Confusio* is the mixing
     together of two liquids belonging to two different owners. Where the liq-
     uids are of the same kind the result will be physically inseparable and will
     be owned in common by both owners. Where the two liquids are of differ-
     ent kinds, the result will always, by definition, be a new species. The test to
     be applied is then that of *specificatio*: can the new species revert to its pre-
     vious constituents? If so, there is no change in ownership; if not, the
     mixer, i.e. specificator, becomes owner of the new thing.
44   at 194.

In this state of matters it seems to me that the case is a pure type for the application of the Roman doctrine of *specificatio*. The oil at the date of the pursuers' claim no longer existed in its original and proper form; a new species had been created, of which the oil was an ingredient, but of which the component parts could not after the creation be again resolved into their original elements. The doctrine of *specificatio* is undoubtedly part of the law of Scotland. It is so recognised by all our institutional writers. The result accordingly in this case is, in my opinion, that the defenders became the sole proprietors of the lard compound, and that the pursuers have a good claim against them for the value of the oil.

Even if it is clear that the Roman principle of the *media sententia* is an established part of Scots law, "so recognised by all our institutional writers", and corroborated in practice by case law, we should not think that Scots law has been altogether unaffected by the natural law doctrines on *specificatio* which have come to play such a decisive role in other European systems. In particular, the founder of modern Scots law, James Dalrymple, Viscount Stair (1619–95), discusses all the main doctrines, that of the Proculians, the Sabinians, the *media sententia*, Connanus' principle of relative value, and Grotius' plea for common ownership. He concludes that any of these solutions may be considered satisfactory, since the real point at issue is rather recompense to the owner or workman for loss suffered. He writes:[45]

> There remains to be cleared that appropriation which is by specification, whereby of materials belonging to other owners a new species is produced, whether the product belongs to the owners of the materials or to him for whom the work is made. As to which the two great sects of the ancient lawyers were divided, Proculus and his followers attributing the property of all the materials to him that made the work, and Sabinus and his attributing the whole to the owners of the materials. But Tribonian midseth the matter thus, that if the product can easily be reduced to the first matter, the owners of the matter remain proprietors of the whole, as when a cup or other artefact is made of metal, but otherwise the materials cede to the workmanship, not only when the materials are consumed, but even when they remain, and cannot be reduced to their first nature ... Connanus is of opinion, that whether the workmanship or the materials be more precious, the property is carried by the value. And Grotius is of opinion, that there ariseth a communion, as in confusion of liquors, proportioned according to the value of the materials and workmanship. Positive law or custom may without injustice follow any of these ways, reparation being always made to the party who loses his interest ...

Thus Stair adopts a neutral stance in relation to all three solutions, emphasising that the question of compensation in reality deprives the question of its significance; for what difference does it make, Stair

---

45   Stair, 2,1,41.

seems to ask, whether the workman becomes owner and must pay the value of the material to the original owner; or the original owner is awarded the new thing but must pay the workman the value of his workmanship?

Only George Joseph Bell (1770–1843), writing at the beginning of the nineteenth century in the wake of the French codification, is openly critical of the *media sententia*. In his *Commentaries on the Law of Scotland and on the Principles of Mercantile Jurisprudence* of 1810, Bell pours scorn on the traditional Roman doctrine:[46]

> It is impossible to enter upon this enquiry without recollecting the famous controversy of the Proculeiani and Sabiniani concerning specification, which, after a course of perplexed and subtile reasoning, turning on imaginary and vain distinctions, was by Tribonian and the other lawyers appointed by Justinian to digest the Roman jurisprudence, decided according to a rule as distant perhaps from plain sense, or any useful purpose, as the opinions which it professed to reconcile.

In a footnote he discusses at some length the alternative solutions of other European legal systems:[47]

> Neither the system of the Proculeiani, nor that of the Sabiniani, nor the middle opinion of Justinian's lawyers, have been universally approved of abroad ... It was not to be expected that a rule founded on this kind of subtilty should be tamely acquiesced in by modern nations, to whom the Roman jurisprudence was rather a fountain than a code of law. And, accordingly, we find the commentators of various countries contesting this point. One commentator, who is quoted by Vinnius, speaks very judiciously on the subject. He considers it as absurd to enter into these distinctions, and holds that in common sense the point on which the attention should be fixed is the comparative value of the rude material and of the manufacture: Connanus lib. 3. *Comm.* 6. Grotius takes another view; he holds that there should be a common property established: *De iure belli ac pacis* 1. 2. c. 8, n. 19. But Vinnius (*Instit. Imper. Com.* p. 148) differs from both, and holds that the rule established by Justinian is the true one; for, without regard to value, the point is, Where in truth does the property lie? And to determine this point, the essential question is, Whether the original subject be extinguished or not? This, on the authority of Grotius (*Manud. ad iuris Holl. lib.* 2. c. 8), he represents as the modern rule of the Dutch states. Pothier seems to approve of Justinian's middle course, with this qualification, that a certain degree of arbitrary judgment should be reserved to determine according to circumstances (*Traité du droit de propriété*, no. 188) ...

Thus Bell's aggressive attack on the traditional Scots law rather dissipates itself in the citation of leading European jurists who had in fact

---

46   Bell, *Comm.*, i, 276; 7th ed., i, 295.
47   *Loc. cit.*, note 1.

upheld the *media sententia*: Grotius himself, Vinnius, and Pothier. That his criticisms have not been taken up in any later works of Scots law perhaps also owes something to the contradictory and entirely positive judgment he passes on the doctrine of *specificatio* in his later work, the influential *Principles of the Law of Scotland* (1829):[48]

> Specification is the forming of a new species from materials belonging to another, a change being produced on the substance, as flour out of corn, wine out of grapes. The questions which occasioned the controversy of the Sabinians and Proculeians are resolved with us according to the "*media sententia*", *on the plain principles of good sense and natural equity*.

It is through another legal case, however, that the views of Connanus and Grotius have bid fair to leave their mark on Scots law. In this case the principles of industrial accession, and in particular *specificatio*, were discussed at length in the course of the judgments. In *Wylie & Lochhead* v. *Mitchell,* which came before the Court of Session in 1870,[49] a workman, Mitchell, had been contracted by Wylie & Lochhead to build a hearse partly from his own, and partly from their materials, the latter consisting of fittings which were to be incorporated into the body of the vehicle. When this work had been carried out, and the vehicle was all but completed, Mitchell went bankrupt. The question arose: to whom did the vehicle with its fittings belong? If it belonged to Wylie and Lochhead, they could as owners, by paying the contractual price for the workmanship, extract the vehicle from the estate in bankruptcy. If it belonged to the workman, however, they must rank with the other creditors for a share of the remaining assets. The court decided that the vehicle was owned in common, according to the shares of each.

It is important, I think, to draw attention to the limits of the scope of the judgment, as indeed was emphasised by the court itself. In particular, the consequences drawn from the decision by the standard Scots law textbooks seem to me questionable. Gloag and Henderson, treating this case under the heading "Confusion of Liquids and Commixtion of Solids", and hence as pertaining to industrial accession, see agreement as the essential factor:[50]

> But, where two or more persons have agreed to contribute to the production of a new subject, either materials or skill and labour, or both, the subject will belong to them as common property in shares corresponding to the value of their respective contributions.

T.B. Smith, with more concision, also emphasises the crucial factor of agreement:[51]

---

48   Bell, *Prin.,* s. 1298.1 (my emphasis).
49   (1870) 8 M. 552.
50   *Introduction to the Law of Scotland,* (7th ed. by A.M. Johnston and J.A.D. Hope, Edinburgh, 1968), 502; in the 9th ed. (by A.B. Wilkinson *et al.,* Edinburgh, 1987), para. 37.8.
51   *A Short Commentary on the Law of Scotland,* (Edinburgh, 1962), 538.

Where, however, several persons have agreed to contribute work or
material towards the production of a new subject, this will vest in
them as common property – *Wylie & Lochhead* v. *Mitchell.*

It should be observed at once that as soon as contractual agreement enters the picture, we are no longer dealing with a question of
industrial accession. It may be recalled that in the relevant *Digest* text
on *specificatio* Gaius poses the case of someone making a new thing
suo nomine; if, by contrast, the workman constructs an object under a
contract, then the law regarding *locatio operis* will apply. As Vinnius
commented on the text of Justinian's *Institutes* which deals with
mixing by consent:[52]

> By the agreement of the owners] This case does not properly
> belong here.

In fact, the question of the acquisition of ownership by the workman
employed to work on an object is one of considerable difficulty. It has
been little discussed, since the crucial question in the circumstances is
rather the degree of care to be taken by the workman. Since this is
agreed to be very high, namely *custodia* or liability for all loss other
than that caused by *vis major*,[53] in the normal case the party commissioning the work will either receive the finished object as specified, or
compensation for the value of the material. The only point at which it
will become important to decide where ownership lies is if the workman goes bankrupt, and the trustees in bankruptcy assert ownership of
the object upon which he was working.

It is unnecessary to enter into this question here. The Roman texts
on the question have recently been treated at length by Nicolaus Benke
in an article in the *Zeitschrift der Savigny-Stiftung*.[54] Certainly, it is by
no means clear that the rules of industrial accession are to be applied
by way of analogy in these circumstances. Clearly, if I employ you to
transport my column, the column remains my property the entire time.
But suppose I employ you to make wine from my grapes. Are we to
hold that, applying the rule of *specificatio*, under a contract of *locatio
operis* there are two intrinsic transfers of ownership here: my grapes
become the workman's property when they are made into wine, and
the property in the wine is passed to me when he hands over the wine
under the contract? By a similar argument, if I employ a workman to

---

52 *Commentarius in Institutiones*, 2.1.27 §3: *Voluntate dominorum]* Haec
    species proprie huc non pertinet. Similarly, in 2.1.28 §1, on mixture of
    solids, which if done by mutual consent results in common ownership, if
    by error, leaves the ownership in the (by definition) separable units unaf-
    fected, Vinnius writes: *Nihil est in hoc ʃ quod ad institutam de accessione
    disputationem pertineat.*

53 See Zimmermann, *Obligations*, 393–412, esp. at 397–404.

54 Nikolaus Benke, "Zum Eigentumserwerb des Unternehmers bei der "*loca-
    tio conductio irregularis*"", (1987) 104 *Z.S.S. (RA)* 156. This article does
    not, however, enter into the treatment of the question by later civilians.

make a vase from my gold, the property would remain with me the entire time. At any rate, the proposition advanced in the Scottish text-books – that in a case of *locatio operis*, in which the workman uses partly his own materials and partly those of the person commissioning the work, the result is necessarily common ownership of the object made (presumably dissolved at the moment when the workman hands over the finished object) – seems to me as a general principle to be highly dubious. The rule ought to be narrowly confined to the circum-stances of the case: supervening bankruptcy in a contract of *locatio operis*. This is essentially stated by Lord Kinloch in his judgment:[55]

> This is not, in my view, to hold it common property in its origin and downwards; it is merely to introduce the equitable mode of dealing with it in the supervening circumstances.

Indeed, in such circumstances it might be considered whether a similar rule should not apply even where the workman had contributed only his workmanship.

Wylie & Lochhead v. *Mitchell* does, however, take on importance in the present context because the judges in the case passed comment on the various principles of industrial accession in arriving at their deci-sion. Doubtless for this reason the above-quoted Scottish textbooks treat the case under the heading of industrial accession. More impor-tant, however, is the fact that another highly influential textbook draws a general conclusion regarding *specificatio* proper, ignoring the crucial factor of the consent of the parties. Thus D.M. Walker sets out the doc-trine of *specificatio* in Scots law as follows:[56]

> Where a person in *bona fide*, as by mistake, makes a new thing from materials wholly belonging to another, if the materials are thereby wholly destroyed, the property in the new thing is with the maker ... but if the materials can be restored to their original state the property in the new thing is in the owner thereof ...

So far so good; this is the familiar *media sententia*.[57] However, on the authority of *Wylie & Lochhead* v. *Mitchell,* Walker advances the further proposition:

---

55 *Loc. cit.*, at 564.
56 *Principles of Scottish Private Law*, 2nd ed. (Oxford, 1975), at 1553, citing this case as authority; 4th ed., vol. 3, 370.
57 We may note in passing that the requirement of good faith mentioned as a condition of acquisition by Walker is generally accepted by the civilians: Cuiacius, *Notae in Institutiones* 2.1.25; Donellus, *Commentaria* 4.12.4; Grotius, *Inleidinge* 2.8.2; Vinnius, *Commentarius in Institutiones* 2.1.25 §2; Noodt, *Commentarius in Digesta* D.10.4; Pothier, *Traité du droit de propriété* 186. An important dissenting voice is that of Ioannes Voet, *Commentarius ad Pandectas* 41.1.21: "*nihil refert utrum in bona fide fuerit, putans materiam suam esse, an alienam sciverit*". On Voet's authority this is stated to be the law of South Africa: cf., Maasdorp's *Institutes* 2.36. However, among the Scottish authorities, Bell clearly insists

> If the new thing be made from materials belonging partly to two or more persons, it belongs to them in common in proportion to the value of the contribution of each.

This conclusion seems to the present writer to be mistaken.

I should like here to advance three propositions:

(1) Where there is a contract between two parties for the making of a new object, the law of industrial accession has no application; the question of a possible transfer of ownership under a contract of *locatio operis* pertains to a separate legal doctrine.

(2) If there had been no agreement in the present case, if, for example, the workman had built the mountings into the vehicle unaware that they belonged to someone else, it would have been a simple case of industrial accession. However, the category would have been that of *adiunctio*, not of *specificatio*. The normal rules of *adiunctio* would then have applied; the fittings would have acceded as accessory to the principal thing, in this case the vehicle, according to the well-established rules of Scots law pertaining to that category of industrial accession.[58] Thus the workman would have become owner of the fittings, (subject, as always, to the obligation to compensate the owner of the material for their value according to the principles of quasi-contractual liability).

(3) In a normal case of *specificatio*, where a workman, on his own account and in good faith, makes a new thing partly out of his own materials, and partly out of those of another, the result in Scots law

---

on *bona fides* (*Prin.*, s. 1298.1): "if the materials, as a separate existence, be destroyed in *bona fide*..." This was accepted on Bell's authority in *McDonald* v. *Provan (of Scotland St.) Ltd.*, 1960 S.L.T. 231. The most explicit formulation of this rule in Scots law is by William Forbes (Professor of Law at Glasgow University 1714–46) in his *Great Body of the Law of Scotland* (at 495): "So be the specifier or workman did *bona fide* for his own use, make the work by mistake of another's matter thinking it his own; but if he knew that the matter he was labouring belonged to another, the new species accrues to that other: 1.12. §3 ff. Ad exhib.". Forbes' work remains in manuscript in Glasgow University Library.

58   Thus in the case itself Lord Ardmillan states at 561: "If, in considering the question of combination or industrial accession which thus arises, the rule '*accessorium sequitur principale*' be held applicable, then I am of opinion that the mountings, being intended and used 'to adorn and complete' the fabric of the hearse, are accessory to the hearse, and that, subject to the equitable principle of indemnification for the value of the mountings, the property of the hearse draws after it the property of the accessory mountings...". For the rules determining principal and accessory in a case of *adiunctio*, Lord Ardmillan here cites the standard Scottish source, Bell's *Prin.*, s. 1298. The hierarchy of tests set out by Bell in this paragraph, each of which traces its origin to a *Digest* text, will be found to derive directly from Pothier's *Traité du droit de propriété*, at 170–76, (which Bell cites on a different point in the same paragraph).

is certainly not common ownership. In fact, in these circumstances, which are covered by a particular rule of the Roman law,[59] the workman will in all cases become owner of the new thing, even where it is reducible to its previous materials.

It is the third of these propositions which is relevant here, and which is, indeed, the simplest to establish. For it is strongly emphasised by the judges themselves that they did not wish the rule adopted in this case to be extended as a general principle to all cases of *specificatio*. That the existing principles of industrial accession were to remain untouched by the present case is emphasised in the judgment of Lord Inglis, the Lord President:[60]

> There are certain rules fixed in the law of industrial accession which it would be unwise to disturb.

Equally decisive is the following ruling by the same judge:[61]

> Neither is it the production of a new subject of property by art and industry, where the materials belong to one party, and the skilled labour is supplied by the other, which is *specificatio*, and in which the law determines the question of property in the manufactured article according to certain rules, which avoid the extreme doctrines both of the Sabinians and the Proculeians.

---

59   The basic text of the *Institutes* on *specificatio*, after setting out the *media sententia*, continues (*Inst.*2.1.25): "But if someone has made a new thing partly out of his own materials, and partly out of those belonging to someone else, as when he has made mead out of his own wine and someone else's honey, or a plaster or ointment out of his own and another's drugs, or a garment from his own and another's wool, it is not to be doubted that in this case he who has made the new thing becomes owner, since he not only contributed his own workmanship, but also provided part of the material". *Ex facie* the meaning of this passage would seem crystal clear: when the workman contributes some of his own materials he will always acquire, whether or not the new thing is reducible. Yet, perhaps because the examples given are all of new things which are irreducible, many jurists have insisted that in this case too the test of reducibility has to be applied. In *International Banking Corporation* v. *Ferguson, Shaw & Sons*, the judges took cognizance of the fact that the new substance was irreducible, even although the manufacturer had used partly his own materials; however, it is to be considered that the point was not explicitly debated, and since the new species was irreducible in any case it would not have affected the outcome. Bankton clearly favours the straightforward meaning of the text (*Inst.*, 2,1,13): "If the materials belonged partly to the workman, and partly to another, the new species belongs wholly, *without distinction*, to the workman" (my emphasis). Again it is William Forbes who exhibits the greatest clarity on the point (*Great Body of the Law of Scotland*, at 495): "When the matter is partly the workman's, and partly a stranger's, the piece of work goes to the artificer, without distinguishing whether it can be cast into its first state or not" (cf. note 57).

60   *Loc. cit.*, at 557.

61   *Loc. cit.*, at 558.

In other words, the traditional Scottish doctrine of *specificatio*, decided according to the *media sententia*, remains wholly untouched by the decision in the present case. Indeed, in adopting the principle of common ownership as a just solution in the particular circumstances of the present case, the Lord President explicitly denies that this doctrine is to apply to the case of *specificatio*:[62]

> We are not entitled to follow this philosophical doctrine to all its just results, and to hold that the same rights of common property will arise from *specificatio* as from *confusio,* because we are restrained by the rules of law fixed as applicable to these particular categories.

In view of these categorical statements of the Lord President, there would seem to be little scope for the proposition that this case establishes authority for common ownership in certain cases of *specificatio*, or indeed that it has altered the established principles of the Scots law of industrial accession in any way whatsoever.

It is nevertheless significant that in the course of their judgments, their Lordships did indeed express negative opinions about the principles applied in industrial accession. These might be thought to lend support to the view that the existing Scots law is in some sense unsatisfactory. Lord Ardmillan writes trenchantly on the subject:[63]

> In thus viewing the question we are led at once into the midst of the celebrated controversy between the Proculeians and the Sabinians – suppressed, yet scarcely settled, by what is called the '*media sententia*' of Justinian. I cannot venture to enter on that alarming field of juridical conflict. I shrink from even treading on the edge of
>
>   ... that Sirbonian bog,
>   Betwixt Damiata and Mount Casius old,
>   Where armies whole have sunk.
>
> Accordingly, I do not mean to occupy the time of the Court by attempting an analysis of the conflicting authorities on this subject.

Lord Kinloch also waxed poetical, feeling that there had passed before him:[64]

> ... lists dressed for a great tournament, with hosts of armed civilians on either side, eager and vociferous for the fray. Proculus on one side, Sabinus on the other, lead their enthusiastic followers. The whole body of commentators is broken into rival factions ...

More specifically, the Lord President explained that he considered it unwise to extend the rules of industrial accession to analogous cases, such as the present, precisely because these rules were so unsatisfactory:[65]

---

62   *Loc. cit.*, at 558.
63   *Loc. cit.*, at 561, quoting Milton, *Paradise Lost*, Book 2, lines 592–94.
64   *Loc. cit.*, at 564.
65   *Loc. cit.*, at 557.

For it may well be doubted whether these rules, or some of them, as fixed in the Roman law and adopted into our own, are really based on natural equity, or whether they can always be reconciled with one another.

He quoted with approval the statement of Grotius to the effect that:[66]

There is scarcely any area of law in which there are so many conflicting opinions of the jurists, and so many errors.

It is almost with regret that the Lord President feels he is unable to extend the equitable principle to the other categories of industrial accession:[67]

We are not entitled to follow this philosophical doctrine to *all its just results*, and to hold that the same rights of common property will arise from *specificatio* as from *confusio*, because *we are restrained* by the rules of law fixed as applicable to these particular categories.

The principle in question was that of common ownership, which he derived from Grotius.
  Lord Ardmillan also concurred:

I have carefully considered the conflicting authorities on this sub-ject, and the result is, that I am satisfied that, amid the refined and subtle speculations of opposing controversialists, the great equi-table principle comes out, that where materials belonging to differ-ent persons are by mutual consent mixed up, or wrought up together, so as to become inseparable, the mutual consent to such contribution creates a common property in the whole mixture or fabric, proportionate to the shares of the consenting and contribut-ing parties respectively.

Thus *Wylie & Lochhead* v. *Mitchell* is in the end ambivalent. On the one hand it is amply stressed that the decision in no way alters the tradi-tional doctrines and solutions applying in the Scots law of industrial accession; on the other, the judgments clearly question, albeit *obiter*, the wisdom of these solutions. So what if we were free to chose, free to emend the existing law?

VIII Towards a European Common Law

In a memorandum issued in 1976, the Scottish Law Commission set out to modernise the Scots law of industrial accession.[68] Two alternatives for the doctrine of *specificatio* are suggested:[69]

---

66 *Loc. cit.*, at 557, quoting Grotius, *De iure belli ac pacis* 2.8.21.
67 *Loc. cit.*, at 558 (my emphasis).
68 Scottish Law Commission, *Corporeal Moveables: Mixing, Union and Creation* (Memorandum no.28, 31 August 1976).
69 *Op. cit.*, at 24. Alternative A is intended to embrace all forms of industrial accession.

Alternative A

> Where materials belonging to another are incorporated into ... a new thing in such a way that the original materials cannot be conveniently separated from ... the new thing, ... the thing shall be deemed to be the common property of all persons who had an interest ... in the materials, or who have contributed by their skill or labour towards the making of the new thing.

While this clearly represents an attempt to treat discrete categories of industrial accession together (*adiunctio, commixtio/confusio, specificatio*), it will be clear that the result proposed as it affects *specificatio* is the common ownership principle of Grotius. The second alternative offered is as follows:[70]

Alternative B

> When a person has by skill or labour transformed materials which do not belong to him into a new thing, the producer becomes owner of it if his skill and labour are more valuable than the materials, but otherwise the owners of the materials become owners of the new thing.

This suggestion incorporates the pure form of the principle of Connanus, as found also in the Swiss civil code.

There is surely an element of irony in the intention of the Scottish Law Commission to modernise current Scots law by proposing solutions which were in fact first adumbrated in the mid-sixteenth and early seventeenth centuries. This irony is heightened by the fact that both solutions were rejected by the continental jurist who has had arguably the greatest influence on the law of Scotland, Arnoldus Vinnius, more than three and a half centuries ago, in the year 1642. Yet this conclusion was reached in a memorandum which clearly aims at a historical and comparative approach to Scots law, citing civilian writings, and discussing various modern European codes. But it must be said that it will contribute nothing to the harmonisation of European law for Scotland to adopt now, at the eleventh hour, the solution of a single, random European code against all others. The point is rather that behind the great diversity of specific rules – the Proculian, the Sabinian, the *media sententia*, the principle of relative value of Connanus, the principle of common ownership of Grotius, and all the changes rung on these principles which have passed into the modern civil codes – there lies a single European civilian tradition. All these systems may have adopted a slightly different solution, but they are nevertheless all speaking the

---

70 *Op. cit.*, at 25. Alternative B is divided into two sections, the first covering *specificatio*, the second adjunction and commixtion.

same language.[71] As regards the best solution in the particular doctrine of *specificatio*, we could perhaps do worse than heed the words of our leading jurist:[72]

> Positive law or custom may without injustice follow any of these ways, reparation being always made to the party who loses his interest ...

---

71 This, of course, does not apply to the non-civilian parts of Europe: cf. *International Banking Corporation* v. *Ferguson, Shaw & Sons, per* Lord Ardwall at 193: "I further wish to say that I do not consider that the English decisions which have been referred to by the Sheriffs and by counsel for the parties can be relied on as safe guides in a case which must be decided according to Scots law. These decisions all proceeded upon the doctrine, or perhaps I should rather say the form of action, formerly known as 'trover', and now as 'conversion', a doctrine and process peculiar to the law of England, and which, so far as I understand it, is in some applications of it at variance with the principles of Scots law".

72 Stair, 2,1,41.

6. DERIVATIVE ACQUISITION OF MOVEABLES

By DAVID L. CAREY MILLER

Introduction

This essay is concerned with the transfer of ownership in moveable property and the extent to which the common law of Scotland reflects the influence of Roman law. Throughout the history of the modern system of Scots law it has been accepted that the area concerned is of Romanist strain. Bell[1] states that the regulation of rights to moveables is "according to the principles of Roman jurisprudence". Sir Thomas Craig in his *Jus Feudale*[2] - the first organised textbook on Scots law - although writing an account of the feudal law, unambiguously accepts the Romanist approach to the transfer of ownership in commencing his treatment of sasine with the proposition that it is universally accepted that there can be no transfer of ownership without an act of delivery.[3]

It is not the case, however, that the Civil law relating to the transfer of ownership in moveable property was received complete and unaltered in Scotland. Stair's system of property - which, it is suggested, may be taken as definitive of the common law - has aspects not from Roman law and, also, does not know certain characteristic features of that system. Before commencing to consider the substantive law two general matters may be considered briefly. These are the prevalence of the use of Roman terminology and what may be called the "essential similarity factor".

In the Scots law of property relating to moveables one finds a quite marked use of Roman terminology. This is unexceptionable given the fact that the Latin labels of Roman law are part of a common European legal language. In the process of the development of the law Scottish writers and judges - in common with much of the rest of Europe - worked in this tradition. But, of course, the adoption of a convenient label or tag does not mean that what it stood for at any particular prior

---

1   Bell, *Prin.,* s. 636.
2   Craig, 2,7,1. See *Sources and Literature of Scots Law* (Stair Society, 1, 1936), 61-63. The 3rd ed. of J. Baillie (Edinburgh, 1732) was translated by Lord Clyde (Edinburgh, 1934).
3   W.M. Gordon, *Studies in the Transfer of Property by Traditio* (Aberdeen, 1970), 210 quotes this passage and goes on to say that he (Gordon) commences his treatment of Scots law with moveables "as illustrating the more complete acceptance of the whole Roman and Romanistic doctrine of *traditio*".

stage has been adopted. In aspects of the Scots law of property Roman terminology is prominent but, not infrequently, an investigation of the law behind the label reveals a distinctive solution.

The "essential similarity factor" is a matter of recognising that a substantial part of the affinity is to do with the similarity between systems which regulate property for purposes which are basically the same. Much of what was developed in Roman law is naturally appropriate to systems of similar orientation. Systems regulating property rights in the context of the primacy of individual ownership of goods inevitably have certain features in common. Thus, for example, it must necessarily be that there can be no transfer of ownership without a legal act by the owner. *Nemo dat quod non habet* is adhered to by English law[4] but it proclaims a principle recognised in Roman and Scots law. It is also the case that certain common conclusions follow from the mere fact of things being open to individual ownership. The conclusion that what is produced by a thing – the "fruits" – belong, in principle, to the owner of the parent item is an example. That one finds truisms of this sort in both Roman and Scots law hardly seems to point to more than a basic affinity between property systems operating in contexts of similar orientation. But the coincidence of principle only goes so far and there is room for different approaches to the ways in which basics are given effect. An example is the requirement of a separate act of delivery for ownership to pass. There is a policy choice as to whether delivery, in some shape or form, is required, or whether the passing of ownership should be allowed on any basis demonstrating the necessary agreement between the parties.

In an attempt to assess the extent of Roman influence in Scots property the more meaningful areas of comparison are those in which there is scope for different rules based upon considerations of policy. It is significant that Scots law does not have anything akin to the Roman law institution of *usucapio* providing for the acquisition of ownership by short prescription. This is, at least partly, an instance of Scots property not following Roman law in a matter in which there is room for different approaches. *Usucapio* served in a residual role in the context of derivative acquisition in Roman law; its absence in Scots law is considered in some detail below.

While the law of Scotland concerning derivative acquisition is essentially Romanist there are enough differences in matters of detail to justify the conclusion that it represents a distinct system. It is not Roman law but it does reflect the influence of that system. In what follows the relevant subject-matter will be dealt with firstly by identifying the Scots law position and secondly by attempting to establish the extent of Civil law influence. The treatment will be under the following headings: I – the basis of derivative acquisition; II – possession as a

---

4   See, e.g., W.W. Buckland and A.D. McNair, *Roman Law and Common Law* (2nd. ed., revised by F. H. Lawson, Cambridge, 1952), 77.

form of title; III – the transferor's title to convey; IV – the requirement of delivery – comprising: (1) general aspects of delivery, (2) particular modes of delivery; and V – an assessment of the extent of the Civil law influence.

I Basis of Derivative Acquisition

In the institutional writings of Scots law – notably Stair – one finds the essential requirements of derivative acquisition analysed from an abstract point of view. Stair's work compares very favourably with that of Grotius – a contemporary late seventeenth century writer – and although Stair's contribution should be seen as part of the general civilian development it is characterised by a strong original quality.[5] One may meaningfully compare Stair's originality and strength of analysis with the more prosaic work of Bankton[6] written "after the general method"[7] of Stair's *Institutions*. Bankton,[8] in stating that derivative acquisition is essentially a matter of the will of the transferring owner, quotes the less than compelling statement from Justinian's *Institutes*[9] to the effect that it is in accordance with natural equity that the wishes of a person who desires to tranfer his property to another should be given effect.[10] Indeed, Bankton's analysis seems circular in that he identifies delivery as "founded in the will of the disposer" but goes on to say that the owner's will "is not understood to be perfected till, in evidence thereof, delivery follows".[11] Stair explains derivative acquisition on the basis of the power of disposal which is essential to the notion of ownership as an ultimate right – "the power of disposal being the characteristic of dominion".[12]

A necessary corollary of this definition of ownership is that, at least as a matter of theory, disposition must be competent by mere act of will. But, of course, Scots law reflects the Romanist tradition of the requirement of a separate act of delivery for the passing of ownership. Stair's account showing the juxtaposition of the prerequisite act of will and the requirement of delivery explains the basis and basics of derivative acquisition in a philosophically valid manner. While, in philosophical terms, disposition must necessarily be valid on the sole basis of an

---

5   See D.L. Carey Miller, "Systems of Property: Grotius and Stair" in *Comparative and Historical Essays in Scots Law*, edd. D.L. Carey Miller and D.W. Meyers (Edinburgh, 1992), 13–31.
6   *An Institute of the Laws of Scotland* (Edinburgh, 1751–3).
7   Stated on the title page.
8   Bankton, 1,1,20.
9   *Inst.*2.1.40.
10   Gordon, *op. cit.*, n.3, 212 n.1, identifies Mackenzie, 2,1,5 with Bankton, 2,1,6, in that both refer to tradition as a mode of acquisition by natural and civil law but seem to follow Justinian rather than contemporary natural law theories to a greater extent than Stair and Erskine do.
11   Bankton, 2,1,20.
12   Stair, 3,2,3.

act of will the rules of a given legal system may freely prescribe "what-soever else is requisite to complete the conveyance".[13] Stair goes on to explain that, as a matter of policy, there must be some form of delivery which achieves a transfer of possession as a prerequisite to the acquisition of a real right by the transferee. In noting the universality of the Romanist requirement of delivery Stair makes clear that Scots law is conforming to legal science rather than merely following Roman law:

> But, for utility's sake, not only the Romans, but almost all nations require some kind of possession, to accomplish real rights, that thereby the will of the owner may sensibly touch the thing disponed, and thereby be more manifest and sure; so the law saith, *traditionibus et usucapionibus, non nudis pactis, dominia rerum transferunter*, with which our custom accordeth.[14]

Bell provides a useful enumeration of the considerations which support a requirement of actual delivery before going on to examine the exceptions – considered in detail below – which must be allowed as a matter of commercial necessity:

> This sort of delivery was well entitled to be held as the true and proper badge of transferred property, as importing full evidence of consent to transfer; preventing the appearance of possession in the transferrer from continuing the credit of property unduly; and avoiding uncertainty and risk in the title of the acquirer.[15]

Bell's statement would appear to reflect a jurisprudence more concerned with the perspective of practicality than considerations of theoretical integrity. The danger of identifying delivery as a manifestation of intention, or as an act following as a matter of consequence of the intention to transfer ownership is that thinking of this sort leaves the way open for transfer by consent. An eighteenth century case seems to manifest the difficulty produced by thinking of delivery as something derived from the intention to pass ownership rather than an independent requirement.[16]

The appearance of the word "sensible" is the only point of similarity between Stair's "utility's sake" passage and what Professor Gordon[17] describes as a "rather scathing" comment about the necessity for delivery by the eighteenth century philosopher David Hume:

---

13   *Ibid.*
14   Stair, 3,2,5. Scots case law concerned with the common law is generally faithful to the *non nudis pactis* principle; see, e.g. *Anderson* v. *McCall* (1866) 4 M. 765 *per* Lord Justice-Clerk Inglis at 769: "I hold it to be clear, and to be a rule of law, without any exception, that while the seller of the goods retains the goods in his own possession, no entry in his books will operate any delivery of the goods to the buyer, actual or constructive".
15   Bell, *Comm.*, i, 178.
16   See *Buchanan and Cochrane* v. *Swan* (1764) Mor. 14208.
17   *Op. cit.*, n.3, 211.

In order to aid the imagination in conceiving the transference of property we take the sensible object and actually transfer its possession to the person on whom we would bestow the property. The supposed resemblance of the actions and the presence of this sensible delivery deceive the mind and make it fancy that it conceives the mysterious transition of the property. And that this explication of the matter is just appears hence, that men have invented a symbolical delivery to satisfy the fancy when the real one is impracticable....[18]

Hume goes on to describe the requirement of delivery as "a superstitious practice in civil laws" and something to be equated with "Roman Catholic superstitions in religion".[19] As Gordon points out this is not a questioning of the utility of delivery but an attack on the notion of what Hume sees as the "perfectly insensible" concept of the transfer of property.

Hume's reductionist approach appears to show a failure to appreciate the significance of the distinction between property (or title) and *de facto* possession. This dichotomy was well developed in Roman law – the centrally important institutions of *mancipatio* and *usucapio* operated on the basis of the distinction – and it is certainly part of Scots law. The distinction was, of course, well understood by Stair and is demonstrated in various of the earlier sections in the first title of book two, concerned with real rights or *dominium*. The importance of the distinction is shown in a passage, of impressive rational strength, essentially concerned with possession:

The second step of real right is possession, which, as it is the way to property, and in some cases doth fully accomplish it, so it hath in it a distinct lesser right than property, which hath no other name than possession, though it be more *facti* than *juris:* and seeing possession is a common precognite to the most of real rights, it fitly falleth in here to be considered, both as it is a fact, and as it is a right; for as it is a fact, it is not only requisite to constitute real rights, but is also an effect thereof, when constitute.[20]

It is interesting that questions concerning the basis and essential requirements of derivative acquisition were debated in Scots law, at least from the time of Stair. The principal features of the system developed in Roman law may have come to prevail in Scotland but not without an indigenous process of analysis and development. This said, it would be incorrect to think that the texts of Roman law and later Romanist learning did not influence the work of Scottish jurists. Stair's analysis proceeds from the premise that the transfer of ownership is essentially a matter of intention but *Corpus Iuris* texts give prominence

---

18   D. Hume, *Treatise of Human Nature* (London, 1739–40), 3.2.4. Quoted by
      Gordon *op. cit.*, n.3, 211–2.
19   *Ibid.*
20   Stair, 2,1,8.

to the *animus* factor. For example, the statement in the *Institutes*[21] that delivery is a mode of acquisition of natural law because it is in accordance with natural equity that an owner's intention to transfer ownership be given effect.

A feature of Stair's system of the transfer of ownership is the extent to which it features the concept of possession. The reason for requiring a transfer of possession may be a matter of policy but its role in Stair's system of conveyance is a pivotal one. The transfer of possession achieves "the accomplishment of the disposition of real rights, so that not the first disposition, but the first possession, by virtue thereof, preferreth".[22] Given that a personal right or obligation is "anterior to, and inductive of, real rights of *dominium* and property"[23] it is perfectly logical that a personal right which becomes a real right by the transfer of possession should, on that account, take precedence over an earlier personal right on the basis of which there was not any transfer of possession.

The lectures of Baron David Hume (the nephew of the philosopher David Hume), delivered over the period 1786–1822, treat the basis of the transfer of property in some detail.[24] Hume is seen by Gordon[25] to differ from Stair and Erskine in taking the view that delivery is a requirement not only of Scots law but also of the law of nature. It is indeed the case that Hume does not distinguish the prerequisite principle of an act of will and the policy requirement of delivery in some shape or form:

> The natural way of transferring property, whether moveable or immoveable, is by an agreement to convey as in property, followed with delivery, real or symbolical, of the thing. These two circumstances (I have said) must concur in any case towards transference of the real right. The delivery of possession shall not transfer it, unless it follows on a suitable contract, on a habile title for transference of property, such as sale, gift, or barter in contradistinction to the more limited titles of loan, pledge, deposit, or the like. On the other hand, the mere consent or agreement to convey as in property is equally ineffectual to transfer, unless this be followed with delivery and possession.[26]

In this passage Hume appears to be summarising the essential features of the common law of Scotland and it must be doubtful whether he had in mind any distinction between natural and domestic law. Arguably, the word "natural" at the beginning of the passage says no more than that agreement followed by delivery is the naturally appropriate method of conveying property. "Natural" in this more colloquial sense

---

21   *Inst.* 2.1.40. See also *Inst.* 2.1.44, 46 and D.41.1.9.3–7.
22   Stair, 3,2,6.
23   *Ibid.,* 3,3pr.
24   The importance of Hume to the development of the law of property in Scotland is demonstrated by K.G.C. Reid in *Stair Memorial Encyclopaedia,* vol. 18, (1993), para. 1.
25   *Op. cit.,* n.3, 212.
26   Hume, *Lectures,* vol. 3, at 245.

can be distinguished from "natural" law in the sense of what, as a matter of pure rationality, is the prerequisite basis of the transfer of property. Hume, it may be noted, emphasises the importance of the transfer of possession as a justification for delivery in that "[i]t is the only ready, practicable, and suitable and patent criterion of right".[27]

Returning to the requirement of an intention to convey there is some question whether Scots law requires a *causa* in the sense of an acceptable basis as a prerequisite to the transfer of title. The requirement of such a *justa causa traditionis*[28] would be consistent with the role of dispositive intent in Scots law. Where a definite basis for the transfer of ownership can be established it is a matter of simple shorthand to infer the presence of an intention to convey where a thing is handed over apparently on the basis concerned. But, of course, the fact that the prerequisite of intention may be inferred from the particular relationship between transferor and transferee does not mean that any such relationship must necessarily be a *sine qua non* of the existence of the requisite intent.

An alternative formulation of the question whether Scots common law required a *justa causa traditionis* is whether the system of the transfer of ownership was causal or abstract. In short, is an underlying valid *causa,* manifesting the necessary intention, required as a prerequisite to the passing of ownership or can the requisite intention to transfer be established without the necessary support of such a basis? The distinction between "causal" and "abstract" systems as terms of art relevant to an analysis of the passing of ownership appears to be attributable to the nineteenth-century German jurist Savigny[29] but it is perfectly possible to apply the distinction to earlier systems.[30]

The emphasis in Scots law on the requirement of an independent act of delivery suggests that the system, in its common law form, should be thought of as abstract.[31] This is because an act of delivery cannot be

---

27   *Ibid.*
28   See R. Evans-Jones and G.D. MacCormack *"Justa causa traditionis"* and W.M. Gordon "The Importance of the *justa causa* of *traditio*" both in *New Perspectives in the Roman Law of Property,* ed. P.B.H. Birks (Oxford, 1989), 99–109, 123–35.
29   *Das Obligationenrecht.* 2 vols. (Berlin, 1851–53), vol. 2, 254–9.
30   For an account of the Roman-Dutch position see D.L. Carey Miller, *The Acquisition and Protection of Ownership* (Cape Town, 1986), 124–34.
31   I have tried to show this in my *Corporeal Moveables in Scots Law* (Edinburgh, 1991), 107–13. It should be noted that although Hume's statement in the passage quoted above, n.26; ("The delivery of possession shall not transfer it, unless it follow on a suitable contract, on a habile title for transference of property, such as sale, gift or barter in contradistinction to the more limited titles of loan, pledge, deposit, or the like") might appear to support a causal theory, the better view is that this does no more than indentify the usual bases of the required intent; to establish Hume's true position one must look at his treatment of defective consent – which I try to do in the work referred to above.

truly independent if the driving intention requirement is derivative. What is relevant for present purposes is that broadly speaking this reflects the position in Roman law which accepted that ownership would pass if, on delivery, the parties were in agreement that it should – even if they were not in agreement as to the underlying basis upon which it passed. A Roman law text[32] in which ownership passes where A hands over money as a gift but B thinks that he is receiving as a loan demonstrates the position of the system in looking to the parties' intention to pass ownership as the matter of primary importance.[33] That the accepted position of Scots common law, as described by Stair, is essentially Romanist in these matters is what one would expect given the strength of the fundamental requirement of a separate act of delivery. The act of delivery may be inferred from relevant events but only on a basis which is sufficient as a bilateral act.[34] The requirement of a separate act of delivery stands, as a hallmark of Roman influence, in contrast to the manifestly causal form, reflected in English common law, in which ownership passes on the basis of the parties' intent expressed in or implied by their contract – a form which, of course, came to prevail over the Scots law of sale as a result of the Sale of Goods Act 1893.[35]

The emphasis upon the requirement of a separate act of delivery does not and should not detract from the primacy of the requirement that the parties must intend that ownership should pass. Certain features of Scots law show that this *animus* aspect is the controlling factor. The corollary of the essence of ownership as a power of disposal is that an owner cannot be deprived against his will or, put in positive terms, that a transfer of ownership must necessarily be motivated by the owner. The signal importance of the intention factor explains why

---

32   D.41.1.36.
33   A better example, avoiding the problem of money as property, is the case of property passing where A believes that he is selling but B thinks that he is receiving a gift. See R.W. Lee, *Elements of Roman Law* (4th. ed., London, 1956), 138.
34   The judgment of the Court of Session in *Gibson* v. *Forbes* (1833) 11 S. 916 went against the pursuers but the court was equally divided on the issue of delivery. The strength of the notion of a legal act of delivery is seen in the argument for the pursuers (at pp.918–19) in a case concerned with the issue whether ownership had passed in wine purchased from a wine-merchant but left in the cellars of the seller. "Delivery was essential to transfer property to a purchaser. The entry of the wine in the books of the sellers, under the name of the purchaser, and the placing of it in special bins, were merely spontaneous acts on the part of the seller, to which the buyer was no party. But there were no *termini habiles* for delivery, real or symbolical, unless there were two parties to the act, one of whom represented the giver and the other the receiver". The issue here was clearly whether there was a sufficient legal act of delivery.
35   As Professor Sir Thomas Smith notes in his Tagore Lectures, *Property Problems in Sale* (Edinburgh, 1978) 13, Professor James Mackintosh, in the first edition of his *Roman Law of Sale* (Edinburgh, 1892), vi, warned against the 1892 Sale of Goods Bill.

the system does not follow the rule, probably of later Roman law, that in a contract of sale ownership only passed upon payment of the price, or upon the buyer giving security for payment, unless the transaction was on a credit basis.[36] Stair[37] specifically notes that in principle delivery passes ownership "and there is no dependence of it, till the price be paid or secured, as was in the civil law". The thinking behind the Romanist rule is that unless the buyer has furnished security, or the seller extended credit, it may be assumed that the seller would only intend to pass ownership on the price being forthcoming. In making an assumption about probable intent in the absence of security or credit, the rule operates to detract from the freedom of the parties to arrange the passing of ownership. The primacy of the parties' intention in Scots law emerges in the recognition that title could be reserved to the seller with the effect of restraining the passing of ownership when delivery occurred.[38]

II Possession as a Form of Title

Consistent with the importance of the transfer of the right of possession – in most cases by the handing over of actual possession – Scots law recognises a presumption that the possessor of a moveable is its owner. A passage from Stair shows the dogmatic logic of the correlation between the role of possession in the constitution of the right and in the proof of ownership:

> In moveables possession is of such efficacy, that it doth not only consummate the disposition thereof, but thereupon the disposition is presumed without any necessity to prove the same.[39]

For present purposes it is significant to note that this device did not come from Roman law in a direct sense. It could, however, be thought of as a rationalisation of what was recognised in Roman law, as a necessary implication of the protection of possession, in the situation in which a claimant to ownership sought to vindicate from a party in lawful possession. As Ulpian noted, the consequence of an interim finding as to possession was that the losing party would have to prove his case as pursuer in an action claiming ownership.[40] Grotius,[41] in his classic work on Roman-Dutch law, makes the point from the opposite perspective of the possessor being relieved of the burden of proof of ownership.

It is possibly arguable that the Scots law presumption arising from possession is consistent with the obligation to which a seller is subject,

---

36   *Inst.*2.1.41.
37   Stair, 1,14,2. See David Johnston "Sale and Transfer of Title in Roman and Scots Law" in *The Roman Law Tradition*, edd. A.D.E. Lewis and D.J. Ibbetson (Cambridge, 1994), 182–98.
38   See Stair, 1,14,4.
39   *Ibid.,* 3,2,7.
40   D.41.2.35.
41   *Inleidinge tot de Hollandsche Rechtgeleerdheid* (The Hague, 1631), 2.2.7.

according to the common law, on the basis of contract. The seller is not, as a matter of course, subject to an obligation to make the buyer owner, rather, only, to give the buyer undisturbed possession. As Stair[42] puts it the entitled buyer "could demand no more but delivery and warrandice". To make the seller subject to an obligation actually to pass ownership could only be justified on the assumption that he could, an assumption which could not be made without detracting from the primacy of the *nemo dat quod non habet* principle. The limitation of the duty of a seller to give a guarantee against eviction in respect of the subject delivered originated in Roman law but has been seen to be somewhat anomalous because of the relative weakness of the position of a Roman possessor against one able to prove a right of ownership.[43] Scots law, arguably, is somewat more logical and consistent in the correlation between the rule that a buyer is entitled to no more than undisturbed possession and the presumption that the possessor of moveable property is the owner of it.

Does Scots law's presumption that the possessor of a moveable is owner of it mean any more than that the claimant to ownership against a party in lawful possession must establish his title? Erskine seems to say no more than this:

> Such is the natural connection between property and possession, that in moveables, even when they have a former owner, the law presumes the property to be in the possessor; so that till positive evidence be brought that he is not the right owner, he will be accounted such by the bare effect of his possession.[44]

This somewhat elaborate description of the presumption does not appear to come down to anything more than Grotius' terse comment that possession relieves the possessor of the need to prove ownership.

Returning to Stair one finds a somewhat more demanding burden upon the claimant to ownership with a corresponding increase in the meaningfulness of the presumption for the possessor. As a matter of consistency with the principle that the transfer of property involves an act of will Stair requires that attention be paid to the circumstances under which the claimant to ownership came to lose possession:

> ...but he must instruct the manner how his possession ceased, as being either taken from him by violence, or by stealth, or having strayed, and being lost or the like; and the reason thereof is, because moveables pass without writ, and oft-times without witness; and therefore, whatever right parties once had to moveables, it is presumed to be transmitted by donation, sale or otherwise, unless it be proved that he lost possession, as aforesaid.[45]

---

42   Stair, 1,14,1.
43   See Buckland and McNair, *cit. sup.*, n.4, 283.
44   Erskine, *Inst.,* 2,1,24.
45   Stair, 2,1,42. See also Stair, 4,30,9.

The *vitium reale* attaching to a thing stolen or taken by violence had an important role in the Roman law of property in that *usucapio* could not take place.[46] To this extent it had implications for possession as a basis for title. The absence of *usucapio* in Scots law – commented on below – means that the problem of a *vitium reale* does not have the particular relevance that it had in Roman law. It should be acknowledged, however, that Stair's prescription of what a vindicating owner must prove against a lawful possessor is an application of the notion of the civilian doctrine of *vitium reale*. This said, one probably seeks in vain for absolute originality, and Stair's application of the concept of deprivation contrary to the will of owner as something to be proved in addition to title by the claimant to ownership against a lawful possessor is an important, and seemingly original, device.[47]

A major difference between Scots and Roman law in respect of moveable property is the absence in the former of a system of acquisitive prescription based upon a short period of possession. Until later Roman law certain moveables were classified, with land, as *res mancipi* and, as such, required a formal act of transfer. Where an informal transfer occured *usucapio* served to give a good title in appropriate circumstances. *Usucapio* also applied in the case of a transfer *a non domino* where the transferee had acquired in good faith on a basis which in the normal course of events would have made him owner; but in the case of property stolen or taken by violence acquisition was barred.[48] In Scots law there is no analogous institution of acquisition on the basis of short possession.

Stair[49] surveys the Roman law in some detail and when he comes to decribe Scots law it is clear that the native system is entirely different:

> ...our common rule of prescription is by the course of forty years, both in moveables and immoveables, obligations, actions, acts, decreets, and generally all rights, as well against those absent as present: we have not these differences which we have shown were in the civil law; and because our prescription is so long, there is little question with us, *de bona fide*.[50]

The transfer of moveable property being free of requirements of form means that the role of *usucapio* in giving a good title where the only difficulty is a defect of form is irrelevant to Scots law. In respect of transfer *a non domino* it is questionable whether the presence of a system of short prescription would be consistent with an emphasis on

---

46   *Inst.* 2.6.2-3.
47   For further comment see D.L. Carey Miller "Systems of Property: Grotius and Stair" in *Comparative and Historical Essays in Scots Law, cit. sup.*, n.5, 18.
48   See *Inst.* 2.6.*pr.*-11.
49   Stair, 2,12,1-10.
50   *Ibid.*, 2,12,11.

the protection of the right of ownership. As indicated a central element in the system of property of Scots law is that, in principle, an owner can recover what he can prove to be his provided he can show that he did not part with the thing in circumstances consistent with a transfer of ownership. To allow acquisition, after a period of possession, against an owner who would otherwise have been able to recover the thing would weaken the protection of ownership which this principle upholds. Looked at in another way, the protection of possession against a claimant to ownership, unable to establish the basis under which he parted with or lost the thing, renders *usucapio* superfluous. In this regard, it is relevant that the possessor is presumed to be owner and, in principle, is in as strong a position as any other acquirer of a moveable on a derivative basis.

III   The Transferor's Title to Convey

The premise ruling derivative acquisition is that no more can be acquired by the transferee than that the transferor is in a position to convey. Two considerations are necessarily involved: (i) the nature and extent of the right of the party from whom the transfer is made; (ii) the competence of the party actually making the transfer when it is someone other than the owner. The second issue is only an indirect property issue in that although the act of transfer seeks to have proprietary consequences it is essentially a contractual act to which questions of capacity may apply. Capacity will not be dealt with in this essay because where it arises it does so as a contractual issue.

  With regard to the right of the party purporting to transfer ownership Roman law recognised that a transfer was limited to the extent of the right residing in the transferee. Ulpian states this axiom and goes on to give the simple example of a transfer of land by an owner being effective to convey title but a purported transfer by a non-owner being without effect:

> *Traditio nihil amplius transferre debet vel potest ad eum qui accipit, quam est apud eum qui tradit. Si igitur quis dominium in fundo habuit, id tradendo transfert, si non habuit, ad eum qui accipit nihil transfert* (Delivery should not and cannot transfer to the transferee any greater right than resides in the transferor. Hence, if someone conveys land of which he is owner, he transfers his title; if he does not have ownership, he conveys nothing to the recipient).[51]

One need hardly seek iteration of this truism in the sources of Scots law. It may be noted, however, that Stair states the positive correlative of the principle in the first section of his title on dispositions:

> In both dispositions and assignations, the disponer or cedent is called author, and the acquirer is called the singular successor, and

---

51   D.41.1.20.

in both, this common brocard takes place, *jus superveniens authori accrescit successori,* that is, whatever right befalleth to the author after his disposition or assignation, it accresceth to his successor, to whom he had before disponed....[52]

It is incontrovertible that Scots law adheres to the maxim *nemo dat quod non habet.*[53] An example is the dictum of Lord Kinnear in *Mitchell* v. *Heys & Sons:*[54]

> The general rule is perfectly well settled that the possessor of corporeal moveables can give no better title to a purchaser or pledgee than he himself acquired from the owner.

It may be noted, however, that a modern writer has suggested that the strength of the recognition in Scots law of the link between possession and ownership, in the case of moveable property, is not consistent with giving full effect to *nemo dat quod non habet.* Having identified the emphasis on and effect of a transfer of possession in Scots law Professor Gow's comments:

> On the other hand it also recognises the general principle that *nemo plus juris ad alium transferre potest quam ipse habet* with its corollary *resoluto jure dantis resolvitur jus accipientis,* and clearly such a principle militates against ownership founded upon possession.[55]

In considering this observation one must examine the role of possession in relation to derivative acquisition and ask whether either the requirement of a transfer of possession to pass ownership or the presumption that the possessor of a moveable thing is its owner do, in any way, gainsay the ruling position of the principle that a transferor cannot convey any more than he has. Insofar as the transferor is owner of a thing, his right of ownership may be passed by a legal act of transfer involving the transferee in obtaining possession. There are two distinct parts to this proposition: the premise of the transferor's ownership and the requirement that he give possession to the transferee. The requirement of a transfer of possession to achieve the transfer of a real right is not inconsistent with the premise principle concerned. As indicated above, the presumption that the possessor of a moveable is the owner is a feature of Scots law distinct from Roman law but, this said, it is not appropriate to see it as detracting from the essential derivative character of an act of transfer. This is so notwithstanding that, as a matter of contractual right,

---

52 Stair, 3,2,1.
53 J.J. Gow *The Mercantile and Industrial Law of Scotland* (Edinburgh, 1964), 118, n.5 regards *nemo plus juris ad alium transferre potest quam ipse haberet* (D.50.17.54) as the "analogous Scots brocard" but the truncated maxim expresses precisely the same principle. See also *Stair Memorial Encyclopaedia,* vol 18, para. 669, n.1.
54 (1894) 21 R. 600 at 610. Lord Kinnear's *dictum* was adopted by Lord Ashmore in *Lamonby* v. *Foulds Ltd.* 1928 S.C. 89 at 100.
55 *Op. cit.,* n.53, at 62.

a buyer can claim no more than vacant possession as his reciprocal entitlement for payment of the price.[56] The limited presumption deriving
from possession does not hold against a claimant to ownership who can
prove his title and show that he did not part with the thing in circumstances consistent with an intention to convey it.[57] That the derivative
principle, as expressed in the maxim *nemo dat quod non habet*, is the
ruling basis is not put into question by the presumption which is not to
do with whether the transferor was owner but whether, in parting with
or losing possession, he intended to pass ownership.

IV The Requirement of Delivery

(1) General aspects of delivery

As already shown the essential active requirements for the transfer of
ownership in a moveable thing in Scots law are intention and delivery.
Stair's analysis of the basis of derivative acquisition has been considered above. As a matter of natural law the parties must necessarily
intend that ownership pass but, as a matter of policy, and following
Roman law, Scots law requires an independent act of delivery. Writers
describe the juxtaposition of the two elements in different ways. Bell –
citing Stair, Erskine and Pothier – identifies delivery as "the *modus* following on a legal *titulus transferendi*"[58] applicable to the derivative
mode of acquisition. Bell goes on to note that given the existence of
"the conventional will to convey" delivery is "the overt act by which the
real right is transferred".[59]

 Hume, accepting that the delivery of possession is a prerequisite
to the transfer of ownership in moveable property, demonstrates the
significance of the requirement in the context of a competition
between purchasers:

> ...the mere consent or agreement to convey as in property is equally
> ineffectual to transfer, unless this be followed with delivery and
> possession: so that if one sell the same subject successively, to two
> persons, he shall have the property, in whose favor delivery is made
> although on the posterior contract.[60]

Hume goes on to say that the prior purchaser has a claim for damages
against the seller. According to Hume it is the "equitable and natural
rule of preference" to give priority to the party to whom delivery has

---

56 See Sir John More's notes to Stair, lxxxviii: "In sales of personal effects,
    (with the exception of ships, or other personal estate, to which by law, or
    usage, a written title is required,) as the possession presumes the property,
    no other title can be required from the vendor".
57 See Stair, 2,1,42; 4,30,9.
58 Bell, *Prin.*, s. 1299.
59 *Ibid.*
60 Lectures, vol. 3, 245. See also Stair, 3,2,6, quoted above n.22.

been made because "[w]ithout delivery, the buyer does not form any real connection with the thing, to make his claim attach on it".[61] This, of course, is consistent with the demarcation in Roman law between the underlying contract and the act of conveyance: the latter being the basis upon which property passed. Accordingly, in principle, the party to whom delivery was made became owner and a disappointed prior purchaser was left with a possible contractual action against the seller.[62] It may be noted that, at least in later civilian development,[63] the subsequent purchaser who obtained delivery was in an impregnable position only if he was in good faith in that he did not know of the prior purchase. Scots law also applies a limitation based upon the good faith of the second purchaser who obtains delivery. Where he knew of the first purchase "the acquirer is partaker of the fraud of his author"[64] and his title is reducible. The vulnerability of a transferee who had knowledge of his transferor's obligation to deliver to a prior party has been recognised in an important domestic development[65] which may owe something to later civilian learning.

Arguably the most important general statement, and an appropriate starting point to consider the details of the requirement of delivery, is the continuation of Stair's text, the initial part of which, quoted above,[66] makes the case for the separate requirement of a transfer of possession:

> It useth here to be debated, whether possession itself be sufficient to accomplish dispositions; or if there must be tradition, or delivery of that possession, by the disponer to the acquirer: the forecited law[67] seems to require tradition, or at least usucapion, or prescription, which doubtless are the most proper ways to accomplish dispositions; yet *utiliter* and *equivalenter*, possession lawfully attained by virtue of the disposition, although not delivered by the disponer, will be sufficient; as if the disponer were not in possession himself, and so cannot deliver it; yet the acquirer may recover it from the detainer, or the acquirer might have been in possession before, by any other title, as by custody, conduction, etc; in which case none require delivery....[68]

This text justifies a change of possession as the rational basis of the act of conveyance. The recognition of this generalised basis makes possible

---

61   *Ibid.*
62   See C.3.32.15*pr.*
63   See J.E. Scholtens "Double Sales" (1953) 70 *S.A.L.J.* 22, n.2.
64   Stair, 1,14,5.
65   See e.g. *Morrison* v. *Somerville* (1860) 22 D. 1082 at 1089. The only comprehensive juristic analysis is a very recent one: see K. G.C. Reid's account in *Stair Memorial Enyclopaedia*, vol. 18, paras. 690 and 695–700.
66   See n.14.
67   *Traditionibus et usucapionibus, non nudis pactis, dominia rerum transferuntur.*
68   Stair, 3,2,5.

a range of modes of transfer – including forms not involving an act of handing over from transferor to transferee – which must necessarily exist in any sophisticated economy. Stair's particular analysis and rationalisation of the role of possession is characteristically distinctive but, this said, one would hardly think of it as innovative given the importance of the transfer of possession in Roman law. As Professor Gordon has shown[69] the "classical lawyers continued to require a transfer of possession in order to transfer ownership of most kinds of property *inter vivos*". The learned author makes this comment as a preliminary to an inquiry into the reason for the emphasis upon a transfer of possession. To put the proposition in context it should be noted that the treatment is commenced with the statement that "[c]lassical law shows no rooted objection to the passing of ownership without the transfer of possession, nor is this surprising considering the clear distinction made between ownership and possession".[70] As Gordon points out the obvious example of a transfer of property *inter vivos* without a transfer of possession was the mancipation of Italic land by parties not present on the land.[71]

At first sight it might appear that, on Stair's analysis, the *mancipatio* case would not be seen as an exception. Stair[72] requires a transfer of possession in all cases involving "the accomplishment of the disposition of real rights". But, as the institutional writer goes on to explain, the requisite possession is not the same in all cases, "for [it is] in some real, in others symbolical": an example of the latter is the transfer of land by infeftment for a transfer of "natural possession makes no real right without seasin".[73] In this instance Stair's apparent pursuit of a consistent rationale would appear to be at the expense of blurring the concepts of actual physical possession *(corpus)* and the right to possession *(animus)*. The statements from Professor Gordon's book, on the other hand, are concerned with possession in the physical sense and, of course, in the context concerned, it is appropriate to show that there are cases in which ownership may be passed without the physical handing over of the thing. Turning again to Stair it would appear to be misconceived to say that the effective act in respect of the transfer of land also involves a transfer of possession. Stair[74] in effect concedes that his generalised requirement of a transfer of possession involves a unified use of the two different notions of possession. The flaw in Stair's analysis is that the basis of the act of delivery cannot be constituted by a transfer of the right to possession because this right only comes to vest in the transferee as a consequence of the act of transfer – however it is identified. In the cases concerned, ownership passes because the

---

69   *Op.cit.*, n.3, 5.
70   *Ibid.*, 4.
71   *Ibid.*
72   Stair, 3,2,6.
73   *Ibid.*
74   *Ibid.*: "possession is not alike in all cases".

intention of the parties must necessarily prevail provided the circumstances justify the conclusion that there has been a change of possession. But, of course, the law draws the line at allowing a transfer of
ownership on the basis of the mere intention of the parties that this
should occur. To do so would be to abandon the delivery requirement.
The position was well understood by nineteenth-century Scottish
judges. In the full court decision of *Moore* v. *Gledden*[75] Lord Neaves,
whose opinion was concurred in by the majority, commented as follows:

> Possession cannot be constituted by mere paction. It is a matter of
> fact, though there also enters into it the existence of an *animus
> possidendi* in addition to an overt act of corporeal possession or
> apprehension. But the outward or visible fact of possession cannot
> be supplied by mere paction, or by anything committed to paper
> merely.

In the circumstances of their being no alternative, and, of course,
always assuming that the intention factor is satisfied, Roman law and
Scots law allow the reasoning that "in so far as X has obtained the right
to possession it must be taken that ownership has passed to him".

Erskine's general treatment of tradition is less original and less systematic than that of Stair but it does appear to be closer to the texts of
Roman law. In relation to immoveable subjects, because they are fixed,
and in relation to incorporeal property, because it is intangible, delivery must necessarily be symbolical and "the symbols used are generally
such as are fittest to express the delivery of the subject made over".[76] In
respect of moveables Erskine makes specific reference to the forms of
constructive delivery mentioned in Justinian's *Institutes*. Rather than
attempting to explain the Civil law rules on a dogmatic basis – as Stair
does – Erskine's general theme is that actual delivery is no more than
the natural mode which may be departed from where necessary.

> Though moveables are capable of real delivery, it is not always nec-
> essary that the *ipsa corpora* of moveables be delivered. If, for
> instance the subjects to be conveyed are under lock and key, the
> delivery of the key to the purchaser is accounted a legal tradition of
> all that is contained in the repository: at least when the question is
> with him who makes the tradition.[77] Notwithstanding the general
> rule, that property cannot be acquired but by tradition, yet where
> the possession or custody of a subject hath been before with the
> person to whom the property is to be transferred, *ex. gr.* if he who
> has been intrusted with the custody of a thing should purchase it
> from the owner, no tradition is necessary for perfecting the pur-
> chase, either real or symbolical.[78]

---

75 (1869) 7 M. 1016 at 1020. See also the earlier case of *Broughton* v. *J. & A.
    Aitchison* 15 Nov. 1809, F.C. in which the issue was whether a change of
    possession had occurred.
76 Erskine, *Inst.*, 2,1,19.
77 *Ibid.*, citing *Inst.* 2.1.45.
78 *Ibid.*, citing *Inst.* 2.1.44.

The extent to which the pragmatic approach of Erskine differs from
Stair's attempt to explain the Roman law rules on a systematic basis is
demonstrated in Erskine's explanation of the *traditio brevi manu* form
of delivery described in the last sentence of the passage quoted above.

> It is commonly said, that in such cases there is a *ficta traditio*: the
> depositary is supposed to give it back to the purchaser, upon the
> title of vendition, which is called by the doctors, *fictio brevis
> manus*. But the plain reason why tradition is not required in that
> case is, because there is no room for it; for no subject can be deliv-
> ered to one who hath it already in his custody.[79]

Bankton's account places the emphasis upon distinguishing the different forms of delivery without making any attempt to identify a unitary
basis in terms of possession. But a useful aspect of his treatment is the
clear identification of a "feigned" delivery category to stand alongside the
accepted classes of actual (or "real") delivery and symbolical delivery.

Symbolical delivery, Bankton notes, is applied in the case of land.
"[P]utting the acquirer in possession" was the proper way of "perfect-
ing feudal rights" but "delivery of a symbol upon the ground of the
fee...was sufficient to perfect the right in place of actual possession".[80]
Symbolical delivery is also applicable in the case of moveables and
achieves the transmission of a real right provided that "together with
the symbol, power and liberty is given to the receiver to take possession, which the owner quits".[81]

The difficulty, apparent in Stair's treatment, of explaining delivery
– assumed on the basis of what can only be an *ex post facto* change – in
the case in which a party holding the thing concerned commences to
do so as owner (*i.e.* comes to possess in the full sense) has been considered above. Bankton avoids any philosophical problem by applying the
"feigned delivery" label.

> A feigned delivery is when delivery is supposed in law, though it
> did not actually intervene: thus, in delivery *fictione brevis manus*,
> as it is called, or short-hand delivery, if one that has the possession
> of the thing already, by loan or pledge, buys it, the property is trans-
> ferred without a new delivery; for it is understood in law as if he
> had restored it to the owner, and reveived it back again from him
> upon the title of purchase....[82]

Stair, Erskine and Bankton – probably in that order of importance
– are institutional writers relevant to the the issue of the role of Roman
law in the development of the common law of Scotland. What their

---

79   *Ibid.*
80   Bankton, 2,1,20 and 21.
81   Bankton, 2,1,22. Bankton cites *Inst.* 2.1.45 as authority for the example
      which he gives: "thus, the delivery of the keys of a granary or cellar to a
      purchaser of the corn, wine, or other things therein, infers the delivery of
      the same".
82   Bankton, 2,1,23. In support of this passage Bankton cites *Inst.*2.1.43.

respective accounts of the principles of derivative acquisition appear to show is that Roman law influence occurred through received knowledge of its rules and principles which were applied in their expositions in a manner which varies from writer to writer. In any event, however, what is apparent is more a matter of a general adherence to Roman thinking and a readiness to have recourse to its rules in expounding the common law of Scotland than any reception as such. The result is three accounts reflecting different approaches but not showing any significant difference in substantive conclusion.

2 Particular modes of delivery

Although Scots law has long been familiar with the main Roman alternatives to actual delivery[83] – *traditio brevi manu, traditio longa manu* and *constitutum possessorium* – the forms concerned have not acquired any higher status than that of instances of delivery subsumed under a classification based on distinguishing the categories of actual, symbolical and constructive delivery.[84] To this extent Scots law, reflecting Stair, shows a certain originality. What is especially interesting is how domestic development has achieved a breakdown between the three heads with the emphasis on an open-ended concept of actual delivery operating from the basis of the prerequisite of a transfer of possession; a notable aspect being the scope for an extended notion of this requirement. A quotation from Bell is apposite:

> ... although delivery of the commodity is necessary to the passing of property, it still is not indispensably required that it should be of that actual and unequivocal kind which places the thing sold within the grasp and in the personal apprehension of the buyer, or of his servants, clerks, and others, whom the law identifies with him and considers as his hands; but that acts of possession less immediate and direct are by construction of law held sufficient, when actual tradition into the buyer's hands cannot be given.[85]

One result of a wide concept of actual delivery is that the need for other forms becomes less pressing. Symbolical delivery tends to be seen as having a somewhat specialised scope and constructive delivery is primarily concerned with the case of property held by a third party.

---

83   See Gordon, *op. cit.*, n.3, 215–22.
84   Alternative labels for "actual" and "constructive" are respectively "natural" and "civil". In *Cabbell* v. *Brock* (1831) 5 W. & S. 476 at 503 Lord Chancellor Brougham adopted the formulation of the Court of Session requiring (in the case – analogous for present purposes – of the creation of a real right of security) a "change of possession, either naturally, civilly, or symbolically". "Natural" needs no explanation; "civil" derives from *possessio civilis* and refers to delivery by the transfer of the right of possession "as owner" but, of course, without the transferee obtaining actual possession – hence the alternative "constructive" delivery.
85   Bell, *Comm.*, i, 181–182.

The handing over of a key to premises in respect of goods contained in the premises was accepted in Roman law[86] but the primary function of this form of delivery appears to have been to give the transferee effective control – possession of the goods: hence the requirement that the key be handed over proximate to the warehouse.[87] To this extent the delivery was not symbolical as, of course, it would have been had the handing over of a merely symbolic key been effective.

Stair's treatment identifies two true forms of symbolical delivery and explains the difference on the basis of the presence of the subject concerned. On the one hand the handing over of a part as "a symbol or token...when the thing to be possest is present" as in the case of the "delivery of a parcel of corns for a stack or field of corns"[88] and on the other hand, a "merely supposititious" representative token, as in the case of "delivery...by a wisp of straw, which ordinarily is in absence of the thing to be possessed".[89] The viability of a transfer based on the giving of symbolical possession – consistent with an emphasis upon the role of intention in the act of transfer – is recognised in early case law. In *Gray* v. *Cowie*[90] the Lords acceded to the following argument.

> That a disposition of moveables upon which there follows symbolical possession, being a competent and valid right, gives the party a sufficient right, albeit the common debtor retain the possession, seeing our law makes no difference between symbolical possession and actual possession of moveables, the right of property of the goods being as validly conveyed by a symbolical possession as by an actual possession.

Erskine,[91] quoting Justinian's *Institutes* 2.1.45, identifies the handing over of a key as an instance of symbolical delivery in the true sense[92] but suggests the possible limitation that delivery would be effective only "when the question is with him who makes the tradition".[93] Hume,[94] it may be noted, denies any symbolical aspect in the case of the handing over of the key to premises in which the goods are stored.

> But this does not happen under the notion of a figurative or symbolical delivery, or, as if the key were given, or taken, as a token or representative of the goods. In truth, in the nature of things, – possession of the key is the essence of a genuine and real substantial delivery. It admits the buyer, and excludes the seller; it conveys the

---

86   *Inst.* 2.1.45.
87   D.18.1.74.
88   Stair, 2,1,15.
89   *Ibid.*
90   (1684) Mor. 9121.
91   Erskine, *Inst.,* 2,1,19.
92   See Gordon, *op. cit.,* n.3, 216.
93   It is difficult to see that this is saying any more than that the transferee would only get a contractual right to the goods.
94   Hume, *Lectures,* vol. 3, 250–1.

goods out of the natural power and command of the one party, and into that of the other, and this just as effectively and substantially, as if the goods were moved into the buyer's own warehouse, out of that of the seller.[95]

The emphasis upon ensuring that delivery is effective from the point of view of achieving the critical requirement of the transfer of the right of possession appears in the tendency to identify what could be seen as symbolical delivery as actual delivery.

Of course, even if – on the principle of Stair's handing over of a wisp of straw[96] – there does not need to be any element of giving actual possession but merely an identifiable overt act, the subject concerned must be identified for the purposes of the act of transfer. What is required in terms of identification may, possibly, sometimes be thought of as making the delivery actual rather than symbolical. This dilution of the classic notion of symbolical delivery appears in a statement in the case of *Maxwell & Co.* v. *Stevenson & Co.*,[97] an appeal from the Court of Session to the House of Lords. But one could hardly say that the perspective of Lord Chancellor Brougham was not consistent with Hume's approach to goods in a warehouse. The *dictum* concerned is as follows:

> If I deliver the key of a warehouse, it is a symbolical delivery of the warehouse, but an actual delivery of the goods in the warehouse; whether it is a delivery of all the goods I have there, there is some little doubt about: but if I deliver the keys, with a delivery-note, directing the stakeholder, the warehouseman, or the King's lock-keeper, to give the goods up, that is a delivery of the goods....

A legacy of Roman law as the system which has exercised a significant influence over the development of aspects of Scots property law is the tendency to identify matters in terms of Romanist concepts and categories. An example of this would appear to be the identification as symbolical delivery of any situation in which a thing, not the actual or full subject to be delivered, is handed over. Accordingly the transfer of the cargo of a ship by a bill of lading is typically identified as an instance of symbolical delivery.[98] As Professor Gordon[99] notes the law "in recognising a true symbolical delivery in the case of bills of lading" has gone beyond the texts of Roman law.

---

95   See also Bell, *Comm.,* i, 186.
96   Stair, 2,1,15; see above n.89.
97   (1831) 5 W. & S. 269 at 279–80.
98   See e.g. *Price & Pierce Ltd* v. *Bank of Scotland* 1910 S.C. 1095 *per* Lord Johnston at 1114: "A bill of lading may be a good symbol of possession while the cargo is subject to the bill of lading." See also T.B. Smith, *Short Commentary* (Edinburgh, 1962) 539.
99   *Op. cit.,* n.3, 215. The role of a bill of lading as an instrument of property was recognised in an early case in which the majority opinion was that "proper possession of the goods was held, not by the shipmaster or owner, but through them, first by the shipper, and then by the indorsee to the bills of lading." (*Bogle* v. *Dunmore & Co* (1787) Mor. 14216 at 14218).

Arguably one may question whether it is apposite to treat the passing of property by a bill of lading as symbolical delivery and, as a broader point, it seems questionable whether there is any case for approaching instances of delivery not known to Roman law from the perspective of the Roman forms.

Delivery providing for the transfer of ownership by one who does not actually hold the thing to one who does not immediately receive it has been important in the context of commercial law.[100] The development in Scots law would appear to have as its ultimate - albeit somewhat remote - source a *Digest* text[101] which provides for delivery on the basis of the thing being placed within the sight, and so subject to the control of, the transferee. This form of delivery was identified in Roman law as *traditio longa manu* - delivery by the long hand. Stair,[102] adhering to his systematic emphasis upon a transfer of possession, explains the process in which property passes even though the thing is "not delivered by the disponer" as the equivalent of actual delivery - possession having been "lawfully attained by virtue of the disposition" the acquirer may recover the thing from the detainer. The requirements of what had come to be identified as constructive delivery are set out in the case of *Pochin & Co* v. *Robinows & Marjoribanks*[103] by Lord President Inglis.[104]

> Constructive delivery may take place, and generally does take place, where specific goods or other moveables being in the custody of some person other than the owner, the owner gives to a purchaser of these goods a delivery order addressed to the custodier, ordering him to deliver to the purchaser these specific goods. When this delivery-order is intimated to the custodier constructive delivery is effected, because the custodier from that time becomes in law holder for the purchaser, just as before he was holder for the seller. But to the completion of such constructive delivery two things are indispensable, - that the custodier shall hold an independent position, and be neither the owner nor in any way identified with the owner of the goods...and that the goods themselves shall be specific in this sense, that they be capable of identification, either as one total undivided quantity stored in a particular place, or at least a specified quantity, forming part of an identified whole.

---

100 Bell, *Comm.*, i, 194–98 pays more attention to this form of delivery than to any other.
101 D.46.3.79.
102 Stair, 3,2,5.
103 (1869) 7 M. 622 at 628–29. See also the Second Division case of *Anderson* v. *McCall* (1866) 4 M. 765 at 770.
104 This dominant figure of nineteenth century Scots law precedes his remarks about constructive delivery with the statement: "[b]y the law of Scotland the property of moveables in no case passes by personal contract, but only by tradition, actual or constructive." With regard to the influence of Lord President Inglis see below, n.120.

Although Roman law did not have a developed form of delivery involving the thing in the *detentio* of a third party there is, as indicated, a possible link between this important form of constructive delivery and *traditio longa manu*. As Professor Gordon has noted, the Scottish form seems to be "a development of the principle implicit in D.46.3.79, that there is delivery by giving instructions which put the thing out of the control of the present possessor and into the control of the acquirer".[105] This is plausible on the basis that the giving of the instructions to a third party is an obvious possible extension of the notion of delivery by an act which brings about a shift of control from transferor to transferee. This said, the development of this form of constructive delivery in the common situation of goods held by a third party has been a domestic response to the needs of commerce. Moreover, there can be little doubt that the need factor was of greater significance than the question of the existence of an appropriate civilian basis.

Traditio brevi manu and *constitutum possessorium* identify modes of delivery which involve a change of circumstances between transferor and transferee.[106] In both modes the emphasis is on a peg upon which to hang the label "delivery" rather than a manifest act of delivery. In the former ownership passes to the transferee on the basis that he comes to possess as owner what he formerly held on a contractual basis.[107] In the latter, rather more controversially, ownership passes to the transferee on the basis that he has acquired the right to possession (as owner) of a thing or goods which remain with the transferor who commences to hold on a contractual basis.[108] Both modes of delivery are facilitated by the analysis of possession which makes clear the difference between the *corpus* and the *animus* aspects and the related difference between a mere holding of the thing and having possession

---

105 *Op. cit.*, n.3, at 217. It is interesting to note that in South African Roman–Dutch law a closely similar form of delivery was developed in the nineteenth century. In South Africa there has been some debate as to whether the basis of what is sometimes identified by the English law label of "attornment" is *traditio brevi manu* or *longa manu*. The view supported by case law appears to accord with that of Professor Gordon – i.e. that it is *traditio longa manu*. On the Roman-Dutch development see my *Aquisition and Protection of Ownership, cit. sup.*, n.30, 152–53.

106 In *Boak* v. *Megget* (1844) 6 D. 662 at 669 Lord Justice-Clerk Hope noted that trade custom and usage sometimes sanctioned forms of delivery in which "the possession of the party is not really looked to...as necessarily proving that the stock apparently on hand is his".

107 See Erskine, *Inst.*, 2,1,19: quoted above n.78.

108 Stair, 2,1,16 appears to be speaking of heritable property in noting that possession may be attained by a mere "conjunction of interest". Hume, *Lectures,* vol. 3, 251, however, recognises an exception to the usual requirement of actual delivery in what amounts to the Romanist device of *constitutum possessorium*. He gives the example of the buyer of a horse leaving it at livery with the seller and assuming responsibility for the farrier's and other charges.

in the sense of a proprietary right, sometimes identified as *possessio civilis* or civil possession. Stair's clear enunciation of this difference probably contributed to the development of the forms of delivery which rely upon it. Stair[109] wrote: "[h]ence ariseth the distinction of possession, in natural and civil; the former being that which is, and the latter that which is holden or repute such".

In *Orr's Trustee* v. *Tullis*[110] Lord Justice-Clerk Moncreiff rejected the proposition urged by counsel for the pursuer that insofar as the law of Scotland "adopted to the full extent" the Roman law doctrine of *traditio,* actual delivery was always required. On the contrary, the court took the view that it was not correct to say that "some ostensible corporeal act – some change in the actual local situation or custody of moveables sold, is necessary to pass the property".[111] Lord Justice-Clerk Moncreiff went on to explain:

> That is only true when possession has not been attained by the purchaser. It is manifestly not true when possession has been attained. The simplest illustration of this is the case in which the thing sold is at the time of the sale in the possession of the purchaser. If a man hire a horse or carriage, and purchase it while his contract of hire is current, the property has passed; for no delivery could make the possession more complete than it was before.[112]

The case of *Eadie* v. *Young*,[113] referred to by Hume[114] allowed delivery in an arrangement in which two horses and carts were sold but retained by the transferor on hire. However, the carrying out of a symbolic handing over of the subjects concerned and the marking of the carts with plates bearing the name of the transferee meant that the case was not an instance of *constitutum possessorium* pure and simple. On the basis of Lord Justice-Clerk Moncreiff's *dictum* in *Orr's Trustee*[115] these acts of physical delivery would not be necessary provided it could

---

109 Stair, 2,1,10. In Scots law the designation "civil possession" has come to connote "possession through the physical detention of another" (see *Stair Memorial Encyclopaedia*, vol 18, para. 121) because the distinction is most meaningful in the circumstances in which A has the right to possession but the thing is actually held by B.

110 (1870) 8 M. 936.

111 at 945. *Traditio brevi manu* has been accepted in Scots law from an early date. In *Hope's Major Practicks*, ed. J.A. Clyde (Stair Society, 3, Edinburgh, 1937) 2,4,3 reference is made to the case of *Park* v. *Findlay* decided in 1621 to the effect that there was no need to deliver "quher the goods wer els in the buyer's possessione". See also *Arbuthnott* v. *Paterson* (1798) Mor. 14220.

112 at 946. See also *Rennet* v. *Mathieson* (1903) 5 F. 591 *per* Lord Moncreiff at 599: "There may possibly be cases in which the property of moveables will pass without delivery, although the seller remains in possession under another title, such as hire or loan".

113 (1815) Hume 705.

114 Hume, *Lectures,* vol. 3, 251.

115 Quoted above, n.112.

be established that a change of possession had occurred as a result of the parties' changed relationship. That the parties were concerned, by one means or another, to ensure that the legal requirements for the passing of ownership were satisfied is rather more plausible than the analysis that the acts manifesting physical delivery were merely intended as evidence that ownership had passed. As Professor Gordon points out, although in principle, delivery by *constitutum possessorium* should be admitted provided there is a definite *causa detentionis,* the case law shows a tendency to require acts which make it "clear to third parties that there has been a change of ownership, despite the fact that there is no change in the physical situation of the goods".[116] The insistence that the creation of a real right of security over moveables requires a physical handing over to the secured party[117] is an analogous concern. In principle the passing of ownership and the creation of security are matters entirely distinct[118] but, this said, it is understandable that the law's long-standing concern to prevent unfair prejudice to third parties is reflected in both forms of disposal of property.

V   An Assessment of the Extent of the Civil Law Influence

There is no doubt that Roman law and civilian learning has been a significant source of influence in the development of the law governing the derivative acquisition of moveable property in Scotland. But, this said, the developed product of Scots law is distinctive both in certain matters of substance and in the way Romanist concepts are applied. The differences of substance appear and, in some instances, are identified in Stair's work which describes a complete and established system reflecting a settled juxtaposition of the essential ingredients of Roman and indigenous law.

An important difference, drawn attention to in Stair's work, is the absence of *usucapio,* acquisitive prescription being a matter regulated by the native law.[119] This institution had a major residual role in the context of derivative acquisition in Roman law. Its general effect was to enhance the security of a title obtained on a derivative basis even, of course, in the *a non domino* situation – provided the property concerned had not been stolen or taken by violence. There is no *usucapio*

---

116   *Op. cit.,* n. 3, 218.
117   See e.g. *Clark* v. *West Calder Oil Co.* (1882) 9 R. 1017 *per* Lord President Inglis at 1024: "A mere assignation of corporeal moveables *retenta possessione* is nothing whatever but a personal obligation and creates no preference of any kind." See also *per* Lord Shand at 1033: "There is no principle more deeply rooted in the law than this, that in order to create a good security over subjects delivery must be given. If possession is retained no effective security can be granted".
118   See *Armour* v. *Thyssen Edelstahlwerke A.G.* 1990 S.L.T. 891 at 895.
119   See Stair, 2,12,11 "our common rule" and 2,12,12 "[b]y our ancient custom" in contrast to the Roman law described in the earlier sections of the title. See above n.50.

in Scots law but a presumption that the possessor of a moveable is the owner operates to give a measure of security to acquisition on an *ex facie* derivative basis. The common law presumption is part of a property system which, in respect of moveable property, seeks to balance the interests of a claimant to ownership and a possessor – what *usucapio* and the associated rules protecting a usucaping possessor did in Roman law in a somewhat different way. Both Roman *usucapio* and the Scots law presumption are subject to the *vitium reale* of theft which operates to preserve the right of vindication of an owner deprived by theft. A corollary of this – and a particularly important feature of the Scottish system – is the limitation of the right of a claimant to ownership by the requirement that he establish, not only his right of ownership, but that he parted with or lost the thing in circumstances inconsistent with the transfer of the right.

In accepting the parties' intention that ownership should pass as the foundation requirement of derivative acquisition Scots law is in accordance with Romanist thinking. But, as Stair shows, the core essential of ownership is a power of disposal and any act of disposition necessarily involves an exercise of that power. Taking the intention essential to its logical conclusion Scots law does not inhibit the role of the parties in determining the passing of ownership. Accordingly, there is no requirement that the price be paid, credit extended or security given for ownership to pass in sale.

Although the basic nature and features of the requirement of delivery in Scots law very much reflects its ancestry, the system has a stronger dogmatic coherence than Roman law. This derives from a certain rationalisation of the requirement of delivery which was influenced by Stair and reflected in a case law which had to develop to meet the needs of commerce. The approach was consolidated in the nineteenth-century juristic works of Hume and Bell. It is something of a paradox that this development, enunciated most strongly in the case law of the era dominated by John Inglis as Lord Justice-Clerk and Lord President, came to a *de facto* end with the coming into force of the Sale of Goods Act 1893 soon after the death of Inglis. The late Professor Sir Thomas Smith QC in his Tagore Lectures commented on the circumstances under which the requirement of *traditio* was, for all intents and purposes, lost to Scots law.

> Lord President Inglis, for many years the Olympian head of the Scottish judiciary and a resolute opponent of the doctrine of the notional transfer of real or property rights by mere consent, died in 1891. For him sale was a contract, while different methods of creation or transfer of property rights were appropriate for immoveables and moveables – in the case of corporeal moveables "tradition" or delivery. However, in the year of Inglis' death, Lord Watson, a Scottish Lord of Appeal whose judicial experience was exclusively in the House of Lords in London, organised and ultimately pressed through, with the support of certain commercial

interests, the inclusion of Scotland in the English Sale of Goods Bill, which became the Sale of Goods Act 1893. Thus the English rules regarding e.g. the "passing of property" in specific goods by agreement were extended to Scotland – but in the context of the sale of corporeal moveables only – so destroying the internal coherence of the law of moveable property in Scotland.[120]

There is no scientific measure of the extent of the influence of Roman law in the development of Scots law in the area of moveable property. It is difficult to see that there could be any plausible challenge to the proposition that the influence was considerable. This has been demonstrated in a comprehensive and convincing manner in Professor Gordon's final chapter "Scots Law" in his *Studies in the Transfer of Property by Traditio* to which I have made frequent reference. It may, however, be possible to arrive at a conclusion with regard to the broad nature of the influence. Commencing with a negative proposition, it was not a reception *in complexu* with Roman law virtually replacing the local law. Rather, Roman law appears, for some centuries, to have had the role of a parallel legal culture – a body of legal principle applied by writers and judges as a point of reference. The tendency towards this approach appears in the passages in Stair and in the other institutional writings referred to in this essay. Perhaps more significant is the fact that one finds the two systems referred to together, but as separate systems, in the developmental context of case law – both in the submissions of counsel and in the opinions of judges. As an example of the former one may note part of what was contended for the respondent in the case of *Paul* v. *Cuthbertson*:[121]

> In considering the question as to what constitutes delivery, it has been resolved, both in the Roman and Scottish law, in such a way as to preclude the possibility of the rule being employed as an engine of fraud and injustice; and, accordingly, in the Roman law, the delivery of the subject was held complete either by transporting it into the possession of the buyer, or by putting it under his power if it could not readily be transported, and even without any visible or overt act;[122] and, in like manner, in the law of Scotland, great latitude is allowed in determining what shall constitute sufficient delivery.[123]

The classic approach of Scots case law can be found in the opinion of Lord Justice-Clerk Inglis, as he then was, in *Hansen* v. *Craig & Rose*.[124] "We must decide it according to the principles of the law of Scotland, and the rules as to risk which we have adopted from the Roman law." The opinion continues:

---

120 *Property Problems in Sale, cit. sup.*, n.35, 14.
121 (1840) 2 D. 1286 at 1291.
122 Citing D.18.6.14.1.
123 Citing Erskine, *Inst.*, 3,3,8.
124 (1859) 21 D. 432 at 438.

The rule *res perit domino* is generally an unbending rule of law, arising from the very nature of property. But the law of Rome and of Scotland introduces an exception to that rule, founded on principles of equity, and expressed in the brocard *periculum rei venditae nondum traditae est emptoris*.[125]

In *Black* v. *Incorporation of Bakers, Glasgow*[126] Lord President Inglis made another statement showing the attitude of the Court of Session to Roman law.

It is material to observe that the *specificatio* in this case is of that complete and immutable kind which, both by the Roman law and ours, is in certain circumstances a mode of transferring or acquiring property.

A more recent acknowledgement of the contribution of Roman law to the development of Scots law in the area of the transfer of moveable property is to be found in *Widenmeyer* v. *Burn, Stewart & Co.*,[127] a case also concerned with the passing of risk. After describing the essential features of the common law Lord President Clyde observed that "[t]hese principles come down to us from the Roman system and are well settled in our own law".[128]

The most recent work of legal scholarship relevant to the common law regulation of the derivative acquisition of moveable property tends, it is submitted, to support the view that the relationship between the common law of Scotland and Roman law has two distinct aspects. Firstly, the obvious influence in development and, secondly, the less well recognised parallel legal culture and point of reference feature. In the recently published "Property" volume of the *Stair Memorial Encyclopaedia* the principal author and co-ordinator, Professor K.G.C. Reid, writes:

The modern law of property in Scotland is laid on the foundations of the Roman law. Many of the general concepts of the modern law, such as *dominium* or real rights or *traditio* or possession or *accessio*, are Roman concepts, and indeed the Roman name is often retained. Much of the content of the law is also Roman in origin, although it may have been substantially altered and developed in matters of detail.[129]

In the same volume the common law relating to the transfer of ownership of corporeal moveables is dealt with by Professor W.M. Gordon under the headings of delivery *longa manu*, symbolical delivery,

---

125 *Ibid.*
126 (1867) 6 M. 136 at 141.
127 1967 S.C. 85.
128 at 98; see also the *dictum* of Lord Guthrie at 102: "[t]he rule of the common law of Scotland as to the incidence of risk under a contract for the sale of goods is embodied in the maxim *periculum rei venditae nondum traditae est emptoris*. The rule was derived from Roman law".
129 *Stair Memorial Encyclopaedia*, vol. 18, para. 2.

delivery *brevi manu* and *constitutum possessorium*.[130] Professor Gordon explains that, as a matter of convenience, the various cases of some form of transaction other than actual delivery recognised in Scots law are "fitted into categories borrowed from Roman law...because Roman law, as understood by the civilian writers, clearly influenced the treatment of this topic by the institutional writers".[131] The important *Stair Memorial Encyclopaedia* work in the property area would appear to support the notion of a parallel system of Roman law applied as a point of reference to Scots law, not only in past development but as a living part of the system. This phenomenon is probably strongest in property and would, in any event, only apply in the areas of private law which have been subject to significant civilian influence.

---

130 *Ibid.,* paras. 620–23.
131 *Ibid.,* para. 619.

7. ROMAN INFLUENCE ON THE SCOTS LAW OF REAL SECURITY

By WILLIAM M. GORDON

This essay starts from the observations of the late John Spencer Muirhead:[1]

> Scots Law follows Roman Law closely in the matter of real security, and for this reason the Roman rules have been set out somewhat fully. There are differences of detail arising out of our system of registration of writs affecting heritage, and some Roman rules, such as the *ius retinendi* and the *beneficium ordinis*, are not adopted by our law.[2] Security by an *ex facie* absolute disposition, by pledge and without possession of immoveable subjects, are all known and the necessity of intimation to make effective security over debts is recognized. Our law, however, does not recognize security over moveables without delivery, and hence chattel mortgages, known to English law, are not known in ours. Our law also does not recognize floating charges.

There have been changes in the law since these words were written. In particular, security over heritable property must now take the form of a standard security and can no longer be created by *ex facie* absolute disposition,[3] without prejudice to existing securities in this form, and floating charges can now be created over the property of companies, industrial and provident societies and European economic interest groupings.[4] The rest stands, for the present at least, and three things are

---

1   *An Outline of Roman Law* (2nd. ed., Edinburgh, 1947), 109 [hereafter, Muirhead, *Outline*]; the text of the quotation is unchanged from the first edition in 1937.

2   The *ius retinendi* was a right to retain a pledge, originally given to secure a specific debt, to secure any remaining indebtedness after the specific debt was paid off – the so-called *pignus Gordianum* recognised in C.8.26(27).1.2 (Gordian, A.D. 239); the *beneficium ordinis* in this context meant that personal action and action against cautioners was to be taken before proceeding to enforcement of any real security – *Nov.* 4.2 (Justinian, A.D. 535).

3   Conveyancing and Feudal Reform (Scotland) Act 1970 (c.35), s. 9(3).

4   They were introduced for companies in 1961 by the Companies (Floating Charges) (Scotland) Act 1961 (c.46), for industrial and provident societies in 1967 by Industrial and Provident Societies Act 1967 (c.48) and for European economic interest groupings by the European Economic Interest Groupings Regulations 1989 (S.I. 1989/638). Extension of floating charges and a new fixed moveable security are proposed in a consultation paper issued by the Department of Trade and Industry, Security over Moveable Property in Scotland (November, 1994).

said or implied which require further examination. The first is that
Scots law follows Roman law closely; the second, the statement which
seems to be implied, is that Scots law followed Roman law in recognising forms of real security corresponding with the Roman forms of
fiducia (*ex facie* absolute disposition),[5] pledge, security without possession of immoveables (hypothec) and security by intimated assignation
of debts (which Muirhead apparently sees as constituted by mandate to
sue intimated to the debtor rather than by hypothec);[6] the third is that
Scots law, unlike English law, does not recognise security over moveables without delivery and so does not recognise chattel mortgages or
floating charges by common law. The refusal to recognise security over
moveables without delivery is a major difference, and even if it has
been lessened by changes in the law since Muirhead wrote, the changes
have been mainly statutory. It is for consideration how far Scots law has
in fact followed Roman law and where and why it differs from Roman
law. It may also be asked what can be learned from Roman law for the
benefit of the modern law.

Borrowing from Roman Law

There is an important difference between Scots law and Roman law in
the matter of security over land. In Scots law heritable securities, which
for practical purposes mean securities over land, have become a distinct category of real security rights; the significance of the distinction,
and especially the historical significance, is somewhat underplayed in
the quotation from Muirhead above. In Roman law, and particularly in
Justinianic Roman law, the distinction between land and moveable
property was not of great legal significance. In classical law it was over-
shadowed by the distinction between things capable of mancipation
(*res mancipi*) and things not capable of mancipation (*res nec mancipi*)
and, while it is true that *res mancipi* included land in Italy and land
treated like land in Italy, land did not have the same dominant place
among the Roman *res mancipi* as land does in the Scots category of heritable property. That land was involved did not in Roman law directly
and specifically affect the modes of constitution of real security, even in
classical law. In classical law (and before) a *fiducia*, a trust which could
be attached to a conveyance of property and which imposed an
obligation to reconvey the property in the circumstances agreed on,
was used to provide for reconveyance of property transferred *ex facie*

---

5   It is not entirely clear that Muirhead had *fiducia* in mind as the parallel to
    the *ex facie* absolute disposition. He may have been thinking of sales with
    a clause of redemption which also existed in Roman law although it is not
    clear that they were used as a means of constituting real security – see
    below.
6   See Muirhead, *Outline*, 107. That it was so conceived in Roman law is
    doubtful but there is a post-Justinianic link with assignation – see M.
    Kaser, "Zum *pignus nominis*", *Études offertes à J. Macqueron* (Aix-en-
    Provence, 1970), 399.

absolutely in security. It could be attached only to a mancipation or an assignment in court *(in iure cessio)*. But while mancipation was the specific form of conveyance of *res mancipi*, including Italic land, assignment in court could be used by a Roman citizen to transfer any kind of property and so *fiducia* as a form of real security was not restricted even to *res mancipi* and so not even to Italic land. Security over non-Italic land would take the form of a pledge or a hypothec. Pledge and hypothec, the other forms of real security available in classical law, were equally applicable to land and moveables, although it is reasonable to suppose that hypothec was more commonly used for land and pledge for moveables.

With the disappearance of *fiducia*, the texts relating to which were not included in the *Corpus Iuris Civilis* or were adjusted for application to pledge and hypothec,[7] pledge and hypothec were left as the only surviving forms of real security in Justinianic law – or at least as the only forms expressly recognised as a means of constituting such security. An *ex facie* absolute conveyance in security would have been competent in Justinianic law but there is little or no trace of such an institution in the *Corpus Iuris*. The law of the *Corpus Iuris*, therefore, did not provide an exact model for a system which made an important distinction between land and moveables and which in the course of its development for various reasons has made much use of *ex facie* absolute conveyances as a form of real security.

It is true that, if *Regiam Majestatem* can be taken to represent Scots law in this matter historically accurately,[8] there appears to have been a stage in the law at which no distinction was drawn between constitution of real security over land and over moveables. In *Regiam* it is simply said that moveables or immoveables are pledged *(ponuntur in vadium)*, and there are indeed fourteenth century documents recording that land was pledged or wadset in the sense that it was expressly given in security by way of pledge.[9] But even in *Regiam* there are the beginnings of a distinct law of heritable security in that the consequences of

---

7   See W.W. Buckland, *A Textbook of Roman Law* (3rd ed. revised by P.G. Stein, Cambridge, 1963), 431–32 and 473–74

8   *Regiam Majestatem and Quoniam Attachiamenta*, ed. Lord Cooper (Stair Society, 11, Edinburgh, 1947) [hereafter *Regiam*], III.2 (*A.P.S.* edition, III.3), taken from *Glanvill*, X.6 (ed. G.D.G. Hall, London, 1965) but quoted as authority by Balfour, *The Practicks of Sir James Balfour of Pittendreich*, ed. P.G.B. McNeill (Stair Society, 21 and 22, Edinburgh, 1962–63) [hereafter, Balfour], "Anent thingis laid in wad", c. I, i, 194, Hope, *Minor Practicks*, (Edinburgh, 1734), 239 and Erskine, *Inst.*, 2,8,4.

9   *Reg. Mag. Sig.*, i, no. 477 – "*impignoravi...omnes terras meas*". The deed is dated in 1372 and is referred to in Hume, *Lectures*, vol. 4, 371. The verb "*impignorare*" may indicate Roman influence although only the forms "*pignerare*" or "*pignorare*" are found in the sources up to Justinian – see Heumann-Seckel, *Handlexikon zu den Quellen des römischen Rechts*, (9th ed., Jena, 1926, reprinted Graz, 1971), s.h.v.

a pledge are treated separately for moveables and immoveables.[10] It is also clear that at latest by the middle of the fifteenth century express pledges were falling out of use because it was the common practice to grant real security over land not by an express pledge but by a grant of the land to the creditor subject to a reversion in favour of the debtor allowing him to redeem the land on payment or satisfaction of the creditor. Such a grant of land subject to a reversion was still referred to as a wadset,[11] but it was on the face of it an absolute grant, while security over moveables was apparently still granted by express pledge.[12]

Craig[13] does suggest a Roman derivation for reversions observing that all the essentials appear in C.4.54.2 (Alexander, A.D. 222), a case of a sale with a clause of redemption, and it is possible that Muirhead had in mind what Craig says and not, or not only, his own knowledge of *fiducia* when referring to the parallels between the Scots and Roman law as including security by an *ex facie* absolute disposition. Craig himself does admit that the word reversion is not found in the Roman texts but he is clear in his opinion that reversions are derived from Roman law. A simple borrowing seems unlikely in the light of what has been said but the possibility of indirect Roman inspiration for the development of wadsets by reversion cannot be dismissed out of hand. The use of Roman law in the course of its reception into other systems was not confined to application of the texts in accordance with their original circumstances. But, as noted, there is not a great deal to suggest that in Roman law itself sales with a clause of redemption were in fact used as a means of creating real security. As the general tendency of the later law was to protect the debtor against potentially oppressive use of the creditor's position and *ex facie* absolute transfers as a form of real security tend to favour creditors there was no reason to encourage them. Sales with clauses of redemption are not prominent in the sources in any context never mind in this context and Craig may simply have assumed derivation from the existence of a parallel.

Heritable Securities

Accepting, then, that Scots law distinguishes between heritable and moveable real securities and taking heritable securities first, it seems

---

10 *Regiam*, III.3 and 4 and III.5 and 6 respectively (*A.P.S.* edition, III.4 and 5 and III.6 and 7).

11 See, for example, Erskine, *Inst.*, 2,8,4 and Hume, *Lectures*, vol. 4, 372.

12 Cf. *The Acts of the Lords Auditors of Causes and Complaints*, ed. T. Thomson (Edinburgh, 1839) [hereafter *Acts of the Lords Auditors*], 65 (11 June 1478), 87 (14 October 1479).

13 Craig, 2,6,2 and 3; see also W. Ross, *Lectures on the History and Practice of the Law of Scotland relative to Conveyancing and Legal Diligence* (2nd ed., Edinburgh, 1822) [hereafter Ross, *Lectures*], vol. 2, 330. Citing no texts, Ross says that "feigned or simulate sales were also known among the Romans for security of debt. The creditor possessed in the character of a purchaser till the debt was paid, and then reinstated the borrower in his right".

that Scots law quite early moved away from the use of express grants in security over land to grants of the land subject to a right of redemption. This development, the creation of the wadset by sale under reversion, was bound to take Scots law into some different paths from Roman law. But even at a stage where an express pledge was apparently normal there are differences from as well as similarities to Roman law, quite apart from the inevitable differences resulting from the use of a different legal procedure for the constitution of security. Starting with the similarities, from the account in *Regiam* it appears that a wadset of land was constituted by delivery of sasine to the creditor; that the land wadset was to be kept safe until the creditor was satisfied;[14] that it was to be returned immediately once the creditor had been satisfied; and that the fruits might be set off against the debt due.[15] All this accords with the Roman law of pledge (and hypothec) as does the rule that a mere agreement to constitute a pledge gives the creditor no action on the pledge, which has still to be constituted by delivery of the object pledged to the creditor,[16] but whether there is derivation from Roman law is another matter. Certainly the name of the institution is not Roman.

Against the similarities must be set the differences. For one thing it seems clear that there was nothing corresponding to the Roman hypothec in the sense of an agreement giving rise to a security right without possession. *Regiam,* in fact, following *Glanvill,* says that the royal courts are not concerned with such agreements or with the priority of different creditors who each claim to have an agreement to have security granted to them over the same thing.[17] Then, where expenses were incurred in maintaining the thing there was no general rule on who should bear them as there was in Roman law where this obligation fell on the debtor; the question of expenses is left to the agreement of the parties.[18] Again, an agreement that the creditor may take the fruits

---

14 According to *Regiam* III.3.2 (*A.P.S.,* III.4) the creditor is liable if the thing deteriorates through his fault where the wadset is for a fixed period (the text refers to moveables but in III.5.5 (*A.P.S.,* III.6) it is indicated that in general the rules are the same for moveables and immoveables); in III.4.3 (*A.P.S.,* III.5) there is no express reference to fault where there has been deterioration and the wadset was for an indefinite period but liability for fault only may be implied. It was held in *Foulis v. Cognerlie* (1566) Balfour, *Practicks,* vol. 1, 196 that liability was for fault and this is the established rule.

15 See *Regiam* III.2.3; III.3.1 and 2; III.4.3; III.6; III.5.1 and 2 (*A.P.S.,* III, 3 to 6).

16 *Regiam* III.4.4 to 6 (*A.P.S.,* III.5).

17 *Regiam* III.4.4 to 6 (*A.P.S.,* III.5). Presumably an action might have lain in an ecclesiastical court for breach of faith in such a case. That is indicated in Balfour's rendering "Anent redemptioun of landis", c. ix, in the second paragraph, *Practicks,* vol. 2, 447. Making reference to *Regiam* he says that claims of breach of faith are pursued "befoir the spiritual Judge" and that disputes between creditors over competing wadsets are not a matter for "the temporal Judge".

18 *Regiam,* III.3.3 (*A.P.S.,* III.4).

rather than setting them off against the debt, which is described as a *mortuum vadium*, a mortgage or dead wad, and which would correspond to the arrangement described as *antichresis* in Roman law, when fruits were taken in place of interest, is said not to be prohibited; but at the same time it is described as a kind of usury.[19] Here the Canon law prohibition of usury affects the arrangement and it is interesting to note that in the wadset of 1372 referred to above the creditor is allowed to take the fruits and rents but this is said to be for service, advice and assistance given – which looks very like an evasion or an attempt at evasion of the Canon law rule against usury. Then, a thing wadset for a fixed period may be forfeited to the creditor on non-satisfaction of the debt if the parties so agree,[20] whereas in the later Roman law such a forfeiture clause, *lex commissoria in pignoribus*, was prohibited as bearing too heavily on debtors.[21] Finally, if there is no such agreement the creditor may dispose of the thing with the authority of the court after allowing the debtor the opportunity of satisfying the debt. Up to a point this corresponds with the Justinianic Roman law but there is not the same elaborate procedure to deal with the possibility that no buyer may be found as there was in Roman law.[22] The impression given over all is that the writer may well have been familiar with Roman law and may well have had it in mind as the background to his exposition but he takes little from Roman law by way of actually moulding the law. Scots law is brought into contact with Roman law, through Canon law, but is not yet deeply affected by it if it is affected at all.

Once wadsets in the form of dispositions subject to rights of reversion became usual the question of protection of the debtor against improper disposal by the creditor arose. The first legislative intervention was the Act 1449 c.19[23] which provided that where the wadsetter had granted leases continuing after redemption "for halfe maill or neir thereby" they should not stand; they should be effective only if granted "for the verry maill or neir theirby". The passing of the Leases Act 1449,

---

19   *Regiam*, III.5.2 to 4 (*A.P.S.*, III.6).
20   *Regiam* III.3.4 and 5 (*A.P.S.*, III.4). In later practice such an irritancy was not necessarily enforced according to its terms, out of consideration for debtors – see Stair, 2,10,6.
21   C.8.34(35).3 (Constantine and Constantius, A.D. 326).
22   *Regiam* III.3.6ff. (*A.P.S.*, III.4). Cf. C.8.33(34).3 (Justinian, A.D. 530) for the Roman procedure.
23   4° ed. c.18 (the language is modernised from the *A.P.S.* version; in the Leases Act 1449 (the Act 1449 c.18, *A.P.S.*, ii, 35–36, c.6) it forms a clause of exception to the main provision protecting tenants in case of alienation of the land. The Act assumes that such a lease is in principle valid as it would be if the creditor had title to the land on the face of it. Balfour, *Practicks*, "Anent redemptiouns", c.vii (vol. 2, 446) cites a case, *Dalrimpil* v. *Kennedie*, 26 February 1567 to the effect that in principle the holder of land under reversion may not set tacks to begin and endure after redemption of the lands although, if there are existing tacks, he may set others in conformity with them.

with which this provision on wadsets is connected, may itself reflect a need to protect tenants against introduction of the Roman principle that a lease as a personal contract was binding only on the landlord and not on a purchaser from the landlord ("sale breaks hire" as it is sometimes expressed). It may thus reflect a Roman influence which from the point of view of tenants was malign.[24] The provision that a lease by a wadsetter is invalid if it is for half the true rent or less may also reflect Roman influence, as it suggests the application of the Roman rule of *laesio enormis* which is vouched for sale in the later empire.[25] In the civilian development of Roman law the rule on *laesio enormis* is commonly extended to lease (and other *bonae fidei* contracts),[26] and it seems too much of a coincidence that the statute corresponds with this extension if there was no consciousness of the Roman, or civilian, rules. There is no express reference to Roman law in the statute, however.

Again, because a reversion was a personal right it could not in principle be asserted against the creditor's disponee unless it was incorporated into the creditor's infeftment so that third parties had notice of it and so notice of the limitation on the creditor's right. Protection for the debtor where the creditor's infeftment was *ex facie* absolute was given by the Act 1469 c.27.[27] This is said to be passed "As touching new inventiones and selling of landes be Charter and saising...", implying that *ex facie* absolute wadsets were relatively new and it allowed the debtor to assert his reversionary right against third parties who had acquired from the creditor. The right to do so was given without insisting that he should have made his reversionary right public by registration. To this extent there is a parallel with the Roman hypothec and a parallel weakness in that third parties may not have notice of the debtor's reversionary right but there is no indication in the legislation that the idea of making reversions into real rights without publication came from Roman law. The 1469 Act did provide for registration of reversions but it was registration for preservation in case the debtor's reversion should be lost, not registration for publication. What would now be seen as an essential safeguard for third parties,

---

24 The principle was, however, restrictively interpreted by medieval Romanists, see E.J.H. Schrage, "Zur mittelalterlichen Geschichte des Grundsatzes 'Kauf bricht nicht Miete'", *Das römische Recht im Mittelalter*, ed. E.J.H. Schrage (Wege der Forschung, vol. 635, Darmstadt, 1987), 281.

25 It appears in two texts C.4.44.2 (A.D. 285) and 8 (A.D. 293) both attributed to Diocletian and Maximian but it is not clear that it is their work – see, for example, A. Watson, "The Hidden Origins of Enorm Lesion", (1981) 2 *Jour. Leg. Hist.* 186.

26 See, for example, Azo, *Summa Codicis, de rescindenda venditione* (Pavia, 1506, as reprinted in *Corpus Glossatorum Juris Civilis,* ed. M. Viora, Turin 1966), vol. 2, 156b – *quod dixi in venditione ad quemlibet contractum bone fidei extenditur;* J. Voet, *Commentarius ad Pandectas* (The Hague, 1734), 18.5.13.

27 12° ed.; c.28 4°; *A.P.S.,* ii, 94–95, c.3

registration of reversions for publication, was effectively provided only by the Registration Act 1617.[28] This Act did not apply to land in burghs so that there was no requirement of registration for publication in burghs at first but registration was extended to burghal land by the Act 1681 c.11.[29]

The Real Rights Act 1693[30] then simplified and improved the rules on priority as between real rights, including rights in security, by giving preference to rights according to their date and order of registration. The statutory provision follows the Roman principle of priority of security rights, *prior tempore, potior iure*,[31] but it is not clear that a specific desire to give effect to the Roman principle played any part in providing a motivation for the legislation. It can be explained as a rational development arising out of the general use of registration of deeds purporting to create real rights in land and the legislation applied to all real rights involving infeftment and not just to security rights. The general principle that infeftments took priority according to their dates was already established.[32]

A further, although earlier, statutory amendment of the law of heritable security was the Diligence Act 1661.[33] This, an extensive measure, among other things restricted the rights of proper wadsetters, that is, wadsetters who took the rents or fruits of land in place of interest as opposed to improper wadsetters who received interest on the debt for which security had been granted and who, if they received the rents or fruits, must set them off against the capital in so far as they exceeded the interest due. As well as making various other provisions in favour of both debtors and creditors the Diligence Act in effect permitted debtors who had granted proper wadsets to convert them into improper wadsets on which they need pay only the legal rate of interest, any surplus of the fruits or rents going to reduction of the debt. In substance this equated the position to the normal position in Roman law but the reason for statutory intervention on this matter is said to be that:

> ...some persons may have taken advantage of the late times and troubles, by taking and acquiring of proper Wodsets of Lands and others, exceeding the Annual-rent of the Sums lent upon the same; and providing neverthelesse, by the right of the foresaids Wodsets and expresse provisions therein, or by writ apart, that they should not be lyable to any hazard of the Fruits, Tennents, War or Troubles...

---

28 Act 1617 c. 16, 12° and 4° eds.; *A.P.S.*, iv, 545–47, c.16. The need was recognised before. For earlier attempts to provide for registration see L. Ockrent, *Land Rights: An Enquiry into the History of Registration for Publication in Scotland* (London, Edinburgh, Glasgow, 1942).
29 *A.P.S.*, viii, 248, c. 13.
30 Act 1693 c.13; *A.P.S.*, ix, 271, c.22
31 C.8.17(18).3(4) (Antoninus, A.D. 215).
32 See Stair, 4,35,8ff.
33 The Act 1661 c.62, *A.P.S.*, vii, 317–20, c.344.

The motive, therefore, does not seem to have been to bring Scots law into conformity with Roman law and it did not produce exact conformity.

Most of the litigation on heritable securities in the form of wadsets of lands in the period from the sixteenth to the beginning of the nineteenth century is recorded in Morison's *Dictionary* under the headings of redemption, reversion, rights in security and wadset, but with some cases appearing separately or additionally under the headings of irritancy and personal and real. Many of the cases are concerned with the various statutory provisions affecting heritable securities and do not involve reference to the Roman law of real security. Nevertheless it is clear that Roman law is there in the background. For example, problems are discussed in Roman terminology, if not necessarily using equivalent Roman concepts, as where attempts are made, generally with decreasing success, to insist on literal compliance with the terms of reversions on the ground that they are *stricti iuris*[34] or *strictissimi iuris*.[35]

Ross,[36] noting the use of Roman terminology, lays most of the blame for what he sees as the introduction of a stricter interpretation on Roman law – "when the Roman law became the law of the land, to the exclusion of our ancient customs, the analogy of the order of redemption to the *actio praescriptis verbis*, in which the party stood bound to precise and literal performance, was observed". He does not give the source of his reference to the *actio praescriptis verbis* although in its general application it was regarded as a *stricti iuris* action.[37] What he describes as "the minuteness of the stipulation itself", which he says was turned against the reverser seeking redemption, may seem more probable, with Roman law providing no more than what appeared to be an appropriate term to describe the strict interpretation. Again, in relation to a provision in a reversion that the debtor must repay the debt with his own money it is argued (successfully) that there is no objection to payment with borrowed money because in the case of a *mutuum* borrowed money becomes the property of the borrower.[38] The principle that a provision is to be interpreted in a way which gives it effect rather than in a way which will result in invalidity is cited.[39] Proper wadset is referred to as *antichresis*.[40] A knowledge and use of

---

34   *Ogilvie* v. — (1547) Mor. 13441; *Finlayson* v. *Wemyss* (1638) Mor. 13463.
35   *Grierson* v. *Gordon* (1630) Mor. 13455; *Earl of Glencairn* v. *Brisbane* (1677) Mor. 13477.
36   Ross, *Lectures*, vol. 2, 361–62.
37   A. Vinnius, *In Quattuor Libros Institutionum Imperialium Commentarius*, on *Inst.* 4.6.28, (Venice, 1768), vol. 2, 324.
38   *Lord Bargeny* v. *Ferguson* (1696) Mor. 13481.
39   *Livingston* v. *Earl of Calander* (1697) Mor. 13481.
40   *Urquhart* v. *Cheyne* (1666) Mor. 16525; *Heckford* v. *Ker* (1675) Mor. 16529 – both instances are from Dirleton and may represent a display of his learning.

Roman law in general is therefore assumed as normal in the discussion of the relevant legal problems.

In some cases, however, there is a more specific use of the principles of the Roman law of security as where it is held that the security affects the whole property until full payment of the debt has been made.[41] It is accepted that once a debt has been paid the security right falls.[42] In *Brown* v. *Storie*[43] there is a learned discussion of whether a creditor who has been granted a power of sale of land by the debtor may proceed to sell at his own hand without obtaining judicial authority. Introduction of a power of sale at the creditor's own hand appears to have been a novelty at a time when the wadset was being replaced as a common form of heritable security by the heritable bond, the immediate ancestor of the bond and disposition in security,[44] and this would account for the full discussion. As well as Scottish authority the parties invoke Brunnemann, Heineccius, Perezius, Vinnius and Voet, arguing on the one hand that in Roman law the praetor's authority was needed and on the other that this was so only where there was no express agreement. It is ultimately held that sale by the creditor is permissible without judicial authority and this would seem to be a victory for Roman law over an older tradition which required judicial authority in all cases, a tradition which is also reflected in discussions of pledge of moveables. There is, then, evidence both of general use of Roman law and of specific use of the Roman law of real security in the reported cases but it must be said that the harvest of such cases in which it is clear that the Roman law of real security was followed is not abundant.

In the nineteenth century, which saw a major simplification of the almost incredibly cumbersome forms of constitution of heritable securities, along with other conveyancing reforms,[45] the only context in

---

41   *Earls of Loudoun and Glasgow* v. *Lord Ross* (1734) Mor. 14114; *Creditors of Auchinbreck* v. *Lockwood* (1758) Mor. 14129.

42   *Governor and Company of the Bank of Scotland* v. *Governor and Company of the Bank of England* (1781) Mor. 14121 – the principle was held not to apply in the circumstances; *Trustees of Brough's Creditors* v. *Heirs of Selby* (1794) Mor. 14118.

43   (1790) Mor. 14125

44   Ross, *Lectures*, vol. 2, 372ff. gives an account of the development of the heritable bond having remarked, at 371, that since 1745 wadsets "have gone much out of fashion" and, at 372, that wadsets had been "of late years revived for the purpose of creating and multiplying voters, in the elections of our county members of Parliament". Hume in his *Lectures*, vol. 4, 370, makes similar remarks in the introduction to his treatment of wadsets and goes on to give a separate account of heritable bonds, at 386ff. He states that a power of sale is normal (at 393) but still records a doubt whether the conveyance following on a sale may be granted by the creditor alone (at 394).

45   See for an account of the background W.M. Gordon, "George Joseph Bell – Law Commissioner", *Obligations in Context. Essays in Honour of Professor D.M. Walker*, ed. A.J. Gamble (Edinburgh, 1990), 79.

which Roman law is still cited in relation to heritable security appears to be exercise of the power of sale, and in particular purchase by or on behalf of the selling creditor. There is direct reference in *Faulds* v. *Corbet*[46] and indirect reference in *Taylor* v. *Watson*[47] where the fuller discussion in *York Buildings Co.* v. *Mackenzie*,[48] with substantial citation of Roman law, is among the authorities relied on. But it is noticeable that English authorities are also relied on both in these and in later cases on sale of the security subjects such as *Davidson* v. *Scott.*[49] The paucity of references to Roman law is partly to be explained by the extent to which litigation arose out of the statutory provisions on heritable security. Some of these were old, in particular the Bankruptcy Act 1696.[50] Others were new, in particular the conveyancing legislation with its provisions for short forms of bonds and dispositions in security. On such relatively narrow questions arising from statute Roman law and the Roman law of real security was not of much direct assistance.

To sum up, it may be said that the Scots law of heritable securities does offer parallels with Roman law but it is far from clear that this is a result of borrowing from Roman law. It seems more accurate to say that Scots law has not so much followed Roman law in the matter of heritable security as drawn upon it when the Roman law has been found helpful. What has been drawn on has been not only the law of real security but a wider pool of ideas made available by study of Roman law. It seems probable that more use could have been made of Roman ideas but much of the law has been founded on conveyancing practice and on legislation. Roman influence has, therefore, tended to be confined to certain fundamental questions; discussion and litigation are dominated by questions arising specifically out of the practice and the legislation.

Securities over Moveables

Security rights over moveables are dealt with in *Regiam* in much the same way as immoveables, as already noted. In fact, the treatment of security rights begins with moveables and the similarities to and differences from Roman law referred to above[51] emerge from the detailed rules which are stated in relation to moveables granted in security. The same question arises, therefore, how far the similarities represent a borrowing from Roman law, accepting that the expositor seems to have been familiar with Roman law. The moveables which are envisaged as the object of security rights are corporeal moveables. Only pledge, referred to as

---

46   (1859) 21 D. 587.
47   (1846) 8 D. 400.
48   (1793) Mor. 13367, rev'd (1795) 3 Pat. App. 378.
49   1915 S.C. 924.
50   The Act 1696 c.5, *A.P.S.*, x, 33–34, c.5. Among other things this provided that a security was good only for obligations contracted before infeftment was given. *Ex facie* absolute dispositions were used to evade this rule and the rule that a security must be for a definite amount.
51   at 161–62.

vadium,[52] is recognised and *Regiam* can be seen as the starting point for what becomes a basic principle of the Scots law of security over corporeal moveables, that the creditor must be given possession of the articles pledged, a principle which contrasts sharply with Roman law.[53] The Scottish principle is explained by later writers as being for the security of commerce so that persons dealing with a potential debtor can assume that he has full title to goods still in his possession and so can safely transact on the basis that no latent real rights will be asserted against an acquirer. The contrast with Roman law is noted as is the very limited number of cases in which security is allowed by way of hypothec, whether legal or conventional, such as the landlord's hypothec or bonds of bottomry.[54] Bell[55] specifically refers to Voet for the proposition that a pledge creditor loses his security if he returns the pledge to the debtor.[56] He also includes Voet among the various continental authorities whom he cites for the proposition that hypothecs are generally restricted in continental states in the interests of commerce.[57] Roman and civilian principles are challenged in this area and the principle that possession must be given to the pledge creditor in order to constitute a pledge effective against third parties is supported because it is not confined to Scotland, but is found elsewhere despite Roman influence.

It is also noted by writers as a rule of Scots law, although it is not always noted as a divergence from Roman law, that a pledge creditor may not sell the pledge at his own hand. The earlier authorities state that judicial authority is always needed, whether by doing diligence or by applying to the court for warrant to sell.[58] In the tenth edition of Bell's *Principles,* s. 1364 (but not in s. 207) the editor has added that sale is allowed also "by special agreement"[59] and no reason is given for

---

52   In the fifteenth century records articles pledged are still said to be "laid in wad" - see, e.g., *Acts of the Lords Auditors*, 65 (11 June 1478), 87 (14 October 1479).
53   It is doubtful whether any significance can be attached to the references to hypothec of moveables and immoveables contained in documents in the *Selkirk Protocol Books 1511-1547*, edd. T. Maley and W. Elliot (Stair Society, 40, Edinburgh, 1993), C79, C223, and (?) C115.
54   See Stair, 1,13,14; 4,25,1; Erskine, *Inst.*, 3,1,34; Bankton, 1,17,3; Bell, *Prin.* s. 1385; *Comm.*, ii, 24-25.
55   *Comm.*, ii, 22.
56   See on this matter *North-Western Bank Ltd.* v. *Poynter, Son and Macdonalds* (1894) 22 R. (H.L.) 1, discussed below.
57   *Comm.*, ii, 24-5.
58   See Stair, 1,13,11 and 13; Erskine, *Inst.*, 3,1,33; Bankton, 1,17,4; Bell, *Comm.*, ii, 22; *Prin.*, s. 207 and (4th ed. 1839) s. 207.
59   No specific authority is cited for the change. Presumably it was based on commercial practice. In *Moore* v. *Gledden* (1869) 7 M. 1016, which is cited without direct reference to the editorial change in the text, Lord Neaves does say at 1020 that there is no power of sale implied in pledge without special stipulation. In the case itself a provision in a contract that contractors' plant brought on to railway company's property should become the

the earlier restriction other than that it is the custom of Scotland. The rule implies that the giving of security is regarded more as a means of putting pressure on the debtor than as providing a means of recovery of the debt through sale of the security subjects. The principle that judicial authority is needed for sale does provide a protection to the debtor which accords with the general approach of Justinianic Roman law although it is not fully in conformity with it. Justinian, in the absence of agreement, allowed sale after formal notice or judicial decree, with a very elaborate scheme for acquisition by the creditor if no purchaser could be found.[60] That Roman law did allow sale at the creditor's own hand if there was specific agreement that he might sell seems to be overlooked when comparisons are made with Roman law in the treatments of pledge before the editorial change to Bell's *Principles* and Roman law is not referred to in support of the change.

There is little reported litigation on pledge before the nineteenth century when commercial practice introduced new applications of the idea of pledge which are linked with the increasing use of commercial paper and the increasing importance of incorporeal moveable property, and other moveable property, as a form of wealth. The new applications included the common use of pledge of documents, assignations of incorporeal property in security,[61] pledge by intimation to an independent custodier and pledge in which delivery takes a more sophisticated form than handing over the thing. In dealing with these situations Roman law is referred to but the judges not infrequently give the impression that they are not wholly equal to the task of using Roman law effectively to help them to sound decisions, perhaps because they are not sufficiently in command of Roman law.

The guiding principle that there must be some overt transfer into the hands of the creditor in order to constitute a security right over moveables is maintained very firmly in the cases. The tone is set by the opinion of Lord President Blair in *Broughton* v. *Aitchison*,[62] a case

------

property of the railway company and could be sold if necessary was treated as creating a good security right, provided that possession was acquired by the railway company, but apparently as a pledge. Presumably the provision was seen as a kind of pledge because it was intended to create security. The main issue was whether possession had been acquired by the railway company so as to constitute a security right.

60 C.8.33(34).3 (Justinian, A.D. 530)
61 Assignation in the form of a *procuratio in rem suam*, with intimation to the debtor, seems to be of Roman origin. The Transmission of Moveable Property (Scotland) Act 1862 (25 & 26 Vict. c.85) provided a simpler form.
62 15th Nov., 1809, F.C. The case concerned a delivery order addressed to a warehouseman who was employed by the transferor. Later cases, including *Anderson* v. *McCall* (1866) 4 M. 765, make it clear that to be effective a delivery order must be addressed to an independent warehouseman but the majority in *Broughton* seem to have regarded the employee as employed partly by the transferee as he was paid to turn over the grain in question to keep it in good condition.

dealing with transfer by intimation to a custodier who was also an employee of the transferor; his opinion is reported at considerably greater length than the opinions of the majority who prevailed (by four to three) in the case itself. Lord President Blair was primarily concerned with the principle of delivery in the transfer of ownership but he is reported as saying that "...if the property of moveables could be transferred *retenta possessione*, there was no reason why a pledge, *or hypothec* [emphasis supplied], might not be constituted in the same way, and to create it the proprietor had nothing more to do than to write an order of delivery to his own servant". Presumably in saying "pledge or hypothec" he meant to imply that "hypothec" would be the more correct term to describe such an arrangement but the statement reads rather oddly.

The principle that delivery is necessary to constitute a security right in corporeal moveables is then commonly but rather inappropriately supported by citation of the Roman maxim *traditionibus, non nudis pactis, dominia rerum transferuntur*, (ownerships of things are transferred by delivery, not by bare agreements), a maxim which is made to apply to all real rights.[63] This maxim, as its wording shows, applied in Roman law to ownership but not to the constitution of real security but it could be used (or misused) to bolster the requirement of delivery for constitution of a security right in so far as Scots law required that security over moveables should in general be constituted by way of pledge and not by way of hypothec. It could also be made relevant to constitution of security by way of intimated delivery order in that in *Hamilton* v. *Western Bank*[64] it was held on appeal that such a delivery order necessarily transferred the ownership of the goods held in store, at least where the store was a bonded warehouse. The necessity is not obvious, except perhaps on the facts of the case, and the more reasonable view that the right created depends on the intentions of the parties is supported by *North-Western Bank Ltd.* v. *Poynter, Son and Macdonalds*.[65] It would be difficult for anyone with an understanding of Roman law to come to any other conclusion as possession can certainly be held through third parties in Roman law and whether

---

63   W.M. Gloag and J.M. Irvine, *Law of Rights in Security Heritable and Moveable including Cautionary Obligations* (Edinburgh, 1897), 188; *Anderson* v. *McCall* (1866) 4 M. 765 per Lord Justice-Clerk Inglis at 769–70. To be fair to Gloag and Irvine they, at 187–88, are critical of the rigidity of the Scots law resulting from this approach.

64   (1856) 19 D. 152. At first instance civilian authority was used to support the view that there was a pledge which would seem more in accord with the parties' intentions.

65   (1894) 22 R.(H.L.) 1. See A.F. Rodger, "Pledge of Bills of Lading in Scots Law", 1971 *J.R.* 193, criticising *Hamilton and Hayman* v. *McLintock* 1907 S.C. 936. He is also critical of the decision in *North-Western Bank* itself in so far as it weakens the principle that pledge depends on physical possession by the creditor. See also G.L. Gretton, "Pledge, Bills of Lading, Trusts and Property Law", 1990 *J.R.* 23 on both points.

possession or ownership is given by delivery of possession depends on the *causa* or basis on which delivery is made.

The various cases in which attempts were made to create security without a clear delivery actually into the hands of the creditor are surveyed in Gloag and Irvine[66] and it is probably sufficient for the purposes of this article to note the difficulty which the courts had in admitting that security had effectively been created where the goods were left in the hands of the debtor and in some measure under his control. The difficulty was felt even where Roman law could give clear assistance and was referred to. One of the cases which caused most anxiety was that in which the debtor purported to hold under a new subordinate title such as lease or hire, delivery in the form of *constitutum possessorium*. This is certainly recognised in Justinianic Roman law, despite some doubts about the classical law. It was even more clearly recognised, and even extended, in the subsequent civilian tradition as a means of transferring ownership and possession, although there is admittedly some suspicion of its use in security transactions, as noted below. So far as transfer of ownership in Scots law is concerned, in *Orr's Tr.* v. *Tullis*[67] it was held that printing machinery purchased from a tenant by his landlord and leased back to him had been delivered so that it belonged to the landlord and did not form part of the tenant's bankrupt estate but there seems to be no instance of a comparable transaction being recognised as creating a security right.

The opportunity of doing so has also been missed in more recent cases involving hire-purchase back to an owner seeking credit on the security of goods which he already owns.[68] Part of the reason for missing the opportunity would seem to be that on the facts the parties involved in the relevant cases did not make a sufficiently serious effort to show that there was a real change in their legal relationships with the thing offered in security – if indeed there was such a change and the deals in question were less shady than some of them appear to have been. It is also true that free use of *constitutum possessorium*, in the form of a clause stating that possession was now held by the acquirer, was viewed with suspicion as a means of constituting security rights over moveables in the period of the *usus modernus pandectarum*[69] on the principle that *donner et retenir ne vaut* or that *mobilia non habent*

---

66   *Rights in Security, cit. sup.*, n.63, 188ff
67   (1870) 8 M. 936.
68   *Scottish Transit Trust Ltd.* v. *Scottish Land Cultivators Ltd.* 1955 S.C. 254; *G. and C. Finance Corporation* v. *Brown* 1961 S.L.T. 408; *Ladbroke Leasing (South West) Ltd.* v. *Reekie Plant Ltd.* 1983 S.L.T. 155 – although there are references to possible use of symbolical delivery to indicate a change of possession. This device, which seems no more than a device, would not be necessary if *constitutum possessorium* were recognised.
69   See W.M. Gordon, *Studies in the Transfer of Property by Traditio* (Aberdeen, 1969), 186 n.3, referring to J. Biermann, *Traditio ficta* (1891), 318-19; J. Voet, *Commentarius ad Pandectas*, 20.1.12.

sequelam (moveables cannot be followed) but Scots law has not accepted either of these principles, or at least has not accepted them in their full rigour. The real issue is whether there has been a genuine transaction when a *constitutum possessorium* takes the form of the creation of a holding on a subordinate title. While suspicion may be in order if a creditor conveniently acquires a security right shortly before his debtor's bankruptcy it does not follow that any transaction which could be used fraudulently must be treated automatically as fraudulent when it has a proper commercial function, given that there are means of setting aside transactions which ought to be set aside as involving prejudice to other creditors.

Rejection of the use of *constitutum possessorium* as a means of constituting a security right is in fact inconsistent with the recognition of hire-purchase, which functionally allows the creation of security without possession,[70] but was recognised in the later nineteenth century as an effective means of protecting the interests of a seller until full payment of the price.[71] In the relevant cases it was in the first place quite properly recognised that an owner who grants out a moveable on a limited title which does not imply a power of disposal does not thereby authorise the taker to dispose of the property by way of pledge or sale. It was subsequently recognised that so long as the hire-purchaser was not bound to buy he or she was not a buyer in possession with the consent of the seller and so enabled to dispose of the property under the Factors Acts or the Sale of Goods Act,[72] and so effectively the seller had security until the buyer chose to exercise his right to buy by paying the balance due. But if hire-purchase is acceptable when a thing is being acquired it is difficult to see any good reason for rejecting it when an owner is genuinely seeking to raise money on security of what he already owns.

A technical difficulty in the way of accepting *constitutum possessorium* in security transactions has been the existence of s.61(4) of the Sale of Goods Act 1893 (now s.62(4) of the Sale of Goods Act 1979). This was enacted to prevent the use of sale as a means of constituting security by *ex facie* absolute transfer of ownership without delivery when the Sale of Goods Act made it possible to transfer ownership by agreement of the parties to a sale. It would be kind to assume that s.61(4) was enacted on the considered view that the recognition of hire-purchase had caused enough damage to the principle of giving publicity to security rights by insisting on a visible change of possession. The more probable reason is that the issue was not thought through and that s.61(4) was more in the nature of a knee-jerk reaction

---

70 See G.L. Gretton, "The Concept of Security", *A Scots Conveyancing Miscellany. Essays in Honour of Professor J.M. Halliday*, ed. D.J. Cusine (Edinburgh, 1987), 126.
71 *Murdoch* v. *Greig* (1889) 16 R. 396.
72 *Helby* v. *Matthews* [1895] A.C. 471.

to the possibility of the creation of security without transfer of possession, based on the idea that the principle of requiring transfer of possession was of unquestionable value.

The result, consciously reached or otherwise, appears to be that it is in order for an owner to obtain what is functionally a security right by parting with possession of a moveable while still retaining his ownership but it is not in order for someone who has (physical) possession of a moveable to use that moveable as security by giving up one title of possession and retaining the moveable on a subordinate title. Thus it is acceptable for an owner to let a moveable on hire-purchase, using it as security for payment of the hire and ultimately the purchase price if the hire-purchaser proceeds to complete the purchase. It is also now recognised as acceptable to use a retention of title clause to obtain security for payment of the purchase price of a moveable and even of other sums due by the purchaser.[73] But it is not acceptable to offer something which one owns as security by transferring it to the creditor and taking it back on hire-purchase unless it is physically handed over or, possibly, symbolically handed over.[74] A symbolical transfer seems a rather primitive idea compared with *constitutum possessorium* and it is difficult to see what difference it would make to the facts. The physical situation of the moveable is not affected by the order in which transactions are entered into and a businessman nowadays would be naive indeed if he believed that everything he saw in the possession of his potential debtor belonged to him unencumbered and would be available to his creditors in a bankruptcy. Even to use *constitutum possessorium* is in contradiction with Roman law's ready admission of hypothec but it recognises the principle that possession must be given to the creditor in so far as that principle has value.

To sum up, with regard to security over moveables, Scots law has diverged quite notably from Roman law, although in the matter of the power of sale it has come closer to it again. Roman law has been followed only to a limited extent and full use has not been made of the possibilities which ideas derived from Roman law could offer to reconcile commercial practice with legal principle. As in the case of heritable security Roman law appears to have been used rather than followed. Arguably it has not been used enough.

Use of Roman Law

The first point to be made with regard to continued use of Roman law is a general one, namely, that it is not enough to refer to Roman law as it might now be understood by a modern Romanist. That distorts the influence which Roman law had in the past by ignoring what was made

---

73   *Armour* v. *Thyssen Edelstahlwerke A.G.* 1990 S.L.T. 891.
74   *Scottish Transit Trust Ltd.* v. *Scottish Land Cultivators Ltd.* 1955 S.C. 254 *per* Lord Carmont at 268; *Ladbroke Leasing (South West) Ltd.* v. *Reekie Plant Ltd.* 1983 S.L.T. 155 *per* Lord Grieve at 158.

of the texts in the development after Justinian. The civilian development must also be considered in assessing what Roman law meant to
those who did refer to it when its application was under consideration
from the fifteenth century onwards. If Roman law is to be used most
profitably, therefore, that use should be based on a sound knowledge
both of the Roman law of antiquity and of the civilian development
based on the *Corpus Iuris Civilis*. But the use made should also be a
critical one. Roman law has never been more than persuasive authority
and so selective use of Roman law is perfectly permissible. Such use is
use in the spirit in which Roman law was applied when it was more frequently cited than it generally is today. It is not enough merely to cite
civilian views as views to be followed. If the civilian development has
diverged from what appears to have been the law of the *Corpus Iuris* as
it was intended to be applied the rationale of such divergence must be
explored.

But Scots law is not bound to follow any particular understanding
of Roman law. There is, therefore, no necessity to follow Roman law as
it was understood in the past if this produces a result that now seems
unsatisfactory. Equally there is no necessity to follow Roman law as it is
now understood unless this can produce a satisfactory result. But it is a
fundamental misunderstanding of the use of Roman law in the past and
an undue narrowing of the potential scope of Roman law to reject a
civilian development because it does not correspond to what Roman
law is now understood to be. Roman law and its civilian development
are a rich heritage available to be drawn upon. That heritage can be and
should be drawn upon as a source of ideas, to be critically assessed for
their continuing usefulness. In this way Roman law can still be used
and profitably used in the spirit in which it was used to assist in building up Scots law in the past.

So far as heritable security is concerned the detailed statutory provisions now made for standard securities probably mean that Roman
law will rarely be called on to help solve specific problems. The fundamental principles have already been built into the new provisions in
the main, based as these are on accumulated experience of earlier
forms of real security, and the problems which arise are likely to be
problems of statutory interpretation. In the case of moveables, quite
apart from any radical change which might result from A.L. Diamond's
review of security interests and the consultation paper now issued by
the Department of Trade and Industry,[75] there is scope for consideration how useful it is to insist on possession to constitute a security
right. Roman law may not provide a model of a satisfactory law of real
security (except in identifying types of security right) but the deficiencies of the Roman law of real security which are noted would seem to

---

75   A.L. Diamond, *A Review of Security Interests in Property* (H.M.S.O., 1989)
     and the consultation paper by the Department of Trade and Industry
     referred to in n.4 above.

result at least as much from the introduction of privileged security rights as from the recognition of security rights without possession as such. Suspicion of hypothecs can go too far. Even if possession is insisted on, Roman law has something to teach on a more sophisticated use of the concept of possession and on the distinction between a pledge and a transfer of ownership in security and there would still seem to be a place for these forms of security right in any new system.

8. OWNERS AND NEIGHBOURS: FROM ROME TO SCOTLAND

By DAVID JOHNSTON

Seventeenth and eighteenth century Scottish cases display a bewildering diversity of views on an owner's right to make unrestricted use of his own property. Some cases state only that no substance must be discharged onto a neighbour's land (*immittere*);[1] others recognise that restriction together with another, *aemulatio vicini*;[2] another mentions *aemulatio vicini* and servitudes;[3] another *aemulatio vicini* and public law;[4] and another still *aemulatio vicini*, servitudes and public nuisance.[5] The diversity cannot be explained as a historical development. But it shows an extraordinary concern at that time with exploring the bounds within which an owner can legitimately exploit his property. The origins of some of these restrictions on ownership are Roman. This essay attempts to explore those origins, and the shaping of Scots law by the adoption of some elements of Roman law and the rejection of others. It also suggests some factors which may have been responsible for the different fates of these Roman institutions in Scots law.

I The Roman Background

(a) Classical and Justinianic law

Roman law provided an owner concerned by his neighbour's activities with a range of remedies. Three of these will be discussed in some detail. In advance, two other remedies should at least be noted. The first is liability under the *lex Aquilia*. Such evidence as there is indicates that there would be no liability under the *lex Aquilia* where any harm done was harm resulting from the normal use of property.[6] So, for example,

---

1   *Mayor of Berwick* v. *Laird of Hayning* (1661) Mor. 12772; *Hall* v. *Corbet* (1698) Mor. 12775; *Gray* v. *Maxwell* (1762) Mor. 12800. This also appears in the form that there must be no prejudice to a neighbour's land going beyond the accidental: *Mayor of Berwick, cit.*; *Mags. of Dumfries* v. *Heritors on the Water of Leith* (1705) Mor. 12776.
2   *Brodie* v. *Cadel* (1707) 4 B.S. 660; *Fairly* v. *Earl of Eglinton* (1744) Mor. 12780.
3   *Gordon* v. *Grant* (1756) Mor. 7356.
4   *Kinloch* v. *Robertson* (1756) Mor. 13163.
5   *Ralston* v. *Pettigrew* (1768) Mor. 12808.
6   P.B.H. Birks, "Cooking the Meat: Aquilian Liability for Hearths and Ovens", (1985) 20 *Irish Jur.* 352–77.

Proculus refused an action to the proprietor of a house in a case where heat damage had been caused to a mutual wall by the neighbour's oven abutting the wall: his reasoning was not that no harm had been done, but that no harm had been wrongfully (*iniuria*) done.[7] The *lex Aquilia* accordingly had a severely limited application to neighbourhood disputes because its focus was on how reasonable or normal the use was rather than how harmful or intolerable it was to the victim.

The second of these remedies is *iniuria*. Labeo discussed the case of a neighbour who made smoke in his house *fumigandi causa*, purely to smoke out his neighbour. He was unwilling to allow an *actio iniuriarum*, while Iavolenus was prepared to do so, provided the intention to injure was proved.[8] Here it is enough to note, first, that proof of that intention would be a serious practical restriction on the availability of the remedy; and second, that the *actio iniuriarum* should in principle lie only if the offending acts are clearly directed at the owner *qua* person, rather than *qua* owner of property. Perhaps this was why Labeo refused it.

With these delictual remedies eliminated from further consideration, it remains to consider three property-related remedies. They (as well as the texts from the *Digest* discussed here) are selected for their significance for later law. This is not a comprehensive account of restrictions on ownership in Roman law.

(i) *damnum infectum*

This remedy concerned damage anticipated from a neighbouring building which was in danger of collapse. Through the praetor, the threatened neighbour could obtain a *cautio* from the proprietor of the ruinous property promising reimbursement for loss caused by its collapse.[9] There were various sanctions in the event of failure to cooperate.

The notion of *damnum* is discussed by Ulpian in book 81 of his commentary on the edict. He makes it clear that the *cautio* was not concerned with damage caused by the fault of an occupier;[10] nor was it concerned with damage caused by *damnum fatale* (to use a modern term) such as earthquake or flooding.[11] What it was concerned with was the case where a legitimate activity, such as building or excavation, caused damage to or on a neighbour's property.[12] The position was

---

7   Proculus, D.9.2.27.10 and *Collatio* 12.7.8; with Birks, *op. cit.*, 366.
8   D.47.10.44.
9   The terms of the *cautio* expressly covered loss in the event of collapse, breaking, excavation, and construction, in each case caused by defect in a building, place or work: O. Lenel, *Das Edictum Perpetuum*, (3rd ed., Leipzig, 1927), 551–52.
10   D.39.2.24.7; here the *lex Aquilia* would no doubt provide a remedy.
11   D.39.2.24.3 and 10.
12   J.M. Rainer, *Bau- und nachbarrechtliche Bestimmungen im klassischen römischen Recht*, (Graz, 1987), 113.

more complicated in the event that no direct physical damage was caused. This emerges from a series of texts in which Ulpian discusses the views of Trebatius and Proculus.

Trebatius is concerned with the case where one neighbour, digging on his own property, has cut off his neighbour's water supply. There is said to be no liability for *damnum infectum*: I cannot be regarded as having caused damage owing to a defect in my work where I have been using my own right (*ius*).[13] The reason for there being no liability is that the excavator was using his own right; that interpretation is confirmed by the citation from Proculus which follows: even if someone has given a *cautio* for *damnum infectum*, he will not be liable under it when he has done something *iure* on his own property.[14]

On the other hand, it emerges from Trebatius' discussion that excavation on one's own land to such a degree that the neighbour's wall collapsed did give rise to a liability under the *cautio damni infecti*. Accordingly, certain actings on one's own property were capable of giving rise to liability under the *cautio*. Where then does the borderline lie? It is true that, in the first case (cutting off water), no direct physical damage has been caused, while in the second (collapse) it has. But this cannot be the whole explanation, since Trebatius himself took the view that the blocking of somebody's light could amount to *damnum* for the purposes of the *cautio damni infecti*; and here too there is no direct physical damage.[15] While it seems odd to distinguish between deprivation of water and deprivation of light, it may be either that the second was regarded invariably as the more serious; or that, in the particular case in question, it was in fact the more serious. In any event, *damnum* in these circumstances appears to have been interpreted restrictively: Proculus distinguishes between being deprived of an existing benefit (to which there was actually no entitlement) and sustaining a loss. Probably only an act which obstructed light to a significant degree would be regarded as going too far, and as constituting *damnum*.[16]

To sum up. First, the liability for *damnum infectum* was a strict liability, but it was dependent on the *cautio* having been given in the first place; without it, a neighbour who suffered damage might well be without a remedy.[17] Second, a liability for *damnum infectum* was a liability for damage inflicted by a neighbour which went beyond a certain limit. In other words, a degree of reasonableness enters into the question whether I have suffered *damnum* at the hands of my neighbour or not.

---

13   D.39.2.24.12.
14   D.39.2.26.
15   D.39.2.25 (Paul, 78 *ad edictum*). It should be noted, however, that another passage in the *Digest* appears to suggest the opposite: D.8.2.9 (Ulpian, 53 *ad edictum*). But this text is to be understood as denying a pursuer the right to an action rather than recourse to the *cautio* for *damnum infectum*: see Rainer, *op. cit.*, n.12, 242–44.
16   Rainer, *op. cit.*, n.12, 124–26, 247–48.
17   D.39.2.6.

(ii) *Servitudes*

Servitudes were of some assistance in restricting neighbours' activities. But certain normal uses of property such as washing, lighting a fire, or walking could not be restrained by servitude.[18] The earliest urban servitudes were restricted essentially to water and light; they did not cover emissions of matter other than water. None the less, there are signs that at least some early jurists were willing to recognise that such things as smoke could be the subject of servitudes, provided they went beyond a certain degree.[19]

The best-known and certainly the most disputed text in this context deals with smoke emanating from a cheese-maker's premises.[20] Ulpian reports an opinion of Aristo that smoke cannot lawfully be discharged from a cheese shop into buildings higher up, unless they are subject to a servitude to this effect. Aristo also holds that it is not permissible to discharge water or any other substance from the higher onto the lower property, as a man is only permitted to carry out operations on his own property provided he discharges nothing onto the property of another; and the discharge of smoke is just like that of water. So the owner of the higher building can bring an action against the owner of the lower, asserting that he has no right to act in this way.[21]

There are certainly some peculiarities in this text, which at the least must have been much abbreviated.[22] In its Justinianic form the text warrants the conclusions that emissions of one sort or another from a neighbouring property could be the subject of an urban servitude; and that they could accordingly be restrained by an *actio negatoria*. So far, however, as classical Roman law is concerned, an owner was required to tolerate a certain amount of water or smoke before the point was reached at which he, on the one hand, could object to it in

---

18   D.8.5.8.6 and D.8.2.19*pr.*
19   Rainer, *op. cit.*, n.12, 104–6; L. Capogrossi Colognesi, *La struttura della proprietà e la formazione dei "iura praediorum" nell'età repubblicana* (Milan, 1976), 501ff., 511; A. Watson, *The Law of Property in the Later Roman Republic* (Oxford, 1968), 177–78.
20   D.8.5.8.5. (Ulpian, 17 *ad edictum*).
21   *Aristo...respondit non putare se ex taberna casiaria fumum in superiora aedificia iure immitti posse, nisi ei rei servitutem talem admittit. idemque ait: et ex superiore in inferiora non aquam, non quid aliud immitti licet: in suo enim alii hactenus facere licet, quatenus nihil in alienum immittat, fumi autem sicut aquae esse immissionem: posse igitur superiorem cum inferiore agere ius illi non esse id ita facere...*
22   So the words which follow *idemque ait* are not, as they ought to be, in indirect speech; and in suggesting that it is not permissible to release any smoke or any water *(non quid aliud; nihil)* they conflict both with the text that follows and with the general proposition that servitudes exist to regulate cases in which one neighbour wishes to go beyond a merely reasonable use of his property. Furthermore, the *nisi* clause at the end of the first sentence is very odd.

the absence of a servitude and his neighbour, on the other hand, must cease or negotiate one. Pomponius, for example, indicates that no servitude was possible to restrain light smoke (*fumus non gravis*), and the same appears to be true of water. If classical law required a degree of tolerance, Justinian appears, in an incomplete and unsystematic manner, to have attempted to make the rights of the owner more absolute and his need for tolerance less.[23]

(iii) *actio aquae pluviae arcendae*

This action provided a landowner with a remedy for damage caused to his land by rainwater, but only if the defender to the action had carried out works — usually the construction of banks or drainage channels — and these had caused the harm.[24] From the terms of the formula it emerges that there was liability in the action only if (i) an *opus* had been built (ii) causing rainwater (iii) which harmed the pursuer's land. These criteria appear to be purely objective; there is no reason why it should matter what the purpose of the *opus* was, provided it caused the necessary harmful results. Three texts merit closer inspection.

Ulpian cites the views of Marcellus:

> ...there can be no action against a person who, by digging in his own land, has intercepted his neighbour's water supply; not even an action for fraud *(actio de dolo)*; and certainly the (first) neighbour should not have one, if he (the second neighbour) did this not with the intention of harming his neighbour but of improving his own land.[25]

Against the background outlined already — that this action lies only where harm is done to land by rainwater owing to the construction of an *opus* — it comes as something of a surprise to find the question of intention raised: how can it be relevant why the water supply was intercepted? How can the action even arise if the rainwater is not (now) actually reaching the neighbour's land? It appears that we have here only the remains of a fuller discussion about what remedies might be available in these circumstances.

Marcellus is said to have denied that an *actio de dolo* would lie. Why he did, is not explained, although the reasoning in the text about the necessary intent for *dolus* is one possibility. There does not appear

---

23   D.8.5.8.6 (Ulpian, 17 *ad edictum*); D.8.2.19*pr.* (Paul, 6 *ad Sabinum*); cf. A.F. Rodger, *Owners and Neighbours in Roman Law* (Oxford, 1972), chapter I, *passim.*

24   The most plausible reconstruction of the formula runs *si paret opus factum esse, unde aqua pluvia agro Ai Ai nocet, quam ob rem Nm Nm eam aquam Ao Ao arcere oportet, si ea res arbitrio iudicis non restituetur,* etc: Lenel, *op. cit.,* n.9, 375–77, with A.F. Rodger, *op. cit.,* n.23, 153–54.

25   Ulpian, D.39.3.1.12 (53 *ad edictum*): *denique Marcellus scribit cum eo qui in suo fodiens vicini fontem avertit nihil posse agi nec de dolo actionem: et sane non debet habere si non animo vicino nocendi sed suum agrum meliorem faciendi id fecit.*

to be a case in which the *actio de dolo* was granted in relation to abuse of rights of this sort. But once the old definition of *dolus* had been abandoned, and the requirement of an attempt to deceive *(aliud simulatum aliud actum)* jettisoned in favour of a broad notion of *dolus* as an absence of good faith,[26] it is not clear why in principle *dolus* could not be committed by deliberately cutting off a neighbour's water supply. There is, however, no evidence of this for classical or later Roman law. Yet it is precisely for this proposition that the text became significant in later law.

Two more texts in this area, both from the jurist Paul, complete the survey. In the first, there is discussion about rebuilding earthworks which have been destroyed by natural forces, in connexion with the question whether they constituted an *opus*.[27] The text asserts that:

> ...this action cannot be used to compel anybody to benefit his neighbour, but can be used to stop him from damaging his neighbour or preventing him from acting within his rights. Although the action for warding off rainwater may be inapplicable here, none the less, I take the view that an *actio utilis* or interdict is available to me against my neighbour if I wish to restore earthworks on his land whose construction will be to my advantage and will not harm him in any way. Equity supports this view even though we may lack a legal right.[28]

For later law the significance of the text lies in the general remarks at the end; there must be some doubts about the reasoning, since it is again unclear why intention should matter; and here it is hard to say that an *opus* has done any damage.

In the second passage Paul reports Labeo saying that:

> If a neighbour has diverted a torrent to prevent water reaching him, and this results in harm to his neighbour, an action to ward off water cannot be brought against him: since warding off water is seeing to it that it does not flow onto one's property. This view is preferable, as long as he took this action with the intention not of harming you but of preventing harm to himself.[29]

---

26 See G.D. MacCormack, "*Dolus* in Republican Law", (1985) 88 *B.I.D.R.* 1–38.

27 A.F. Rodger, (1988) 105 *Z.S.S.(R.A.)* 726, 727.

28 D.39.3.2.5 (Paul, 49 *ad edictum*): *...nam hac actione neminem cogi posse ut vicino prosit, sed ne noceat aut interpellet facientem quod iure facere possit. quamquam tamen deficiat aquae pluviae arcendae actio, attamen opinor utilem actionem vel interdictum mihi competere adversus vicinum, si velim aggerem restituere in agro eius qui factus mihi quidem prodesse potest, ipsi vero nihil nociturus est: haec aequitas suggerit etsi iure deficiamur.*

29 D.39.3.2.9 (Paul, 49 *ad edictum*): *idem Labeo ait, si vicinus flumen torrentem averterit ne aqua ad eum perveniat, et hoc modo sit effectum ut vicino noceatur agi cum eo aquae pluviae arcendae non posse: aquam enim arcere hoc est curare ne influat. quae sententia verior est, si modo non hoc animo fecit ut tibi noceat sed ne sibi noceat.*

This laconic passage appears to come from the section of Paul's commentary on the notion of harm *(nocere)*.[30] Here the neighbour's grievance appears to be that his water has been cut off; so it is not a case of "warding off" *(arcere)* water; and there can be no liability in the action.[31] Accordingly, it is difficult to see why the motivation of the other party should make the slightest difference: it will still not be *arcere*.[32]

(iv) *Summary*

Where a neighbour wished to restrain an activity on neighbouring property which was resulting in emissions of one sort or another onto his own, there were several possibilities: (i) if the emission was of a nature such that it could be made the subject of a servitude, the *actio negatoria* would be available; (ii) if not, the *cautio damni infecti* could be sought; (iii) in the event that it was an emission of rainwater owing to a construction on neighbouring land, the *actio aquae pluviae arcendae* could be brought. All of these remedies were independent of fault on the part of the neighbour; all depended purely on the objective fact of damage arising owing to activity on the neighbouring land; but not all damage was regarded as material for the purposes of *damnum infectum*; nor was any degree of use enough to warrant a servitude, so that considerations of reasonableness were impliedly introduced.

If, however, there was no emission but the damage took another form − blocking off light or cutting off water − the remedies were more restricted. Clearly, if there was a servitude, the *actio confessoria* would be available. In the absence of a servitude, the remedies can have been only (i) *damnum infectum,* in the event that the deprivation was regarded as serious enough to qualify as *damnum;* (ii) *dolus.* Yet both of these remedies had their limitations: *damnum infectum* because it depended on a *cautio* having been given in advance; and the *actio de dolo* because it required proof of evil intent.

(b) *The Later History of Roman Law*

Some of the texts on servitudes and on *damnum infectum* suggest that an owner was not entirely at liberty on his own property; some of those relating to the *actio aquae pluviae arcendae* imply that an owner's motivation in carrying on activities on his own land might be material. Those hints were taken in later law: these texts laid the basis for a doctrine of abuse of rights.

---

30   A.F. Rodger, (1988) 105 *Z.S.S.(R.A.)* 726, 727.

31   Cf. H. Burckhard in his continuation of Glück's *Ausführliche Erläuterung der Pandecten*, vols. 39–40, part 3 (Erlangen, 1881), 227ff.

32   Again, therefore, this seems to point towards abbreviation of a possible discussion about what a neighbour deprived of water actually could do; the gloss *(noceat)* on this text suggests that there will be liability in the *actio de dolo*.

In Scots law and in other legal systems abuse of rights (at least in this context) is conventionally known as *aemulatio vicini*[33]. That term, however, does not appear in the *Corpus Iuris Civilis*. If there was any such doctrine in classical or Justinianic Roman law,[34] it did not go under that name. The sole appearance of *aemulatio* is in a passage from book 2 of Macer's *de officio praesidis* which is preserved in the *Digest*. It reads:

> A private individual is permitted to construct a new building even without the emperor's authority, except if it relates to the emulation of another city *(ad aemulationem alterius civitatis)* or furnishes material for sedition or is a circus, theatre or amphitheatre.[35]

The context is plainly public law (that was the subject of Macer's book, and the text appears in the *Digest* title *de operibus publicis*) and in particular public spending. Unnecessary projects are not to be allowed to consume funds or even space where their only motivation is that a particular town should be one up on its neighbour. This has nothing to do with restrictions on private owners when their acts are informed by malice.[36]

The *Digest* passage, therefore, will not take us far. We need to consider the content with which the word *aemulatio* was invested by later lawyers. The gloss on this *Digest* text appears already to have considered a wider context.[37] It states that this text applies to works in public places; and that such works are permissible where there is an intention that they be donated to the public and they are useful or necessary to the *res publica*. So far, there is nothing very exceptional about this. The gloss goes on, however, to consider the question of building on private land and recounts two views. The first is that I can build on my own land even *ad emulationem*, since everyone is entitled to do as he will on his own land, provided he does not emit anything onto another's land. There then follow references to passages from the *Digest* to vouch that proposition, dealing variously with *damnum infectum*, the *actio aquae pluviae arcendae*, and the vindication of servitudes.[38] The second view is that the restriction of *aemulatio* applies even to building on private land, principally (it seems) because this *Digest* text itself does not distinguish according to the type of land in question. Clearly,

---

33 Cf. for South African law, J.E. Scholtens, "Abuse of Rights", (1958) 75 *S.A.L.J.* 49–59.

34 The uncertain mentions in the texts cited are almost its only support. The prevailing modern opinion seems to be that at least in Justinianic law there was a general principle of abuse of rights: see e.g. M. Kaser, *Das römische Privatrecht*, vol. 2, (2nd ed., Munich, 1975), 63; but the evidence even for this is not strong.

35 D.50.10.3*pr.*

36 *Contra*, the lone voice of A. Palma, *Iura vicinitatis* (Turin, 1988), 167.

37 Gl. *novum ad h.l.* Cf. also the gloss on other texts discussed above, notably gl. *non teneri me* on D.39.2.24.12.

38 D.39.2.24.12; D.39.3.1.11–12, 17; D.8.5.8.5.

on the first view the text is irrelevant to building on private land. None the less the significance of this gloss is that a text concerned with public law had already been assimilated into a general discussion of private-law restrictions (such as *immissio*) on an owner's right freely to make use of his property; and that the restriction in question was based on the owner's motive rather than on the nature of the activity he was carrying on.

After the Gloss, *aemulatio vicini* as a restriction on ownership seems to have been accepted almost universally by the writers of the *ius commune*, as a generic term for a restriction which depended on the subjective rather than the objective, on motive rather than activity.[39] Why then was such a restriction called *aemulatio*? Conceptually, abuse of rights comes closer to *dolus* than to anything else. Yet the weight placed by the writers of the *ius commune* on the last title of the *Digest, de diversis regulis iuris antiqui* must have caused them difficulties.[40] For there it is stated quite bluntly that "nobody who makes use of his own right is regarded as acting with *dolus*".[41] The fact that this rule was derived from a context — wills — quite remote from neighbourhood relations would not have been regarded as a solution to the problem: a rule phrased so generally made it difficult for jurists to develop a theory of abuse of rights under the name of *dolus*. It may therefore be for this reason that the term *aemulatio* was seized upon: it had already become acclimatised in an environment of private law restrictions on the use of property.

II Scots Law

From this range of possibilities, ancient and early modern, what remedies did Scots law forge? The writers and the cases will be considered in turn.

(a) Institutional and Other Writers

The writers are not much concerned with setting out a general theory of the content of ownership and an exhaustive account of the restrictions to which it may be subject. All of them, naturally, recognise the existence of servitudes; beyond that, uniformity proves elusive.

Stair, in the course of his discussion of stillicide, says only that "no man may dispose so upon his own ground as to put any positive prejudice, hurt or damage upon his neighbour's".[42] Although "positive prejudice,

---

39   A list of these writers is given in V. Scialoja, "*Aemulatio*" in his *Studi giuridici*, vol. 3 (Rome, 1932), 216–59 at 219–21.
40   See P.G. Stein, *Regulae Iuris* (Edinburgh, 1966), e.g. at 148ff.
41   D.50.17.55 (Gaius 2, *de testamentis, ad edictum urbicum*): *nullus videtur dolo facere, qui suo iure utitur.* For the *palingenesia (si quis omissa causa testamenti)*, see D. Daube, "*Zur Palingenesie einiger Klassikerfragmente*", (1959) 76 *Z.S.S.(R.A.)* 149–264 at 215.
42   Stair, 2,7,7.

hurt or damage" is not defined, the examples he gives (damming or gathering water such that it then flows onto a neighbour's land) all involve direct physical damage to property. The notion of "positive prejudice" is clarified somewhat by a later passage dealing with the servitudes of light and prospect:[43]

> ...the owner of every ground may build thereupon at his pleasure, though thereby he hinder the view and prospect from his neighbour's tenement, or the coming of the sun-beams or light thereto, which being but in relation to the extrinsic benefit of that which is not in, but without, the tenement, is not accounted a positive damage, from which the owners of neighbouring tenements must abstain.[44]

The thought seems to be that here the effect on neighbouring property is not sufficiently direct. So it seems that building so as to block a neighbour's window could not be restrained in the absence of a servitude; and no point appears to exist at which the deprivation of light might constitute positive damage. Nor is anything said about restrictions if the motive for building was purely malicious.[45]

Bankton, discussing the same topic, urban servitudes, does not mention the question of physical damage. He does, however, refer to an additional restriction on use, *aemulatio vicini*:[46]

> There may be as many several kinds of these servitudes as there are different methods, whereby the natural liberty of using one's property in building thereon may be restrained, for the advantage of neighbouring tenements. It is lawful for one who is subject to no servitude, to build on his own ground or otherwise use it tho' his neighbour's house should be thereby entirely darkened or rendered uninhabitable;[47] but it must be done for one's own benefit, and not purely out of envy to his neighbour, or in *Aemulationem vicini*, for, in such case, the law would not indulge a malicious humour.

But what form this lack of indulgence takes is not revealed. And in the absence of *aemulatio vicini* or a servitude, no restriction on an owner's activities is noted.

Erskine, in a more general discussion of legal limitations on the right of property,[48] notes that "the law interposes so far for the public interest, that it suffers no person to use his property wantonly to his

---

43   Stair, 2,7,9.
44   Contrast Paul, D.39.2.25.
45   Although Stair was plainly familiar with *aemulatio vicini*, since he himself reports a case which concerned it: *Farquharson v. Earl of Aboyne* (1679) in Stair, *Decisions of the Lords of Council and Session 1671–81* (Edinburgh, 1687), 727; Mor. 4147.
46   Bankton, 2,7,15.
47   Here he refers to D.8.5.15–17.
48   Erskine, *Inst.,* 2,1,2.

neighbour's prejudice; *interest enim reipublicae ne quis re sua male utatur*. But where the proprietor's act is of itself lawful, though it should be in its consequences detrimental to his neighbour, *utitur jure suo*, he is allowed to make use of what is his own in the manner most beneficial to himself; and though his neighbour suffer damage, he has no redress unless the act of the other was *in aemulationem*". Here too nothing is said about physical damage; and nothing about nuisance.[49] So Erskine is broadly in line with Bankton.

By far the fullest discussion, however, is found in Kames' *Principles of Equity*. According to Kames there is a rule which regulates harm done by a person in prosecuting his own rights.

> This rule consists of two branches: the first is, That even the prosecution of my own right will not justify me in doing any action that directly harms another; and so far my interest yields to his: the second is, That in prosecuting my right I am not concerned with any indirect or consequential damage that another may suffer; and so far the interest of others yields to mine....[50]

As an example of the first branch of the rule, Kames gives the case of draining a higher field by opening a passage into a lower neighbour's field. This cannot be done, because it causes direct damage. After further examples, Kames concludes that all "are governed by a practical rule, That we must not throw anything into our neighbour's ground, *Ne immittas in alienum*, as expressed in the Roman law. But the principle goes a great way further, obliging us to abstain from every operation that has directly the effect to make our neighbour's property useless or uncomfortable to him...".[51]

The second branch of the rule allows the digging of a pit in my own land for gathering water, although it intercepts a spring that supplies my neighbour with water; equally, I may build a house upon my march, although it intercepts the light from my neighbour's house.

> But with regard to this branch of the rule, there is a limitation founded entirely upon equity; which is, That however lawful it may be for a man to exercise his right for his own benefit where the harm that ensues is only consequential; yet that the exercise is unlawful if it be done intentionally to distress others, without any view of benefiting himself...justice will not permit a man to exercise his right where his intention is solely to hurt another; which in law-language is termed the acting *in aemulationem vicini*. In all cases

---

49   If Erskine intended to set out an exhaustive account of limitations on property, his doctrine is certainly too broad: cf. note (a) to this passage in Nicolson's edition. But, in cases where physical damage was caused, it is not clear that Erskine would have said that the owner *utitur jure suo*; while the cases cited by Nicolson to controvert Erskine's doctrine are cases concerning damages where fault on the part of the owner has been proved.

50   *Principles of Equity* (2nd ed., Edinburgh, 1767), 58.

51   *Op. cit.*, 59.

of this nature a court of equity will give redress by voiding the act, if that can be done; otherwise by awarding a sum in name of damages.[52]

This interesting analysis has little in common with the Roman rules just discussed. The first, direct, branch of the rule derives from D.8.5.8.5, and the context of servitudes, at least so far as the reference to non-emission of matter into a neighbour's property is concerned. But it has been elaborated by Kames to incorporate anything that makes property useless or uncomfortable to its owner. Since this is said to fall under the first, direct branch of the rule, with the qualification that there must be a direct effect on the neighbouring land, it comes very close to a doctrine of nuisance.[53] The second branch of the rule is broadly in line with the other writers (apart from Stair): there is no restriction on interception of light or water (in the absence of a servitude) at common law. But it may be restrained if motivated by *aemulatio vicini*, a doctrine that is here said to be equitable.

To sum up. The Roman institutions which feature in one or more of these writers are servitudes, the related concept of *immissio,* and *aemulatio vicini.* The only restraint referred to by all the writers is a servitude in favour of neighbouring property. Stair and Kames appear to be broadly in line in distinguishing between direct and consequential damage to neighbouring property, although Kames (with all the other writers) recognises that *aemulatio vicini* operates as a further restriction where the damage caused is only consequential. Stair does not. Kames is the only writer to mention *immissio* expressly; the doctrinal origin of Stair's restriction of "positive prejudice" is unclear. Bankton and Erskine say nothing about direct damage to neighbouring property. The extent of the writers' actual differences in doctrine is perhaps exaggerated by their different concerns in writing these passages. It is safe, however, to say that their apparent differences in doctrine left much scope for different approaches to be canvassed in the courts. The proper course is accordingly to see how far these various views are represented in the cases.

(b) Six Main Cases

Very little can be extracted from cases before the eighteenth century. Some early cases mention *aemulatio vicini* as an allegation directed against someone who establishes a new fair near an existing one, so detracting from the value of its business.[54] But these do not assist the present discussion, beyond indicating that the term was then known in Scotland. At the end of the seventeenth century, in *Hall* v. *Corbet,*[55] the

---

52 *Op. cit.,* 59–60.
53 Cf. Bell, *Prin.* (10th ed.), s. 974.
54 *Falconer* v. *Laird of Glenbervie* (1642) Mor. 4146; *Farquharson* v. *Earl of Aboyne* (1679) Mor. 4147; *Mags. of Stirling* v. *Murray* (1706) Mor. 4148.
55 (1698) Mor. 12775.

parties were in dispute over the construction of a chimney. The defender argued that he could use his property freely, subject only to the restriction of *immissio*. The court took the view that the pursuer required to show prejudice in order to restrict building by the defender. The precise relationship between *immissio* and prejudice is not clear; it seems likely that *immissio* is a form of prejudice, and that prejudice involves physical damage, as in Stair's account.

Fuller reports appear only in the eighteenth century. It will be enough to consider six of these.

(i) *Brodie of Letham* v. *Sir James Cadel of Muirton*[56]

The pursuer complained that the defender was disrupting his fishing on the river Findhorn. The defender had fishing rights upstream of the pursuer, and so it was possible that disruption downstream was driving the fish upstream. The pursuer argued that (i) all laws condemn the pretence of private utility where an act is evidently done *in aemulationem vicini*; (ii) everyone can do as he will on his own property, but always with the exception *ne quid immittat in alienum*. In support of the first proposition reference was made to some Scottish cases; in support of the second to some passages from the *Digest*.[57] The court found that the defender had acted *in aemulationem vicini* by anchoring off the pursuer's property, since it appeared that there were other places at which he could safely anchor.

Unfortunately, the report provides no indication how the court reached its decision; perhaps it was on the view that there was no possible reason for anchoring in that place unless there was a malicious motive. The relevance of the arguments on *immissio* is not very clear. But, taken together with *Hall* v. *Corbet*, they demonstrate that that restriction on ownership had a certain currency around 1700; the doctrine of D.8.5.8.5 was playing a part in the development of the law.

(ii) *Fairly* v. *Earl of Eglinton*[58]

The defender had built a dam on the river Irvine where it ran through his property. It caused the river to back up, affecting the good running of a mill upstream owned by the pursuer. The pursuer sought to have the defender ordained to remove, or at least lower, his dam. The defender offered to pay to have the pursuer's mill raised to a height such that it would function properly notwithstanding the dam. The offer was refused. It was held on a reclaiming petition (reversing the decision at first instance) that the defender could not lawfully build a dam so as to cause the water to back up and interfere with the pursuer's mill; that the pursuer was not obliged to accept the defender's offer; and that, while the court might have restrained the pursuer from

---

56   22nd Mar. 1707; 4 B.S. 660.
57   Notably, D.8.5.17.2 and 8.2.19, both concerned with damp.
58   (1744) Mor. 12780.

acting *in aemulationem vicini* had he had no mill, *aemulatio* could not be alleged in a case where the pursuer could show prejudice.

Unusually, it was the defender who pled *aemulatio vicini*, arguing that the pursuer could not show that he would suffer loss if the proposed alterations were made to his mill. Unusually again, each party wished to argue that an owner's rights were unrestricted: the pursuer because he did not wish to have his own mill altered; the defender because he did not wish to have to take his dam down. The same passages from the *Digest* were cited by each party, with different emphasis. The defender cited the *Digest* to support the propositions that he should be allowed to alter the pursuer's dam where this was to his advantage and would not prejudice the pursuer; and that the pursuer's motive in refusing to allow this was material.[59] The pursuer argued that (i) no person's property is subject to the will of another, and cited the expression *in suo hactenus facere licet quatenus nihil in alienum immittat* from D.8.5.8.5 ("a man is only permitted to carry out operations on his own premises to this extent, that he discharge nothing onto those of another"); (ii) a man cannot be restrained from making use of his own property whatever consequential damage may ensue to a neighbouring proprietor, since such restraint resolves into a servitude; (iii) want of interest might limit a man in the exercise of his property where the exercise was harmful to others: "To do an action in itself lawful, with the view to hurt another, without any benefit to myself is in law language acting *in aemulationem vicini*".[60] These propositions too were vouched by texts from the *Digest*: nobody is obliged to employ his own property for the benefit of another; no action lies against somebody who has been making use only of his own rights; and to found an action there must be *immissio*.[61]

The most intriguing aspect of the pursuer's analysis is that it was carried out largely in terms of servitudes: to prevent an owner from an activity causing merely consequential damage to his neighbour amounts to a (negative) servitude. The owner's right is regarded as absolute, unless qualified by servitude or involving *immissio*. Otherwise the only restriction recognised is want of interest, effectively *aemulatio*. What the court appears to have decided is that the

---

59   D.39.3.1.12 and 2.5, both cited at 12784 in the report of Clerk Home, the fullest report of this case.

60   The similarity between these arguments and those favoured by Kames is not accidental: Kames was counsel in the case: see the preface to the volume in which he reports this case, *Remarkable Decisions of the Court of Session 1730–1752* (Edinburgh, 1766).

61   D.8.5.8.5; D.39.3.1.12 and 2.5; D.39.2.26; Mor. 12786. Reference is also made to J. Heringius, *Tractatus singularis de molendinis* (1663) as cited by Dirleton. No doubt this refers to Dirleton's doubt *an extrui possit molendinum quod noceat vicino?* in *Some Doubts and Questions on the Law especially of Scotland* (Edinburgh, 1698), 128, which refers to Heringius q. 14 n.30, to the effect that where a lower mill causes interference with an upper mill it can be prohibited from operating.

backing up of water to the pursuer's mill did amount to damage or prejudice; and that it therefore fell within a recognised restriction on an owner's use of his property (*immissio*). The relevance of *aemulatio* does not appear to have been doubted, but to have been confined to the case where loss was not being sustained.

(iii) *Gordon v. Grant*[62]

This was a case about muirburn. A plantation of the pursuer's had suffered fire damage owing to unseasonal muirburn carried on by the defenders; and the pursuer concluded for damages, as well as for declarator that the defenders were not entitled to raise muirburn within a certain distance of his plantation and should raise it only on certain terms. After proof, only the declaratory conclusions were insisted in.

While, as might be expected, some attention was directed to delictual arguments, other issues too were raised.[63] The defenders accepted that no man can use his property *in aemulationem vicini*, but maintained that otherwise no man can be restricted from "profitable or necessary acts of property, though they may, or even must, hurt that of his neighbour, unless he be liable to a servitude". They cited works to show that an owner's activities could only be restrained by servitude, and to illustrate the question of *aemulatio vicini*: a text from the *Digest*; Bankton; the *Practicae observationes* of the German judge Andreas Gail; and the commentaries of the Dutch jurist Zoesius on the *Digest*.[64]

The pursuer argued that freedom to use one's property applied only where "a man's operations are confined to his own property, and the effect of them is not *immittere* any thing destructive upon that of his neighbour". The report does not make the defenders' response to this argument clear, although it records no admission that any kind of damage to neigbouring property might restrict an owner's rights. The court's reasoning is also left unclear; but the defenders were assoilzied.

---

62   (1765) Mor. 7356.
63   On the question whether the defenders were at fault in raising muirburn when and where they did, D.9.2.30.3 was cited. On the argument put forward regarding *damnum infectum* see section III.
64   D.39.3.21; Bankton, 2,7,15; A. Gail, *Practicarum observationum libri II* (1578) 2.39. H. Zoesius, *Commentarius ad digestorum libros L* (1645) 39.3.4 and 5 are concerned with two passages discussed above, D.39.3.1.12 and 2.9, on the *actio aquae pluviae arcendae*. For present purposes the most significant points made there relate to (i) *animus nocendi*, which is said to be gathered from an objectively harmful action which is maliciously and unjustly aimed at harming a neighbour, and not caused by any utility or need of the actor; (ii) the notion of *damnum*, and the distinction drawn between consequential harm and harm as the principal purpose of an act: "somebody who has used his own right to do what is to his advantage cannot be said to do wrong, even if he has incidentally harmed another; although he would be liable if he acted principally with the desire of harming his neighbour".

It may be that it was thought the case should properly turn on fault (an argument which the pursuer had apparently abandoned) or *aemulatio vicini* (an argument of no real plausibility in this context). But it may be thought that the arguments about *immissio* or physical damage had some merit and could have been given closer attention.

(iv) *Dewar* v. *Fraser*[65]

The pursuer had begun to build lime kilns on his property close to its boundary with the defender's property, when he was faced with a suspension at the instance of the defender. The pursuer argued that this was the most convenient location, and that he was not motivated by *aemulatio vicini*. He made reference to *Gordon* v. *Grant* and much of the authority cited there.[66] Reference was also made to Voet's commentary on the *Digest,* where it is said that the *cautio* for *damnum infectum* will not be given where a neighbour is carrying on works on his own property for his own advantage and by his own right, although they may be harmful to neighbours. (The harm referred to there, however, is indirect harm by cutting off water or light).[67]

The defender argued that *aemulatio vicini* was a restriction on the free use of property; that his house would become altogether uninhabitable "on account of the smoke and noisome smell and vapours" and that "this case is very different from those in which one neighbour by operations carried on upon his own property, may deprive another of an advantage he had formerly enjoyed, as depriving him of a prospect..." for in this case actual damage (of what sort, is not reported) would be done to his property. Kames' report mentions that a rule — *quod non licet immittere in alienum* — which derives from D.8.5.8.5, was considered but found not to apply. The reason was that the emissions of smoke were not direct, but the chance consequence of the way the wind happened to be blowing. That consideration, however, plays no part in D.8.5.8.5 itself.[68]

Here again therefore the court appears to have been faced with submissions both about *immissio* and about *aemulatio vicini.* *Immissio* appears to have been interpreted restrictively. When that argument failed, the defender was left only to argue for *aemulatio vicini*, and the basis in fact for that argument is unclear. So the court found for the pursuer. But it did observe that if, without loss or inconvenience, he could have located the kiln somewhere less noxious, he was bound to yield that far on the principle of neighbourhood.

---

65   (1767) Mor. 12803.
66   D.39.3.21; Bankton, 2,7,15, both cited for the proposition that a servitude is needed to restrict an owner's actings on his own land; Zoesius, *loc. cit.*, n.64, for the question of motive.
67   J. Voet, *Commentarius ad pandectas,* (The Hague, 1704), 39.2.5, citing D.39.2.24.12–26 and D.39.3.21.
68   *Fumi autem sicut aquae esse immissionem,* says Aristo in that text.

(v) *Ralston* v. *Pettigrew*[69]

The defender had built a brick kiln about thirty feet from the pursuer's land. It was proved to have killed part of the hedge between the two properties and damaged some trees and bushes on the pursuer's land. The defender set out the restrictions he understood to apply to a property owner's free use of his property, and argued that "Every person is entitled to use his property in the way that may be most profitable to him, though a consequential damage should thence arise to his neighbour. From this general principle have sprung the variety of servitudes that make such a figure in the law, and which are nothing else but restraints from using one's property to the prejudice of others. Such are the servitudes, *altius non tollendi, ne luminibus officiatur,* etc. The necessity of those servitudes for such restraint clearly evinces the general principle...This general principle admits of two limitations only; one, that the exercise of one's property must not be merely in *aemulationem vicini*; the other, that it must not be a public nuisance". The pursuer argued that in this case there was no need to consider *aemulatio*: "The proper place for that limitation is where something has been done, which, though disagreeable, or even prejudicial to a neighbour, yet does not directly encroach upon, or destroy any part of his property". The court found for the pursuer, finding a third limitation beyond the two contended for by the defender, namely physical damage to neighbouring land. The reasoning goes no further than that: the report notes simply that the Lords "found that the defender was obliged to remove said kiln" and remitted the case to the Lord Ordinary. No citation of authority, beyond reference to the case of *Dewar,* is reported.

It is unclear whether the court relied on *immissio* (which it could have derived from the reference to *Dewar*); on positive prejudice, which it might have derived from Stair; or on some third possibility, such as nuisance. But the decision clearly rested on physical damage and not on *aemulatio.*

(vi) *Glassford* v. *Astley*[70]

The defender's windows overlooked the pursuers' garden. To prevent him looking, the pursuers built a wooden screen in front of the windows. The defender pulled down the screen; the pursuers sought to have him ordained to reinstate it and interdicted from interfering with it thereafter; at the same time the defender petitioned to have the pursuers restrained from rebuilding it.

The defender's argument was based on *aemulatio vicini* (there was no relevant servitude). It was argued that "Nothing will be allowed to be built which causes a great evil to a neighbour unless it is of considerable or serious use to the person who builds; and particularly

---

69   (1768) Mor. 12808.
70   (1808) Mor. s.v. "Property", App. no. 7.

nothing will be allowed to be built which without any serious use to the builder directly and immediately hurts a neighbour. These are the established doctrines of what is called the law of nuisance. They are recognised in the laws of all countries". The defender went on to cite Blackstone; a number of institutional writers and Scottish authorities (in particular *Dewar* and *Ralston*); and a good deal of civilian authority: Gail, Gratian, Heringius, Mevius and Menochius. This is the fullest citation of civilian authority given in any of the reported cases.

So far as the civilian authority is concerned, it is enough to refer to Mevius' commentary *ad ius Lubecense*, in which most of the other writers are cited. Mevius notes the various accepted arguments in favour of there being *aemulatio vicini*: where the builder obtains no use from the building but the neighbour sustains damage (*damnum*); where any benefit to be derived from the building is exceeded by the cost of building it; where the builder obtains a slight benefit but the neighbour suffers serious detriment (*detrimentum*); where the building is for the purpose of spying on the neighbour, for example looking into his bedroom or other private chamber, or is built *in contemptum* of the neighbour; where the neighbours are so hostile that they would not have built what they built had they not been enemies. There is, notes Mevius under reference to Menochius's work *de praesumptionibus*, a presumption that an enemy does everything he can to harm his enemy.[71]

The defender appears to have gone to great lengths to argue his case, but he was unsuccessful at all stages. The conclusions to be drawn from this case are mixed. First, the solid line of civilian authority cited by the defender shows not only that *aemulatio* was a recognised concept but also the presumptions which applied in determining whether or not it was present. Little attention appears to have been paid to that question in the earlier cases. Second, the propositions which are said to be "the established doctrines of what is called the law of nuisance" are in fact quite familiar from civilian authority on limitations on ownership. The references to Blackstone and to nuisance (in a manner suggesting that it was something of a novelty) are signs of what was to come, about which there will be a little more to say in the final section. Third, the defender's argument that one may not build something which "directly and immediately hurts a neighbour" does not, in terms of earlier authority, apply to the case where lights are blocked, and no positive prejudice is sustained. Fourth, after such extensive researches into the civilian tradition, it is disappointing that the defender did not exploit the potential of the *Digest* more fully. Here was a case in which Trebatius' assertion that the blocking of light amounted to *damnum* was entirely apposite. Yet it was not cited. Why, must be a matter of

---

71   D. Mevius, *Commentarii ad ius Lubecense* (1679) 3.12.7.30–32; citing in particular A. Gail, *op. cit.*, n.64, 69.28 and J. Menochius, *de arbitrariis iudicum quaestionibus et causis* (1672) 2.156.9 and *de praesumptionibus commentaria* (1588) 29.26.

speculation: perhaps because of the contrary assertion in D.8.2.9, which would make any advocate hesitate to peril his case on one sentence from Trebatius. Less attractively, perhaps because knowledge of the *Digest* in Scotland was not what it had been.[72]

From these cases a few conclusions may be drawn. First, there is much uncertainty surrounding the *immissio* principle: it appears to have been decisive in *Fairly* and possibly in *Ralston;* but it was rejected in *Dewar* and apparently in *Gordon.* Linked to this is some confusion on the question whether physical damage to neighbouring property (whether or not consisting in *immissio*) constitutes a restriction on ownership. While this is accepted in most cases, it is rejected in *Gordon* and apparently also in *Dewar.* The argument in both those cases depends to some degree on Bankton; it may be that the confusion is to be laid at his door. Second, the cases (and most of the writers) accept that *aemulatio* is a restraint on action on one's own property. Prior to *Glassford,* nothing is said about how *aemulatio* is to be identified, but in *Dewar* there is a hint that the court is feeling its way to a presumption that, if other land equally convenient to the kiln builder and much less inconvenient to the neighbour is available, to insist on the troublesome land may be *aemulatio*. Third, it appears to be accepted by the writers, and by the court in *Ralston,* that *aemulatio* relates only to cases in which the neighbour suffers no physical damage; his remedy if he does suffer physical damage is to be sought elsewere. In principle therefore it might be expected that the remedies available in the event of *aemulatio* should be limited to suspension, interdict and specific implement, and that damages should not be available.[73] *Aemulatio* has therefore a severely limited role to play, quite independently of the fact that there may be difficulties in proving it.[74]

III Some General Conclusions

The Roman scheme of remedies was permeated by the notion of reasonableness. The term *damnum* covered cases in which activity by one owner had affected another beyond a reasonable degree, so that even the right to light could be protected by the *cautio* for *damnum infectum*, if its infringement went beyond what was reasonable. Equally,

---

72 See J.W. Cairns, "The Formation of the Scottish Legal Mind in the Eighteenth Century" in *The Legal Mind*, edd. N. MacCormick and P.B.H. Birks (Oxford, 1986) 253–77 at 266, 276.
73 *Contra,* Kames, *op. cit.*, n.50, 60.
74 Nowadays its role is even slighter, since (i) nuisance is a settled institution in our law and (ii) it is accepted that in nuisance the proper question is whether the victim is being exposed to something *plus quam tolerabile* (*Watt* v. *Jamieson* 1954 S.C. 56). It follows that *aemulatio* can only ever be relevant (a) in cases where no nuisance is committed, notably interception of water or light, or (b) theoretically (though implausibly) where what the victim is exposed to is not *plus quam tolerabile* but the motive of the neighbour is none the less malicious.

servitudes regulated cases in which a proprietor was faced with emissions from neighbouring property going beyond what was reasonable.

In Scotland in the seventeenth century a promising start appears to have been made in looking to the Roman texts to develop criteria for regulating owners' use of their property. From the context of servitudes was elaborated the doctrine that an owner could not carry on activities on his own land which resulted in *immissio* into his neighbour's property. From the civilian writers was derived the concept of *aemulatio vicini*.

The second of these doctrines turned out to have a secure future. Yet the jurisprudential potential of the first doctrine, *immissio*, was not fully exploited, and it seems to have disappeared from view in the second half of the eighteenth century.[75] Several reasons suggest themselves. The proximate cause was perhaps the restrictive interpretation placed on *immissio* in the case of *Dewar* (and perhaps also in *Gordon*), which made it unsuitable as a remedy except for direct emissions of such things as water. Lying behind this, however, is the fact that a doctrine that no *immissio* to any degree was permissible must have caused problems in practice. Interpreted strictly, it would have curtailed the use of property significantly. In classical Roman law *immissio* had to go beyond what was reasonable before it could be restrained. The more extreme doctrine, to which Justinian subscribed, and which Scots law inherited, was impractical and probably did something both to discredit the doctrine of *immissio* altogether, and to encourage the courts to interpret it restrictively.

Difficulties with the *Digest* may have had a more general effect. The Roman scheme of remedies set out in the *Digest* was hard to comprehend as a system of law. The same text could be cited for quite different propositions, as the case of *Fairly* shows. Officially, contradictions in the *Digest* did not exist; but where it was a matter of attempting to understand the notion of *damnum* or the degree of *immissio* which was permissible without a servitude, the Roman texts told an incoherent story.[76] Its incoherence was due to the fact that the system of law set out in the *Digest* had never applied as a whole at any historical time. It is clear that, without the *Digest,* the revival of Roman law in civilian systems would have been quite impossible. But it seems reasonable to suppose that the prospects of reception for a given Roman legal institution were affected by the degree to which the texts could successfully be reconciled, and a clear and coherent doctrine extracted from them.

Be that as it may, another factor in the swift rise and fall of *immissio* must be the fact that the reception of Roman doctrine in Scotland

---

75   Contrast the very different development in Germany, where the notion of *immissio* has been much elaborated by case law on para. 906 *B.G.B.*

76   On the right to light: D.8.2.9 versus D.39.2.25; on emissions: D.8.5.8.5 versus D.8.5.8.6. On other such problems, A. Rodger, "Roman Law in Practice in Britain", (1993) 12 *Rechtshistorisches Journal* 261–71 at 269.

had been only partial. Gaps gaped in the scheme of available remedies. In the first place, Scots law did not adopt the institution of *damnum infectum* in any systematic way. The few instances in the reports make it clear that the *cautio* did not play a central role in regulating the rights of neighbours *inter se*. Stair mentions it only in passing; Morison, in the section of his *Dictionary of Decisions* dealing among other things with *damnum infectum*, seems to have been able to find only one case to report: it concerned damage caused by the collapse of a ruinous building, and the notion of *damnum infectum* was introduced by a defender eager to argue that there was no liability in the event of collapse unless the *cautio* had been given in advance.[77] The defender's argument was rejected; the pursuer could actually argue that *damnum infectum* was a remedy unknown to the law of Scotland. The decision itself appears to turn on foreseeability of damage owing to the ruinous state of the building, and so on fault.[78] Such other cases as there are indicate that the institution of *damnum infectum* was not unknown, but do not suggest that it played a central role.[79]

In the second place, in Scots law the right to light depended on a servitude; the right to prevent building beyond a certain height equally depended on a servitude.[80] From the very fact that servitudes existed as a class of property right, the extreme conclusion was drawn that, where there was no servitude, ownership must be unrestricted.[81] That view had been espoused by civilian authors such as Voet, so the development in Scotland was not a purely local phenomenon.[82] Yet in Roman law no such conclusion could have been drawn from the fact that in a given case no servitude existed.

The absence from Scots law of the differentiated notions of *damnum infectum* and of servitudes which appear in the Roman sources meant that the Roman institutions which actually were received could not alone provide a satisfactory scheme of remedies in relation to neighbourhood rights. Nor could this be arrived at by seizing on the single institution of *immissio* and overhauling it. A more radical solution was required. This solution seems in the late eighteenth century to have been identified in nuisance. Some of the early cases had

---

77   Stair, 2,7,7; Morison s.v. "Reparation", section X; *Hay* v. *Littlejohn* (1666) Mor. 13974. The defender's argument turns on D.39.2.6.
78   See esp. the brief report in the decisions appended to Dirleton, *op. cit.*, n.61, no. 66, p. 28.
79   *Duke of Gordon* v. *Braco* (cited in *Mags. of Aberdeen* v. *Menzies* (1748) Mor. 12787); *Gordon* v. *Grant, cit. sup.*, n.62; *Sharp* v. *Robertson* (1800) Mor. s.v. "Property", App. no. 3.
80   Stair, 2,7,9; Bankton, 2,7,29; *Somerville* v. *Somerville* (1613) Mor. 12769; *Mags. of Dumfries* v. *Heritors on Water of Leith* (1705) Mor. 12776.
81   *Fairly, cit. sup.*, n.58; *Ralston, cit. sup.*, n.69. Note, however, that there might be administrative restrictions on building, introduced by the Dean of Guild: see, e.g., *P.F. of Edinburgh* v. *Dott and Paterson* (1789) Mor. 13187.
82   Voet, *loc. cit.*, n.67.

already recognised the existence of nuisance as a restraint on antisocial activity or on noise;[83] but its place as a restriction on ownership was not yet secure. With the advent of the nineteenth century came not just an increase in the influence of English law but also industrialisation. Neighbourhood rights came to be of greater significance. An area of law in which civilian influence had not yet been deeply absorbed or coherently ordered was vulnerable.[84]

To return to Roman legal institutions. In contrast with *immissio*, it is striking that the reception of *aemulatio vicini* never faltered, and that it became an established doctrine of Scots law. The term (probably even the concept) did not exist in classical or Justinianic Roman law, but it had been refined into a coherent concept by generations of Glossators and Commentators. It was here that Roman texts drawn from the context of *damnum infectum* and the *actio aquae pluviae arcendae* played their true role in Scots law. For they mattered now not for what they said about those remedies but because of their potential as quarries for broader concepts. Concepts of motive and intention were duly extracted from them. Where Roman law had been concerned with an objective focus on *damnum* and the question of reasonable use, the same materials were now turned to a subjective focus on *animus*. The doctrine of *aemulatio vicini* is a clear illustration of the fact that the Roman law which was received in Scotland was the *ius commune*, rather than classical or Justinianic law.[85] And among the advantages which it had to offer was that there was no need to face and resolve conflicts in the *Digest;* quite simply, because the doctrine of *aemulatio vicini* did not appear there.

Roman law influenced various institutions of Scots law to varying degrees. This essay, apart from following a few threads of Roman influence from antiquity into eighteenth century Scotland, has attempted to suggest how the influence of individual doctrines of Roman law was affected by their accessibility in the *Digest;* and how the reception of only part of a Roman scheme of remedies, because manifestly incomplete, made the Roman institutions which were received vulnerable to replacement by a more coherent doctrine. Finally, the essay has attempted to show how much the reception of Roman legal thought in Scotland owed to the civilian writers, as opposed to their Roman predecessors; and how the true significance of Roman texts for the law of Scotland may often rest in concepts and meanings which the Roman jurists themselves never contemplated.

---

83   *Fleming* v. *Ure* (1750) Mor. 13159 (noise from a fencing school);·*Kinloch* v. *Robertson* (1756) Mor. 13163 (noise from a blacksmith's forge); *Clark* v. *Gordon* (1760) Mor. 13172 (a "house of office" held not to be a nuisance).

84   On nuisance in general, see N.R. Whitty in *Stair Memorial Encyclopaedia*, vol. 14 (1988) s.h.v.

85   For the significance of this point in connexion with other legal institutions, cf. R. Evans-Jones "Unjust Enrichment, Contract and the Third Reception of Roman Law in Scotland", (1993) 109 *L.Q.R.* 663–81.

9. ROMAN LAW COMES TO PARTICK

By ALAN RODGER

I Introduction

"The Conveyancer's calling is not destitute of excitement or interest". With these and similar encouraging and uplifting words Professor Menzies was wont to address those gentlemen whose destiny it was to be to inhabit the distinct realm of Conveyancing[1] — for Conveyancing truly "is a foreign country: they do things differently there". Those of us who live in the more ordinary realm of Scots law must look to statute and to the courts for our law; our giants are men such as Lord Watson, Lord Atkin and Lord Reid. In the realm of Conveyancing, they mostly live without reference to the courts and their giants have names such as Menzies, Montgomerie Bell and Halliday. Indeed when the courts are occasionally bold enough to enter the conveyancers' territory and to lay down a rule or clear up an apparent ambiguity, conveyancers can be somewhat slow to praise their efforts — especially in so far as those efforts seem to disturb the consensus by which the conveyancing community had been wont to conduct their affairs.[2]

But largely because conveyancers are by nature cautious and careful, most problems which can be anticipated are in practice regulated by the deeds and styles which are in everyday use. At the very heart of the conveyancer's work lie the sale and transfer of property, especially land and other heritable property. Not surprisingly therefore the basic rules of such transactions have long since been regulated by professional practice and come before the courts only comparatively rarely — especially since conveyancers are in the habit of referring disputes to the arbitration of those mysterious oracles, "the professors of conveyancing".

Among the basic rules of sale are the rules relating to risk, i.e. the determination as to which of the parties bears the risk of accidental damage to or destruction of the property after a contract for its sale has been concluded. Against the background of a general understanding

---

1   A. Menzies, *Conveyancing according to the Law of Scotland,* revised by J. S. Sturrock (Edinburgh, 1900), 3.
2   The decision in *Winston* v. *Patrick* 1980 S.C. 246 is a well-known example, while Lord Penrose has stirred up a fine controversy in *Sharp and Souter (Receivers of Albyn Construction Ltd)* v. *Thomson and Woolwich Building Society* 1994 S.L.T. 1068. Cf. R. Rennie, "Dead on Delivery" 1994 S.L.T. (News) 183.

that the common law rules of sale, which derived from Roman law, apply to heritable property just as much as they once did to moveable property, conveyancers have long been in the habit of including in missives clauses which actually lay the risk on the seller up to the time when the property passes to the purchaser.[3] Presumably it is for this reason that the law reports contain little authority on risk as it applies to transactions involving land. But just occasionally something slips through the fingers of the conveyancers and happily − for lawyers at least − in 1972 a slightly unusual agreement to purchase tenement property in Glasgow was followed by a fire which severely damaged the property. The result was a litigation in which the Inner House of the Court of Session had to consider the common law of risk. This gave them the opportunity for one of those forays into the foothills of Roman Law which come to be cited by writers concerned with enumerating the sources of Scots law and explaining the ways in which it differs from English law.[4] This article looks at the decision of the Court of Session and its Roman law background and then more briefly at the light which the decision casts on the relationship between Roman law and Scots law today.

II The Facts

The basic facts of the case are fairly straightforward. Glasgow Corporation were concerned to promote a compulsory purchase order and entered into negotiations with Sloans Dairies to buy certain premises which they owned in Partick. Since the order was not confirmed by the Secretary of State, the Corporation offered to buy the property from Sloans Dairies who accepted the offer in April 1972. The purchase price was fixed, but the agreement included a clause that "The date of entry will be a date to be agreed between the parties as at which vacant possession of the creamery and shop will be given". In June 1972, before any agreement on a date of entry had been reached, a fire broke out and damaged the buildings which had to be demolished. Despite this, Sloans Dairies tendered a disposition of the subjects and demanded payment of the price. When the Corporation refused to pay the agreed price, the Dairies raised an action against the Corporation for payment. In the event the Court of Session held that the risk would have passed to the defenders provided that the pursuers would have been willing to give the defenders possession of the subjects.

In both the Outer House and the Inner House it was held that the law which applied was the same common law of sale based on Roman

---

3   See e.g. J.P. Wood, *Lectures on Conveyancing* (Edinburgh, 1903), 550; J.M. Halliday, *Conveyancing Law and Practice*, vol. 2 (Edinburgh, 1986), paras. 15−115 and 15−116; *Stair Memorial Encyclopaedia*, vol. 6 (1988), para. 569.

4   E.g. *Stair Memorial Encyclopaedia*, vol. 22 (1987), para. 555.

law[5] as had formerly applied to the sale of moveable property before being superseded by the Sale of Goods Act 1893.[6] The general principles of that law are not in doubt and were not disputed: risk passes to the purchaser when the sale is perfect and a sale is perfect if the parties, subjects and price are agreed, but not if the contract is subject to a suspensive condition.[7] But on the particular issue there was little prior authority to guide the court and none which was directly in point. So the judges were forced in varying degrees to try to apply what they conceived to be the relevant principles of Roman law.[8] Those principles were derived from Justinian's *Institutes*[9] and D.19.1.30[10] together with an excerpt from Voet in translation and certain passages from the books of Moyle[11] and de Zulueta[12] on sale in Roman law.

III   A Risky Quotation from Voet

Lord Dunpark's opinion contains the most detailed treatment of the Civil law authorities. It has to be said that rather a lot of the material in it was never likely to contribute greatly to the solution of the particular problem before the Court. For instance, Lord Dunpark embarks on an investigation of the basis of the Roman rule *periculum rei venditae nondum traditae est emptoris* (the risk of a thing which has been sold but not yet transferred is on the buyer). One cannot but admire his courage since the topic has been debated for centuries without any generally accepted conclusions being reached.[13] It is hardly surprising therefore that Lord Dunpark's account is not entirely satisfying. He claims to find the equitable reason for the risk rule in both Roman and Scots law in the fact that in words attributed to Voet "all the benefit of the thing goes with the risk".[14] This is not an immediately compelling solution since the aim is supposed to be to identify why the risk lies where it does, whereas this formula presupposes that we know where

---

5   A.D.M. Forte, "Must a Purchaser Buy Charred Remains? — An Analysis of the Passing of Risk on Civilian Principles" (1984) 19 *Irish Jur.* 1 at 7ff. suggests that the Court too readily accepted that the Roman rules applied. *Sed quaere.*
6   Now replaced by the Sale of Goods Act 1979. For the background to the 1893 Act, see A. Rodger, "Codification of Commercial Law in Victorian Britain", (1992) 108 *L.Q.R.* 570.
7   See e.g. *Hansen* v. *Craig & Rose* (1859) 21 D. 432; *Widenmeyer* v. *Burn, Stewart & Co.* 1967 S.C 85.
8   For the Roman law background see now Zimmermann, *Obligations*, 281ff. with refs.
9   3.23.3.
10   1977 S.C. 238
11   J.B. Moyle, *The Contract of Sale in the Civil Law* (Oxford, 1892).
12   F. de Zulueta, *The Roman Law of Sale* (corrected edition, Oxford, 1957).
13   Zimmermann, *Obligations*, 290ff. with refs.
14   1977 S.C. 237. The passage comes from T. Berwick, *A Contribution to an English Translation of Voet's Commentary on the Pandects* (London, 1902), 136.

the risk lies and tells us that all the benefit goes with the risk. Could Voet really have argued so loosely? Happily not. The proposition is the work not of Voet but of his translator who misunderstood the Latin. This can best be seen from the text of the relevant passage from Voet:

> *Quamvis enim plerumque res suo pereat domino & a venditore ante traditionem dominium rei non recedat, non tamen eo minus periculum ante traditionem ad emtorem pertinet; tum quia eum etiam omne rei commodum sequitur, tum quia statim a perfecta venditione venditor incipit esse speciei debitor, quem rei interitu liberari placuit.* (For although a thing perishes at the risk of its owner and the ownership of a thing does not pass from the seller before transfer (*traditio*), none the less risk is on the purchaser before transfer; both because all the benefit of the thing also goes to him, and because from the time the sale is perfect the seller immediately starts to be the debtor in respect of the individual item, who, it has been held, is freed [from his obligation] by the destruction of the thing).

Therefore what Voet actually said in the first of the reasons which he gave in the relevant passage was *"periculum ante traditionem ad emtorem pertinet...quia eum etiam omne rei commodum sequitur..."*,[15] i.e. "risk is on the purchaser before transfer...because all the benefit of the thing goes to him...". In other words Voet said the reverse of what Berwick makes him say and Lord Dunpark's reason rests on a mistranslation.[16] Unfortunately there is actually nothing in the Roman sources to suggest that Voet's explanation really accounts for the origin of the Roman rule. There are three Roman texts which link the burden of risk and the enjoyment of benefit (*commodum*): D.18.6.7*pr.*, C.4.49.12 and *Inst.*3.23.3. But all presuppose that the purchaser bears the risk and therefore they do not tell us anything about why that was the case. Indeed their form would suggest that the rule on risk was fixed before that on the benefit which follows it. The view of Brodie[17] and others which Lord Dunpark adopts is therefore erected on a somewhat shaky foundation.

Instead of chasing up other minor points in Lord Dunpark's opinion, it is preferable at this point to turn to the core of his reasoning. He takes the basic principle of the law to be "that, on the conclusion of a perfect contract for the sale of heritable property, the risk of damage passes from the seller to the buyer".[18] The question was therefore whether on the facts of this case the contract was "perfect". The parties and subjects were determined, as was the price. The argument of the defenders was that none the less the contract was not perfect because the date of entry had not been agreed.

---

15 *Commentarius ad Pandectas* (Louvain, 1698), 18.6.1 (citations omitted and punctuation modified).
16 Berwick appears to have translated the passage as if *eum* were *id.*
17 G. Brodie (ed.), *Supplement to Stair's Institutions of the Law of Scotland* (Edinburgh, 1831), 857. Cf. 1977 S.C. 237.
18 Cf. at n.7 *supra.*

One important aspect of that argument was based on aspects of
Scots law in which Roman doctrines play no particular part.[19] The issue
was whether a date of entry was essential for there to be a binding contract of sale of heritable subjects. The defenders in effect conceded that
a fixed date of entry was not essential and that concession appears to
be in line with what is now regarded as settled law.[20] The result of the
concession was significant because the position came to be that "It is
accepted that the missives concluded a binding legal contract".[21]

IV   Types of Condition

Even though the defenders thus accepted that the contract was binding, they nevertheless presented an argument based on the proposition
that the date of entry provision introduced "a suspensive element".[22] It
is a little difficult to reconstruct precisely how the point was argued,
but referring to the date of entry, Lord Justice-Clerk Wheatley asks "Did
this constitute a suspensive condition or was it simply a resolutive condition?" He goes on to record that the defenders contended that it was a
suspensive condition, which prevented the contract from being perfect, while the pursuers argued that it was "simply" a resolutive condition and so they had a prestable right from the time of the conclusion
of the contract.[23] The Lord Justice-Clerk then proceeds by way of examining the terms of the contract and concludes that all that the defenders were entitled to was a valid conveyance and to be valid a
conveyance would not have required to refer to the date of entry. He
therefore holds that from the time when the contract was completed
the defenders had had a prestable right to delivery or possession of the
subjects on the date of entry and that accordingly the risk had passed to
them by the time of the fire.[24]

Certain aspects of this analysis are not altogether easy to follow. In
particular it will be observed that his Lordship begins by recording the
pursuers' argument that they had a prestable right to the price but ends
up with a conclusion based on the defenders' right to delivery or possession of the subjects. More importantly, however, the idea of the date
of entry being a resolutive condition is surely rather strange.

In Roman law sales could be made subject to suspensive or resolutive conditions.[25] The distinction is similar to that in Scots law where

---

19   For a discussion see Forte, *op. cit.*, n.5, 4ff.
20   *Gordon District Council* v. *Wimpey Homes Holdings Ltd.* 1988 S.L.T. 481
     and the discussion in G.L. Gretton and K.G.C. Reid, *Conveyancing*
     (Edinburgh, 1993), 51ff.
21   1977 S.C. 233.
22   1977 S.C. 233.
23   1977 S.C. 234.
24   1977 S.C. 235.
25   On the whole subject of the Roman law on conditions and *dies* see now
     the account in Zimmermann, *Obligations,* Chap. 23.

obligations subject to a suspensive condition are regarded as contingent.[26] A sale subject to a suspensive condition was not perfect and risk did not pass to the buyer unless the condition was fulfilled. On the other hand a resolutive condition would not prevent the sale from being perfect, but the occurrence of the condition would mean that the contract was at an end. So I could agree to purchase a particular load of corn from you, "unless my ship arrives by 1 September". The sale is perfect and the risk passes — subject to the possibility of the contract coming to an end if the ship does indeed arrive before 1 September.[27] In *Sloans Dairies*, however, the pursuers at no time contended that the occurrence of the date of entry would have operated in this fashion. On the contrary, entry was something which would have been contemplated as an ordinary and indeed essential stage in the working out of the contract and the conveyance, rather than as an event which would have led to the contract coming to an end. In fact on any normal analysis — and certainly on any analysis which would have been adopted by Roman jurists — the date of entry was not a resolutive condition. Indeed one suspects that the pursuers would never have sought to describe it as a resolutive condition if the defenders had not first argued that it was a suspensive condition. Faced with the argument that the date of entry was one kind of condition, the pursuers apparently countered with the argument that it was the other.

Some of the confusion may stem from not distinguishing clearly enough at this point in the argument between conditions which relate to the operation of a contract as a whole and conditions which merely relate to one of the obligations in a contract.[28] An agreement to buy your car if it passes the relevant statutory mechanical test next month does not take effect pending the purification of the condition. On the other hand you may sell me your house and agree to give me entry on 1 October if you have found suitable alternative accommodation by then. The contract of sale is not suspended since the condition relates only to the performance of one of the obligations under the contract. Now since, as we saw,[29] it was agreed in the present case — and on the authorities rightly so — that the missives constituted a binding agreement, it follows that the date of entry provision did not operate as a suspensive condition of the first kind. Rather it related to the operation of

---

26   W.M. Gloag, *The Law of Contract* (2nd ed., Edinburgh, 1929), 272. It is not clear whether the Scottish Law Commission employ a different analysis when they say that if a suspensive condition is not fulfilled "the contract will fall": Scottish Law Commission, *Passing of Risk in Contracts for the Sale of Land*, Discussion Paper No. 81 (March 1989), para. 2.1.

27   Cf. D.18.3.2 (Pomponius, 35 *ad Sabinum*). The subject was of course rather complicated: W. W. Buckland, *A Textbook of Roman Law* (3rd ed. by P.G. Stein, Cambridge, 1963), 494ff.

28   Cf. W.W. McBryde, *The Law of Contract in Scotland* (Edinburgh, 1987), paras. 4–08ff.

29   At the end of Part III.

one of the obligations under the missives. The Lord Justice-Clerk was proceeding on that basis when he said: "[t]he parties, the subjects and the price were specified. Was anything further required to be done to give the buyer, i.e. the defenders a *jus ad rem specificam*? The answer is 'No'". He added that the defenders "would have a prestable right to delivery or possession of the subjects on the date of entry, however that date was determined, and that was a right which they enjoyed from the 'perfection' of the contract and thus at the time of the fire".[30]

V The Date of Entry

It may be useful to recall the wording of the relevant provision: "The date of entry will be a date to be agreed between the parties as at which date vacant possession of the creamery and shop will be given". The form of this term is not perhaps that which one immediately associates with a typical condition and, of course, the purpose of the term is simply to identify the date on which the pursuers would require to perform their contractual obligation to give the defenders possession of the creamery and shop. Until that date arrived the defenders could not have demanded immediate entry to the subjects.[31] None the less the term did not provide for entry on a specified date such as 1 October and indeed at first sight it seems to leave the position rather uncertain since the date required to be agreed between the parties.[32] Suppose that, despite their best endeavours, the parties could not agree. Would there then have been no date of entry under the missives and therefore no date on which the defenders could have demanded entry? Rather surprisingly perhaps, the Court solved this conundrum by holding that, failing agreement, the date of entry under the missives would be determined by Section 28 of the Conveyancing (Scotland) Act 1874,[33] a provision which really seems to deal with the date of entry to be implied into a disposition which does not contain one. However that may be, by invoking this section, the Inner House judges were able to conclude that there was no lacuna since the date of entry under the missives was either to be a date agreed between the parties or, failing agreement, the first term of Whitsunday or Martinmas after the conveyance.

VI The Problem as one of *Dies*

As we saw,[34] the Lord Justice-Clerk presents the arguments on the passing of risk in terms of types of condition. Lord Dunpark's final position

---

30   1977 S.C. 234. Cf. Lord Dunpark at 239. Cf. also the Lord Ordinary (Stott) at 228.
31   1977 S.C. 242.
32   Cf. Gretton and Reid, *Conveyancing, cit. sup.*, n.20, at 51ff.; Forte, *op. cit.*, n.5, 5ff.
33   1977 S.C. 233ff. *per* Lord Justice-Clerk Wheatley.
34   In Part IV.

is somewhat different. He sees the date of entry provision as essentially concerned with a *date*, viz. the date when certain critical obligations became enforceable. He says that, although when the missives were concluded the defenders had no right to demand immediate entry, they did acquire a personal right to become proprietors of the subjects at some future date to be fixed by agreement. "It is the vesting of that right which is material — *dies cedit* — not the date when the performance may be demanded — *dies venit*".[35] The use of this particular terminology and his conclusion that the right is not suspended but vests forthwith are significant. They indicate that Lord Dunpark was thinking of the problem in terms of the effect of *dies* rather than in terms of the effect of a condition on the passing of risk. He was really using Roman terminology to define the issue before the court along the following lines: does the date of entry clause viewed as some kind of *dies* provision prevent the contract of sale from being "perfect" for the purposes of the passing of risk?

Unfortunately it cannot be said that defining the question in terms of *dies* makes it any easier to answer in terms of Roman law at least, for Zulueta points out that we "are even less informed" on the subject of risk and *dies* than we are on other aspects of the topic of risk in connexion with sale.[36] This is largely because both Gaius and Justinian's *Institutes* do not mention the topic at all and the few texts in the *Digest* which may have a bearing on the topic are scattered in different titles.[37] Precisely because the matter is not treated prominently in the *Institutes* or *Digest,* it does not feature prominently either in works which are based on them. So for instance in his section on risk, Pothier discusses the effect of conditions but makes no mention of *dies*[38] and a similar pattern is found in the work of the Scottish writer, Mungo Brown, who is heavily influenced by Pothier.[39] One of the few texts which touches on an aspect of the topic and which purports at least to give us the opinion of Papinian is contained in the Vatican Fragments[40] which were not discovered until 1821. Not surprisingly Brown's book on sale — which appeared in the same year and so before the new text had even been published — makes no mention of this text. Even where the topic of *dies* is mentioned in the context of risk, because of its absence

---

35   1977 S.C. 242. One might have expected Lord Dunpark to contrast the date when the defenders could enforce their right to demand entry with the vesting of the right to demand entry on that date rather than with the vesting of the right to become proprietor on that date.

36   Zulueta, *The Roman Law of Sale, cit. sup.*, n.12, 32.

37   E. Seckel and E. Levy, "Die Gefahrtragung beim Kauf im klassischen römischen Recht", in E. Levy, *Gesammelte Schriften*, vol. 2 (Cologne and Graz, 1963), 167 at 213.

38   R.J. Pothier, *Traité du Contrat de Vente* (first published, Paris, 1762) nos. 307ff.

39   M.P. Brown, *Treatise on the Law of Sale* (Edinburgh, 1821), para. 365.

40   V.F. 16. The text is however not without its difficulties. Cf. Zimmermann, *Obligations,* 285 with refs., esp. Seckel-Levy, *op. cit.,* n.37, 215ff.

from the *Institutes* and *Digest* it tends to come in as something of an afterthought.[41] This pattern is carried over into modern discussions in Scots law where even after *Sloans Dairies* there tends to be no mention of the effect of *dies* on risk.[42]

VII Conditions and *Dies*

The absence of a proper discussion of the topic of *dies* in the treatment of risk by the *Institutes* and *Digest* means not only that there are very few texts on it, but also that we are in consequence extremely badly informed about the views of the Roman jurists. Of course we know quite a lot about their attitude to conditions and *dies* in general. At the very simplest level the jurists distinguished between provisions which set a particular day for an obligation to come into force (*dies certus*) and those which specified a time by reference to an event which was bound to occur but at a moment which could not be predicted (*dies incertus*).[43] It was a characteristic of either kind of provision and hence of *dies* that it related to a time which was bound to come. In Scots law obligations of these kinds are known as future obligations.[44] An example of the former type would be a contract for the sale of Whiteacre to take effect on 1 June next — one can predict precisely when the contract of sale will come into effect. An example of the latter would be a sale of Whiteacre to take effect one month after your father's death: the sale is bound to come into operation since your father is bound to die, but, since no-one knows when this will happen, the precise date when the contract will come into effect is uncertain. These are no mere academic distinctions since different legal consequences might follow, depending on whether the contract was subject to *dies certus* or *dies incertus*.

The Roman jurists were also very well aware that one could not decide whether something was truly an example of *dies* rather than a condition simply by looking at its form. Something which looked like a condition might really be *dies*[45] and something which looked at first sight like *dies* might actually turn out on inspection to operate as a condition.[46] Indeed the complications did not end there since a provision could combine elements of *dies* and condition.[47] If then one were

41   E.g. B. Windscheid, *Lehrbuch des Pandektenrechts*, vol. 2 (9th ed. by Th. Kipp, Frankfurt am Main, 1906), para. 390, n.10; Zulueta, *The Roman Law of Sale, cit. sup.*, n.12, 32.
42   E.g. Gretton and Reid, *Conveyancing, cit. sup.*, n.20, 68ff.; *Stair Memorial Encyclopaedia*, vol. 18 (1993), para. 651.
43   In fact it has long been recognised that the use of the terminology in the *Digest* is by no means uniform. See, e.g., F.C. von Savigny, *System des heutigen römischen Rechts* vol. 3 (1840) 204ff.
44   Gloag, *The Law of Contract, cit. sup.*, n.26, 271.
45   D.45.1.45.3 (Ulpian, 50 *ad Sabinum*); Savigny, *System, cit.*, vol. 3, 206.
46   Savigny, *System, cit.*, vol. 3, 207.
47   D.36.2.22*pr.* (Pomponius, 5 *ad Quintum Mucium*); Savigny, *System, cit.*, vol. 3, 207.

trying to analyse the *Sloans Dairies* problem in Roman terms, it would be necessary first to decide into which category the date of entry provision fell.

Lord Dunpark does not seem to have had any doubt about the matter. Having committed himself to an analysis in terms of *dies*, he really approaches the term on the basis that *dies cedit* and so the right to demand entry had vested in the defenders even though the date for demanding performance of the sellers' obligation to give entry (when *dies venit*) had not yet arrived. In other words, in Scots law terms, he regards the obligation to give entry as future rather than as contingent. Since the terminology of *dies* does not seem to be used much in modern Scottish contract law,[48] it may be that Lord Dunpark is thinking of the law of succession where *dies* has a role to play and the terminology is freely employed.[49] At all events it seems clear that his Lordship takes the view that a date of entry which will fall on a date to be agreed or else at the legal term following the conveyance of the property is sufficiently certain not to prevent the risk passing to the purchaser.

Lord Dunpark's approach has been criticised by Professor Forte who equally uncompromisingly asserts the opposite opinion. He thinks that the entry date provision "imports a suspensive condition into the contract...which requires to be purified before the sale will be perfect". He apparently takes the view that the mere presence of what he regards as a suspensive condition attaching to one of the terms is sufficient to prevent the contract from being perfect for the purposes of the passing of risk.[50] It is not entirely clear what the basis for his conclusion is, but nothing which he cites in his article would seem to vouch it. In particular the Roman texts which indicate expressly that a contract of sale is not perfect until any suspensive condition is purified appear to relate to a suspensive condition which is attached to the contract as a whole rather than to one particular obligation under that contract.[51] So they are not directly in point.

None the less, and without necessarily adopting Forte's approach, one can at least wonder whether the position is indeed as straightforward as Lord Dunpark's opinion implies. Even if one starts from the position that the term should be regarded as an example of *dies*, it is a somewhat *incertus dies*. The date of entry is not a calendar date, which would be the most definite. Nor is it a straightforward example of a

---

48 See, however, the discussion in W.A. Wilson, *The Scottish Law of Debt* (2nd ed., Edinburgh, 1991), paras. 1.10ff., with a rare but appropriate misprint in 1.11.

49 See e.g. R.C. Henderson, *The Principles of Vesting in the Law of Succession* (2nd ed., Edinburgh, 1938) 7ff.

50 *Op. cit.*, n.5, 6ff. Forte does not deal with the point that Lord Dunpark is proceeding on the basis of *dies*, but this may be because he rejects the Court's use of Section 28 of the 1874 Act to supplement the contract.

51 Cf. Buckland, *Textbook, cit. sup.*, n.27, 494ff.

date which is bound to occur though one cannot predict when.[52]
Rather, the term requires the parties to agree and that at the very least
imports a stage of uncertain date between the completion of the contract and the date when the purchasers could enforce their right of
entry. Moreover that stage introduces what looks like a further element
of uncertainty since there can be no guarantee that the parties will
reach agreement on the date. Even if the statutory provision can be
prayed in aid to introduce a fall-back date if the parties do not agree,
that date is itself somewhat precarious since it is determined by reference to "the date of the conveyance" which presumably means the date
of execution by the seller and therefore depends on when (or even
whether) the seller executes the disposition.

But the more one looks at the provision the less clear it becomes
that it is really a straightforward case of *dies*. In particular the provision
for agreement surely imports a measure of doubt as to whether the date
will ever materialise and that doubt is not entirely removed by the
statutory provision which requires the sellers to act before it can come
into effect. Given these elements it seems likely that the Roman jurists
would have reached the conclusion that the date of entry provision
should really be regarded as operating to a large extent as a form of
condition attaching to the sellers' obligation to give entry under the
contract. In Scots law terms the obligation would begin to look more
like a contingent than a future obligation.

Even if that is correct, what we cannot tell unfortunately is what
opinion the Roman jurists would have held about the effect of such a
term on the passing of risk under a contract of sale. Indeed in one
sense the question is almost meaningless since the date of entry is a
concept which derives from Scottish conveyancing law and which
formed no part of a contract for the sale of land in Roman law. In that
sense the issue simply could not have arisen in this form. On the other
hand a Roman seller of land was obliged to give the purchaser peace-
able possession of the land and doubtless arrangements were often
made to postpone the actual transfer of possession until some time
after the conclusion of the contract of sale. So in that sense similar
issues must have arisen. The difficulty is that we are simply not told
in the texts what the position was and commentators have been reduced
to speculating. Speaking of sale in general, Zulueta suggests that
"Deferred delivery may be assumed to be in the seller's interest and the
risk to be on him".[53] It is far from clear, however, that the advantages in

---

52   For a discussion of some of the issues which such a provision would have
     raised if attached to a contract of sale in classical Roman Law, see A.
     Rodger, "*Emptio Perfecta* Revisited: a Study of Digest 18,6,8,1" (1982) 50
     T.v.R. 337. That article derived from an initial attempt to understand *Sloans
     Dairies* in terms of Roman law.
53   *The Roman Law of Sale, cit. sup.*, n.12, 32. He is following the approach in
     the Seckel-Levy article, *cit. sup*, n.37, 231.

the postponement of the date of entry in the present case were exclusively or even predominantly with the sellers. Of course, they continued to draw the rents from the property and so to derive that benefit.[54]
On the other hand the Corporation were really the prime movers in the
whole transaction which originated in a compulsory purchase scheme.
In such a situation the local authority will have no particular desire to
take over the property and pay out the price or compensation before
they are ready to proceed with any scheme for redevelopment and so it
will undoubtedly have suited the Corporation to leave the sellers in
possession in the meantime. Very probably therefore in this case the
arrangement to postpone the date of entry was in the interest of both
parties. Against that background Zulueta's test, which has in any event
no basis in the Roman texts, does not produce any clear result.

Only certain very general points can safely be made in regard to
the approach of the Roman jurists to the point. First, Professor Daube
has remarked that "the attitude of Roman law to conditions is highly
opportunistic"[55] and so the jurists might well have adopted a flexible
approach — to be coloured by the particular facts of any case before
them. That makes it really impossible even to attempt to go further in
reconstructing what the decision might have been in the case of the
unusual *Sloans Dairies* provision coupled with Section 28 of the 1874
Act. Secondly, it is in any event most unlikely that there would have
been any single agreed solution, since Roman law thrived on differing
views and on debates among the jurists which could carry on from generation to generation in the absence of anything like a modern appeal
court to issue an authoritative ruling. Lastly, we are concerned with the
operation of sale, one of the *bonae fidei* contracts, and in advancing
any solution a jurist would have had regard to the requirements of good
faith which governed such contracts.

Given these uncertainties and differences between the systems,
there is no real way of knowing whether the Scottish judges' decision
would have met with the approval of their Roman predecessors. Nor
does it perhaps matter very much since the Second Division had to
apply what they conceived to be the law of Scotland in 1977.

VIII   Roman Law and Scots Law Today

Consideration of the problems thrown up by *Sloans Dairies* prompts a
few remarks on the role of Roman law in our legal system today.

Nowadays the courts have to grapple with Roman law only rarely.
The cases where they are called upon to do so generally involve topics
which, for some reason, have not been much litigated. This is because,

---

54   1977 S.C. 235. It is not clear from the report whether they were also able
to continue using their shop and creamery.

55   D. Daube, "Slave-Catching" (1952) 64 *J.R.* 12 at 22, reprinted in D. Daube,
Collected Studies in Roman Law, edd. D. Cohen and D. Simon (Frankfurt
am Main, 1991), 501 at 509.

even though some aspect of our law may ultimately derive from Roman law and the *ius commune*, there will be no need to go back to those older materials if a *corpus* of relevant case law already exists.[56] To a large extent *Sloans Dairies* conforms to this pattern. Since the doctrine of risk applies only where the damage is accidental and is not the fault of either party to the contract, there will be relatively few occasions when it would be called into play. Since our common law of sale was superseded for moveable property in 1894 the potential field of application of the Roman principles on risk has been confined to sale of heritable property and, as was noted in the Introduction, the well-established practice of conveyancers will mean that, even in those few cases where it might otherwise apply, the matter will usually be regulated by the provisions of the missives. *Sloans Dairies* was therefore an unusual case and that explains why, although the legal doctrine in question was ancient, the first litigation on the point could occur as late as 1977. Since the question had not been before the courts previously, there was little Scottish authority to guide the judges and this in turn accounts for the need felt by Lord Dunpark in particular to examine the Roman law materials to see whether they offered guidance on the appropriate decision in Scots law.

It is hard to avoid the impression that the judges were not entirely at ease in dealing with the Roman law materials and, although this is harder to detect from the pages of the report, it is likely that the same applied to counsel. It certainly applies to the *Session Cases* reporter who was plainly unfamiliar with the material and as a result produced many unfortunate citations. The Lord Justice-Clerk avoided the difficulties by simply adopting[57] the results of Lord Dunpark's "exhaustive study" of the civilian materials.

Moreover his endorsement of Lord Dunpark's analysis was merely *obiter* since he had felt able to decide the case without entering too deeply into the matters which Lord Dunpark discussed.[58] This is not as surprising as it might at first sight seem since, as we have noted, the Roman law materials cited to the Court did not actually provide a neat answer to the problem which had to be solved. Indeed quite possibly it was precisely because those materials did not contain the answer that the case ever reached the Court of Session. If it had been possible to identify some passage which dealt with the matter in a clear-cut way, the case might well not have been fought. This would suggest that paradoxically the Scottish courts may tend nowadays to be asked to look at Roman law materials when they do not provide the answer to the problem in issue rather than when they do.

---

56   Cf. generally A. Rodger, "Roman Law in Practice in Britain", (1993) 12 *Rechtshistorisches Journal* 261 esp. at 267ff.

57   1977 S.C. 235. Lord Wylie agrees with both the Lord Justice-Clerk and Lord Dunpark even though their opinions do not proceed on an identical basis, e.g. on the matter of *dies*.

58   1977 S.C. 235.

Finally the opinions of the judges do not give the impression that they felt that the Roman law which they were applying was law which had developed over a period of two thousand years or more. The texts which they mention come from Justinian's *Institutes, Code* and *Digest* which date from the sixth century. Although the seventeenth- and early eighteenth-century writer Voet is also referred to, this is merely for his supposed view about the basis of the Roman rule on risk.[59] That is a particularly unsatisfactory reason for citing Voet, since if one wishes to understand as a matter of history what the origins and principles of a rule of ancient Roman law were, then the correct place to look is in the writings of modern Romanist scholars who will at least have approached the matter in a scientific manner.[60]

For the most part the citations in Lord Dunpark's judgment jump backwards and forwards in time without seeking to describe the development of the law. There are direct or indirect references to the views of Voet, Pothier,[61] Justinian, Julian,[62] Moyle, Windscheid and Powell[63] and it is not entirely clear how one distinguishes the weight to be given to the views of writers spanning the ages from at least the second to the twentieth century. In any event the selection of views is arbitrary in the extreme. If Voet, why not Cujacius? If Pothier, why not Domat? At certain points moreover the views of the jurists who are mentioned seem to have been invoked for propositions which the writers might not have supported. For instance Lord Dunpark[64] records a very strange argument of defenders' counsel based on a passage in Moyle[65] and his reference to a disputed theory of Windscheid. That theory is in turn based on the premise that in a contract of sale the seller does not so much agree to transfer the property as actually transfer it.[66] It is far from clear that any such theory would fit well into the framework of the sale and transfer of land in Scots law, but in any event Lord Dunpark rightly points out that counsel's argument really stands Windscheid's theory on its head. Is this single indirect and unsatisfactory allusion to Windscheid really a sufficient recognition of the contribution of the nineteenth-century Pandectists?

---

59 See Part III.
60 For a convenient survey of modern scholarship see R. Monier, *Manuel élémentaire de droit romain,* vol. 2 (Paris, 1948), 147ff.
61 1977 S.C. 238 quoting Lord McLaren.
62 1977 S.C. 238 quoting Lord McLaren who cited D.19.1.30 (Africanus, 8 *quaestionum*) giving the views of Julian (*ait*). On the nature of the work see F. Schulz, *History of Roman Legal Science* (corrected edition, Oxford, 1953), 230ff.
63 1977 S.C. 241 where the correct reference is to R. Powell, "Eviction in Roman Law and English Law", in *Studies in the Roman Law of Sale Dedicated to the Memory of Francis de Zulueta,* ed. D. Daube (Oxford, 1959), 78 at 86.
64 1977 S.C. 240.
65 *The Contract of Sale in the Civil Law, cit.sup.,* n.11, 91.
66 *Lehrbuch des Pandektenrechts, cit. sup.,* n.41, vol. 2 para. 321.

If there are signs that the Roman law material caused particular problems for the Court in *Sloans Dairies*, then those problems probably stem largely from the fact that the courts do not often have to handle these authorities nowadays and so are not particularly familiar with them. Nor is there any particular reason to think that the position will change significantly in future. The downgrading of the study of Roman law in the universities gives no cause for optimism about the future handling of such issues. On a happier note we may notice that, since *Sloans Dairies* was decided, Professor Zimmermann has provided a very significant new source of information on all matters relating to the development of the civilian doctrines in the sphere of obligations. Had his *Law of Obligations* been available in 1977, it could undoubtedly have helped to focus the arguments in the case, even if in the end the judges would still have been left with the hard work of actually deciding the point.[67]

---

67   I am grateful to Professor David Johnston who at short notice read a draft of this article and gave me useful advice of which I have tried to take account. I should also like to thank the Hon. Lord Davidson for a number of corrections.

10. FROM "UNDUE TRANSFER" TO "RETENTION WITHOUT A LEGAL BASIS" (THE *CONDICTIO INDEBITI* AND *CONDICTIO OB TURPEM VEL INIUSTAM CAUSAM*)

By ROBIN EVANS-JONES

Introduction

The main purpose of this chapter is to examine the content of the central claim of the law of repetition in Scots law, the *condictio indebiti*, to attempt to understand why, notwithstanding its central position, the content of the *condictio indebiti* has proven to be so elusive, and to establish a structure which not only resolves the tensions within the *condictio indebiti* itself, but which provides a model for the future development of the modern Scots law of unjustified enrichment as a whole.

This examination of the *condictio indebiti* will also make it possible to identify some general characteristics of modern Scots law. In this context Scots law has a clear civilian basis. However, since the *condictio indebiti* has developed in some respects beyond earlier conceptions, it should not be viewed in Scotland exclusively in the light of Roman law. The elusive nature of the *condictio indebiti* can be understood, and then authoritatively defined, only after an appreciation of the manner in which it was transmitted into modern law. The Scottish experience of the *condictio indebiti* also shows how its law is still often extremely historical in character.

The historical nature and relative uncertainty of private law[1] are among features of the Civil law tradition which led most civilian legal systems to codification. Codification, on one level, can be seen as the choice of what is best from the alternatives presented to a legal system from its past. In Scotland, because of the nature of its legal history for the last two hundred years, the choice now often needs to be made from alternatives provided both by its own traditions and by English law. No country in the world has undergone such a direct attack on the fundamental conceptions of the *condictio indebiti* as Scotland. This attack comes mainly in the form of a voice which has argued that Scots law should abandon the *condictio indebiti* and follow English law by understanding it as "mistake".[2] The mixed legal system might be seen to

---

1 This uncertainty results from the richness of the civilian culture. For example, in respect of the *condictio indebiti* it has given rise to a range of interpretations of the content of the claim.
2 P.B.H. Birks, "Restitution: A View of Scots Law", (1985) 38 *C.L.P.* 57 at 63; "Six Questions in Search of a Subject – Unjust Enrichment in a Crisis of Identity", 1985 *J.R.* 227.

be in the enviable position of being open to, and therefore well placed to select, what is best from both the Civil and Common law traditions. However, the "mixed" character of Scots law results largely from the fact that one legal culture has merely been replaced by another. We will see from the examination of the *condictio indebiti* that the new culture, unsurprisingly, always tends to interpret the law deriving from the (earlier) civilian culture in the light of its own understandings which are often heavily influenced by English law. So, for example, in addition to the suggestion that the *condictio indebiti* should be abandoned in favour of "mistake", we find that in Scotland, notwithstanding judicial dicta to the contrary, there is now a widespread conviction that error forms an essential feature of the cause of action of the *condictio indebiti*. The attraction of this understanding is seen to be that it allows a typology of claims to be established in which "error" corresponds with "mistake" of English law.[3] Such an approach in fact masks what are important differences of structure between the modern Civil law and the Common law in this context.[4] This examination of the *condictio indebiti* will attempt to identify these differences and to evaluate their strengths. It will conclude that there is one solution – which, as it happens, looks to classical Roman law for its inspiration – which is functionally and conceptually superior to the rest.

The framework of the Scots law of unjustified enrichment was created by the institutional writers mainly on the basis of the Civil law.[5] Since the beginning of the nineteenth century its development has lain almost exclusively in the hands of the courts. It is only now, towards the end of the twentieth century, that the law of unjustified enrichment is attracting widespread academic attention in Scotland. The academic attention will certainly result in important developments of the law, the direction of which will be determined by a series of choices which will themselves contribute to the overall quality of the Scottish legal system. It is important for a number of reasons to build a strong civilian culture in Scotland. At the very least, whenever the law is in a state of uncertainty, the existence of such a culture will allow a more informed choice to be made from the range of solutions presented to the legal system. The importance of this ability to be informed about one's own

---

3   See the discussion by N.R. Whitty, "Some Trends and Issues in Scots Unjust Enrichment Law", 1994 *J.R.* 127. See also D.R. Macdonald, "Mistaken Payments in Scots Law", 1989 *J.R.* 49.

4   Those who are of this opinion ignore the fact that the *condictio indebiti* must by definition always relate to what is "undue". In attempting to assimilate Scots law and English law they tie the former into a destructively narrow range which is not shared by English law since "mistake" is not restricted to transfers which are "undue".

5   See most recently, H.L. MacQueen and W.D.H. Sellar, "Unjust Enrichment in Scots Law", in *Unjustified Enrichment. The Comparative Legal History of the Law of Restitution*, ed. E.J.H. Schrage (Comparative Studies on Continental and Anglo-American Law, 15, Berlin, 1995), 289–321.

law is underlined by the observation that the conception of the *condictio indebiti* which looks to classical Roman law for its inspiration has been adopted as functionally best by all the civilian codes of the twentieth century. Yet, this is the conception of the *condictio indebiti*, perhaps because it is furthest from English law, which, if the arguments found in this chapter are found to be convincing, will only just have escaped with its life in Scotland.

Repetition and the Condictio

It has recently been argued, and seems universally to have been accepted, that the Scots law of unjustified enrichment is ordered according to the nature of the benefit received. "Repetition" is taken as that part of the law of restitution which concerns the exact return of money.[6] However, there are grounds on which to argue that an important underlying order of the law of restitution is according to the manner in which the enrichment was acquired.

"Repetition" is literally a reclaim of a specific thing or a fixed amount, the accent being upon "reclaim". Sometimes in Scots law the term "repetition" is restricted to claims arising under the *condictio indebiti*[7] but more usually it is also seen to include claims under all the other named *condictiones*.[8] The institutional writers before Bell did not speak of a law of repetition as such, they merely identified a distinct part of the law of restitution as that governed by the *condictiones* in respect of which the term "repetition" is sometimes used.[9]

Repetition is of Money or Money and Property?

A feature of the law of repetition in Scots law is that it is usually, but not invariably, presented as the recovery of money with one of the recognised *condictiones*[10]. The belief that repetition is restricted to claims of money has recently been given still further academic support by P.B.H.

6   See P.B.H. Birks, *op. cit.*, n.2 above.
7   Mackenzie, 3,1,15; Bell, *Prin.* s. 531; Bell's *Dictionary and Digest of the Law of Scotland* (Edinburgh, 1890), "Repetition".
8   See W.M. Gloag, *The Law of Contract* (2nd ed., Edinburgh, 1929), 57, 60; *Encyclopaedia of the Laws of Scotland* (Edinburgh, 1931), "Repetition"; W.M. Gloag and R.C. Henderson, *Introduction to the Laws of Scotland* (9th ed. by A.B. Wilkinson and W.A. Wilson, Edinburgh, 1987), 160; D.M. Walker, *Principles of Scottish Private Law* (4th ed., Oxford, 1988), vol. 2, 507. Cf. T.B. Smith *A Short Commentary on the Law of Scotland* (Edinburgh, 1962), 626; D.M. Walker, *The Law of Contracts and Related Obligations in Scotland* (London, 1985), 584; W.W. McBryde, *The Law of Contract in Scotland* (Edinburgh, 1987), 204.
9   See esp. Stair, 1,7,9; Mackenzie, 3,1,15; Hume, *Lectures,* vol. 3, 173.
10   Hume, *Lectures,* vol. 3, 172; Gloag, *op. cit.*, 57, 60; *Encyclopaedia of the Laws of Scotland* (1931), "Repetition"; Gloag and Henderson, *cit. sup.*, n.8, 160; Walker, *Principles, cit.*, vol. 2, 507. Cf. Bell, *Prin.* s. 531 discussed by Birks, 1985 *J.R.* 227 at 236; T.B. Smith, *A Short Commentary*, 626; Walker, *Contract, cit.*, 584; McBryde, *op. cit.*, 204.

Birks[11]. Crucially, but without developing it further, Birks remarks that "while the claim to the money is denoted 'repetition' this usage is not strongly insisted upon".[12]

Stair applies the *condictio indebiti* to both property and money and in this regard he is followed by Bankton[13] and Bell.[14] He says that *indebite solutum* is where any party "delivereth or payeth that which he supposeth due".[15] He then uses the word "repetition" of *indebiti solutio*. He says, "There is this exception against *indebite solutum*, that it cannot be repeated".[16] A possible implication is that "repetition" covers both property and money except that the context suggests that Stair probably had only a claim for money in mind in the particular instance where the word "repeated" was used. Erskine expressly applies the *condictio causa data causa non secuta* to transfers of property.[17] Bell, who was the first of the institutional writers to identify "repetition" as a distinct category of the law, saw it as including transfers of property though only under the *condictio indebiti*.[18]

There is nothing in the word "repetition" itself which means that it is restricted to claims of money. It is taken from the Latin *repetitio* and is best translated as "a demanding back".[19] In Roman law the term *repetitio* is used in connection with transfers both of property and money under the *condictiones*,[20] though, since there was no specific implement in this context, the *condictio* necessarily sounded in money.[21]

The belief that "repetition" is limited to claims of money is likely to have resulted from four main factors: the legacy of Roman law where the *condictio* sounded in money, the dominance of the *condictio indebiti* in the scheme of repetition allied to an understandable but misleading translation from Latin of its basis, and the fact that in practice recovery of money still comprises the vast majority of claims under the *condictiones*.

The basis of a claim under the *condictio indebiti* is *indebiti solutio*.[22] *Solutio* is often translated, perfectly correctly on one level, as "payment". "Payments" of course, *stricto sensu*, involve only the transfer

---

11   1985 *J.R.* 227 at 235ff; (1985) 38 *C.L.P.* 57 at 62ff.
12   (1985) 38 *C.L.P.* at 63.
13   Bankton, 1,8.
14   Bell, *Prin.* ss. 530, 531.
15   Stair, 1,7,9.
16   *Ibid.*
17   Erskine, *Inst.*, 3,1,10.
18   Bell, *Prin.* s. 531.
19   See A. Berger, *Encyclopedic Dictionary of Roman Law* (Philadelphia, 1953), 675.
20   See, for example, D.12.6.32*pr.*; D.12.6.63.
21   The operation of the *condictio* in Roman law was complicated especially by the conception of *iusta causa traditionis*. See most recently R. Evans-Jones and G.D. MacCormack, *"Iusta causa traditionis", New Perspectives in the Roman Law of Property*, ed. P. B.H. Birks (Oxford, 1989), 99.
22   See, for example, Stair, 1,7,9.

of money.[23] In fact *solutio* in this specialised context is understood more broadly and should be translated as "to discharge a legal duty" of which "payments" are only the most common examples.[24] A person who transfers a piece of property may also act to discharge a legal duty.[25] For example, the seller delivers the object of the contract to perform and discharge the duty to deliver imposed upon him by the contract of sale.[26] The buyer on the other hand, because he transfers money, is said "to pay" the price.[27] Notwithstanding that one party "delivers" and the other "pays", both transfers amount to a *solutio* because the purpose of each was to discharge a legal duty. The term "discharge" is used to encompass both the "paying" by the buyer and the "performing" by the seller.[28]

Stair includes recovery of property under the *condictiones* but may possibly have reserved the term "repetition" for claims to recover money. Bell on the other hand creates a distinct category of law called "repetition" which includes claims to recover property. This illustrates nicely the forked stick on which modern Scots law has perched itself. The difficulty has arisen as a result of systematisation of the law which has led lawyers to speak, not merely of individual claims of repetition concerning money, but of a distinct body of law called "repetition". The Roman law origin where the *condictiones* were the paradigm "claiming back" remedies led to the modern Scots law of repetition being seen as that governed by the *condictiones*. An association of the term "repetition" with money claims has subsisted in the minds of many at the level of individual claims. When the term "repetition" is used of the body of the law governed by the *condictiones* sometimes it is assumed that the *condictiones* are still exclusively about the recovery of money.[29]

Scots law associates claims of repetition with the recovery of money but has named a body of law "repetition" which is not exclusively about the recovery of money. It is difficult to know which way to jump to resolve the dilemma. With reference to repetition as a *body* of law, we should note that it is simply incorrect to restrict it to claims of money. This usage conflicts with institutional authority and it imports an undesirable result in the sort of example discussed: the buyer under a void contract will have a claim of repetition to recover the money price but the seller would not have a claim of repetition to recover the object.

---

23   See Mackenzie, 3,1,15; Erskine, *Inst.,* 3,1,3; 3,3,54; Hume, *Lectures,* vol. 3, 172.
24   The approach of Stair.
25   See for example, D.12.6.63; Stair, 1,7,9.
26   Sale of Goods Act 1979 s.27.
27   Sale of Goods Act 1979 s.27, s.28.
28   Erskine, *Inst.,* 3,1,3.
29   See esp. *Encyclopaedia of the Laws of Scotland, cit. sup.,* n.10, "Repetition".

Since there is absolutely nothing in the word "repetition" which shows that it is restricted to claims of money, it is best understood as that part of the law of unjustified enrichment which concerns the recovery of property or money with one of the recognised *condictiones*. However, such a formulation begs the further question; what are the distinctive features of this part of the law? In other words, what are the essential features of the law of repetition?

The Main Features of a Claim of Repetition

(1) There must have been a *transfer* of wealth in a particular manner and of a particular sort by the pursuer to the defender;

(2) there must be a recognised *cause of action* in the law of repetition; the enrichment must have been unjustified. An unjustified enrichment is one which is retained "without a legal basis". Transfer retained without a legal basis covers the following fact situations: (i) undue transfers i.e. transfers made to discharge a legally recognised duty which fail (*condictio indebiti*), transfers made to create an obligation or gift which fail (*condictio obligandi/donandi causa dati*) and transfers which fail because their purpose is immoral or illegal (*condictio ob turpem vel iniustam causam*); (ii) transfers made for a purpose (normally discharge of a legal duty) which succeeds temporarily but which then fails (*condictio ob causam finitam*); (iii) transfers made for a future purpose (normally outwith contract) which fails (*condictio causa data causa non secuta*) and (iv) residual causes of action (*condictio sine causa*).

The origin of the single unifying principle "retention without a legal basis" is attributed to the Roman jurist, Papinian.[30] The importance of the principle lies in the fact that it both unites the individual causes of action arising from the named *condictiones* and it imports controlled flexibility by allowing new causes of action which fall outwith the recognised claims to be accommodated. Reinhard Zimmermann sums it up nicely as follows:[31] (it was) "the general principle that had justified the granting of specific enrichment actions and (which) could now be used to expand, but at the same time suitably contain, the range of claims".[32]

---

30 D.12.6.66.

31 *Obligations*, 852.

32 See Bankton, 1,8; *Carrick* v. *Carse* (1778) Mor. 2931; *Patten* v. *Royal Bank* (1853) 15 D. 617 at 619; *Bell* v. *Thomson* (1867) 6 M. at 68; *Agnew* v. *Ferguson* (1903) 5 F. 879 at 884. While the *condictio sine causa* is certainly recognised in Scots Law its potential has not been exploited in modern times.

Transfer and the Nature of the Enrichment

Two factors need to be distinguished in this context: (a) how the enrichment was passed from the pursuer to the defender; and (b) the nature of the enrichment. Both show the influence of Roman law.

In Roman law the *condictio*, to begin with at least, lay to recover only fixed sums of money or specific pieces or fixed quantities of property which had been transferred by a *datio*.[33] *Datio*, literally translated as a "giving", had a technical meaning in Roman law which is not wholly appropriate for modern Scots law. Nevertheless, *datio* was seen by the Scottish institutional writers to express a fundamental feature of the law of repetition: the enrichment for the reversal of which the *condictio* lies must have been passed by a *transfer* of money or property. The very word "repetition" (a demanding back) indicates that in this context what is claimed is something that had been transferred to the defender from the patrimony of the pursuer which the latter is now seeking to recover.

Dare can be translated as "To give, (or) hand over a thing for the purpose of making the receiver the owner thereof".[34] In modern Scots law the conditions for the passage of ownership of moveables are not entirely clear.[35] For this, amongst other, reasons it is not appropriate to insist that a passage of ownership should be a pre-condition for raising a *condictio*; transfer of possession is sufficient. *Dare* in the sense of a "giving", with its historical association with a passage of ownership, is an unsatisfactory translation for modern Scots law.

The requirement of *datio* is satisfied in modern Scots law by a "transfer". A transfer should be understood as the passage of wealth of a particular sort (fixed sums of money, specific pieces or fixed quantities of property) which the pursuer *consciously intended* to confer on the defender for a particular purpose. Stair speaks firstly, from the point of view of the transferee, of the duty of restitution extending "to those things, *quae cadunt in non causam*".[36] He then speaks in turn of a "transfer", "delivery" or "payment".[37] Bankton speaks of things "given" or "delivered" or money "paid".[38] Erskine speaks mainly of "giving" but in the context of the *condictio indebiti* also of "paying".[39]

The transfer of wealth must have been consciously intended by the pursuer; he must have had a particular purpose in mind when he made the transfer. So, for example, as regards the *condictio indebiti*, the transfer is made to discharge a legal duty. The dual notions, "will" and

---

33   F. Schwarz, *Die Grundlage der condictio im klassischen römischen Recht* (Münster and Köln, 1952), 7.
34   A. Berger, *Encyclopedic Dictionary, cit. sup.*, n.19, 424.
35   D.L. Carey Miller, *Corporeal Moveables in Scots Law* (Edinburgh, 1991), 106–114. See also K.G.C. Reid, "Unjustified Enrichment and Property Law" 1994 *J.R.* 167.
36   Stair, 1,7,7.
37   *Ibid.*, 1,7,8; 9.
38   Bankton, 1,8.
39   Erskine, *Inst.*, 3,1,10; 3,3,54.

"purpose" can be detected in Stair. In respect of the *condictio ob turpem vel iniustam causam* he says, "the *will* of the owner, and his *purpose* to transfer the property is effectual...".[40]

Although the transferor intends to confer the benefit on the defender his purpose fails for some reason. For example, in claims arising under the *condictio indebiti* he intends to discharge a legal duty but discharge fails because his intention is vitiated normally, but not exclusively, by error.

Transfer and Acquisition by Wrongs

The identification that where he makes a *transfer* the pursuer *intended* to confer a benefit on the defender allows us to understand a difficult passage in Stair.

In the context of a discussion of the *condictio ob turpem vel iniustam causam* Stair says:[41]

> As for these things which are attained by force and fear, they have their original from delinquence and come not under this consideration.

This statement needs to be read in conjunction with Stair's introductory remarks on the *condictiones*:[42]

> The duty of restitution extendeth to those things, *quae cadunt in non causam*, which com[e] warrantably to our hands....

The *condictiones*, in Stair's estimation, lie where the benefit is acquired "warrantably". By this is meant that it should have been acquired by a transfer from, not by a wrong against, the pursuer. This approach again can only be understood in the light of Roman law. The return of things acquired by force and fear gave rise, not to a *condictio*, but to a regime of *restitutio in integrum* under the *actio quod metus causa*.[42] As has recently been argued, it may be appropriate to treat *restitutio in integrum* as a remedy of unjustified enrichment.[44] However, one should note that different remedies were at issue in Stair's treatment according to the manner in which the enrichment was acquired.

The Cause of Action: condictio indebiti

It is helpful to look first at the operation of the *condictio indebiti* in Roman law[45] and then at the manner of its reception by the Scottish institutional writers.

---

40   Stair, 1,7,8.
41   *Ibid.*
42   *Ibid.*, 1,7,7.
43   See, for example, *Love* v. *Downie* (1606) Mor. 16480.
44   D.P. Visser, "Rethinking Unjustified Enrichment", 1992 *Acta Juridica* 203.
45   The international literature is extensive. I have followed in the main the treatment of F. Schwarz, *op. cit.*, n.33. Cf., esp. S.E. Wunner, "Der Begriff *causa* und der Tatbestand der *condictio indebiti*" (1970) 9 *Romanitas* 459; B. Kupisch, *Ungerechtfertigte Bereicherung* (Heidelberg, 1987).

Within the denotation "*condictio indebiti*" there is no suggestion that the remedy lay in respect of a failure of purpose. This is explicable by reference to its history. In classical Roman law the *condictio* was a single remedy applied to different fact situations. One of these fact situations was where a person had made a transfer *solvendi causa* and its purpose failed. The term *causa solvendi* represents the proper range of the *condictio* in this context. The word "*causa*" should be translated as, "purpose" and "*solvendi*" as, "of discharging a duty". Thus the *condictio* lay wherever a person transferred money or an object in order to discharge a legal duty and this purpose failed.

The classical Roman lawyers spoke of a single remedy (*condictio*) which they applied to different fact situations. One of the fact situations was *indebitum solutum*, where a transfer was made to discharge a duty which was undue. The unitary nature of the *condictio* was obscured by the compilers of the *Corpus Iuris Civilis* who allocated a specific name to each *condictio* arising in each main fact situation. Each individualised *condictio* was then allocated its own title in Justinian's *Corpus Iuris Civilis*. *Condictio indebiti* was the name given to the remedy which lay to recover transfers made *solvendi causa* which failed. The name *condictio indebiti* is chosen because the transfer of an *indebitum* (what was undue) represented the central case in which a transfer which was made to discharge a duty failed.[46]

Justinian's compilers did not intend to transform the law in any substantive manner when they named the remedy appropriate to cases of "discharge" as the *condictio indebiti*. *Condictio indebiti* was a shorthand formed on the basis of the central case to which the *condictio* applied in this context. Like most shorthands, this one is potentially misleading. The concept "*indebitum*" (undue) covers the vast majority, but not all, cases to which the *condictio* "*indebiti*" applies. For example, a person who mistakenly thinks himself heir pays a genuine creditor of the estate. Repetition is permitted even although the creditor receives what is due to him because the debt of the true heir was not discharged.[47] The word *indebitum* has to be understood to denote a wider range of cases than those where there is absolutely no debt or duty.

The *condictio indebiti* strictly construed applies to all cases where the purpose underlying the transfer was to discharge a duty (*causa solvendi*) and this failed. For example, X pays 100 to Y as the price under a sale which turns out to have been void *ab initio*. The purpose underlying the transfer (or payment) of 100 was X's attempt to discharge his duty to pay the price under the contract of sale. The transfer failed because the duty was not discharged. The duty was not discharged

---

46   Or at least the term *indebitum*, which was classical in origin, applied to a wider range of cases than those in which it could be said that there was no debt (*non debitum*). I am grateful for Christian Emunds of the the University of Freiburg for this observation.

47   See R. Evans-Jones, "Identifying the Enriched" 1992 S.L.T. (News) 25.

because, unknown to X, there was in fact no duty to pay in view of the nullity of the contract.

Sometimes the fact situation *indebitum solutum*, to which a *condictio* is applicable, is met in early Scots law. This represents more closely the approach of the classical Roman lawyers. More commonly Scots law now identifies the claim where a person has made a transfer which has failed to discharge a duty as the *condictio indebiti*. The word "*indebiti*" emphasises that the claim lies in respect of what was undue. The underlying idea of a failure to discharge a duty is generally not encountered in modern Scots law because what, in essence, was a shorthand is taken to represent the necessary and sufficient conditions of the claim. This approach, as stated, has its limitations.

Transfer without a Legal Basis and the condictio indebiti

The normal case for the application of the *condictio indebiti* is where a transfer is made to discharge a duty which the transferor thought was due; most commonly under the law of obligations. An obligation may depend for its existence on a valid transaction like, for example, a contract. Where the *condictio indebiti* is available the transaction underlying the transfer will usually be void. In such circumstances one can think in terms of the transfer having been made without a legal basis. The legal basis is the state of affairs which creates a duty which is discharged by the transfer. When reference is made to the transfer having been made without a legal basis, instead of focusing on the fact that there is no duty (*indebitum*), the focus is on the *reason* why there is no duty. This distinction is important from the evidentiary point of view. In order to be entitled to recover, a transferor is obliged to prove that there has been no discharge of a duty. He will do this by proving that there was no duty which in turn he will show by the fact that the legal basis on which he made his payment was defective or did not exist; because, for example, the contract in fulfilment of which he made the transfer was void. In other words, the pursuer establishes that his transfer was undue by proving that no legal basis existed for it when it was made.

Knowledge and Error

The *condictio indebiti* applies to cases of "discharge". A person who "transfers" in this connection does so to discharge a duty which he necessarily believes to exist. If, in fact, there was no duty, usually the transferor must have been acting in error. If when he made his transfer, the transferor "knew" that there was no duty his purpose cannot normally have been to discharge a duty and therefore the *condictio indebiti* is usually not appropriate.

The requirement of error is clearly stated by Gaius in his *Institutes*:[48]

---

48   Gaius, *Inst*.3,91. See also, for example, D.19.2.19.6.

> *Is quoque qui non debitum accepit ab eo qui per errorem solvit, re obligatur.* (He too who receives what is not due to him from one who pays in error comes under a real obligation).

The same requirement is expressed by Ulpian in the opening text of the *Digest* title on the *condictio indebiti*:[49]

> *Et quidem si quis indebitum ignorans solvit, per hanc actionem condicere potest; sed si sciens se non debere solvit, cessat repetitio".* (A person who, in ignorance, pays what is not owed may recover what he gave with this action, but if he pays knowing that he is not under an obligation there is no repetition).

Gaius and Ulpian are referring to the same requirement, but they present it differently. Gaius refers to the "error" of the person entitled to recover, whereas Ulpian refers to the "ignorance" of the person entitled to recover and to the "knowledge" of him who is not entitled to recover. The difference is important because it helps us to understand that when one speaks of "error" as a requirement of the *condictio indebiti* – and here it is difficult to avoid the double negative – one means that the transferor should not have "known" that there was no duty.[50] As stated, if the transferor knew that there was no duty his purpose cannot have been to discharge a duty and therefore the central condition of the *condictio indebiti* is not normally satisfied. We should note the intimate connection between knowledge/ignorance/error and the foundation of the *condictio indebiti* in the idea of discharge of a duty.

Proof of Error

In classical Roman law, in the standard claim, error was a negative requirement of the *condictio indebiti*.[51] This meant that the pursuer himself was not obliged to prove error. He had merely to prove that he made a transfer which was received by the defender and from which discharge of a duty did not result. In other words the pursuer had to prove that he gave an *indebitum* from which error was then presumed in his favour. The defender was able to defeat the claim by showing that, when he made the transfer, the pursuer knew that there was no duty. The onus of proving knowledge was therefore on the defender.

The classical regime was obscured by Justinian. Particularly influential was an interpolated text, D.22.3.25*pr.*, according to which the onus of proof of error was on the pursuer.[52] The contradictory testimony

---

49   D.12.6.1*pr.* See also, for example, D.12.4.7*pr.*; 12.6.26.8; 12.6.37; 12.6.50; 18.1.16*pr.*

50   Some scholars like Beseler and Solazzi have argued that the term "error" is an interpolation. This view is not generally accepted; see Wunner, *op. cit.*, n.45, 463.

51   See Schwarz, *op. cit.*, n.33, 96ff.; Also H. Koch, *Bereicherung und Irrtum* (Berlin, 1973).

52   See the discussion of C.F. von Glück, *Ausführliche Erläuterung der Pandecten nach Hellfeld: ein Commentar* (Erlangen, 1868), vol. 13, 112ff.

found in the *Corpus Iuris Civilis* was reconciled by the Commentators, Baldus and Bartolus, in a manner which proved to be influential in the *ius commune*.[53] Founding on the Accursian Gloss, they suggested that the onus of proof was indeed on the pursuer but that there was a presumption of error on proof of an *indebitum*. The attraction of this solution was that whereas it recorded the principle found in the Gloss that the onus of proof was on the pursuer, since a presumption was created for error on proof of the *indebitum*, in practice the position was indistinguishable from that which placed the onus of proof entirely on the defender. This artificial accommodation of legal precedent was finally rejected by some of the German Pandectists in the nineteenth century whose influence led to the re-establishment of the principle which is enshrined in modern German law[54] that the onus of proof of knowledge is on the defender.[55] In Scotland we also find that some of the institutional writers present the onus of proof of knowledge as being on the defender.

Knowingly to Pay a Non-existent Debt and Gift

The deliberate payment of a non-existent debt is often dealt with in conjunction with gift. It is generally thought that classical Roman law distinguished the two cases since an *animus donandi* is necessary to constitute a gift and a person who deliberately pays a non-existent debt, strictly speaking, may not have an *animus donandi*.[56] Classical law sometimes utilised the concept of gift because it was similar in its effect to a payment of a debt in the knowledge that it was not due, both transfers being irrecoverable.[57] A complete assimilation of gift and the deliberate payment of a non-existent debt is found in the *Digest* but this is thought to be the work of Justinian:

> D.50.17.53: *Cuius per errorem dati repetitio est, eius consulto dati donatio est.* (Repetition lies for what is given in error but what is given knowing (that it is not due) is a gift).

This complete assimilation of gift and knowingly to pay a non-existent debt is widely reproduced in the Scottish institutional writers. It is important since it indicates the limits within which they clearly thought that the requirement of "knowledge" had to be operated in the *condictio indebiti* in Scots law. As we will see, there are different qualities of "knowledge" and only such knowledge as should be construed like a gift is effective to bar recovery of the undue transfer.

---

53   See Schwarz, *op. cit.*, n.33, 99ff.
54   Para. 814 B.G.B.
55   See G.F. Puchta, *Pandecten* (Leipzig, 1856), 466ff. who recognises that D.22.3.25*pr.* is interpolated. But cf. the approach of Glück, *op. cit.*, n.52.
56   Schwarz, *op. cit.*, n.33, 111ff.
57   For example, D.46.2.12. D.12.6.50 mentions the case of a man who pays knowing that he does not owe but with the intention of reclaiming at a later date. He cannot recover although he clearly did not intend a gift.

Error of Fact, Error of Law, and the Excusability of the Error

Classical Roman law, in principle, made no distinction between error of fact and error of law since in both cases the transferor had made a transfer in ignorance of the fact that it was undue. One exception, for very special reasons regarding *fides,* was found in the context of payments made under a *fideicommissum.*[58]

Justinian's compilers generalised the rule that they found applied to *fideicommissa* that an error of law barred recovery.[59] By drawing the distinction, on a general level, between different sorts of error, the compilers came to elevate the notion of "excusability" of error to a general precept of the *condictio indebiti.*[60] Only certain forms of error were excusable and gave rise to a claim. In the time of Justinian the requirement of error therefore fulfilled a double function. Its primary purpose remained, as it always had been, to show that the transferor did not know that what he gave was undue. Its secondary function was to penalise those whose lack of knowledge was of facts or rules of law which should have been ascertained. In this context it is worth recording the observation of Fritz Schulz[61] that, viewed from the standpoint of a law of unjust enrichment, the sound and clever classical system was obscured and confused by what is one of the worst parts of Justinian's law.

The *Corpus Iuris Civilis* provides conflicting testimony on the effect of error of law depending on whether it reproduces the classical or Justinianic approach.[62] The Glossators set out to reconcile the texts by means of elaborate distinctions involving four different gradations of the word *indebitum*. Error of law and the "excusable" rule were given effect in such a narrow range of cases that, quite unwittingly, the Glossators virtually re-established the position of classical law. The tradition of the Middle Ages, the Humanists and of Roman-Dutch law, though there were always some who took a contrary view, also sought to minimise the distinction between error of law and error of fact in the context of the *condictio indebiti*. It is interesting that Vinnius founds on the notion of gift in this regard. He says that all persons who pay in error of law and of whom it cannot be said that they intended a gift should be entitled to recover. The idea of gift is used to draw the limits within which it was thought that the error requirement was to be understood in the *condictio indebiti.*[63]

---

58   Schwarz, *op. cit.*, n.33, 101ff. See also T. Mayer Maly, "Rechtsirrtum und Bereicherung", *Festschrift für Heinrich Lange* (Munich, 1970), 293.
59   Schwarz, *op. cit.*, n.33, 105ff.
60   D.22.6.9.2; 22.3.25*pr.*
61   *Classical Roman Law* (Oxford, 1951), 611.
62   In this section I reproduce the results of the research conducted by Professor D. Visser of the University of Cape Town to whom I am extremely grateful for providing me with the materials.
63   Vinnius, *Comm. in Institutiones* 3,28,6.

The Institutional Basis of Scots Law

The legacy of Roman law on the *condictio* is both massive and varied. The teaching of the *ius commune* on issues like error of law was often highly involved and arcane. This raises the issue; how did, and how should, Scots law orient itself to this teaching? The answer is given by the early Scottish institutional writers since they present the form in which Roman law was received into Scotland. On the *condictio indebiti* Scots law took the following approach:

(i)   some of the early institutional writers speak, not of *condictio indebiti*, but of *indebiti solutio* (transfer to discharge a duty which was undue). This reflects the approach of classical Roman law and identifies the cause of action in *condictio indebiti* as the undue transfer;

(ii) we will see that the reception of the knowledge/error requirement reflected different strands of the civilian tradition but that the burden of proof of knowledge/error was seen to be on the defender;

(iii) gift is often mentioned to indicate the limits within which the error requirement is to be operated in the *condictio indebiti*. It is expressly referred to in an early case to show that the burden of proof of knowledge lay, not on the pursuer, but on the defender;[64]

(iv) apart from Mackenzie,[65] no distinction is made between error of law and error of fact;

(v)   the rule that error must be "excusable" was not received in Scotland.

The early institutional writers provided Scotland with an interpretation of the *condictio indebiti* which was the product of their choice from the vast and complex body of learning which Roman law and the *ius commune* provided on the subject. The institutional writers appear, in this context, overwhelmingly to have chosen the approach of classical Roman law. The choice of the classical model was a happy one for Scotland. The primary focus was given to whether the transferee had a legal basis to retain what he had received. If he did not, the presumptions operated in favour of the transferor and the consequence of his error was remedied without any moralistic enquiry as to whether he should, in the circumstances, have known that the duty was undue. The classical system which formed the basis of Scots law was also very simple and effective.

The choice of the classical system is likely to have been governed purely by an appreciation of what was best in the legacy of Roman law. However, in this regard we should also remember that the reception of Roman law came relatively late in Scotland and followed closely on the

---

64   See *post* p. 231.
65   Mackenzie, 3,1,15.

great age of Humanist learning which had made classical Roman law accessible to modern legal science for the first time.[66]

Modern Scots Law

Scots law recognises a claim in unjustified enrichment called *condictio indebiti*. There is, however, a deep-seated disagreement in Scotland as to its nature. There are two main approaches: (i) as its name suggests, the cause of action in the *condictio indebiti* is constituted by the fact that a transfer was undue (*indebitum*) subject to a defence, provable by the transferee, that the transferor knew that he was not obliged to make the transfer. Founding on this formulation the *condictio indebiti* is also given to recover an undue transfer made under compulsion; (ii) the *condictio indebiti* concerns only the recovery of undue transfers made in error as to their being due. Error is seen to be a feature which the pursuer needs positively to establish as part of his claim and consists of the erroneous belief that he was under a legal liability to pay; (iii) analogous in some respects to the error approach, is that advocated by Peter Birks[67] who suggests that the cause of action in the *condictio indebiti* should follow English law and be rendered as "mistake". Mistake has to be proved by the transferor but differs from the "error" approach in that it permits recovery in circumstances where the mistake is not only as to legal liability. This view has been presented as Scots law in a modified form by W.J. Stewart.[68]

The difference of formulation – whether knowledge excludes the *condictio indebiti* or whether error as it has been defined is a feature which has positively to be established – may seem small but it has major structural and functional consequences. In a paper entitled "The Taxonomy of Unjustified Enrichment in Scots Law"[69] which is part of his inspirational work on unjustified enrichment, Niall Whitty writes as follows:

> The *condictio indebiti* is generally defined as an action for the recovery of money or property unduly paid under an erroneous belief that it is due...In Roman law, error was an essential requirement.[70] In Scots law the great weight of Institutional and judicial authority is to the effect that error is an essential requirement of the *condictio indebiti*. Contrary judicial dicta are sparse and must be regarded as loose usage or made *per incuriam*. This view is not accepted by Dr. R. Evans-Jones.

---

66 See the comments of Cujas on D.22.3.25; *Comment. Lib III Quaestionum Pauli, Opera*, vol. 5 (Prati, 1838).
67 *Op. cit.*, n.2.
68 *The Law of Restitution in Scotland* (Edinburgh, 1992), 67.
69 Delivered at the seminar on the Scots law of unjustified enrichment convened in Parliament House in Edinburgh in October 1993. I am grateful to Niall Whitty for permission to quote from this paper.
70 D.12.6; C.4.5; Zimmermann, *Obligations,* 849, 850. Zimmermann does not in fact support the point.

The authority for the proposition concerning error in the *condictio indebiti* is given firstly as Roman law. We should also note that Whitty admits that in Scots law there is a contrary view that error is not an essential feature of the claim but this is seen to be the result of loose usage or carelessness.

To resolve the dilemma it is helpful to give a brief summary of Roman law and then to look at how Roman law was transmitted into Scots law.

Summary of Roman Law

The picture presented by Roman law in the *Corpus Iuris Civilis* is a confused one. In classical law the pursuer did not have to prove error, merely that a transfer was undue. That, no doubt, is why it is called a *condictio indebiti*. If the claim was conceived in terms of error which the pursuer had to prove, one might have anticipated that it would be called a *condictio erroris*.

On the other hand, through his interpolation of D.22.3.25*pr.*, Justinian certainly elevated error to a positive feature of the *condictio indebiti*. This difference of approach is, coincidentally, reflected in the formulation of Gaius who speaks positively of error and that of Ulpian who speaks of knowledge. Gaius' use of the term "error" was a shorthand for the more cumbersome "knowledge" rule and did not have any significance for his time regarding the burden of proof.

Summary of the Later Tradition of Roman Law

As a result of the debates in its post-Justinianic history the civilian tradition identified three main approaches: (i) proof of knowledge acts as a defence; (ii) where the claim is presented in terms of error, a presumption of error will be raised from proof that the transfer was undue. Under both these approaches the *condictio indebiti* therefore concerns the recovery of the undue transfer, subject, in practice, to a defence of knowledge. However, (iii) the testimony of Justinian in D.22.3.25*pr.* which placed the burden of proof of error on the transferor, although attacked by the Humanists, necessarily also survived because it is recorded in the *Digest*.

Scots Law

Roman law and the *ius commune* are one thing, Scots law quite another. What understanding of the *condictio indebiti* was received into Scots law in the works of the institutional writers?

Institutional statements of the essentials of *condictio indebiti* are as follows:

Stair:[71]

---

71   Stair, 1,7,9.

Restitution extendeth to *indebite solutum*, when any party through error delivereth or payeth that which he supposeth due, or belongeth to another....

Mackenzie:[72]

[The *condictio indebiti*] arises from the Payer's ignorance, therefore if he knew what he payed was due, he will not get Repetition, but what he payed will be looked upon as a Donation....

Bankton:[73]

[The *condictio indebiti* arises] where one, thro' error, delivers or makes payment of what was not, but which he believed to be due.

Erskine:[74]

Indebiti solutio, or the payment to one of a debt not truly due to him is...called by the Romans *condictio indebiti*. This action does not lie...If he who made the payment knew at the time that no debt was due...for he who deliberately gives what he knows is not due is presumed to intend a present; so to found this action the sum must be paid through mistake or ignorance.

Bell describes the *condictio indebiti* as an action for:[75]

Whatever has been delivered or paid on an erroneous conception of duty or obligation.

However, he then presents knowledge as a defence.[76] He says:

If the payment have been made with full knowledge of the person who makes it that he is under no debt or obligation, it is held a donation, and irrevocable.

The important point to note from the above statements on the *condictio indebiti* is that Scots law received both the error approach and the approach formulated in terms of knowledge. As regards the latter it is clear that knowledge acted as a defence. What perhaps is not entirely clear is whether those who presented error as part of the definition of *condictio indebiti* would have regarded the burden of proof as lying on the pursuer or whether they followed the view that error was to be presumed from the fact that a transfer was undue. Stair, we should note, speaks of the cause of action as *indebitum solutum* (undue transfer) which would strongly suggest that notwithstanding his express mention of error he expected that it would be presumed from the undue transfer.

Erskine devotes most space to the relationship between knowledge and error. The actual cause of action is again presented as *indebitum*

---

72   Mackenzie, 3,1,15.
73   Bankton, 1,8,23.
74   Erskine, *Inst.*, 3,3,54.
75   Bell, *Prin.*, s. 531.
76   *Ibid.*, s. 533.

solutum which is defined as "the payment to one of a debt not truly due to him". Knowledge is clearly presented by Erskine as a defence and yet, like Gaius, he also shows that the knowledge rule can be presented in terms of error.

The value of this brief historical survey is that it shows that Roman law and the *ius commune* present (at least) a double tradition concerning the *condictio indebiti* and that this double tradition was received into Scots law. The error formulation may be founded upon to support the contention that *condictio indebiti* is restricted to cases of error as to liability. Due partly to the influence of English law, recent commentators who adopt this approach in Scotland have always assumed that the burden of proof of error lies on the transferor.

Proof of Error in Scots Law

The four main elements of a claim under the *condictio indebiti* are: (i) that the pursuer made a transfer which was received by the defender or his representative; (ii) that the transfer was made to discharge a legally recognised duty; (iii) discharge of the duty failed because the transfer was undue (*indebitum*) (iv) the pursuer did not know that there was no duty to discharge when he made his transfer (error).

Under a negative approach proof of knowledge acts only as a defence. The pursuer establishes his claim by proving (i) and (iii). The defender can defeat the claim by proving knowledge (iv). By proving knowledge, the defender normally establishes that the transfer was not made to discharge a duty (ii), a fact that had been presumed in favour of the pursuer when he proved the *indebitum*.

Under a system of law which places the onus of proof of error on the pursuer (positive approach) it is possible, following Baldus and Bartolus, to allow a presumption of error on proof of the *indebitum*. This appears to have been the approach of Stair. Alternatively, in what is a very heavy burden indeed, in addition to the *indebitum*, in order to establish his error, the pursuer may be obliged to prove that he had no means of knowing that the duty was undue. All these approaches are now encountered in Scots law in what is a confused picture. A central question is therefore to determine which approach is best. We will do this by examining the reasons why the perception that knowledge should act as a defence has generally been favoured in the modern Civil law tradition.

Firstly there is a presumption against gift. If a person who makes an undue transfer is required to prove, in addition to the fact that the transfer was undue, that he acted in error, it normally conflicts with common sense and with the presumption against gift. This can be illustrated by reference to modern case law. For example, a businessman pays his rival what he owes but due to an oversight the bill is overpaid. Are we to assume that the businessman intended a gift until he can prove, independently of the undue transfer, that he acted in error. In *Dalmellington Iron Co. Ltd.* v. *Glasgow and South Western Railway*

Co.,[77] the pursuers raised a claim to recover overcharges under an agreement with the defenders. It was proved that the charges were undue. Lord Rutherfurd Clark then said that:[78]

> It cannot be imputed to (the pursuers) that they desired to pay more than they could help.

That is the precise issue! Proof that the transfer was undue was seen to create a presumption of error rebuttable only by proof of knowledge by the defenders.

The second factor leading to the perception that knowledge should be a defence even if the claim is presented in terms of error concerns the problem of proof itself. Error is a subjective state of mind which can only be proved by reference to objective states of affairs. Especially in the light of the presumption against gift, a presumption of error is seen to be created by proof that a transfer was undue. Again we can illustrate this by reference to Scottish cases. In *Carrick* v. *Carse*[79] the Court observed:

> when payment is made *sine causa*, it will be presumed to have proceeded from error, and not donation, unless the contrary can be proved.

In *Balfour* v. *Smith and Logan*[80] a *condictio indebiti* was held competent on the grounds of error. Lord Mure said:[81]

> there is here, I think, a sufficient averment of ignorance...for there is a distinct statement by the pursuer that he was in *doubt* [my emphasis] whether the sum claimed was due....

Although the state of mind of the pursuer was concededly one of doubt, ignorance was attributed on the basis of proof by the pursuer that the transfer was undue.

In the well-known case of *Glasgow Corporation* v. *Lord Advocate*[82] the pursuers paid tax in response to a demand which they immediately claimed was *ultra vires*. They made representations to the Secretary of State for Scotland which were unsuccessful and finally paid in fear of incurring penalties. When it was proved that the tax was undue they sought to recover in a *condictio indebiti* on the grounds of error. The reason why the pursuers pled error notwithstanding their earlier protestations was because they had made a transfer which was undue. However, the Court held that the error was one of law and repetition was therefore denied.

---

77   (1889) 16 R. 523.
78   at 533.
79   (1778) Mor. 2931.
80   (1877) 4 R. 454.
81   at 461.
82   1959 S.C. 203.

Some of the problems attendant on requiring a pursuer to prove, independently of the fact that a transfer was undue, that he was in error at the time of paying can be illustrated by reference to the case in English law, *Kelly* v. *Solari*.[83] An action for money had and received was brought by the plaintiff, one of the directors of a life assurance company, to recover a payment made under a policy which had lapsed due to non-payment of the premium. The directors had been informed that the policy had lapsed but they had forgotten this fact by the time they made the payment. Thus, payment was made with the full means of knowledge that it was undue and the question for the Court was whether the means of knowledge should be treated as equivalent to knowledge itself. The Court sensibly came to the conclusion that only actual knowledge existing at the time of payment barred recovery. As regards the matter of proof the issue was this. The plaintiff under English law has to prove mistake in order to be entitled to recover. But once, quite rightly, the Court recognised that having had the means of knowledge should not preclude recovery, how was the plaintiff to prove that he forgot? Abinger, C.B.[84] rather weakly said; "I have little doubt in this case that the directors had forgotten the fact, otherwise I do not believe they would have brought this action". Thus, although the cause of action was "mistake", it was difficult to imagine how "mistake" could be established other than by proof that the payment was undue.

The Subjective or Objective Nature of Error

Knowledge/error is ascertained from an examination of the facts to determine the state of mind of the transferor at the time of payment. The central factor on the basis of which error is attributed to the pursuer is that he made a transfer of what was undue. A legal system which seeks proof of error from factors beyond the transfer of what was undue imposes a heavy burden on the pursuer. He may have to prove, for example, that although he was in possession of the receipt for payment he did not have it before him when he made the second payment which was undue; although the receipt was in his drawer he has to prove that he did not actually open the drawer at the critical moment. There are some judicial *dicta* in Scotland which suggest that the pursuer bears this burden but others suggest that he does not. The best solution is to place the burden of proof on the defender to prove that he is entitled to retain something which the pursuer has had to prove was undue.

The attribution of error is sometimes made from the fact that a transfer was undue even although the transferor's state of mind was clearly quite different. We have seen that in *Balfour* v. *Smith and Logan* the state of mind of the pursuer was concededly one of doubt but that the Court was prepared to attribute error because the payment which

---

83   (1841) 9 M. & W. 54, 152 E.R. 24.
84   *Ibid.*, at 58.

was made was undue. Similarly, in *Glasgow Corporation* v. *Lord Advocate* the pursuers pled error notwithstanding their immediate protestations that the tax was undue. This also can be viewed as a case where a payment made in doubt as to the existence of legal liability is treated as a payment in error as to legal liability.

Is Error an Essential of Condictio Indebiti*?*

The answer to this question is complex. Clearly if error is seen as a positive feature of the *condictio indebiti*, however difficult it might be to operate in practice, error must necessarily be an essential feature. The limitations of such an approach will be examined later. However, the history of the *condictio indebiti* and the nature of its reception into Scots law show that "error" should be understood as a shorthand for the rule that knowledge excludes recovery of the undue transfer. Seen in these terms it is at least misleading to present the issue in terms of error as an essential of the claim. We will also see that by founding on the tradition of "knowledge", in what is a profoundly important step, the *condictio indebiti* has been developed in Scotland in a similar manner to that in Civil law jurisdictions, beyond both "error" and "knowledge". The error cases, it should be stressed, nevertheless remain the core cases to which the claim applies.

The Cause of Action

Stair presents the cause of action of *condictio indebiti* as *indebitum solutum* (undue transfer).[85] Typically an undue transfer will be made as a consequence of error but error is unlikely to have been a positive feature of the claim for Stair. The relationship between the cause of action and error is more clearly stated by Erskine. He also presents the cause of action as *indebitum solutum* which he defines as "the payment to one of a debt not truly due to him". He then says that recovery is excluded "If he who made the payment knew at the time that no debt was due".[86]

Neither Stair nor Erskine mentions the idea of a failure to discharge a duty as the foundation of the *condictio indebiti*. Nevertheless such a conception can still be of assistance when one wishes to identify the range of this, and analogous, claims in modern law.

The Duty May Be Legally Recognised Not Only Legally Enforceable

The typical type of case to which the *condictio indebiti* applies is that where, but for the transferor's error, discharge of the duty could have been enforced in law. For example, if I fail to pay the price under a sale, the seller can enforce payment but I may recover what I gave where the sale turns out in fact to have been void. The *condictio indebiti* is often

---

85   Stair, 1,7,9.
86   Erskine, *Inst.*, 3,3,54.

presented as if it applies only to cases where the transfer is legally exigible. For example, Hume says:[87]

> To make way for this action, it must also be clear, that the payment was made out of error, – under a mistaken impression of a necessity to pay.

This perception has been supported by modern scholars. Gloag says that the belief must have been that the money was "legally exigible",[88] and Birks speaks of the *condictio indebiti*'s "definitional limitation to liability mistakes". As is shown by Birks's remark, the idea that the duty must have been legally enforceable is drawn from the word "*indebitum*". The central idea is that of "owing" and discharge of duties which are "owed" in law, it is thought, can always be enforced.

In fact there are cases to which *condictio indebiti* applies where the transfer is not legally enforceable, merely legally recognised. A person subject only to a moral duty such as that created by a natural obligation cannot be forced in law to discharge his debt.[89] He may pay in the knowledge that he is not bound in law. Such a payment is construed like a gift.[90] Alternatively he may pay in the erroneous belief that he is under an enforceable legal duty. No action lies to recover what was given on this occasion since he transferred, not an *indebitum*, but something which was due. Erskine states that "as the action for repayment is introduced merely from equity, it cannot be admitted where the sum was due in equity".[91] Hume says that the person who receives payment of a debt due on a natural obligation is not enriched.[92]

The availability of the *condictio indebiti* in this context arises where, due to error of the transferor, no natural duty exists for the transfer; for example, he pays the wrong person; or the extent of the natural obligation is exceeded; for example, instead of 100, in error he pays 200. The discharge of the natural obligation provides the legal basis to retain the transfer. If no natural obligation exists the transfer is necessarily retained without a legal basis.[93]

---

87   Hume, *Lectures,* vol. 3, 173ff.
88   *Op. cit.,* n.8, 63.
89   Bankton, 1,8; Erskine, *Inst.,* 3,1,4; Hume, *Lectures,* vol. 3, 172; Bell, *Prin.,* s. 532.
90   *Thomson* v. *St. Mary's Chapel* (1838) 16 S. 82; *Henderson* v. *Alexander* (1857) 29 Sc. Jur. 559; *Masters and Seamen of Dundee* v. *Cockerill* (1869) 8 M. 278 *per* Lord Neaves at 281.
91   Erskine, *Inst.,* 3,3,54.
92   Hume, *Lectures,* vol. 3, 172.
93   This has possible relevance in the context of the recovery of payments under *sponsiones ludicrae.* See R. Evans-Jones, "Repetition of Payments in *sponsiones ludicrae*", (1993) 61 *Scottish Law Gazette* 11. For Roman law see D.36.1.66*pr.* discussed by Schwarz, *op. cit.,* n.33, 239. Cf. *County Properties and Developments Ltd.* v. *Gordon Harper* 1989 S.C.L.R. 597.

*Transfer to Create an Obligation (*causa obligandi*)*

Roman law gave a *condictio* in circumstances which are distinct from, but closely analogous to, those to which the *condictio indebiti* is applicable.[94] The compilers, no doubt because of its narrow range, did not allocate a title to this particular *condictio* in the *Corpus Iuris Civilis* and the result is that it is not mentioned by the Scottish institutional writers. Nevertheless, it is clear that the circumstances to which this *condictio* applies need to be accommodated within modern law on an analogy with the *condictio indebiti*.

This *condictio* lies to recover the transfer which is made *to create*, not, as in *indebiti, to discharge*, a legal duty where the purpose of the transfer fails. For example, money is lent by a person who lacks capacity. The money cannot be recovered under contract, nor, if it has been consumed, under the law of property. The legal basis for the retention of the money by the transferee is the creation of a valid loan. Since no loan came into existence the money is recoverable under the *condictio (obligandi causa)*. In Scots law, because of special developments in Roman law, the case of money lent to a person who lacks capacity is dealt with in the law of recompense.[95] It is clearly undesirable that similar transactions should be classified differently depending on which party makes the transfer. Classifications such as "recompense", which order cases (partly) according to the measure of recovery, are rightly being discarded in favour of classifications like "unjustified enrichment" which look to the source of the obligation to restore what has been received. Peculiar here because they distort modern classifications, the tramlines of Roman law need to be ignored on this occasion and the case of money lent to the *incapax* also recognised as an application of the *condictio obligandi causa*, subject, if necessary, to a special measure of recovery.

Gift

Gifts sometimes go wrong, usually because, in error, they are made to the wrong person or they are overpaid. This normally happens when the gift is fulfilled by a person acting under instructions from the donor. Are gifts which fail in this manner recoverable and if so, how?

A gift is a pure gratuity and can neither be compelled nor is it morally due as under a natural obligation. Can gift therefore be accommodated within the notion of "due" which is central to the *condictio indebiti*? To an extent it can.

Roman law had a restricted conception of contract. As a result gift did not fall within the range of transactions fulfilment of which could

---

94   D.12.1.19.1. The *condictio obligandi causa* attributed to the jurist, Julian. See Schwarz, *op. cit.*, n.33, 240ff.

95   The treatment in this section is an over-simplification. Due to a complex history in Roman law these cases have ended up in the law of recompense; see Scottish Law Commission, *Recovery of Benefits*, vol. 1, at 135.

amount to discharge of a duty. In Roman law we therefore find vitiated gifts of one sort dealt with under the *condictio causa data causa non secuta*.[96] However, modern legal systems classify gift as a contract with important consequences for the classification of some claims arising from gift.

Transfer to Discharge a Duty and Gift

The transfer made *donandi causa* (as a gift) in some cases fits within the core requirement of the *condictio indebiti* that the transfer must have been made to discharge a duty.

Since gift is a contract it generates enforceable obligations in certain circumstances. Where the gift is agreed in the appropriate form in advance of its fulfilment there is no difficulty in seeing that the transfer which completes the gift is made to discharge the obligation thought to have been created by the contract. If this contract is void or if the gift is otherwise vitiated the transfer is recoverable with the *condictio indebiti* in the normal manner.

Problems arise when trying to apply the same reasoning to the spontaneous gift case where the contract cannot be identified so easily as a separate component from the transfer by which it was fulfilled. For example, spontaneously I hand X 100 for his birthday in mistake for Y. It is possible to argue that a contract would have existed but for the error, but it is difficult to conceive of such a contract creating obligations or of the transfer having been made to discharge a duty.

The spontaneous gift case is closely analogous to the transfer whereby a person seeks to create an obligation. However, it differs from that case in that the purpose of the transfer is not to create an obligation but to create a valid gift. It is therefore best to allocate a separate category to spontaneous gifts. The transfer in this instance should be classed as having been made *to create* a valid gift. The validity of the gift is the legal basis for the donee to retain what he has received. If no gift is created the transfer is recoverable with the *condictio (donandi causa)*.

Gift and the Defence of Knowledge

A possible difficulty in applying the *condictio* to the gift case is the rule that a transfer which is made in the knowledge that it is undue cannot be recovered. A person is not bound to make a gift. Does it therefore follow that in all cases the transferor knows that what he gave is undue?

In cases of gift it is certainly true that the transferor knows that he is under no obligation before he makes the transfer. However, this is no different from saying that before he enters, say, a contract of sale, he knows that he need not enter that contract. Knowledge is relevant to the *condictio* in a different sense. The question is whether, when he makes the gift, the transferor's knowledge of its terms is vitiated. Did he

---

96   See C.4.6.

know when he made the transfer those facts which he now claims operate to make the gift invalid? A gift will normally only be defective where the donor's knowledge of its terms was vitiated in some important respect. In other words, it is not the knowledge of whether the transfer was enforceable in law which is relevant, but the knowledge, at the time of transfer, of those factors which, at the moment of raising the *condictio*, it is claimed prevented a valid gift from being executed. The creation of the valid gift is the legal basis for the donee to retain what he received.

Summary

The *condictio* in this context is available where a transfer has failed which was made (i) to discharge a duty (*solvendi causa*); (ii) to create an obligation (*obligandi causa*) and (iii) to execute a gift (*donandi causa*). Category (i) is governed by the *condictio indebiti*. Categories (ii) and (iii) are closely analogous to (i); they are the reverse of the same coin and, subject to exceptions, are governed by the same rules, like that regarding knowledge. All are cases where the purpose of the transfer is to create or discharge a legal relationship and this purpose fails. All are unified by the idea that the transfer is retained without a legal basis because it was either undue or because there was no loan or gift created by the transfer.

The Case Law

The case law shows that Scots law has experienced some difficulty with the idea that the transfer must have been "due". Nothing is known in modern law of the classifications *obligandi* and *donandi causa.* It is only when we return to early case law that we find that the gift which fails is treated as recoverable on the grounds that it is held without a legal basis.

Moore's Executors v. *McDermid*[97]

An agreement was concluded between debtor M and his creditors to the effect that he should be discharged on paying a certain proportion of his debts. All the creditors agreed with the exception of the defender who insisted on, and was given, full payment of the debt owing to her. Following M's death his executors gave effect to a wish he had expressed that, if his estate permitted, those creditors who had discharged his debts should be given payment in full. *Per incuriam* the defender was paid a second time. Her defence to the *condictio indebiti* brought to recover the over-payment was, *inter alia*, that the pursuers knew that the sum was not due to her in law.[98]

---

97   1913 S.L.T. 278 and 298.
98   The expression of the desire on the part of M that his creditors be paid in full cannot have been effective to make them beneficiaries under a will.

The Lord Ordinary[99] conceded that the pursuers knew that the sum was not legally due to the defender but he regarded it as sufficient that the executors supposed that the defender was entitled in accordance with the expressed desire of the deceased. The case therefore presents the proposition that the *condictio indebiti* is available where the pursuers paid in the knowledge that nothing was owed in law provided they did so in implement of what they conceived to be their "duty" and the amount which it was their "duty" to pay was exceeded. Unsurprisingly the defender appealed.

The payments made to the creditors, including the second payment to the defender, are best construed either as gifts[100] or, better, as the fulfilment of a natural obligation of the deceased to his creditors.[101] The issue is therefore whether a person who makes such a payment on the basis of a fundamanetal error of fact may recover what he gave. The Lord Ordinary, to whose opinion the Inner House adhered, reaches the correct result but he is disturbed by the operation of the knowledge requirement of the *condictio indebiti* and its relationship to a "necessity" to pay.

Masters and Seamen of Dundee v. *Cockerill*[102]

The Fraternity of Masters and Seamen of Dundee established a fund to provide annuities, *inter alia*, for the dependants of deceased seamen. Cockerill, who had made the required contributions to the fund, disappeared for sixteen years. In the belief that he was dead the Fraternity paid his wife the annuity appropriate to his status plus a gratuity of thirteen shillings per annum. Cockerill returned alive and the Fraternity raised the *condictio indebiti* to recover both the annuity and the gratuity. Lord Benholme said that "the key to the solution of this case lies in the distinction between an onerous and a gratuitous payment".[103] The Fraternity was successful in respect of the annuity on the grounds that it would have been under a legal obligation to the wife in respect of this sum had the defender been dead. The money given as a gratuity was regarded as a pure charitable payment and not recoverable.

The case might be read so as to show that a gift is irrecoverable even if made under a fundamental error of fact.[104] At first sight it is certainly odd that the two separate payments (annuity and gratuity) were both made on the basis of the same error of fact but only the former was held to be recoverable. The likely problem is that the Court approached the facts through the eyes of the *condictio indebiti* which led it to the conclusion that only payments which are legally "due" were recoverable.

---

99 The Inner House adhered on appeal.
100 See *McIvor* v. *Roy* 1970 S.L.T. (Sh. Ct.) 58.
101 See *Macfarlane* v. *Nicoll* (1864) 3 M. 237 *per* Lord Deas at 243.
102 (1869) 8 M. 278.
103 at 281.
104 See Birks (1985) 38 *C.L.P.* 68.

The above two cases arose in modern times and highlight some of the difficulties which arise when the *condictio indebiti* is made to do a job for which it was never designed. It is precisely because of the decision in *Cockerill* that Birks advocates the abandonment in Scotland of the *condictio indebiti*. However, there is a different approach found in the early Scottish case law where it was clearly understood how the *condictio* should operate in this context. In *Findlay* v. *Munro*,[105] the pursuer successfully recovered the value of an ox which had been delivered to the defender's house by mistake. The case was treated as one in which a gift was sent by mistake to the wrong person. The Lords found the defender liable to make a return as having the ox *sine causa*.[106] *Sine causa* in this context describes the cause of action and should be translated as "without a legal basis".[107]

The Condictio Indebiti *Developed and Retention Without a Legal Basis*

The fact situations covered by the individual nominate *condictiones* are themselves capable of development by the courts in a number of ways. The *condictio indebiti* normally lies to recover transfers made to discharge a duty which was perceived to exist at the time of the transfer but it can clearly be applied by analogy to the situation where I pay a sum to discharge a debt which I erroneously think I will incur in the future.

In respect of further developments of the *condictio indebiti* we need to recall the double tradition of the reception. Under one tradition error is presented (conceivably) as a positive feature of the claim. However, the tradition that *condictio indebiti* concerns the recovery of undue transfers subject to a defence of knowledge does not present error as part of the cause of action. This tradition has been founded on by some Scots lawyers. It has been seen that the defence to *condictio indebiti* is formulated in terms of knowledge in order to permit recovery of an undue transfer provided the intent of the transferor was vitiated at the time of transfer. Error is merely one of a possible range of vitiating factors. Thus undue transfers made under compulsion are treated as recoverable by *condictio indebiti* since the compulsion, like error, vitiates the intent of the transferor.[108] To give the *condictio*

---

105 (1698) Mor. 1767.

106 *Folio Dictionary*, 1, 107.

107 Incorrectly classified under "mistake" by W.J. Stewart, *op. cit.*, n.68, 67. It is difficult to imagine how "mistake" can be extracted from the expression *sine causa*.

108 *Arrol* v. *Montgomery* (1826) 4 S. 499; *Macfarlane* v. *Nicoll* (1864) 3 M. 237. Discussed by R. Evans-Jones and D. McKenzie, "Towards a Profile of the *condictio ob turpem vel iniustam causam* in Scots Law", 1994 *J.R.* 60; *British Oxygen Co.* v. *S.S.E.B.* 1959 S.C. (H.L.) 17 *per* Lord Merriman at 48. Cf. the approach in Scottish Law Commission, *Recovery of Benefits*, vol. 2, 201ff. Note at 206 *British Oxygen* (1958 S.C. 53 at 79 *per* Lord Patrick) is quoted as authority for the proposition that the *condictio indebiti* does not apply to recover an excess sum paid to a public utility for performance

indebiti to recover an undue transfer made under compulsion may seem like a small step but it has the major consequence that the claim is immediately freed from any restriction to liability mistakes. The result is to create a single category of unjustified enrichment based on the notion "undue transfer". The potential of this development can be illustrated by reference to another Scottish case where the cause of action is seen as an undue transfer subject to a defence of knowledge.

Firstly, it is important to observe that not all knowledge excludes recovery – only such knowledge as shows that the transferor should be treated as if he intended a gift operates to bar the claim. Thus, for example, the transferor who paid under compulsion knows that he was not obliged to pay but due to the compulsion his transfer is not construed like a gift. Scottish jurisprudence remains rudimentary on this point, but the close connection between knowingly making an undue transfer and gift can be detected in the statements of Mackenzie, Erskine and Bell referred to earlier. A more refined approach to the operation of the knowledge rule is either to regard only such behaviour as amounts to a *venire contra factum proprium*[109] as barring recovery or to bar recovery only when good faith viewed in the context of "knowledge" so demands.

In *Agnew* v. *Ferguson*[110] a tenant had regularly paid royalties to his landlord without deducting a sum to which he was entitled. The landlord regularly refunded the excess. When the landlord changed, the tenant paid on the same basis but the new landlord refused to repay the undue payment. A *condictio indebiti* was successfully brought to recover the excess. One problem was that the tenant had paid in the knowledge that he was not obliged to pay. There was certainly no error as to legal liability which is necessary under the "error" formulation of *condictio indebiti*.

Lord Justice-Clerk Macdonald allowed recovery because the payment was undue and had been made, as he conceived, under compulsion not error. Lord Trayner also allowed recovery on the basis of the *condictio indebiti* which he formulated as follows:[111]

> I regard this as a simple case of *condictio indebiti* – money paid which was not due – and which the receiver of that money has no title, moral or legal, to retain.

---

of a duty which it was bound to perform for less than it exacted. Lord Patrick, founding on the error approach, in truth merely observes that the facts do not fit well within the *condictio indebiti*. If the *condictio indebiti* is strictly construed this is concededly the case.

109 Behaviour which is inherently contradictory in the sense that a person cannot be allowed to succeed in an appeal to the law to put right factors which he, in full knowledge, willingly brought about by his own actions. See D. Reuter and M. Martinek, *Ungerechtfertigte Bereicherung* (Tübingen, 1983), 183; E. Riezler, *Venire contra factum proprium* (Leipzig, 1912); H.W. Dette, *Venire contra factum proprium nulli conceditur* (Berlin, 1985).

110 (1903) 5 F. 879. The case is not without its analytical oddities.

111 at 884.

To complete the eclectic picture which Scots law presents, Lord Moncreiff in the same case formulated the *condictio indebiti* mainly in terms of excusable error. But interestingly, under the influence of the character of the other judgements, he said that the *condictio indebiti* lay in cases of "excusable error or *misunderstanding*" (my emphasis).[112]

Error under the *condictio indebiti*, in the view of Lord Moncreiff, meant error as to legal liability. There was no error as to legal liability in this case since the transferor knew perfectly well that he did not have to pay. Therefore the claim would have failed under a strict error approach. The payment was, however, made on the basis of the misapprehension that the new landlord would repay the excess. This was why Lord Moncreiff extended the *condictio indebiti* beyond error to "error or misunderstanding".

Alternatively, as Lord Trayner put it, the question was whether the receiver had a moral or legal title to retain the "undue" transfer. The knowledge approach to the *condictio indebiti* allowed the Court to evaluate all the facts to determine whether the transfer should be construed like a gift. Since the transfer was made under a misunderstanding of sufficient gravity the knowledge rule was not seen to bar recovery in this instance.

Some Scots lawyers like Niall Whitty try to restrict the *condictio indebiti* to error alone with the result that he regards developments in the courts beyond this narrow conception as careless oversights which should be discounted. Peter Birks, as stated, has suggested that Scots law should follow English law by rendering the cause of action of the *condictio indebiti* as "mistake". The primary advantage which Birks saw in this approach was precisely that it freed the claim from a restriction to liability mistakes, albeit this step had already been taken before Birks' intervention.

These tensions of classification are primarily due to reasons of history. Scots law received the main *condictiones* of Roman law like the *condictio indebiti* and the *condictio causa data causa non secuta*[113] which Stair unified under the principle "retention without a legal basis (*sine causa*)". We have seen how the general claim "retention without a legal basis" was successfully applied as a cause of action in the early case law. Scots law then lost sight of the general claim in the face of the named *condictiones*, partly no doubt because of the decline in civilian learning, but, more proximately, because the named *condictiones* appear most commonly in the world of practice and therefore are more familiar. Only exceptionally is it necessary to revert to the general claim. The problem is that the named *condictiones* do not accommodate a range of cases which it is proper for a law of unjustified enrichment

---

112   at 885.
113   See the contribution of G.D. MacCormack in this volume and R. Evans-Jones, "Unjust Enrichment, Contract and the Third Reception of Roman Law in Scotland", (1993) 109 *L.Q.R.* 663.

to recognise. One response to this dilemma has been for the judiciary
to advance beyond the classical image of the most important individual
named *condictio*. In a development which is witnessed elsewhere in
the civilian tradition, the *condictio indebiti* has been applied beyond a
narrow restriction to liability mistakes. Provided this development is
limited by the proper bounds of the general principle it is entirely
understandable and right, given the constrictions within which Scots
law has had to operate, that the *condictio indebiti* should be developed
in this way. It is a new beginning which, if it is recognised for what it is,
is the gradual re-creation of the claim to recover what is retained without a legal basis from a foundation of the *condictio indebiti*. In more
emotive terms, it is the hand of vitality reaching out for life from a
world which has become artificially constricted and in which, if it
remains, the *condictio* as a whole is doomed to die. It is because Birks
chose only to look into the dark world of constriction that he advocates
the abolition of the *condictio indebiti* in favour of mistake. And yet it is
precisely the development of the *condictio indebiti* beyond error
which attracts the criticism of scholars like Whitty.

The systematic re-introduction of a classification "retention without a legal basis" will ease the tensions in Scots law as it now stands
since not only can deviations from the strict error approach to the *condictio indebiti* be accommodated within the broader classification but
it will also remove the barriers presented by artificially narrow conceptions like "error as to liability". Thus, for example, in *Agnew* v. *Ferguson,*
since strictly there was no error as to liability, instead of treating the
claim as a *condictio indebiti*, one could classify it differently. The case
might have been analysed in a number of different ways; for example,
in terms of the payment of another's debt or in terms of contract on the
grounds that Ferguson took over the contractual undertakings of the
old landlord to his tenants. However, the Court chose to proceed on the
basis that it was a straightforward claim in the law of unjustified enrichment. Agnew had made his payment on the assumption that the agreement with his old landlord also governed his transfer to Ferguson. This
agreement therefore formed the legal basis for the transfer of the
excess, but, since no such agreement was seen in fact to have existed,
the excess had to be returned on the grounds that it was retained without a legal basis. It is no coincidence that Lord Trayner on this occasion
formulated the *condictio indebiti* (no title moral or legal to retain what
was received) in terms which suggest very strongly indeed that he had
"retention without a legal basis" in mind. In other words, in the language of the *condictio indebiti* he described the claim to recover what
is retained without a legal basis.

In circumstances in which retention without a legal basis is used
to accommodate claims which fall outwith the recognised causes of
action in the law of repetition it is important to be cautious. A desire to
meet such a claim should not provide an avenue to undermine the rules
of three-party enrichment, or any other area of the law for that matter.

The great strength which Birks saw in mistake as compared with the *condictio* was its flexibility and potential range. The comparison was unfair since Birks chose to compare "mistake" only with the *condictio indebiti* which he construed very narrowly. Also when illustrating the range of "mistake", Birks[114] and W.J. Stewart[115] illustrate its dangers since they run foul of the rules of three-part enrichment or use it to explain decisions of Scots law which very clearly proceeded on different grounds.

The Absorption of the Condictio ob Turpem vel Iniustam Causam *by the* Condictio Indebiti[116]

The *condictio ob turpem vel iniustam causam* (henceforth *condictio t.i.)* receives a surprisingly detailed treatment in the institutional works of both Stair and Bankton. Yet, apart from very occasional and brief mentions[117] it appears effectively to have vanished from modern law. How is this to be explained?

The Three-fold Classification of the Condictio t.i.

Following Roman law, Bankton[118] makes the following three-fold classification of cases to explain the broad circumstances and fundamental criteria governing the operation of the *condictio t.i.:*

> If things are given for an unlawful cause, distinction must be made as to the several cases; for where the unlawfulness was in the giver, and not in the receiver, in such a case the thing is not to be returned, even tho' the fact for which it was given was not performed; but if the unlawfulness was in the party receiver, and not in the giver, then the thing must be restored, even tho' the cause of giving was performed: if the turpitude was both in the party giver and receiver, then he that is in possession has the advantage by the rule *in pari casu potior est conditio possidentis;* so that the bond given on such consideration is void, but if payment is made, it is not to be repaid.

------

114   *An Introduction to the Law of Restitution* (Oxford, 1985), 151 on *Aiken* v. *Short* (1856) 1 H. & N. 210, 156 E.R. 1180.
115   *Op. cit.,* n.68, 65ff. Cf. for example, his treatment of *Wallet* v. *Ramsay* (1904) 12 S.L.T. 111 and *G.M. Scott (Willowbank Cooperage) Ltd.* v. *York Trailer Co. Ltd.* 1970 S.L.T. 15 with that of R. Evans-Jones, "Identifying the Enriched", 1992 S.L.T. (News) 25; also cf. his treatment of *Findlay* v. *Munro* (1698) Mor. 1767 with that advocated in this paper.
116   See also R. Evans-Jones and D. McKenzie, "Towards a Profile of the *condictio ob turpem vel iniustam causam* in Scots Law", 1994 *J.R.* 60.
117   *Cantiere San Rocco* v. *Clyde Shipbuilding and Engineering Co.* 1923 S.C. (H.L.) 105 at 122; *Encyclopaedia of the Laws of Scotland, cit. sup.,* n.10, "Repetition", which attempts to build a profile largely on English case law authority.
118   Bankton, 1,8.

History[119]

In classical Roman law the *condictio t.i.* was a modality of the *condictio causa data causa non secuta* (henceforth *condictio c.d.*) and was thus not an independent remedy. It was given what seemed like an independent status in the *Corpus Iuris Civilis* by the allocation of its own titles,[120] but in practice it was still a modality of the *condictio c.d.*

The *condictio c.d.* lay to recover money or property which was transferred for a lawful future purpose which did not materialise. As a modality of the *condictio c.d.*, in its core function, the *condictio t.i.* necessarily also lay to recover money or property which was given for a future purpose. The purpose must have been in the power of the transferee to achieve and have been one which was regarded by the law as offensive and to be discouraged because it offended against morality or law. Until the accomplishment of the immoral or illegal purpose the transferor could bring the *condictio c.d.* to recover what he transferred. Once the purpose for which the transfer was made had been achieved the *condictio c.d.*, by definition, was no longer available. Provided the transfer was for an immoral or illegal purpose the appropriate claim was under the *condictio t.i.*

The *condictio c.d.* in Roman law lay fundamentally in respect of agreements which lay outwith contract. An important result is that it, and therefore necessarily the *condictio t.i.*, did not lie to recover what was transferred to discharge a legal duty (*causa solvendi*) which was, and still is, the main area of application of the *condictio indebiti*. Thus, in Roman law, a clear distinction existed between the *condictio t.i.* and the *condictio indebiti*.

In modern law the major reason explaining the disappearance of the *condictio t.i.* is that it has been absorbed by the *condictio indebiti*. The reason concerns the history of contract. Once the principle *pacta servanda sunt* resulted in the recognition of all agreements seriously intended to have legal effect as contracts, the majority of agreements in respect of which the *condictio t.i.* had traditionally been available were no longer regarded as lying outwith contract.[121] If a transfer is made under such an agreement, the purpose of the transfer is now to discharge the obligation under the contract. If discharge fails the appropriate remedy is the *condictio indebiti*. It is helpful to give an example to illustrate this change of conception. In Roman law a transfer made to bribe an official would not be a contract since the agreement underlying the transfer fell outwith the recognised group of contracts. In principle the *condictio t.i.* was applicable. In the eyes of modern law, however, the agreement is a contract which (we assume) is void as a

---

119 See the treatment of H. Honsell, *Die Rückabwicklung sittenwidriger oder verbotener Geschäfte* (Munich, 1974).

120 D.12.5; C.4.7 and 9.

121 See R. Evans-Jones, "Unjust Enrichment, Contract and the Third Reception of Roman Law in Scotland", (1993) 109 *L.Q.R.* 663.

pactum illicitum; the question of the validity of the contract is decided by reference to the moral or legal prohibition not, as in Roman law, by reference to the restricted notion of contract itself. Thus, the transfer to the official is conceived as having been made to discharge the obligation under a contract which is void. In principle the *condictio indebiti* will lie to recover the undue payment. The limiting factor on the availability of the *condictio indebiti* itself in a case like this is the rule *potior est conditio possidentis* which will apply if both parties were at fault.

Two Generalisations

In modern law the *condictio indebiti* has absorbed the function of nearly all of the *condictio t.i.* This is an important conclusion for two main reasons:

(i)   according to the Scottish institutional writers the only application of the *condictio t.i.* is to the case where a transfer has been made to a payee who alone is reprehensible in the eyes of the law. Since the *condictio indebiti* has absorbed the function of the *condictio t.i.* this statement has to read to cover it, and indeed all of the *condictiones*. The receipt of the transfer for a purpose which was contrary to morals or law will normally render the contract underlying the transfer void on the grounds that it is a *pactum illicitum*. The transferor may then raise the *condictio indebiti* on the grounds that there has been an undue transfer. The immoral or illegal purpose, by rendering the contract void, is merely one of a range of circumstances which trigger the conditions (void contract) for the application of the *condictio indebiti*;

(ii) the *in pari delicto* rule that where both parties are *in culpa, potior est conditio possidentis* is stated by the institutional writers to be a bar to the *condictio t.i.* alone. It is, however, a rule which must apply to the whole of the law of repetition. Again this can be shown by reference to the *condictio indebiti*. Where a payment is made under an agreement in which both parties are in breach of a moral or legal prohinition the contract will normally be void and the *condictio indebiti* applicable in the usual manner. If the *in pari delicto* rule did not apply to the *condictio indebiti* its purpose to bar recovery where both parties were in *culpa* would be undermined in the vast majority of the cases to which it was intended to apply. Thus, in modern law the *condictio t.i.* should be seen to incorporate rules like *in pari delicto* which apply to the whole law of repetition; it should not be regarded as an independent remedy. This is a factor which explains its effective disappearance from modern Scots law.

Compulsion

On the basis of doubtful authority there is now pressure to apply the *condictio t.i.* as an independent remedy to recover enrichment acquired by improper compulsion.[122] This pressure arises in the context of a perception that the *condictio indebiti* is restricted to cases of "error" and that the extension by the courts beyond this narrow field is wrong. Suffice it to say that many other jurisdictions with a *condictio indebiti* now allow it to recover undue transfers made under compulsion.[123] As stated, the tensions created by such a development could be avoided in Scotland by the express recognition of "retention without a legal basis" as a cause of action, but until this is done it is entirely proper that the *condictio indebiti* should have been developed in Scots law beyond a restriction to error as to liability.

The Structural and Functional Problems of Error and Wrongful Compulsion

Whether it is this, or that, *condictio* which lies to recover the undue transfer made under compulsion might seem like an exercise akin to balancing angels on the end of a pin. In fact the answer to this particular point goes to the root of the whole classification of the law of unjustified enrichment. The purpose of those who wish to present the cause of action of *condictio indebiti* exclusively as "error" and *condictio t.i.* as "improper compulsion" is to enable the creation of a taxonomy of unjustified enrichment in Scotland similar to the "unjust factors" of English law. To each "unjust factor" of English law an equivalent *condictio* is allocated in Scots law with a roughly similar cause of action as the English "unjust factor". The civilian tradition has progressively reduced the importance of "error" to the point where, in the most modern codes, it is eliminated completely. To present "error" as the cause of action of *condictio indebiti* therefore throws into reverse what, in modern thinking, for both structural and functional reasons, is seen to be the best conception of its essentials.

We have seen that Whitty wishes to restrict the *condictio indebiti* to "error" but Birks wishes to extend it to "mistake". A fundamental feature which both these suggestions have in common is that they select a narrow, subjective, state of mind as the cause of action. The twentieth century European civilian codes – the German, the Greek, the Italian and the Dutch – have all rejected the error approach to *condictio indebiti*.[124] Thus, the idea that the cause of action of *condictio indebiti* is the undue transfer subject to a defence of knowledge is not the result of oversight or carelessness, but in fact the tradition which has come to be seen as superior by the Civil law. Why?

---

122 Scottish Law Commission, *Recovery of Benefits*, vol. 2, 201ff.

123 For example, for German law, see the Palandt commentary on the German Civil Code para. 814 and for South African law, *Commissioner for Inland Revenue* v. *First National Industrial Bank* 1990 (3) SA 641 (A).

124 The *condictio indebiti* is the principal component of the claim to recover transfers which are retained without a legal basis.

The idea that a transfer or payment is recoverable because it is "undue" is straightforward and is generally perceived to be a fundamentally correct basis on which to reverse enrichments. Error merely explains why an undue transfer was made and is not the factor which requires the transfer to be reversed. Furthermore, "undue" or, much better, "without a legal basis" is a broad unitary notion which ties together similar types of claim. This in turn makes the law simple to understand (especially in its "undue" clothes) and simple to operate. By contrast, under the "unjust factors" approach, instead of a single, broad and objective conception like "undue transfer" similar claims are divided up in a manner which obscures their "undue" unity according sometimes, as in the case of error, to the subjective state of mind of the pursuer at the time of the transfer. We will also see in relation to *Woolwich* that human affairs are so complex that it is sometimes difficult to fit behaviour into restrictive legal categories like error, mistake or wrongful compulsion even although it is perfectly clear that the transfer was made under such circumstances that it should be returned. An approach based on restrictive classifications like error or wrongful compulsion will, in difficult cases, be found wanting.

English law has embarked on an experiment the end result of which remains entirely unknown. For example, a new "unjust factor" of "ignorance" has recently been recognised, but only by some. Does Scots law really wish to be sucked into that puzzle, or into the problems arising from *Woolwich* where, because influential scholars reject "undue" as the cause of action notwithstanding that it is the clear (indeed stated) basis of the decision, no-one really seems to know quite why the undue payments were recoverable? Surely English law, in time, will also have to accommodate the case of the undue transfer made in doubt as to legal liability. Doubt falls short of mistake or ignorance and therefore in principle does not give rise to a claim. Yet undue transfers made in doubt as to liability are common cases in the law of unjustified enrichment which are accommodated under an approach which sees the cause of action of *condictio indebiti* as the undue transfer subject to a defence of knowledge since doubt falls short of knowledge and therefore does not activate the defence.

Woolwich Equitable Building Society v. *Inland Revenue*

It is now appropriate to evaluate the approach to *condictio indebiti* outlined above in the light of the recent reformulation of the English law of restitution by the House of Lords.

The plaintiffs, the Woolwich Equitable Building Society, made three payments amounting to £56.998 million in response to a tax demand under the Income Tax (Building Societies) Regulations 1986. The Woolwich disputed the vality of the regulations but nevertheless paid. It paid because it feared for its reputation in being the only Building Society to fail to pay in terms of the regulations and also because it feared the imposition of penalties. It was accepted by all the judges that, as a practical matter, the Woolwich had little choice but to make the three payments.

The Woolwich immediately sought judicial review that the regulations were *ultra vires* and void. At first instance the regulations were held to be void but this decision was overturned on appeal. However, on further appeal, the House of Lords held that the regulations were indeed void.

Since the regulations were void the case raised the further issue of restitution. After the decision at first instance that the regulations were void the Revenue, exercising what it believed to be its discretion in such matters, repaid the principal sum plus interest, but only interest from the date of the first decision that the regulations were void. The Woolwich, however, claimed interest from the time of payment. In order to substantiate this claim for additional interest – which amounted to approximately £7 million – the Woolwich had to show that they had a right to recover the principal sum at common law. If such a right existed, the obligation in respect of the principal sum and the liability to pay interest upon it arose from the moment that the payment was made.

The existence of such a right at common law was denied at first instance but affirmed by the Court of Appeal. The Revenue appealed to the House of Lords. As stated by Lord Slynn the fundamental question before the Committee was as follows:[125]

> Does the citizen have the right to recover from the revenue money demanded by the revenue and paid by him which was not due in law because the law was *ultra vires*?

The problem was that English law does not provide a *prima facie* cause of action to recover the undue transfer but only provided an action of restitution where the plaintiff, on the facts relevant to this case, could prove mistake or duress. I have already mentioned the potential problems with such an approach. Since the Woolwich paid in response to a demand the validity of which it immediately challenged it was perceived not to have paid by mistake. If it were to have been mistaken the Woolwich would have failed in its claim because, as the law stands, payments in mistake of law are irrecoverable. On the other hand, while the judges admitted that as a matter of fact the Woolwich had no choice but to pay it was subjected to no wrongful compulsion by the Revenue. Duress as a cause of action therefore also failed.

The response of a majority of the Committee (Lord Keith and Lord Jauncey dissenting) was to reformulate the English law of restitution so as to recognise a right at common law to recover money paid to a public authority pursuant to an *ultra vires* demand. However, because of the terms in which the judgements were presented considerable uncertainty exists as to the precise content of this new principle. Ewan

---

125 [1993] A.C. 70 at 199.

McKendrick writes that:[126]

> The vital task which ..remains to be carried out (in respect of *Woolwich*) relates to the identification of the unjust factor.

This suggests that while the Woolwich was held to be entitled to recover it is still not entirely clear why.

The Woolwich *Unjust Factor and the Undue Transfer*

Considerable effort has been expended by English academic commentators,[127] and the Scottish Law Commission, on trying to clarify the precise basis of the *Woolwich* decision. For the purposes of my observations on the *condictio indebiti* it is helpful to identify the attitude of the House of Lords to the notion "undue transfer" which has received scant attention.

Lord Browne-Wilkinson said:[128]

> In the present case, the concept of unjust enrichment suggests that the plaintiffs should have a remedy. The revenue demanded and received payment of the sum by way of tax alleged to be due under regulations subsequently held by your Lordships' house to be *ultra vires*...Yet the revenue maintains that it was under no legal obligation to repay...If the revenue is right, it will be enriched by the interest on money to which it had no right...In my judgement, this is the paradigm of a case of unjust enrichment.

The "paradigm" to which Lord Browne-Wilkinson referred is the retention of money by the Revenue to which it has "no right". This appears indistinguishable from the idea of retention of money which was not due.

Lord Goff presented the leading judgement for the majority. Having reviewed the English authorities which showed that recovery was not permitted in a case such as this he said:[129]

> But a formidable argument has been developed in recent years by leading (English) academic lawyers that this stream of authority should be the subject of reinterpretation to reveal a different line of thought pointing to the conclusion that money paid to a public authority pursuant to an *ultra vires* demand should be repayable, without the necessity of establishing compulsion, on the simple ground that there was no consideration for the payment...I have a strong presentiment that, had the opportunity arisen, Lord Mansfield would have seized it to establish the law in this form. His

---

126 "Restitution of Unlawfully Demanded Tax", 1993 *L.M.C.L.Q.* 88 at 98.
127 See esp. McKendrick, *op. cit.*, n.126; J. Beatson, "Restitution of Taxes, Levies and Other Imposts: Defining the Extent of the *Woolwich* Principle", (1993) 109 *L.Q.R.* 401. Also T. Hill, "Restitution from Public Authorities and the Treasury's Position: *Woolwich Equitable Building Society* v. *I.R.C.*", (1993) 56 *M.L.R.* 856.
128 at 197.
129 at 166.

broad culture, his knowledge and understanding of Roman law, his extraordinary gift for cutting through technicality to perceive and define principle, would surely have drawn him towards this result.

Later Lord Goff says:[130]

> The revenue's position appears to me, as a matter of common justice, to be unsustainable...To the simple call of justice there are a number of possible objections. The first is to be found in the structure of our law of restitution, as it developed during the 19th and 20th centuries. The law might have developed so as to recognise a *condictio indebiti* – an action for the recovery of money on the ground that it was not due. But it did not do so. Instead, as we have seen, there developed common law actions for the recovery of money paid under mistake of fact, and under certain forms of compulsion. What is now being sought is, in a sense, a reversal of that development, in a particular type of case....

The important point to note is that the reversal which Lord Goff had in mind is the re-establishment of the English equivalent of the *condictio indebiti*; namely recovery of payments made for no consideration. When commenting on Lord Goff's approach McKendrick observes:[131]

> "no consideration" would appear to mean simply that a benefit was transferred which was not due; in other words, it would be tantamount to the introduction of a *condictio indebiti*.

The primary difficulties which McKendrick sees in such an approach is that it would render all gifts recoverable (which it would not, at least in Scots law) and that it would undermine the mistake of law rule (which he admits is ripe for abolition anyway).

Scots Law and Woolwich

One response to *Woolwich*,[132] has been to proceed on the assumption that the *condictio indebiti* lies only in cases of error. Since there was held to be no error or duress on the facts in *Woolwich* it is assumed that Scots law would provide no remedy in a similar case were it to arise in Scotland. We should observe that in the light of this approach the remarks of Lord Goff that a *condictio indebiti* would have met the justice of the plaintiff's claim must seem profoundly puzzling. The explanation lies in the fact that Lord Goff's idea of a *condictio indebiti* is based on what is now the dominant civilian tradition that the cause of action of the *condictio indebiti* is the undue transfer subject to a defence of knowledge. How might the *condictio indebiti* conceived in such terms confront *Woolwich*?

---

130 at 172.
131 *Op. cit.*, n.126, at 95.
132 This approach was developed in the seminar on the Scots law of unjustified enrichment held in Edinburgh, October 1993; see note 69.

The question, was the transfer undue, had been resolved earlier by the House of Lords. This is therefore unproblematic. The further question concerns the defence of knowledge. Two approaches are possible depending on whether one takes an objective or subjective approach to the evaluation of knowledge.

The Objective Approach: Doubt

The issue whether the regulations under which the Revenue had made its claim were valid was one which had earlier had gone to the House of Lords. Although the Woolwich had always claimed that the regulations were void, could they be sure if this issue had to be appealed to the House of Lords? Objectively it might be perceived that the Woolwich paid in doubt as to their liability. Doubt falls short of knowledge, therefore the knowledge defence does not operate to bar recovery. The difficulty with taking this approach is that to pay in doubt as to the law is perceived to be as reprehensible as paying in ignorance of the law, and, as things stand, payments in ignorance (or error) of law are irrecoverable.

The Subjective Approach: Knowledge

The House of Lords did not take the objective approach. The Committee held that the Woolwich knew that the regulations were void. Does the knowledge defence therefore bar recovery? Not necessarily. The reason is that only such knowledge as should be construed like a gift bars recovery. The Committee as a whole were of the view that the Woolwich had no choice but to pay. Lord Goff believed that the Revenue's position as a matter of common justice was unsustainable and that a *condictio indebiti* would have met the justice of the Woolwich's claim. The clear suggestion is that because of the demands of *bona fides* he would not have allowed the knowledge defence to operate. There was no *venire contra factum proprium* on this occasion.

The "knowledge" approach to the *condictio indebiti* allows a court to evaluate all the facts of the case to determine whether the undue transfer should be recoverable. The court is not restricted to narrow legal classifications like error or duress. In *Woolwich* a transfer was made which was undue. Since in fact the plaintiffs had no choice but to pay, notwithstanding the absence of "error" or "duress", there is every indication that the "knowledge" defence would not have been allowed to operate to bar recovery had the *condictio indebiti*, rather than the English law action for money had and received, been the claim before the House of Lords.

Conclusions

At the beginning of this chapter it was observed that uncertainty can be one feature of private law at a particular stage of development of a civilian legal system. This uncertainty need not, of course, be viewed as something negative but as the product of an extremely rich tradition. The richness of the Scots law on the *condictio* is enhanced by the periodic overlays which it has received from English law. In this context its mixed legal system really does place Scotland at the interface between the Civil and Common law worlds. The understanding of the *condictio indebiti* developed in this chapter is a product of the richness of Scotland's legal tradition and, as the foundation of the general claim "retention without a legal basis", it offers clear advantages over the alternatives. It hopefully also shows that our Civil law tradition continues to raise issues and offer solutions which are of great importance to the development of modern Scots law.

11. THE *CONDICTIO CAUSA DATA CAUSA NON SECUTA*

By GEOFFREY D. MacCORMACK

Background: The Roman Law.

In Roman law the general term *condictio* was used to express a range of remedies which had in common the fact that one person asserted a claim to recover money or property alleged to be owed to him by another. One can speak of the *condictio* as an action which lay to recover a debt, provided it is understood that the debt did not arise from a legally enforceable agreement. In the latter case the appropriate remedy was constituted by the specific contractual action, for example the *actio empti* (sale), *locati* (hire) or *mandati* (mandate). Since the *condictio* was introduced into Roman law before the recognition of agreement as an independent source of legal obligation, it could be brought to recover what was alleged to be due under certain real (*mutuum*) or formal (*stipulatio*, contract *litteris*) contracts. Here the ground of obligation constituting the debt lay not in agreement but in the receipt of property or the accomplishment of a verbal or written formality. The *condictio* is not in these cases conceived as enforcing an agreement or as providing a sanction for breach of an agreement.

Typical cases in which a *condictio* lay were those in which it could be said that the defender had been unjustly enriched at the expense of the pursuer, in particular through an attempt to retain property which he had received from the latter. The Roman jurists did not formulate a general category of unjust enrichment or devise a general unjust enrichment action. What they did was to develop a number of particular grounds upon which a *condictio* might lie, and distinguish the nature of the *condictio* according to its ground. It is with one of these *condictiones* that we are concerned in this paper, that entitled in the *Digest* the *condictio causa data causa non secuta*.

As is made evident by its name the *condictio causa data causa non secuta* provides a remedy where someone has given money or property to another on the clear understanding that the recipient will make a counter-performance or that a particular event should occur. Should the counter-performance or event not take place, in principle the *condictio* lay to recover the value of what had been given. The word "*causa*" in the title of the *condictio* expresses the fact that the property was given for a particular purpose which fails to materialise. Sometimes it is rendered by the technical term of English law "consideration". Of the examples of the *condictio* 's operation found in the relevant *Digest* title, some contemplate a counter-performance and hence fall into the category of the innominate contracts, and some are predicated upon a "purpose" other than an act to be performed by the recipient. To the first case belongs the situation in which someone gives money to another on the understanding that the latter manumits a named slave, or does not take legal proceedings against the donor.[1] To the second case belongs the situation in which property is given as dowry with respect to a marriage to take place in the future[2] or that in which property is given as a *donatio mortis causa*.[3]

It is clear that in the second class of case there is no question of the *condictio* being used to enforce a contract since the parties to the action had not entered into a contractual relationship. However, the first situation is more problematic since the parties had in fact concluded a contract which became enforceable not on agreement but on performance by one of them. Where one party to an innominate contract had paid money or delivered property to the other who subsequently failed to make the expected counter-performance, the former had the *condictio* to recover the value of what he had given. Could it be said that under these circumstances the *condictio* was given the force of a contractual action? As to this, two points should be made. First, the *condictio* in origin was not a contractual action because it was available before such arrangements were recognised as contracts at all. Second, after recognition of the innominate contracts through the introduction of the *actio praescriptis verbis* by which one party, on performance, could recover damages to the extent of his interest from the defaulting party, the *condictio* continued to be available to recover what had been given. However, the nature of the remedy did not change. The principle upon which it lay was not that the defender had failed to carry out his agreement (the basis of the *actio praescriptis verbis*) but that the *causa* for the initial payment had failed to materialise.[4] While it is clear that in the law of Justinian a party to an innominate contract who had made a payment could sue the defaulting party either by the *actio praescriptis verbis* or by the *condictio causa data causa non secuta*, it seems that the latter was the appropriate one to bring where all that was sought was recovery of what had been paid.[5]

Although the prime instance contemplated for the *condictio*'s application seems to have been the case where some external event

---

1   D.12.4.1*pr*, 3*pr.*–2.
2   D.12.4.6–9.
3   D.12.4.12.
4   F. Chaudet, *condictio causa data non secuta. Critique historique de l'action en enrichissement illégitime de l'art. 62 al.2 CO*, (Lausanne, 1973), 72ff. argues that in Roman law the *condictio* was progressively regarded as a contractual action (pointing, for example, to the requirement in some texts that fault on the part of the recipient was a condition for the availability of the action).
5   D.19.5.7; 19.5.17.2.

prevented satisfaction of the purpose or the recipient was unable to make the requisite counter-performance, there are texts which simply allow the person who had initially made the payment to change his mind and sue to recover what he had paid at any time before satisfaction of the purpose or actual performance by the other party (*locus poenitentiae*). For example, Ulpian states that a person who has given another money in order that he manumit a particular slave may bring the *condictio* to recover what he had paid either where the recipient had failed to manumit or where he himself had changed his mind.[6]

There are also texts which suggest that, in the event of the recipient not performing his part of the agreement, the *condictio* would lie only if failure to perform had been due to his fault. The most explicit of these texts is a constitution attributed to the emperor Diocletian which states that, where money has been given for a *causa* that fails not through the fault (*culpa*) of the recipient but through chance (*fortuitus casus*), it cannot be recovered by the *condictio*.[7] Other texts, however, do not seem to impose such a restriction. Celsus allows the *condictio* where money has been given to another on the understanding that the recipient should give a particular slave who dies before he can be transferred. There is nothing to suggest that the death must have been due to the recipient's fault.[8]

From this brief discussion one can establish the following broad conclusions for the law of Justinian:

(i)   The *condictio causa data causa non secuta* might be brought to recover property paid either where an innominate contract had been concluded but the counter-performance had not followed, or where property had been given for some purpose that remained unsatisfied.

(ii) In the case of the innominate contracts the *condictio* was not conceived as an action by which to enforce the contract; it lay, possibly to the exclusion of the *actio praescriptis verbis*, to recover what had been paid for a *causa* that failed to materialise.

(iii) Some texts explicitly allow the *condictio* to be brought at any time prior to realisation of the *causa*, even on the ground of a simple change of mind on the part of the pursuer.

(iv) There is textual authority for the proposition that, where property or money had been given for a counter-performance, the *condictio* might lie only where the failure of the counter-performance was due to the defender's own fault.

It is not possible here to trace the subsequent complex history of the *condictio causa data causa non secuta* in the writings of the

---

6   D.12.4.3.2.
7   C.4.6.10, generally regarded as interpolated and as stating the position of Justinian, not Diocletian.
8   D.12.4.16.

Glossators, Commentators, Canonists, Humanists or Pandectists. Two points only may be made, one general and one specific. Generally it appears that through the influence primarily of the Canonists[9] all agreements came to be regarded as actionable contracts unless tainted with fraud, duress, illegality or the like. The result was that the innominate contracts of the old Roman law came to be analysed in the same way as the consensual contracts. The appropriate remedies were those founded on breach of the agreement. Hence there no longer remained a role for the *condictio causa data causa non secuta* in the field of contract, though it might still be of relevance in non-contractual situations.

Specifically it is worth noting that the great seventeenth-century French jurist Jean Domat, whose influential work entitled *Les lois civiles dans leur ordre naturel* first appeared in 1694, constructed a scheme of obligations similar to that adopted by Stair. This scheme distinguished sharply between obligations derived from "covenants", that is those which arose from the consent of the parties, and those derived from the receipt of what was not due or the possession of another's property without a covenant. The former were enforced by actions derived from the contract, the latter by the *condictiones indebiti* or *causa data causa non secuta*.[10] It is interesting that only a few years earlier Stair had adopted a similar distinction in his *Institutions of the Law of Scotland*.

Treatment in the Institutional Writers

In emulation of the model first established for Scots law by Stair, the institutional writers all treat the *condictio causa data causa non secuta* as lying in respect of an obligation which is not derived from a contract. Stair himself had preferred not to follow the Justinianic classification of obligations (contract, delict, quasi-contract and quasi-delict) on the ground that it did not reflect their true cause or ground. Instead, he drew a broad distinction between obediential (derived from the will of God and founded in nature) and conventional obligations (derived from the will of man and founded in agreement or contract).[11] Among the obediential obligations were those of restitution, that is, "the obligations, whereby men are holden to restore the proper goods of others".[12] The duty to restore might arise in a number of ways unconnected with any engagement or contract on the part of the person under the duty. One of these ways was constituted by the fact that someone's goods had come into another's hands for a cause which failed. Stair referred to "those goods *quae cadunt in non causam,*

---

9   See H. Capitant, *De la cause des obligations* (Paris, 1923), 315ff.
10 The edition consulted for this essay has been the English translation by William Strachan published in London in 1722 under the title J. Domat, *The Civil Law.* See particularly book I, title 1, section 1, paras 2-4, 7; section 2, paras 3-4; book 2, title 1, introduction and section 1, para 10.
11 Stair, 1,3,2ff.
12 *Ibid.,* 1,7,1.

which coming warrantably to our hands, and without any paction of restitution, yet if the cause cease by which they become ours, there superveneth the obligation of restitution of them; whence are the *condictiones* in law *ob non causam* and *causa data, causa non secuta*". Although he cited no Roman authority, he gave as an example a situation well known in the Roman texts, that where something was given in contemplation of a marriage that never took place.[13]

Bankton distinguished between natural and civil obligations, the former being grounded in the law of nature alone and lacking the sanction of human positive law, the latter being either civil alone or mixed, that is, both grounded in natural equity and equipped with a civil sanction.[14] Restitution was described as a "natural obligation", presumably falling within the "mixed" category.[15] Among the grounds for restitution were: "where the cause of the delivery ceases, the thing must be restored to the giver: hence were introduced by the law, the several condictions, *sine causa, causa data non secuta* etc., as things given in contemplation of marriage which does not follow". None of this essentially diverged from Stair.

Bankton did, however, add some further examples of the *condictio*'s operation, namely:

> ...a bond given in hopes of getting the money which is not delivered, and every deed or grant that depends upon mutual consideration, not given or performed, must be restored to the granters: the recital or narrative of the rights, in such cases, is suffcient to instruct the cause for which they were granted, and make way for restitution, though there is no express condition annexed in the deed; but where a bond bears no cause or consideration for which it is granted, it will not thereupon be annulled, for it is presumed gratuitous.[16]

This is not an easy passage to interpret. In particular it is not entirely clear whether Bankton was describing two classes of case to which the *condictio* applied, both characterised by the expectation that, where something was given or done, a counter-performance would result, but one arising from contract and the other not. The initial words "a bond...delivered" almost certainly refer to the case in which there was no contract between granter and recipient. But do the succeeding words which speak of grants depending upon "mutual consideration" suggest that Bankton was now thinking of the case in which a contract had been made? The general tenor of the passage points to the conclusion that Bankton was considering only one class of case, namely that in which no contract had been made between the granter of the deed or bond and the recipient. When speaking of "mutual consideration" he

---

13   *Ibid.*, 1,7,7.
14   Bankton, 1,4,12; 15.
15   *Ibid.*, 1,8,1.
16   *Ibid.*, 1,8,21.

was adverting to the situation in which the deed declared on its face
the nature of the counter-performance to be made in return for the
grant.

The specific problem he mentioned arose where the deed did not
expressly say that the benefit was to be conferred provided that a particular return was made. Was such a grant therefore to be treated as a
gift? Bankton's reply was that, where the narrative of a deed made it
clear that the benefit granted was dependent upon a certain event,
then, even though no express condition had been inserted in the opera-
tive words of the deed, the "condition" to be implied from the narrative
was still to take effect. The illustration he provided is instructive. He
cited a case of 1684[17] in which under a disposition of lands certain persons who were constituted heirs to the lands undertook to ensure that
the immediate beneficiary received them free from any encumbrances.
The narrative referred to the fact that it was "just and rational" for the
designated persons to undertake the obligation since they had been
made heirs. Where a creditor to whom the lands had been pledged subsequently realised his right, so extinguishing the heirs' right to inherit,
the Lords held that the obligation imposed by the deed was also discharged, since it had been undertaken *causa data*, and *causa non
secuta*. It is significant that the arrangement between the granter and
the prospective recipents of the lands did not amount to a contract.[18]

Erskine followed Stair in his classification of obligations, his understanding of restitution, and his citation of the Roman *condictio causa
data causa non secuta* illustrated with the example of something given
for a marriage that failed to take place.[19] He differed in two particulars.
First, he expressly cited texts from the *Digest* title 12.4 for his propositions, and, second, he adddded an important qualification not found in
Stair or Bankton:

> If it becomes impossible that the cause of giving should exist by any
> accident not imputable to the receiver, no action lies against him,
> unless he has put off performing it when it was in his power to per-
> form, before that accident happened.

This looks like a version of the rule found in some Justinianic texts to
the effect that the *condictio* will lie to recover what was paid only if the
failure of the *causa* was attributable to the recipient's *culpa*.[20] In fact
the text which Erskine cites in support[21] deals with a very specific situation in which money has been given for the manumission of a slave
who dies before the manumission has been accomplished. The jurist

---

17   *Newton's Decis.* 66, wrongly cited as 96.
18   See the discussion of the Bankton passage in R. Evans-Jones, "Unjust
     Enrichment, Contract and the Third Reception of Roman Law in Scotland",
     (1993) 109 *L.Q.R.*, 663.
19   Erskine, *Inst.,* 3,1,9; 10.
20   See, for example, C.4.6.10 cited above.
21   D.12.4.5.4.

(Ulpian) discusses the circumstances under which the money should, or should not, be refunded. Erskine's words later caused the courts some difficulty.[22]

Bell in his *Principles* merely devoted a few words to the *condictio*.[23] Like his predecessors he treated it as falling under the general head of "rights arising from implied obligations independent of convention" and under the specific head of "restitution". All he said, after referring to the obligation to restore goods received by mistake was "and so one to whom a thing has been transferred, or an obligation undertaken and fulfilled, on a consideration which has failed, is also liable to restitution under the condition *causa data causa non secuta*".[24] No illustrations of the operation of this condition are given.

Some general points may be made about the treatment by the institutional writers of the *condictio causa data causa non secuta*. By and large, as Buckland noted in his discussion of the *Cantiere* case,[25] the institutional writers do not directly draw upon the texts found in the *Corpus Iuris Civilis*. They appear rather to have adopted the Roman rules as they had been received in the *ius commune* of continental Europe.[26] Buckland himself refers to the special significance in this regard of the Pandectist tradition, where it is assumed that failure of the cause for whatever reason will ground the right of recovery.[27] The result is that the majority of the institutional writers take for granted the fact that the *condictio causa data causa non secuta* would lie to recover a payment where the counter-performance had failed through no fault of the recipient.[28] It was only Erskine who in fact actually cited the *Digest*, and significantly it was only Erskine who used language capable of the construction that the *condictio* should permit recovery only where the counter-performance had failed through the fault of the recipient.

All the institutional writers quite clearly treat the *condictio* as giving an effect to an obligation which is not conceived as grounded in contract in the sense of an agreement voluntarily entered into by the parties. The obligation is grounded on the principle of natural equity which dictates that, what one has received for a "consideration" or

---

22   See especially the judgments in the *Cantiere* case discussed below.
23   Bell, *Prin.*, s. 530.
24   This language already appears in the 4th edition of the *Principles,* 1839, the last to be prepared by Bell himself.
25   See W.W. Buckland, "*Casus* and Frustration in Roman Law and Common Law", (1932–3) 46 *Harvard L.R.* 1284ff.
26   For the *ius commune* see O.F. Robinson, T.D. Fergus and W.M. Gordon, *European Legal History*, (2nd ed., London, 1994), chapter 7.
27   So Dernberg in para. 142 in the second volume of the seventh edition of his *Pandekten* (though he also records the opinion that the recipient may keep what he has received unless he has been at fault in failing to make the counter-performance).
28   See especially Zimmermann, *Obligations,* 858ff. (citing the opinion of Donellus).

purpose that fails, should be restored to the giver. Further the *condictio* is treated as having a very limited role in Scots law. No more than a few lines is devoted to it by any of the writers, and virtually no instances of its application by the courts are cited. This is particularly remarkable in view of the fact that the early apprenticeship cases which invoked the principle *causa data causa non secuta* were decided in the latter part of the seventeenth or the early part of the eighteenth century. The *condictio causa data causa non secuta* in the minds of the institutional writers occupied a role greatly subordinate to that of the *condictio indebiti* which received considerable discussion. There is mention of the latter but not the former remedy in Erskine's *Principles*.[29]

However, the words used by some of the institutional writers to describe the operation of the *condictio* could readily be transposed to a case in which there was a contract between the parties and one sued to recover what he had paid in fulfilment of its terms, where the other had altogether failed to perform his part. Of particular significance in this regard is the use of the phrases "mutual consideration" (Bankton) and "consideration which has failed" (Bell). The substitution of the word "consideration" for the word "cause" in the formulation of the rules governing the applicability of the *condictio* provides a convenient bridge for the transition from the non-contractual to the contractual class of case. The definition offered by Bell, the last of the institutional writers, was especially suitable for use in a contractual situation.

The Cases

Since the judgment of Lord President Inglis in *Watson and Co.* v. *Shankland*[30] marks a watershed for the application in Scots law of the *condictio causa data causa non secuta*, we may divide the cases into two groups, those decided before 1871 and those decided after that date. Of the first group it can be simply said that they show very little trace of the active application of the *condictio* . Nor is it possible to discern any firm principle on the basis of which the courts at this time were prepared to grant recovery of what had been paid on the ground *causa data causa non secuta*. We can confine ourselves to decisions in which there is a specific reference to the *condictio* or the principle *causa data causa non secuta* either in the arguments or in the judgments. There are in fact a number of other decisions in which, although no such specific reference occurs, application of the *condictio* would in principle have been appropriate.[31]

We may take first the three apprenticeship cases, the two earlier of which make some reference to *causa data causa non secuta*, whereas

---

29   Erskine, *Prin.*, 3,3,17.
30   (1871) 10 M. 142.
31   See, for example, *Lawson* v. *Auchinleck* (1699) Mor. 8402; *Charteris* v. *King's Advocate* (1749–50) Mor. 7293; *Maule* v. *Maule* (1822) 2 S. 26; *Ewing* v. *McGavin* (1831) 9 S. 622; *MacFarquar* v. *MacKay* (1869) 7 M. 766.

the third does not. In the 1683 case of *Ogilvy* v. *Hume*[32] a bond containing a promise to pay had been given to the master in respect of the fee due under the arrangement. Where the master died before the expiry of the term of the apprenticeship, the widow sought to recover from the apprentice the payment promised under the bond. The defender alleged that, in view of the circumstances in which the apprenticeship had been ended, he was entitled to retain a portion of the money. He alleged as the ground of his claim *causa data causa non secuta*. Hence this is not a case in which the *condictio* was brought to recover what had been paid on account of a purpose that failed, but one in which the principle underlying the *condictio* was invoked to justify retention of a sum of money which otherwise would have been due under a promise. The court (no reason for its decision being reported) upheld the defender. One may infer that, should the apprentice fee actually have been paid, the court would have allowed the *condictio causa data causa non secuta* to lie for recovery of the appropriate proportion. It appears that the court was not looking at the matter in terms of the rights and duties created by the contract between the apprentice and the master. Rather it accepted the argument that, since the purpose for which the payment had been promised had partially failed, the debtor was entitled to a corresponding partial release of his debt.

In another apprenticeship case, *Cutler* v. *Littlejohn*,[33] where the master died some time before the expiry of the term fixed by the indentures, the court held that the apprentice was entitled to recover a third of the fee fixed. Unfortunately the ground of the decision is not clear. The defender had cited the *condictio causa data causa non secuta* in argument, urging that it would not lie, since there had been no total failure of *causa*. The pursuer appears to have raised two rather different arguments. On the one hand, citing Stair's remark on things "*quae cadunt in non causam*", he asserted that the *causa* had failed (*sine causa*) with respect to the unexpired term of the apprenticeship. Hence the defender was under an obligation of restitution with respect to such part of the payment as was referable to this period. On the other hand, citing a passage from the *Digest* title on *locatio conductio*,[34] he argued that under the contract of hire the reward agreed for the service was only payable if it was fully rendered; if not, the hirer was entitled to a proportionate reduction. In other words the pursuer sought a remedy either from the law of restitution or from the law of contract. The court, in upholding the pursuer's claim, did not make clear which argument it accepted or upon which it relied. It is, however, inferable, especially from the fact that both the defender and the pursuer raised arguments directed to the applicability of the *condictio causa data causa non secuta*, that the court was prepared to allow the *condictio* in

---

32   2 B.S. 34.
33   (1711) Mor. 583.
34   D.19.2.38.

this case, even although, alternatively, it might also have allowed the claim in contract to succeed.

On the basis of the decisions in *Ogilvie* and *Cutler* one might be prepared to argue that the Lords were prepared to allow a remedy under either the principle *causa data causa non secuta* or the contract of hire, where the master had died before the expiry of the term of the apprenticeship. However, the third of these cases, *Shepherd* v. *Innes*,[35] suggests that the court came to entertain a decided preference for the latter rather than the former approach. In this case it was the apprentice who died before the term of his apprenticeship came to an end. The master sought payment of the apprentice fee in full. Neither the parties or the court made any reference to restitution or to *causa data causa non secuta*. The case was argued purely in terms of the rights and duties incurred under the contract. The Lord Ordinary, whose judgment was approved by the Lords, held that the money promised as fee remained due under the contract, since non-performance, that is, the failure of the apprentice to receive his full training, could not be attributed to any fault on the part of the master.

We have located only two other eighteenth-century cases which turned on the applicability of the principle *causa data causa non secuta*. One is *Rule* v. *Reid*,[36] a case in fact relied upon by the defence in *Cutler* v. *Littlejohn*. Rule had drawn up a bond promising to pay Reid and others a sum of money in consideration of their taking charge of his funeral and going to trouble and expense in looking after the education of his children. On Rule's death Reid had taken part in the funeral arrangements but had been too ill to superintend the education of the children, being confined to his house until the day of his death. Consequently, when payment of the bond fell due, Rule's son refused to pay anything to Reid's representatives, invoking the principle *causa data causa non secuta*, and arguing that the condition for payment had not been fulfilled. The Lords upheld the claim for payment and rejected the defender's arguments on the ground that Reid had in fact complied with the condition for payment by overseeing the funeral and accepting the curatory of the children. The arguments and the decision appear to have turned not upon the rights and duties established by contract, but upon the the scope of a claim in restitution founded upon the principle *causa data causa non secuta*.

The other case, *Mary Provan* v. *Calder*,[37] was concerned with the recovery of a payment alleged to have been made on account of a marriage that did not take place. The issue was whether the defender was liable on a bill for £100 which he had initially given to her, which she had then handed to a third party for safe keeping, and which the defender had obtained from that party. He argued that "the bill was

---

35 (1760) Mor. 589.
36 (1707) Mor. 6364.
37 (1742) Mor. 9511.

granted *intuitu matrimonii*, and consequently must fall to the ground as *causa data, causa non secuta*, since marriage has not followed".[38] To this the reply was made that in fact the bill had not been granted *intuitu matrimonii* since "the true cause of granting it was, to induce the pursuer to accept the proposal; and as she did accordingly accept of Calder's proposal, it can never be said that the bill was either granted *sine causa*, or that it is in the case of *causa data non secuta*".[39] The Lords upheld the pursuer, but the ground of the judgment is not reported.

From the evidence so far surveyed we can draw two conclusions. First, there is very little explicit recourse to the *condictio* or principle *causa data causa non secuta* in the pre-1871 case law. Second, such evidence as there is shows that either the *condictio* or the principle itself might occasionally be invoked in cases where restitution of what had been given was sought on the ground of a failure of purpose, and no obvious remedy in contract was available. Where a remedy in contract was *prima facie* available, as in the apprenticeship cases, the courts after an initial willingness to allow restitution on the ground *causa data causa non secuta*, possibly as an alternative to the contractual remedy, finally appear to have come down in favour of the latter alone.

All this changed with the opinion of Lord President Inglis in *Watson* v. *Shankland*,[40] a case which ushered in a new era for the development of the *condictio causa data causa non secuta* in Scots law. The essential facts in that case were that a charter-party was concluded between the pursuers as charterers and the defenders as owners under which the former made an advance payment of freight. When the ship was lost at sea, the charterers sought repayment of the sum advanced. The decision in favour of the defenders turned in the end upon the construction of a particular clause of the contract. Yet the importance of the case lies in the statement of the general law found in the judgment of Lord President Inglis. His Lordship sought to ascertain the principles which would govern the matter in the absence of any contrary provision in the contract. He identified the relevant area of law as that of restitution, and argued that in accordance with the principle *causa data causa non secuta* the amount of freight prepaid was recoverable where the cause on account of which it had been given failed to materialise. The Lord Justice-Clerk together with Lords Deas and Ardmillan expressed agreement with the general principles of law stated by the Lord President. The relevant part of his opinion runs as follows:

> There is no rule of the civil law, as adapted into all modern municipal codes and systems, better understood than this – that if money is advanced by one party to a mutual contract, on the condition and

---

38   *Ibid.*, at 9513.
39   *Ibid.*, at 9514.
40   (1871) 10 M. 142.

stipulation that something shall be afterwards paid or performed
by the other party, and the latter party fails in performing his part
of the contract, the former is entitled to repayment of his advance
on the ground of failure of consideration. In the Roman system the
demand for repayment took the form of a *condictio causa data
causa non secuta* or a *condictio sine causa* or a *condictio indebiti*
according to the particular circumstances. In our own practice
these remedies are represented by the action of restitution and the
action of repetition. And in all systems of jurisprudence there must
be similar remedies, for the rule which they are intended to enforce
is of universal application in mutual contracts.

   If a person contract to build me a house, and stipulates that I
shall advance him a certain portion of the price before he begins to
bring his materials to the ground or to perform any part of the
work, the money so advanced may certainly be recovered back if he
never performs any part, or an available part, of his contract. No
doubt if he perform a part and then fail in completing the contract,
I shall be bound in equity to allow him credit to the extent to which
I am *lucratus* by his materials and labour but no further; and if I am
not *lucratus* at all, I shall be entitled to repetition of the whole
advance, however great his expenditure and consequent loss may
have been.

   There seems no ground in reason or general legal principle why
the rule should not apply to an advance made by a charterer to the
master of a ship of a part of the stipulated freight, the consideration
of the advance being the performance of the contract work of carrying and right delivery of the goods. If the consideration on which
the advance is made fail by the non-completion of the voyage, the
advance is *pari ratione* repayable to the charterer.[41]

The most important part of this passage for our purposes is Lord
President Inglis's reference to the three *condictiones* of the Roman law.
Although his language is not without ambiguity, one may interpret his
thought in the sense that he took the *condictio causa data causa non
secuta* to express for Scots law a non-contractual claim in restitution
founded on the fact that the purpose for which money or property had
been given had failed to materialise. He was not saying that the *condictio* would lie for the recovery of money which had been paid in accordance with the terms of a valid contract on the ground of a failure of
the consideration in respect of which the payment had been made.

   What suggests that this was the way in which Lord Inglis understood the role of the *condictio* in Scots law is a close reading of the last
paragraph quoted above together with a later passage in his judgment.
These passages formed the basis of the interlocutor actually pronounced by the court. In the later passage he states that the advance by
way of freight can be understood neither as a loan nor as a payment
made in terms of the contract. It is rather "an advance on the credit of

---

41   *Ibid.*, at 152.

the owners" which "creates a debt due by them, though with a post-poned term of payment".[42] The interlocutor itself states that the payment "is to be held as an advance in consideration of the subsequent performance of the contract...and that if there is a failure of consideration by the voyage not being accomplished...the charterers are entitled...to recover the amount of the said advance".[43]

We now proceed to consider the way Lord President Inglis's *dicta* have been applied in subsequent cases. *Davis and Primrose Ltd.* v. *Clyde Shipbuilding and Engineering Co. Ltd.*[44] was a case in which a contract for the supply of engines to a foreign firm had been concluded prior to the outbreak of the First World War. An advance on the purchase price had been paid, but war rendered the performance of the contract impossible. A question arose as to who was entitled to the prepaid portion of the purchase price. The Lord Ordinary (Lord Dewar), holding the contract to be dissolved, found that the principle stated by Lord President Inglis governed the case. Since the sellers had not performed their part of the contract, they were not entitled to retain the money they had received from the purchasers, but must account for it to the pursuers who were a creditor of the latter. Lord Dewar in his quotation from Lord President Inglis omitted the reference to the Roman *condictiones*. He formulated the principle as follows: "It is, I think, an established rule of the law of Scotland that where one party pays a sum of money to the other party on condition that something shall be paid or done in return for it, and that consideration fails, the money paid may be recovered".[45] What is significant about the Lord Ordinary's approach is that he appears to have approached the matter purely from the perspective of the rights and obligations created by the agreement between the parties. He was not invoking or relying upon an alternative remedy derived from the law of restitution, and to this extent he misunderstood the real tenor of Lord Inglis's remarks.

We now come to the most central of the decisions on the role of the *condictio causa data causa non secuta* in Scots law, *Cantiere San Rocco S.A.* v. *Clyde Shipbuilding and Engineering Company Ltd.*,[46] the only one to offer a view of the law by the House of Lords as well as by the Inner House. This decision established two important points. First, in contracts where one party had made a payment to the other, and the latter through supervening impossibility was unable to perform his part of the contract, the *condictio causa data causa non secuta* lay for recovery of the payment. Second, this remedy, although available in a

---

42   *Ibid.*, at 153.
43   The House of Lords upheld the decision of the Inner House but did not support the statement of the law affirmed in the interlocutor, ordering the removal *inter alia* of the words quoted in the text (1873) 11 M. (H.L.) 51 at 56.
44   1917, 1 S.L.T. 297.
45   *Ibid.*, at 299.
46   1922 S.C. 723; 1923 S.C. (H.L.) 105.

case of contract, and therefore made subject to any contrary expression
of intention by the parties, was clearly identified as being non-contractual in nature, located in the law of restitution. Although their
Lordships in *Cantiere* relied heavily upon the *dicta* of Lord Inglis in
Watson v. *Shankland,* they made an important extension in the scope
of the *condictio* . Whereas Lord Inglis had been speaking of the *condictio* as a possible remedy for the recovery of money which had not been
paid under a contract, the judges in *Cantiere,* although treating it as a
non-contractual remedy, applied it to a case in which recovery was
sought of money paid in accordance with the terms of a contract.[47]

The essential facts were that a firm of engineers in Scotland just
prior to the outbreak of the First World War entered into a contract
with an Austrian firm of shipbuilders for the supply to the latter of a set
of marine engines. The price was to be paid in instalments, the first
being received on the signing of the contract. The declaration of war
between Britain and Austria made future performance of the contract
legally impossible. After the war the shipbuilders, now Italian in nation-
ality, sought repetition of the instalment price. Lord Hunter before
whom the case first came in the Outer House relied firmly on the law of
restitution as stated by Stair and Erskine, as well as on the *dicta* of Lord
President Inglis. He held that the principle *causa data causa non
secuta* applied in Scots law to a case in which money had been paid
under a contract in respect of a consideration that failed due to the outbreak of war, and that the principle grounded a remedy not in contract
but in restitution.[48]

The Inner House by a majority overturned the judgment of Lord
Hunter. Lord President Clyde who gave the leading judgment for the
majority accepted that in the law of restitution as stated by Stair a price
paid under a contract which had been annulled or had been abrogated
by the defenders might be recovered from the latter on the principle
causa data causa non secuta. But this rule did not apply where the
contract had been neither annulled nor abrogated, but simply rendered
legally impossible of performance due to the outbreak of war.
Furthermore, he relied upon the statement in Erskine that "if it has
become impossible that the cause of giving should exist by any accident not imputable to the receiver, no action lies against him, unless he
hath put off performing it when it was in his power to perform, before
that accident happened". A supervening legal prohibition or impossibility was sufficiently analagous to an "accident not imputable to the
receiver" to fall within the scope of Erskine's exception.[49] This was in
fact a very important point which caused considerable difficulty in the
House of Lords.

---

47   I owe this insight to Dr R. Evans-Jones. See the essay cited in n.18 at 664.
48   1922 S.C. 723 at 726ff.
49   *Ibid.,* at 739ff.

With the Lord President's judgment may be contrasted the powerful dissenting judgment of Lord Mackenzie.[50] Lord Mackenzie, although relying upon the same institutional and other authority as Lord President Clyde, drew a different conclusion. He first, citing as authority the *dicta* of Lord President Inglis, clarified the position by establishing an important proposition, namely, that, although the pursuer's case involved the construction of a contract, the remedy sought lay not in contract but in restitution. The law of Scotland, he asserted, provides such a remedy, unless the contract contained an express term to the contrary. This means that in a case where a remedy in restitution, based on the principle *causa data causa non secuta*, is applied in favour of a party to a contract, the remedy is subsidiary to any possible contractual remedy designed to give effect to the actual terms of the contract. However, Lord Mackenzie proceeded to obscure the relationship between the remedies in restitution or contract by arguing that the common law of Scotland implies into contracts a rule corresponding to the statement by Stair permitting restitution on the ground of a failure of *causa*. If this were correct, one would imagine that the remedy for restitution was in fact founded upon the terms of the contract, intended to enforce them, and therefore operated as a contractual remedy. It would be as though, to use Stair's phrase, a pact of restitution had been implied in the contract. Lord Mackenzie disposed of the statement in Erskine on which Lord President Clyde had relied by stating that it applied only to the case where property received under the contract had in fact been destroyed. Finally, he asserted the very broad proposition that "the *condictio causa data causa non secuta* is but a particular example of the general rule of equity that no-one should be enriched without sufficient consideration".[51] This is an important formulation, in that one begins to see the shift in the language describing the essential condition for the availability of the *condictio*, from "failure of *causa*" to "unjust enrichment".

On appeal the House of Lords reversed the Inner House and in effect sustained the judgments of Lords Hunter and Mackenzie.[52] The Lord Chancellor, the Earl of Birkenhead,[53] gave a more thorough review of the Roman law than is usually found in the cases on the *condictio causa data causa non secuta*. We need not scrutinise this closely – it is derived largely from the leading textbook of the time, Roby's *Roman Private Law*, vol. 2[54] – except to note that Lord Birkenhead adopts Roby's formulation of the principle underlying the *condictio*, namely: "a person who had given to another any money or other property for a purpose which had failed could recover what he had given, except where there had been no fault on the respondent's part and he had not

50   *Ibid.*, at 734ff.
51   *Ibid.*, at 737.
52   1923 S.C. (H.L.) 105.
53   *Ibid.*, at 108ff.
54   *Ibid.*, at 77.

been enriched thereby".[55] The significance of this proposition is that it predicates the right of restitution not only upon the failure of purpose but also upon the occurrence of two further conditions: that there should have been fault on the part of the recipient and that he should have been enriched. In so far as Lord Birkenhead took Roby's proposition to be also the law of Scotland, it is not clear how he understood the precise operation of these two conditions. He contents himself with the citation of the institutional authorities and Lord President Inglis's *dicta*. On their basis he allowed in the present case a remedy in restitution, especially stated to be non-contractual, on the ground of *causa data causa non secuta*. The statement in Erskine, which would have led to a different result, is dismissed, essentially on the ground that it would not have been intended to subvert the statement of the law found in Stair.

The other principal judgment in the House of Lords was given by Lord Shaw of Dumferline who treated the facts as disclosing a classic case of restitution under both Roman and Scots law.[56] The importance of his judgment is that he very clearly, more so than Lord Birkenhead, adverts to unjust enrichment as the basis of the *condictio causa data causa non secuta*. Like the Lord Chancellor he relies on Roby, but expressly holds that Roby is to be taken as stating also the law of Scotland on unjust enrichment, that is, "enrichment by means of the thing being received and the consideration and return failing – the principle of preventing that underlies as a reason the doctrine of restitution".[57] This principle he finds applied also in the apprenticeship cases, as well as to be that stated by Lord President Inglis. The statement in Erskine he analyses in the same way as Lord Mackenzie, that is, he confines its operation to the case in which the specific property given has ceased to exist. Again he agrees with Lord Mackenzie in denominating the remedy of restitution in the present case as non-contractual.

It may be observed that, with the exception of Lord Clyde, the judges of the Court of Session or House of Lords who relied upon Lord Inglis's judgment in *Watson* v. *Shankland* cited only the first part of that judgment. This contained the general remarks which might be interpreted as supporting the proposition that the *condictio* lay to recover what had been paid under a contract where the consideration had failed. The more restrictive part of the judgment which emphasised that, in the particular case, the money advanced on account of freight had not been paid under the contract, but in order to secure its performance, was cited only by Lord Clyde.[58]

---

55   1923 S.C. (H.L.) 105 at 109.
56   *Ibid.*, at 115ff.
57   *Ibid.*, at 117ff.
58   1922 S.C. 723 at 733–34.

We will return to some of the points raised in the judgments given in the *Cantiere* case after we have considered the treatment of the *condictio* in subsequent decisions. Almost all these cases concern the application of the *condictio* as a remedy to recover what had been paid under a contract. One, however, involved a situation in which no valid contract had been concluded between the pursuer and the defenders. In *Came* v. *City of Glasgow Friendly Society*[59] the pursuer had paid premiums under a purported contract with the defenders which was held to be void. An argument advanced by the pursuer was that, as she had not obtained what she sought, namely, a policy for her own benefit, she was entitled to recover the premiums paid under the principle *causa data causa non secuta*. Of the judges in the Inner House who upheld her claim only Lord Anderson explicitly referred to this principle. He decided the case on the "unimpeachable" ground that the pursuer was entitled to repayment of the premiums on the principle of *causa data causa non secuta*, since she had not obtained from the Society what she had desired to obtain.[60]

The other cases to be considered have been heavily influenced by the opinions of the House of Lords in the *Cantiere* case, especially that of Lord Shaw. First, however, we should note an observation of Lord Atkin in the *Fibrosa* case[61] which appears to have been overlooked by the Scottish courts. Lord Atkin referred to the interesting suggestion in the *Cantiere* case that Scots law restricted claims for restitution to the amount by which the defender had been unjustly enriched, thus allowing a retention by way of expenses and the like. He himself, without delivering a final opinion, thought that, although such a rule might have existed in Roman law, there was no direct authority for it in Scots law, and that Lord President Inglis's *dictum,* to which great weight should be accorded, was against it.[62]

Nevertheless, in a sheriff court decision,[63] it was precisely the "interesting suggestion" in *Cantiere* which Lord Atkin appeared to reject that appealed to the court. In this case A had given a mandate to B to purchase a motor car for him and had provided B with money for that purpose. B in good faith paid the money to C in the expectation of obtaining a car which was never delivered. Where A sought to recover what he had paid from B, Sheriff Walker repelled the action. One of the reasons which he advanced concerned the scope of the *condictio causa data causa non secuta* in Scots law. Like the House of Lords in *Cantiere* he relied upon a statement taken from a textbook of classical Roman law to the effect that the *condictio* lay to recover gratuitous enrichment. Hence, any expenses legitimately incurred by the defender in respect of the transaction on account of which recovery was sought

---

59   1933 S.C. 69.
60   *Ibid.*, at 78.
61   [1943] A.C. 33.
62   *Ibid.*, at 54.
63   *McQuarrie* v. *Crawford* 1951 S.L.T. (Sh. Ct.) 84.

could first be deducted. The sheriff found that Scots law had adopted this rule and cited in support *dicta* of Lords Birkenhead and Shaw in *Cantiere*. He noted Lord President Inglis's *dictum* (relied upon by Lord Atkin) to the effect that the pursuer under the *condictio* would be entitled to repetition of the whole advance however great the expenditure incurred by the defender, but held that this was restricted to a case where the contract had been rescinded and *restitutio in integrum* sought owing to the fault of one of the parties. In the present case neither party had been at fault, B had not been enriched through the payment and hence was not liable to A under the *condictio causa data causa non secuta*.

In another sheriff court decision, *Kirkpatrick* v. *Kirkpatrick*,[64] enrichment also came to the fore. This was an action of repetition for part of the purchase price paid in respect of a contract of sale which had ultimately been reduced by the Court of Session. The defender argued that there was a right to retain the amount paid, since she had a claim for damages arising out of the fact of the pursuer's occupancy of the land that had been the subject of the now reduced sale. Sheriff Smith repelled the action on the ground that the defender had not necessarily been unjustifiably enriched by the receipt of the money towards the purchase price. He took the basis of the pursuer's claim to be the principle *causa data causa non secuta*, and relied upon Lord Shaw's remarks in *Cantiere* which suggested that this principle benefited a pursuer only to the extent of the defender's unjust enrichment. It is significant that in this case the contract had been reduced, so that no contractual action would have lain for recovery of the purchase price.

An important question came before both the Outer and Inner House in the case of *Zemhunt (Holdings) Ltd.* v. *Control Securities p.l.c.* during the years 1991 and 1992.[65] The facts were that the pursuers made the successful bid at an auction of heritable property owned by the defenders. Under the contract they paid a substantial sum of money by way of a deposit, the balance to be paid at a later date. On the purchaser's failure to pay the balance by the due date the seller resiled from the contract. Thereupon the purchaser sought recovery of the deposit, relying in part upon the *condictio causa data causa non secuta*. Lord Marnoch in the Outer House rejected the action on the ground that, while there was no basis in contract for treating the deposit as forfeited, restitution, being a remedy based in equity, should not be granted to a pursuer who had been responsible for the termination of the contract. He said:

> I can see that a claim for restitution of a deposit might succeed where a contract is frustrated, or where it is terminated by breach on the part of the seller. Where, however, it is terminated as a result

64   1983 S.L.T. (Sh. Ct.) 3.
65   1991 S.L.T. 653 and 1992 S.L.T. 151.

of breach on the part of the purchaser himself, I see no basis for allowing a remedy which, of concession, is based in equity.[66]

The Inner House, while coming to the same result as Lord Marnoch, argued the case on a different basis. Their Lordships all held that under the law of contract the money paid as deposit was to be treated as forfeited on the ground that the pursuer had repudiated the contract. Lord Clyde, with whom Lords Ross and Morrison agreed, held that the *condictio causa data causa non secuta* had no application to the circumstances of the present case where the money paid as deposit in effect was a guarantee that the purchaser would fulfil his contractual obligation.[67] Lord Clyde himself left open the question whether the *condictio* could be available to a party in breach of contract. However, Lord Morrison expressed the view that the *condictio* might still lie under such circumstances. He said:[68]

> A breach of contract by the payer of part of the price which is sought by him to be recovered, following rescission of the contract by the payee on the ground of that breach, does not *per se* effect the equity of the claim for restitution. This is because the ordinary remedies for breach of contract are available to the payee and the payer is already fully accountable by the operation of these remedies. The view which I have expressed is at least consistent with the principles laid down in the case of *Cantiere*...and it is directly supported by a passage in Gloag on *Contract* 2nd ed. p.59.

Thus, of the four judges who heard the case, only two expressed an opinion on the scope of the *condictio*. One (Lord Marnoch) held that it would not lie at the suit of a party who had himself committed a material breach of contract. The other, Lord Morrison, took the diametrically opposite view in holding that it might avail a party in such circumstances. Both appealed to equity by way of justification.

Undoubtedly the most significant and authoritative decision given by a Scottish court on the scope of the *condictio* since *Cantiere* is that of the Inner House in *Connelly* v. *Simpson*. The pursuer sought restitution on the principle *causa data causa non secuta* of money paid to the defender as the purchase price of shares in a company which he had never received, since the company of which the defender was a director had gone into voluntary liquidation. Lord Cowie in the Outer House[69] upheld the claim and cited in support Lord President Inglis's *dictum* that, where the person paying had not been enriched at all he was entitled to repetition of the whole, however great the defender's loss had been. He referred to Lord Shaw's reliance upon the rule in Roman law as stated in Roby's textbook to the effect that money paid could not be recovered if there had been no fault and no enrichment

---

66   1991 S.L.T. 653 at 655.
67   1992 S.L.T. 151 at 156.
68   *Ibid.*, at 155.
69   1991 S.C.L.R. 295.

on the part of the recipient. Here in fact there had been fault on the defender's part in his placing of the company into voluntary liquidation without discussing the matter with the pursuer. Without directing himself expressly to the point about enrichment, although he seemed to have accepted Lord Shaw's *dictum* as a correct statement of the law, Lord Cowie founded his judgment upon the fact that, whether or not the defender could be said to have been enriched, he was certainly at fault. He added the further interesting observation that "equity does not play any part in the right of a party to recover money paid for a consideration that has failed", provided that he has not himself been enriched and that the exception stated by Lord Shaw does not apply.[70]

Lord Cowie's approach was rejected by a majority of the judges sitting in the Inner House. The majority judgments are of particular importance, since for the first time we find judicial recognition of the genuine ground of the decision in *Watson v. Shankland*. Lord McCluskey emphasised that Lord President Inglis had been concerned to distinguish between an advance of money on account of freight, or to secure the building of a house, and the payment of a sum due under contract, as by way of price. Only in the former case was there to be recovery of the advance by means of the *condictio causa data causa non secuta*, should the condition upon which the advance had been made not occur, that is, the freight never be earned or the house built. His Lordship further held that in *Cantiere* the opinion of Lord President Inglis was approved only in the context of frustration of contract. The *condictio* would not lie where failure of consideration had resulted from material breach on the part of the defender. In the present case the payment was not in the nature of "an advance or a type of conditional loan", and hence the pursuer's remedy was confined to damages for breach of contract. The *condictio*, Lord McCluskey concluded, "may be invoked by the creditor only where there has been no wilful breach of contract by the debtor giving rise to a claim for damages".

Lord Sutherland came to a similar conclusion, though he did not frame it in quite the same language. He also accepted that Lord President Inglis in *Watson* had made a "vital distinction" between an "advance on the one hand, which is recoverable on failure of the consideration, and a payment or pre-payment on the other hand, which is not". Hence, in the present case, the *condictio* would lie only if the payment made by the pursuer could be construed as "an advance towards the price which would not be due and payable under the contract until delivery of the shares". This in fact was not the situation, since the payment constituted payment of the price itself; the pursuer must therefore be left to his remedy for damages for breach of contract.[71]

---

70   *Ibid.*, at 299.
71   I would like to thank Mr Neil Whitty of the Scottish Law Commission for making available a transcript of the judgements delivered in the Inner House before the case was reported in 1994 S.L.T. 1096. The quotation from Lord McCluskey's conclusion is at 1106H; those from Lord Sutherland's opinion are at 1109E and 1110D.

The decisions given by the Scots courts on the scope of the *condictio causa data causa non secuta* prior to *Connelly* v. *Simpson* suggested that, where one party to a contract has paid money to the other in respect of a "consideration that had failed", he would be able to recover what he had paid provided (i) the recipient had been unjustifiably enriched by the payment, or (ii) that if not unjustifiably enriched this fact had been due to his own fault. There was also some authority for the view that the remedy would not be barred solely through the fact that the party seeking it had brought about a material breach of the contract. Since the decision of the Inner House in *Connelly*, it seems to be clear that, in cases of contract, the *condictio* will lie only where the failure of consideration has resulted from frustration (supervening impossibility) and not from material breach on the part of the defender.[72]

Academic Opinion

With very few exceptions the modern literature has virtually nothing to say about the role of the *condictio causa data causa non secuta* in Scots law. Textbooks, where they mention it at all, tend to treat it as a remedy derived from quasi-contract, whose principal sphere of operation lies in the context of frustration of contract.[73] The rule is stated in the form: where there has been total failure of consideration under a contract, any money paid is recoverable through the *condictio*. The emphasis is upon the fact of failure of consideration, not upon the reason for it. Hence, it appears to make no difference whether the failure of consideration results from some event outside the control of the parties (such as the outbreak of war), or has been induced through the fault of one of them. Indeed, some writers state explicitly that, where one party has repudiated the contract or has committed a material breach, the other party, in addition to any possible contractual action for damages, has the *condictio* to recover what has been paid or delivered to the former.[74] It has also been said that, where a party is entitled to rescind a contract, he can still be compelled, through the *condictio*, to restore any payment received from the other party.[75]

---

72 But cf. J.A. Dieckmann and R. Evans-Jones, "The Dark Side of *Connelly* v. *Simpson*" 1995 *J.R.* 90.
73 T.B. Smith, *A Short Commentary on the Law of Scotland*, (Edinburgh, 1962), 626 where the principle *causa data causa non secuta* is considered under the general head of "quasi-contract"; D.M. Walker, *The Law of Contracts and Related Obligations in Scotland*, (2nd ed., London, 1985), para. 31.59.
74 W.M. Gloag, *The Law of Contract*, (2nd ed., Edinburgh, 1929), 59–60; Walker, *op. cit.*, para. 15.36. Such statements have now, in the light of the Inner House decision in *Connelly* v. *Simpson,* to be regarded as too wide.
75 Gloag, *op. cit.*, n.74, 59. This statement is approved by Lord Morrison in the passage from his judgment in *Zemhunt* quoted above. It has also been endorsed by W.J. Stewart, "Restitution, Unjust Enrichment and Equity", 1992 S.L.T. (News) 47 at 50, in a comment on the *Zemhunt* case.

Criticism of the course which Scots law took as a result of the *Cantiere* case was voiced by W.W. Buckland. His criticism seems to have remained unknown in Scotland; certainly until very recently it has never been cited. Probably the fact that it appeared first in an article on Roman law and the Common law published in an American legal periodical[76] and subsequently in a book on Roman law and Common law[77] militated against awareness of its existence by writers on Scots law. Buckland's principal point was that, although the judges in the *Cantiere* case who sought to decide it according to the rules of Roman law as accepted into Scots law were correct in their approach, they were incorrect in their identification of the relevant area of law. Instead of focusing upon the innominate contracts and the availability of the *condictio causa data causa non secuta* to recover what had been paid, where the recipient had failed to perform, they should have looked at the *bona fide* consensual contract of sale and studied the rules on the allocation of risk. Under those rules risk remained with the seller until the contract was perfected, that is, *inter alia*, until the goods bought were deliverable. In the *Cantiere* case the seller bore the risk constituted by the impossibility of performance induced by the outbreak of war, and therefore was required to return what he had received from the buyer.[78] Thus, in Buckland's view, the court in *Cantiere* reached the right result, but employed the wrong reasoning. The fundamental point was that the *condictio causa data causa non secuta* had nothing to do with contracts of sale.

Buckland considered the reason for the House of Lords going astray was its search for Roman law not in the texts of the *Digest* but in the Scottish legal classics. This criticism cannot be accepted without qualification. It is true that the House of Lords relied upon the institutional writers, but Lords Birkenhead and Shaw interpreted these writers in the light of statements on unjust enrichment found in a textbook of classical Roman law. Further, it might be argued that Buckland himself was in error in suggesting that the courts should have sought their model in the classical Roman rules of sale rather than in the law of the *condictiones*. The appropriate model was not classical Roman law at all but the *ius commune* which supplied the background to the thinking of the institutional writers themselves.

As we have seen, the institutional writers do not in fact provide any direct or unambiguous authority for the application of the *condictio causa data causa non secuta* to contracts of sale. Yet it is true that the language with which they framed the rules on the availability of the *condictio* was capable of application to contracts of sale in which there had been a total failure of consideration through an event which made

---

76   See n.17 above.
77   W.W. Buckland and A.D. McNair, *Roman Law and Common Law: A Comparison in Outline* (2nd ed., revised F.H. Lawson, Cambridge, 1965), 241ff.
78   (1932–3) 46 *Harv.L.R.* 1285–86.

subsequent performance impossible. At this point we should consider the opinion of Lord Cooper expressed in an article on frustration of contract in Scots law.[79] He argued that frustration in Scots law had always been understood in terms of "unintentional enrichment" rather than "discharge of contract". The institutional writers, he suggested, had analysed frustration in terms of novation. The frustrating event entailing failure of consideration extinguished the original contract and replaced it with the substitute obligation of restitution, thus opening the way for the availability of the *condictio causa data causa non secuta*. With all due respect to his Lordship's learning and authority, it is doubtful whether the evidence supports this interpretation of the institutional treatment of restitution. What may have been the case is that some of the judges who later had to deal with the legal consequences of frustration so understood the institutional writers, though even this is by no means certain. The courts have not treated frustration as replacing the original contractual obligation with an obligation derived from restitution, since they assume that the contractual obligation survives the frustrating event.

Finally, we may signal a powerful critique of the course taken by modern Scots law with respect to the development of the *condictio causa data causa non secuta* as a remedy for loss arising from contract. This is the study of R. Evans-Jones to which reference has already been made,[80] written after the decision of the Outer House in *Connelly* but before that of the Inner House. Evans-Jones advances cogent reasons for holding that the judicial development of the law on the *condictio* since *Watson* v. *Shankland* has not proceeded with sufficient analytic rigour.[81] In particular he argues that the much cited and authoritative opinion of Lord President Inglis has been misunderstood by the House of Lords in *Cantiere*, since the critical distinction between "advance on account of freight" and "payment of money due under a contract" drawn by the Lord President had been overlooked.[82] Evans-Jones also

---

79   Lord Cooper, "Frustration of Contract in Scots Law", (1946) 28 *Journal of Comparative Legislation and International Law*, 3rd ser., Pt. 3, 1.

80   Cited at n.18.

81   The study may also be read as a criticism of a thesis advanced by W.J. Stewart in his book, *The Law of Restitution in Scotland*, (Edinburgh, 1992), to the effect that Scots law should substitute for the *condictio causa data causa non secuta* a general restitutionary remedy to apply *inter alia* "where, at the time the claim is initiated, a state of non-reciprocation exists arising from the non-materialization of a state of affairs which was either bargained for or arising from the conditional basis of the original transfer to the defender by the pursuer" (at 138).

82   This point has now in effect been accepted by the Inner House in *Connelly*. Neither Lord McCluskey nor Lord Sutherland, of course, suggested that there had been any misunderstanding on the part of their Lordships in *Cantiere*. The former stated (1994 S.L.T. 1096 at 1105K–L) that "when the passage from *Watson* v. *Shankland* was approved in *Cantiere San Rocco*, the context was plainly not one of breach of contract

argues that the suggestion that a party who commits a material breach of the contract has the *condictio* to recover what he has paid, where the other party has rescinded, is ill-founded, since rescission of the contract itself yields a restitutionary remedy independent of the *condictio*.

A last observation may be made by way of conclusion. Through a process of interpretation of the rules stated by the institutional writers, an interpretation which at best can be regarded as of doubtful accuracy, the courts have arrived at a result which distinguishes Scots law sharply from the position obtaining in the main civilian systems of continental Europe.[83] Whereas German[84] and French law ascribe a very limited role to the *condictio causa data causa non secuta*, excluding it from any operation in the contractual sphere, Scots law has moved in the opposite direction and extended the availabilty of the *condictio* from the field of restitutionary obligation alone to that of the contractual.[85]

---

but of external frustration of contract", and the latter (at 1110B–C) held *Cantiere* to be "ample authority for the proposition that money paid in advance may be recovered under the *condictio* where the reciprocal consideration is for some future event to be performed and that event, for whatever reason, never occurs".

83   For English law see the interesting discussion between Professors Atiyah and Birks on the relationship between restitutionary remedies and the law of contract: P.B.H. Birks, "Restitution and the Freedom of Contract", (1983) 36 *C.L.P.* 141; P.S. Atiyah, *Essays on Contract*, (Oxford, 1986), 47ff.

84   See J. Faber, "*Rückforderung wegen Zweckverfehlung: Irrungen und Wirrungen bei der Anwendung römischen Rechts in Schottland*", (1993) 1 *Z.Eu.P.* 279.

85   This is an expanded and revised version of a paper originally delivered at the meeting of the Scottish Legal History Group held in Edinburgh on 17 October 1992. I would like to express my gratitude to those who participated in the meeting for their comments, and in particular to the editor for a constant supply of information and help.

12. THE DEVELOPMENT OF REMEDIES FOR PERSONAL INJURY AND DEATH

By DONNA W. McKENZIE *and* ROBIN EVANS-JONES

In this essay we re-evaluate the development of part of the Scots law of delict.

Roman Law

XII Tables

Gaius tells us that the XII Tables contained provisions on certain forms of physical assault *(iniuria)*.

> *Inst.*3.223. *Poena autem iniuriarum ex lege XII tabularum propter membrum quidem ruptum talio erat; propter os vero fractum aut collisum trecentorum assium poena erat, si libero os fractum erat; at si servo, CL; propter ceteras vero iniurias xxv assium poena erat constituta...*(Under the Twelve Tables the penalties for outrage used to be: for destroying a limb retaliation, for breaking or bruising a bone 300 asses if the sufferer was a free man, 150 if a slave; for all other outrages 25 asses...).

The purpose of these early provisions on *iniuria*, by providing for retaliation or fixed pecuniary penalties, was to penalise physical assaults. Since the victim received a sum of money, the penalties necessarily also provided compensation in some cases of injury, whether to a slave or a free man, but this was not their primary purpose.

The provisions of the XII Tables provided the basis for the development of the much more wide ranging classical law delict of insult *(iniuria)* whereby any wanton interference with another person's rights, whether by physical assaults, by defamatory words or by other behaviour, was sanctioned with the *actio iniuriarum*.

Lex Aquilia

Traditionally thought to be a plebiscite of 287 B.C., the *lex Aquilia* provides the real origins of the modern Scots law on injury to the person and damage to property. It contained two short provisions which were of importance in this context. Chapter one gave the owner a direct action for the highest value in the previous year against the person who wrongfully *(iniuria)* killed his slave or beast.[1] The precise scope of chapter three when it was first introduced has been the subject of

---

1   Gaius, *Inst.*3.210.

much debate.[2] The traditional view is that it dealt with serious wounds to slaves and animals and serious damage to inanimate objects and provided the owner with a direct action for the highest value of the slave, beast or object within the thirty days prior to the act causing the loss.[3]

A number of special features of the Aquilian delict should be noted.[4] It was called *damnum iniuria datum* (loss caused by wrongful damage) and provided remedies to the owner of property which had been damaged or destroyed.

When the *lex* was first introduced the loss must have been caused in specific ways; chapter one spoke necessarily of "killing", but chapter three, restrictively, only of loss by "burning, breaking or crushing" (*urere, frangere, rumpere*). In time these three verbs became obsolete once *rumpere* was understood as *corrumpere* (spoiling). With this development chapter three became applicable to all forms of loss caused by damage to property provided there had at least been some form of physical alteration.[5]

The direct Aquilian action itself lay only against the wrongdoer who had caused the loss directly (*corpori corpore*). Where the damage was caused indirectly it was only later, after the development of praetorian actions *utiles* and *in factum*, that a remedy was provided.[6]

The wrongdoer must have been at fault (*iniuria*). In time this came to be understood as meaning that he must have been guilty either of deliberate or non-deliberate fault (*dolus* or *culpa* including *culpa levissima*).[7]

The actions arising from the *lex Aquilia* were penal; in other words, in early and classical law, they were concerned with the imposition of a penalty on the wrongdoer, albeit the penalty necessarily also fulfilled a compensatory function. The fact that compensation was not the primary purpose of the remedies is reflected in their penal features: they were passively intransmissible, they imposed a liability for the full loss against each wrongdoer which was not discharged by another paying the amount of the loss, and the application of the time rules meant that the wrongdoer often had to pay more than the amount of the owner's actual loss. Also, to any sum recoverable was added *lucrum cessans* and *damnum emergens*.[8] A special penal feature of the Aquilian remedy was that the wrongdoer who had unsuccessfully denied liability had to pay a double penalty.[9]

---

2   D.9.2.27.5.
3   See G.D. MacCormack, "On the Third Chapter of the *lex Aquilia*" (1970) 5 *Irish Jur.* 164.
4   See MacCormack, *op. cit.* and Zimmermann, *Obligations*, 953ff.
5   Gaius, *Inst.*3.217.
6   Gaius, *Inst.*3.219.
7   D.9.2.5.1; 44*pr.*
8   Gaius, *Inst.*3.212.
9   Gaius, *Inst.*4.9.

Formally the *lex Aquilia* retained its penal characteristics under Justinian but by this time ideas as to its nature had already begun to change. It was no longer perceived to be concerned fundamentally with the imposition of a penalty but rather with exacting compensation for loss resulting from a wrongful act.[10] The penal features of the remedy nevertheless survived to be transmitted through the *Corpus Iuris Civilis* to the mediaeval lawyers on whom this testimony exerted an important, but ultimately not decisive, influence.

Another feature of Justinian's law which proved to be important for later developments in the *ius commune* was its treatment of the praetorian extensions of the *lex Aquilia*.

> Inst.4.3.16. *...sed si non corpore damnum fuerit datum neque corpus laesum fuerit, sed alio modo damnum alicui contigit...placuit eum qui obnoxius fuerit in factum actione teneri.* (but if damage was neither inflicted directly nor was there any injury to the body but loss occurred in some other way...it was accepted that an action *in factum* lay against the wrongdoer).

This statement can be read as to suggest that an Aquilian action *in factum* was available where loss had occurred, but not by damage to property. In other words there is the possibility that Justinian made the important step of freeing the Aquilian actions from their limitation to claims for damage to property. Modern scholarship has suggested that this was not the case.[11] Justinian, it is argued, was dealing with the case where, although there had been no actual damage or alteration, there had at least been an interference with property resulting in its loss; as, for example, where, through compassion, I release your slave who escapes. Thus, by the time of Justinian, it is thought that interference resulting in loss of property had merely come to be treated as analogous to damage to property resulting in loss. The lawyers of the *ius commune*, we will see, took a radically different view of the authority of Justinian in this context and thereby laid the ground for the application of the *lex Aquilia* to a much wider range of cases including those of pure economic loss.

The Free Person

The *lex Aquilia* introduced remedies for damage to property, which a free person concededly was not. The basic stance of Roman law towards injury to the free person is expressed in the following two texts:

> D.9.2.13*pr.* Ulpian (18, *ad edictum*) ... *directam enim non habet, quoniam dominus membrorum suorum nemo videtur* ... ([The free man] does not have a direct action, since no one is considered owner of his own limbs ...).

---

10   G. Rotondi, *"Dalla "lex Aquilia" all'art. 1151 cod. civ."* in *Scritti Giuridici*, vol. 2 (Milan, 1922), 465 at 501.

11   See for example, B. Nicholas, *An Introduction to Roman Law* (Oxford, 1962), 221.

D.9.3.7 Gaius (6, *ad edictum provinciale)...liberum corpus nullam recipit aestimationem.* (The body of a free man cannot be made the subject of any valuation).

When it was first introduced, since it dealt with damage to property, the *lex Aquilia* did not envisage claims for injury to the free person. There were nevertheless some important bridges which started Roman law down the road which ultimately led to the recognition, not only of an Aquilian remedy for injury to, but also for killing, a free person. The rights of the *paterfamilias* over a son-in-power were analogous in certain respects to those of an owner over his slave. Since the estimation of damages had been developed to include not just the value of a wound itself, but also the loss resulting from the wound to a slave, an Aquilian action came to be given to the *paterfamilias* for certain losses arising from injury to his son-in-power.[12] An *actio utilis*, not just to the *paterfamilias*, but to a free man *in his own name*[13] for losses arising from injury to himself seems to have arisen out of the case of the free man who in good faith was acting as a slave.[14]

On the basis of development of the *lex Aquilia* which had introduced a remedy for destruction of or damage to property, Roman law, by the time of Ulpian, gave an *actio utilis* under the *lex Aquilia* to the free man for certain losses arising from wrongful injury to himself. Where injury resulted from a deliberate physical assault, since the time of the XII Tables, and ultimately in the form of the *actio iniuriarum*, a remedy had always been available under the delict of *iniuria*. The importance of the Aquilian extension was that it provided a remedy to the freeman who had been the victim of a wrongful but non-deliberate act. In other words, the stage was reached where the negligent act causing injury to the free person gave rise to a claim in his own name to recover losses such as medical expenses and lost earnings.

The recognition of an Aquilian claim for the killing of a free person was not reached by Roman law itself. This step was first taken by mediaeval scholars founding on the authority of Roman law. Since Roman law did not give such a remedy, this fundamental step was probably taken in the first instance on the basis of a distortion of the earlier authority.[15]

The Glossators

The struggle between the established authority of Roman law and new ideas as to the function of law which is characteristic of the *ius commune* in this field can be found even in the works of the Glossators.[16]

---

12   D.9.2.5.3–7*pr.*
13   D.9.2.13*pr.*
14   See Zimmermann, *Obligations*, 1017.
15   See R. Feenstra, *"Die Glossatoren und die actio legis Aquiliae utilis bei Tötung eines freien Menschen"*, in *Das römische Recht im Mittelalter,* ed. E.J.H. Schrage (Darmstadt, 1987), 205.
16   See Rotondi, *op. cit.*, n.10, 506.

The Glossators saw their task to be one of mere exposition of Roman law but some were bolder than others in respect of what they extracted from the old sources. There is no text in the *Corpus Iuris Civilis* which unequivocally gives an Aquilian action for the killing of a free man. Azo, however, was prepared to give an *actio utilis* for the killing of a free man on the authority of Roman law where, for example, Bulgarus would not. The authority for the new remedy was D.9.2.7.4.[17] The complicated text considers whether an action under the *lex Aquilia* should be available in respect of a killing in a wrestling or boxing match without indicating, in its first section, whether the fighters were free men or not. The action is in fact denied in the *Digest* but only because "the damage is held to have been done in the cause of fame and valour (*gloriae causa*), not of wrongdoing". Could one draw the inference that an Aquilian action would have been given had the killing of a free man not been carried out *gloriae causa*? Obstacles in the way of granting the action were the authority of texts like D.9.3.7 which said that the body of a free man could not be made the subject of any valuation and D.9.2.15.1 which suggested that the Aquilian action was not available to the heir of the free man. However, other texts like D.9.2.36.1 were used in support of granting the remedy. The end result was that other Glossators besides Azo, like his pupil, Roffredus, were also prepared to give the heir the Aquilian action where a *paterfamilias* had been killed.[18]

The Ius Commune

Two broad themes can be identified in the *ius commune*. Firstly the character of Aquilian liability was completely transformed, not by scholars, but by practice. Secondly, the new conceptions came to be given a theoretical underpinning by the natural lawyers who created a general compensatory action for damage to patrimony on the basis of the Aquilian liability. It was the modernised notions of Aquilian liability presented in the form it was given by the natural lawyers which formed the basis of Scots law found in the works of some of the Scottish institutional writers.

A major transformation of Aquilian liability which was accomplished by the seventeenth century was that it lost all trace of its earlier penal nature. Punishment was increasingly seen as the function of public law.[19] The Aquilian action therefore became a purely compensatory claim. This development was a long process which necessarily had to be accomplished in the face of the authority of Roman law itself. The development in this context is therefore about the triumph of new ideas over established authority. It is probably no accident that the breadth of this transformation could only have been achieved by practitioners

---

17   Feenstra, *op. cit.*, n.15
18   Feenstra, *op. cit.*, n.15, 227.
19   See Stair, 1,9,2.

who were less tied to the doctrines of Roman law than the contemporary scholars.

The time rules relating to the assessment of damages were never received by the *ius commune*. Damages were assessed by reference to the value of the object at the time of damage. In the case of injury, beyond medical expenses and lost income, the victim could recover *pecunia doloris et deformitatis*, and, in cases of killing, the heir could recover the expenses of the burial and compensation for loss of support.[20] Under the influence of the Canon law[21] it eventually became accepted that delictual actions were passively transmissible against the heir of the wrongdoer. Less resistant to the demands of change than passive intransmissibility was the cumulative liability of Roman law which gave way more quickly to a regime whereby if one wrongdoer paid the full amount of the damages the others were released.[22]

While the development of the Aquilian action into a compensatory claim was achieved in spite of the authority of Roman law, it was precisely by founding on Roman law that the Aquilian claim was given the range which it achieved in the *ius commune*. In this context the potential of a wide interpretation of Justinian *Inst.*4.3.16 has already been mentioned. The differences in Roman law between direct actions and praetorian actions *utiles* and *in factum* was not received. The testimony of Justinian in *Inst.*4.3.16 was read as being to the effect that the Aquilian claim in any form was not restricted to cases of damage to property or injury to the person. All patrimonial loss, even pure economic loss, in principle was recoverable. It will be shown that this breadth of the Aquilian claim, under the influence of natural law doctrine, was transmitted to Scotland.

The degree of transformation of Aquilian liability in the *ius commune* under the influence of practice, Germanic law, Canon law and statute is nicely expressed by the famous statement of Thomasius:[23]

> *actio nostra, qua utimur, ab actione legis Aquiliae magis differat, quam avis a quadrupede.* (our action in use today differs more from the *actio legis Aquiliae* than a bird from a quadruped).

Certainly, the understanding of Aquilian liability had been completely transformed. The contribution of Roman law to the *ius commune* was nevertheless fundamental; the contemporary ideas of law and its function did not arise out of a legal and cultural vacuum. Thus, although Roman law exerted an influence which was partly restrictive, it was nevertheless on its shoulders that the new developments were built.

---

20 H. Coing, *Europäisches Privatrecht 1500–1800*, vol. 1 (Munich, 1985), 508ff.

21 See, with citations, Zimmermann, *Obligations*, 1019ff. and Rotondi, *op. cit.*, n.10, 520.

22 Stair, 1,9,5.

23 *Larva legis Aquiliae detracta actioni de damno dato receptae in foro germanorum* (Halle, 1703), s.1.

The Natural Lawyers[24]

The concept of a general compensatory action for causing harm through fault (*culpa*) was developed by the natural lawyers. This provided a doctrinal basis for the modern Aquilian claim created by practice during the period of the *ius commune*. Under the rubric *de damno per iniuriam dato* Grotius established a three-fold classification of obligations depending on whether they arose from *pactio – maleficium –* or *lex*.[25] The distinctive feature of *maleficium* was *culpa*. Grotius said:

> *Ex tali culpa obligatio naturaliter oritur si damnum datum est, nempe ut id resarciatur.* (If damage is caused by such *culp* a natural obligation certainly arises to pay compensation).

Under the (new) general obligation to compensate for loss arising from a wrong, *damnum* was understood extremely broadly, as was the notion of *culpa*. In Scots law, the general action was seen to embrace all compensatory claims arising from the nominate delicts of Roman law, not only those arising from causing injury and death to the person or from causing damage to property, but even, for example, from damage to reputation which in Roman law had been indemnified under the *actio iniuriarum*.

Scots law from the time of Stair certainly recognised a general obligation to compensate for harm caused wrongfully. The complicating factor was that, beside the general obligation to compensate for harm, Scots law continued to recognise some nominate wrongs like assythment. It is the relationship between the general obligation to compensate for harm caused by a wrong and assythment which explains the problematic development of the Scots law of personal injury and death.

Scots Law

The details of early Scots law are now lost, although McKechnie[26] gives some glimpses of what may be the earliest specific provisions of a broadly reparative nature. The Laws of the Bretts and the Scots, repeated in four chapters of the *Regiam Majestatem*,[27] are regarded as being of doubtful authenticity. They were essentially tables of "fines" payable for causing death or injury, liability being strict, which are traditionally thought to have substituted monetary penalties for the blood feud. Although the victim would have received payment of a sum of money, the compensatory function of the remedy was purely incidental.

---

24   For a more detailed treatment with full citation, see esp. Rotondi, *op. cit.*, n.10, 527ff; Zimmermann, *Obligations*, 1031ff.
25   *De iure belli ac pacis* (1625), 2.17.1.
26   *Introduction To Scottish Legal History*, (Stair Society, 20, Edinburgh, 1958), Chapter XX.
27   Probably the earliest Scots legal treatise, now generally dated to the fourteenth century.

In time this may have been remedied to a certain extent by "judicial patching"[28] and the growth of a practice of regarding the fixed penalties as guidelines only, which might be departed from where justice manifestly demanded.[29] The "tariff" system was in any event formally proscribed in 1305.[30] There then developed, in the early to mid fourteenth century, a remedy for personal injury and death in the form of assythment.

In relation to property, the remedies available in early Scots law were concerned with interference with possession rather than directly with damage to property. The *Regiam* mentions actions of novel dissaine, which were in course of time superseded by remedies such as ejection and spuilzie, all of which are first and foremost possessory remedies.

Scots law established a system which operated on the basis of nominate delicts such as assythment and spuilzie until the time of the institutional writers when the more sophisticated ideas of delictual liability developed by the *ius commune* and the natural lawyers were introduced. This development commenced with Stair. T.B. Smith describes it thus:[31]

> The trend of Civilian Europe has been to supersede nominate delicts or categories of liability, and – with minor exceptions – to give reparation in a general *actio in factum*, based on *culpa* or fault and inspired by the Aquilian action of Roman law. In Scotland from Stair to Bell, the Institutional writers, who provide the authoritative foundation for modern law, are unanimous in adopting this approach to delictual liability...[t]here was general liability for unjustifiable harm causing damage.

This interpretation presented by Smith is not widely accepted and we would agree that it is, to some extent, misleading. Writers such as McKechnie,[32] Black,[33] and Walker[34] argue that the development of a general remedy for personal injury and death based on *culpa* did not in fact occur until the end of the eighteenth century. They suggest that until that time the sole remedy for personal injury and death was assythment which had replaced the obsolete tariff system. They argue that it was only during the course of the eighteenth century, when assythment had ceased to be viable, that a new remedy based on *culpa* which had its roots in Roman law was developed by the courts. The first application of this new remedy is cited as the unreported case of *Gardner* v. *Ferguson* in 1795.

---

28   See Robert Black, "A Historical Survey of Delictual Liability in Scotland for Personal Injuries and Death", 8 *C.I.L.S.A.* 46 at 50.
29   *Ibid.*, at 52–53.
30   By Edward I.
31   *Studies Critical and Comparative* (Edinburgh, 1962), at 155.
32   *Op. cit.*
33   *Op. cit.*
34   See, e.g. "The Development of Reparation", (1952) 64 *J.R.* 101.

The principal understanding on which this order of development proceeds is that assythment was available only in respect of injury or death resulting from the commission of a crime. However, since all behaviour which caused injury or death was criminal, assythment could always be claimed where loss had been suffered. During the eighteenth century some wrongful conduct which caused injury or death came to be regarded no longer as criminal. As a result assythment could not be claimed in such cases notwithstanding the fact that the conduct was wrongful and had caused loss. It was this gap which was filled by the courts by the application of the Aquilian remedy of Roman law. This approach, which will hereafter be referred to as "traditional theory", thus postulates a very late reception of Roman law in the area of personal injury. Scots law is seen to have been isolated from the European developments in this field until the coming of the Roman fairy prince at the beginning of the nineteenth century. Nevertheless, in relation to damage to property, traditional theory accepts that the principles of Roman law had been received by the earliest of the institutional writers. There is nothing inherently implausible in such a differential rate of reception of Roman law. However, we will argue that the differential lies, not so much in the scale or rate of reception of Roman law in this context, as in the resilience of the indigenous Scottish legal institutions against which the received civilian law had to compete.

The Institutional Writers

Stair

Stair deals with delinquence in a section entitled "Reparation, Where of Delinquences, and Damages thence Arising".[35] It is significant that he attributes the principle of reparation to natural law:[36]

> Obligations of delinquence are introduced by the law of nature…In reference to man is the obligation of repairing his damage….

Damage itself is given a very wide definition. Stair says[37]:

> Damage is called *damnum, a demendo* because it diminisheth or taketh away something from another, which of right he had.

Stair also emphasises the general nature of the remedy and specifically departs from the named delicts of Roman law as the basis for reparation. He says:[38]

> Delinquence in the Roman law is reduced into these four, *furtum, rapina, damnum, iniuria*; wherein we shall not insist, but follow

---

35   Stair, 1,9. It is significant that this is the first use of reparation as a *nomen generalis*.
36   Stair, 1,9,1; 2.
37   *Ibid.*, 1,9,3.
38   *Ibid.*, 1.9.4.

private delinquences and obligations and actions thence arising...so far as they use to be civilly prosecute.

The clear suggestion is that, under the influence of natural law teaching, Stair was introducing a general principle of reparation. This represents a significant step forward in the development of Scots law.

Stair identifies five "rights and enjoyments" where "damages and delinquencies may be esteemed".[39] These are life, members and health; liberty; fame, reputation and honour; content, delight and satisfaction; and goods and possessions. Most important for our purposes are the first and last categories.

In relation to the right to life, members and health, Stair states:[40]

As, first, our life, members and health; which though they be inestimable, and can have no price, yet there are therewith incident damages reparable, and that either *lucrum cessans* or *damnum emergens*. So the life of any person being taken away, the damage of those who were entertained and maintained by his life, as his wife and children, may be repaired. So likewise the loss any man hath in the expense of his cure, or the loss of his labour, and industry in his affairs, is also reparable.

Stair's treatment of damage to property is relatively brief in a passage which clearly sets out a general right to reparation for damage to property. He states:[41]

[t]he last damage is in goods and possessions; the redress whereof is more clear, because the things themselves are more valuable and estimable.

Having dealt with the issue of joint wrongdoers and accessories to delinquencies, Stair then continues:[42]

We come to the obligations by delinquences, which are civilly cognosible by our custom, according to their known names and titles in our law, which though they do rather signify the acts or actions, whereby such obligations are incurred or prosecuted, than the obligations themselves, yet will they be sufficient to hold out both. These are either general, having no particular name or designation: and such are pursued under the general name of damage and interest; which hath as many branches and specialities, as there can be valuable and reparable damages; besides those of a special name and nature, which are chiefly these, assythment, extortion, circumvention...

Of assythment, Stair states:

Assythment, as it signifies the reparation made, so it insinuates the obligation to repair damage, sustained by slaughter, mutilation, or

---

39   *Ibid.*
40   *Ibid.*
41   *Ibid.*
42   Stair, 1,9,6.

other injuries to the members or health of the body. But it is chiefly pursued by the wife, children or nearest of kin of the party slain. In other cases it is competent to the party mutilated or hurt, or otherwise prejudged by the mutilation or hurt. And though the private interest be only for reparation of the damage and loss; yet our custom applieth much which is penal therein, to the injured. And therefore consideration is had of the estate and ability of the offender, and the assythment is accordingly modified, all circumstances being considered.[43]

It has generally been assumed that assythment was seen by Stair as the exclusive remedy for damage to life, members and health. This seems unlikely. In *Black* v. *North British Railway Company*,[44] Lord President Dunedin, correctly we would suggest, identified the relationship between assythment and the general action for damages when he stated:

> Originally...the two actions stood side by side – at least that is what I should gather from the way in which Stair treats the subject in Book 1, Title 9, sections 4, 6 and 7[45].

The suggestion that Stair gave a general remedy for reparation for personal injury and death quite separate from that of assythment is supported by the following points. Firstly, the wording used in relation to the conditions for assythment is significantly different from that used in relation to the general right to reparation for damage to life, members and health. Assythment is said to arise principally from "slaughter" and "mutilation". By contrast, the general right is framed in neutral terms. Reference is made to life being "taken away", and, in the case of injury, simply to "loss".

Secondly, in relation to assythment, the remedy is granted to the party mutilated or hurt, or, in the case of death, to the "wife, children or nearest of kin". On the other hand Stair allows the general remedy in the case of death to those "entertained and maintained" by the deceased's life "as his wife and children". The use of the word "as" suggests that the wife and children are intended only as examples of potential pursuers. Under the general remedy reparation for loss of support is presented as the sole qualifying criterion for the claim whereas assythment is available on a basis of proximity of family relationship which need not coincide with the existence of any ties of support between the victim and the pursuer.

Thirdly, as previously shown, Stair states that assythment contains much that is penal. By contrast, the general right is formulated in purely compensatory terms.

---

43 *Ibid.*, 1,9,7. It should be noted, however, that the reported instances of a surviving party pursuing assythment were far less numerous than those of relatives seeking assythment for a death.
44 1908 S.C. 444.
45 at 453.

Fourthly, Stair contrasts the general remedy of damage and interest with particular customary named remedies including assythment. He may have envisaged that the general action would apply to cases involving damage to an interest, such as life, members or health, where a specific remedy (in this case assythment) was not applicable. However, we should note that the general remedy based on fault has "as many branches and specialities as there can be valuable and reparable damages". Therefore it was in fact so broad that, potentially at least, it overlapped entirely with (the reparative features of) assythment.

Fifthly, Stair draws a distinction between civil reparation and reparation arising from crime. He says:[46]

> ...we...follow private delinquences...in so far as they use to be civilly prosecute. For though, in public crimes, which are criminally pursued, there is competent a reparation, either from the nature of the crime, *or from law and custom*, yet that is incident to a public right and not ordinary (emphasis supplied).

Assythment was the customary remedy of reparation for injury arising from crime and this is likely to have been one of the obligations "incident to a public right" contrasted with the "ordinary" civil right to reparation.

Finally, if one considers the trend of the case law from *Gardner* v. *Ferguson* onwards, sometimes the general claim for reparation for loss caused by fault was accepted in place of criminal assythment with great ease. In *Black* v. *Cadell*[47] Stair is specifically cited as the originator of the general reparative principle. The case involved an action for compensation for the death of a father brought by his children. The defenders argued, *inter alia*, that the action was incompetent on the ground that it was in essence an action of assythment which had to be based on a crime, and furthermore, on a crime where a prosecution had proceeded, which was not the case in this instance. Notwithstanding the arguments of the defence, the pursuers were successful. On appeal, the pursuers relied heavily on Stair's statement of the general right. They argued that:

> The father of the respondents was deprived of his life in consequence of the culpable negligence of the appellant; and according to the law of Scotland, they are entitled to damages, in reparation of the severe loss and injury they have suffered...It is said that assythment is only due where the fact of slaughter is brought home to the defender directly, not where the death is a consequence only of his negligence. The respondents have no occasion to inquire, whether this doctrine be correct respecting a proper process of assythment; *because their action is not what is technically called an assythment, but is an action for reparation and damages for the injury they have suffered...* (emphasis supplied).

Again the pursuers were successful and the appeal was dismissed. McKechnie states that "one fears that their Lordships read into a 17th

---

46   Stair, 1,9,4.
47   (1804) Mor. 13905; (1812) Paton 567.

century work the ideas of a later age".[48] Stair, we would suggest, was read according to his natural and intended meaning.

Mackenzie

Mackenzie divided obligations into contract, *quasi* contract, malefices and *quasi* malefices. He makes the broad general statement that we are "tied and obliged to men by...committing malefices against them".[49] This is a statement of a general principle of liability. Similarly, in his classification of actions, he refers to reipersecutory actions as those "by which we pursue that *quod patrimonio nostro abest* – commonly called damage and interest".[50] In his discussion on crimes, which are divided into public and private, he states that "private Crimes, called also *delicta* in the *Civil law*, oblige the committers to repair the Dammage and Interest of the private Partie".[51] This discloses a general obligation of reparation, stated in wide terms. Mackenzie does not distinguish between types of damage, such as damage to property or injury to the person but simply mentions the general obligation to give reparation which would be wide enough to cover all such cases.

Virtually no mention is made by Mackenzie of delictual or *quasi* delictual obligations in his section on obligations. The reason seems to be that he treats such obligations as a branch of the law of crime.[52] Assythment itself is mentioned only in relation to crime. Thus, although delict is seen to create an obligation to repair loss the likelihood is that Mackenzie regarded assythment, which he defines as a claim to repair losses,[53] as the appropriate remedy in such cases.

Bankton

Bankton also seems to present assythment as the sole remedy for personal injury and death. He deals with reparation under the heading "Reparation arising from Crimes or Delinquencies"[54] and states that these will be considered only in so far as they give rise to a civil claim for damage. He considers first crimes, stating that where a party has committed a crime, he is subjected to punishment and to an obligation founded in nature to repair the damage of the party aggrieved:

> ...because, by the dictates of reason, the offender must suffer the punishment due to the public, and repair the damage of the party aggrieved.[55]

---

48   *Op. cit.*, n.26, at 274.
49   *Institutions*, 3,1,4.
50   4,1,12.
51   4,4,2.
52   3,3.
53   4,4,25.
54   Bankton, 1,10.
55   1,10,1.

The separate civil and criminal consequences of an act are therefore clearly identified.[56] He then turns to delinquencies, stating:

> Delinquencies, as they are civilly cognoscible with us, have their known names and titles in our law; and these are assythment, injury, damage, extortion....[57]

At the commencement of his section on assythment he states:

> Offences whereby wrong is done without any advantage to the offender, either concern the life, members and health; and the satisfaction due to the person wounded or maimed, or, in case he is killed, to his wife or nearest relations, is termed Assythment; or one's fame or reputation, and the offence is specially named Injury; or his goods, and is called Damage, when the intention is not for Lucre.[58]

Assythment itself is defined by Bankton thus:

> "A consideration given to repair the damage sustained by death, mutilation, or other harm done to the life, members or health of the body"; when a person is killed, the Assythment is made to the wife, children or next of kin of the deceased, and is due either by the principal offender, or the accessaries; and the rank and quality of the person maimed, and circumstances of the offender are considered....[59]

In direct contrast to Stair, assythment is presented as the sole remedy for damage to the life, members or health of the body. Although Bankton does mention the concept of a general right to reparation at the outset of the chapter, he concentrates on listing the types of delinquencies which give rise to a remedy. Where Stair concentrates on general principles, and aligns these with the named remedies, Bankton gives consideration only to the latter. His treatment is therefore constrained by the requirements of those remedies. Nevertheless we should note that the wording used by Bankton to define assythment seems to have been influenced both by Stair's description of the general right and his description of assythment. Stair speaks of "life, members or health" in reference to the general right and of "mutilation" in relation to assythment. Bankton on the other hand defines assythment as relating to "death, mutilation or other harm". "Mutilation" is combined with the neutral word "death" which recalls Stair's use of the neutral phrase "life being taken away" used only of the general right. Furthermore, Bankton's description of damages in assythment is virtually the same as Stair's description of what could be claimed under the general remedy:

---

56 The point is reiterated in 1,10,235 where he makes it clear that a civil action for damages will not bar a public prosecution, nor vice versa.
57 1,10,13.
58 1,10,14.
59 1,10,15.

> ...he is entitled, by way of Assythment, to the expences of the cure, and loss of time while under it, which is always due, and is the immediate damage.[60]

Since he concentrates on the named remedies, Bankton gives much fuller information than Stair on these delicts. On damage to property, he refers directly to Roman law and the principles of the *lex Aquilia*. He says:

> Damage is likewise a general term, but here it is particularly understood of that damage which arises from diminishing, spoiling or destroying one's goods, without any advantage to the offender.[61]

The conjunction of the words importing damage in itself brings to mind the formulation of chapter three of the *lex Aquilia*, but Bankton specifically states:

> The damage here understood must be *Damnum injuria datum* as it was called in the civil law, and was repaired by the *lex Aquilia*.[62]

Bankton describes damage as something "occasioned by some fraud or fault of the committer",[63] excluding that which happens accidentally, unless the other's neglect gave occasion to the misfortune. He then explains that some damage, such as that caused in self-defence is lawful. On the issue of liability, he states that the "smallest fault or neglect"[64] will impose an obligation on the defender and he refers specifically to D.9.2.44 where Ulpian states that under the *lex Aquilia*, the slightest degree of fault (*culpa levissima*) sufficed. The issue of the basis of liability (fault, as opposed, for instance, to accident) is therefore clearly highlighted in questions of damage to property, and the reference to *levissima culpa* shows a clear awareness of the degrees of fault employed by Roman law and the *ius commune*. He points out, again recalling Stair, that damage has "as many branches as there are ways whereby our valuable and repairable interests may be damnified, wherof divers instances are given in the title of the Digest, *ad leg. Aquil.*",[65] and he gives various examples, although it is clear that the original Roman rules have been modified and adapted where appropriate.

In Bankton we detect more directly the influence of Roman law which in some of the other institutional writers has been consolidated and reduced to statements of broad general principles under the influence of the approach of the natural lawyers.

---

60 1,10,19. Although additional factors like "status" are taken into consideration in assythment.
61 1,10,40.
62 *Ibid.*
63 *Ibid.*
64 1,10,41.
65 *Ibid.*

Erskine

Erskine treats of "obligations arising from delinquency" only briefly.[66] He begins by stating:

> *Alterum non laedere* is one of the three general precepts laid down by Justinian...In consequence of this rule, every one who has the exercise of reason, and so can distinguish between right and wrong, is naturally obliged to make up the damage befalling his neighbour from a wrong committed by himself.[67]

This is the statement of a general obligation to repair based on natural law. As in Stair, damage is understood very widely: "every thing by which a man's estate is lessened, is damage or loss", and was probably intended to be sufficiently broad to cover cases of pure economic loss.[68]

Liability arises from the commission of wrongs. Erskine explains that "every fraudulent contrivance or unwarrantable act by which another suffers damage, or runs the hazard of it, subjects the delinquent to reparation".[69] Further, wrong "may arise not only from positive acts of trespass or injury, but from blameable omission or neglect of duty".[70] Erskine in fact relies directly on the *Digest* in various matters in his treatment, for example in stating the principle that liability must rest on blameworthy conduct and in explaining the rule that whilst it is the wrongdoer who has the obligation to repair, he who gave a mandate or order for the act is also liable. He also refers specifically to the *lex Aquilia* on the matter of damages, explaining that they are not to be estimated by the *pretium affectionis*, but by their real worth, except where attended by fraud.[71]

Erskine does not distinguish between types of damage or injury since all fall within the general formulation. Although there are no examples of personal injury or death cited by Erskine himself, his editors, as Stair's editors did, evidently considered these cases to fall within the general formulation since they cite such cases as examples of liability arising from *culpa* or negligence in the editorial notes to the relevant sections. As indicated, Erskine refers to assythment only in his treatment of crimes. He mentions it briefly in the context of crimes where it may be due, for example, for demembration and mutilation,[72]

---

66 *Inst.*, 3,1,12.
67 3,1,13.
68 3,1,14. Erskine states, for example, in 3,1,13: "a jailor by whose negligence a prisoner for debt is suffered to escape, becomes liable to the creditor in the sum due", which may be regarded as giving a remedy for pure economic loss.
69 3,1,13.
70 *Ibid.*
71 3,1,13–15
72 4,4,50.

and in the context of extinction of criminal liability especially by pardon.[73]

Hume

Hume distinguishes between obligations which arise *ex delicto* and those which arise *quasi ex delicto*.[74] It is clear from his treatment that delictual obligations are seen to arise from deliberate wrongs. *Quasi-*delict by contrast comprises wrongs which arise fundamentally from negligence. He says:

> In some instances, a man is made liable, as a *quasi* delinquent for the consequences of his own negligence or inadvertency, which, where it is prejudicial to others, the law considers as approaching to or savouring of a delinquency.[75]

Classified under quasi-delict by Hume we find cases like *Black* v. *Cadell* and *Mary Sawers* v. *Patr. Graham*. The latter unreported case which was decided in 1799 he describes as follows:

> ...damages and the expenses of cure were awarded to a woman, who had been hurt by falling into a well, situated in a lane in a town, and which the owner had neglected duly to fence and inclose, during the time of repairs.[76]

Bell

In his *Principles*, under the heading "Of Reparation of Injuries", Bell sets out the general rule thus:

> The rights of individuals, either to property or to personal liberty, safety, or reputation, are not only protected by penal law, but in civil law they furnish, when invaded, ground of action for reparation.[77]

Bell divides this class of civil remedies into two types, delict and quasi-delict. He says:

> A delict is an offence committed with an injurious, fraudulent or criminal purpose.[78]

On the other hand:

> Gross negligence or imprudence, though it should bear no such character of fraud, malice, or criminal purpose as to subject the person to a criminal cognisance, is, as a ground for an action of damages, held as a delict, to the effect of making the person guilty

---

73   4,4,105.
74   *Lectures,* vol. 3, 120 and 186.
75   *Lectures,* vol. 3, 186.
76   *Ibid.*
77   s. 543.
78   s. 544.

of the negligence or imprudence liable to indemnify the person who suffers by the fault. These are by lawyers called *quasi*-delict[79] .

Within this general scheme, Bell treats personal injuries separately. Under the heading "Of Protection of Person and Character", he separates out assythment[80] from reparation for injuries by negligence.[81] Bell states that assythment is applicable only when a crime has been committed by the defender, and that it has in practice given place to the action for damages for personal injuries. He contrasts assythment with injuries caused by "negligence and gross disregard of the safety and interests of others"[82] which are the province of the aforesaid action of damages. Once again, assythment is related to crime and contrasted with the ordinary damages claim. Bell, however, was writing at a time when the damages action had already asserted itself in the case law.

Summary

It is clear that all the institutional writers recognise that a "wrong" gives rise to an obligation of reparation and that such a claim is distinct from one which imposes a penalty on the wrongdoer. In this sense they all recognise a general obligation to repair loss arising from "delinquence". However, we should note a difference as regards the meaning of "delinquence" amongst some of the writers resulting from the structure of their approaches.

Stair dispenses with the Roman four-fold classification of obligations which arise from contract, *quasi*-contract, delict and *quasi*-delict. His first level of classification is between obediential and conventional obligations.[83] Obediential obligations are then divided according to the *content* of the response, not according to the *source* of the obligation. Thus, his section on "delict" is entitled: "Reparation, Where of Delinquences, and Damages Thence Arising".[84] A complicating factor is that having approached his classification from the point of view of "reparation" Stair reverts to a classification which looks to the source of the obligation at least in so far as it arises from delinquence. He does not, however, ever recognise a category of *quasi*-delict. Since he does not recognise *quasi*-delict as a separate source of obligation, for Stair "delinquence" arose either from a deliberate or non-deliberate wrongful act or culpable omission. That this was indeed the case is made explicit by Erskine who followed Stair in his classification of obligations as obediential or conventional. Erskine says: "Wrong may arise not only from positive acts of trespass or injury, but from blameable omission or neglect of duty".[85]

---

79   s. 553.
80   s. 2029, "Reparation or Assythment for Homicide".
81   s. 2030.
82   s. 2030.
83   1,3,2.
84   1,9.
85   *Inst.*, 3,1,13.

Those institutional writers who maintain a classification which recognises both delict and *quasi*-delict as a source of obligation give a narrower definition to "delict" than Stair and Erskine. For example, we see from Hume that delict is seen to be a deliberate wrong whereas a *quasi*-delict is either a non-deliberate positive wrong or a culpable act of omission. Thus, when Stair says that "delinquence" gives rise to an obligation to repair loss this principle is wider than a similar statement if made by Hume for whom a delict is a deliberate wrong. In effect, although using the term "delinquence", Stair is expressing a general principle that "fault", whether by positive act or omission, gives rise to an obligation of reparation.

The recognition of a general obligation to repair harm resulting from fault does not by itself explain the relationship between such a principle and assythment. Writers like Mackenzie and Bankton do not appear to give the general principle an identity which is clearly separate from the nominate delicts, at least as regards death and injury. Thus, we assume that they saw assythment as the appropriate claim in all such cases. Erskine on the other hand speaks only in terms of the general principle which arguably leaves the boundaries of its relationship with assythment unclear. The critical difference in Stair is that he clearly identifies the nature of the relationship between the general principle and assythment. He deals with harm to "Life, members and health" twice, once under the general obligation and once in terms of assythment. Each treatment is also made in quite different terms. The general obligation is said to be purely reparative and assythment partly penal. His formulation of the general claim in terms of "the life of any being taken away" contrasts strikingly with assythment which is said to lie in cases of "slaughter" and "mutilation". The formulation "life being taken away" strongly suggests that one application of the general claim which Stair had in mind was to a case where assythment as he defined it might be inappropriate; namely where death did not result from a positive act of the wrongdoer but from a culpable neglect of duty. Certainly this is precisely what Stair was understood to have meant by the later law.

Stair recognised a general obligation to repair loss caused by fault as, broadly speaking, did the other institutional writers. In the field of death and personal injury this had to compete with the developed indigenous institution of assythment which could not simply be supplanted. Stair's solution was to place both claims side by side and to show how the general principle could incorporate cases which might fall beyond the bounds of assythment. The width of the general obligation also meant that it had the potential to incorporate assythment in so far as the latter was seen to be a purely reparative claim. Erskine apart, the other early institutional writers merely used the general obligation to explain a common feature of the recognised nominate delicts from which they did not give it any clear independence. Assythment was seen to be the appropriate claim in cases of death and injury. In view of his more neutral presentation of its terms, Bankton may have seen a claim of assythment as appropriate where Stair would have applied the general obligation. Mackenzie presents assythment purely as a claim to recover loss but he construed crime so widely as to include all public and private wrongs (*delicta*).

The Decline of Assythment and the Rise of the General Action for Damage and Interest

Assythment is traditionally presented as a remedy arising from the damage sustained through a criminal act. In *Eisten* v. *North British Railway Company*[86] Lord President Inglis states boldly that the action involved in that case could not be an action of assythment because, *inter alia*, "no crime has been committed by the defenders".[87] This statement was accepted as definitive in later cases.[88] Similarly, assythment for the institutional writers seems to be used in a sense associated exclusively with crime. Erskine and Mackenzie mention it only in connection with their treatment of crimes, although again we should note that Mackenzie construes crime so broadly as to include delict. Stair does deal with assythment as part of his title on reparation but it is nevertheless likely that for him it was also to be restricted to criminal acts.

Although normally associated with crime, prior to the case of *Eisten*, we can detect a view that crime was not necessarily an essential element of assythment.[89] In *Greenhorn* v. *Addie*[90] Lord President McNeill stated that assythment "is almost always used in its proper sense in reference to crimes" but "so far as it is a technical word, it has reference to compensation arising out of crime or delict, although it may also have a more general meaning".[91] This highlights the fact that there appears to have been a dual use of the term "assythment". Sometimes it was used in a "proper" sense to describe the composition payable on the commission of a crime, but sometimes it was used more loosely to describe the right to reparation for personal injury generally, even where there was no criminal prosecution. This dual use is

---

86   (1870) 8 M. 870.
87   At 983.
88   For example, in *Black* v. *North British Railway Company* 1908 S.C. 444 at 453 Lord President Dunedin says that the test of assythment "is not doubtful, being that laid down in *Eisten,* viz., was the act complained of a crime?" and in the last reported case on assythment, *McKendrick and Others* v. *Sinclair* 1971 S.L.T. 17, 234 and 1972 S.L.T. 110, on appeal in the House of Lords, it was held that guilt of a crime was a condition precedent of assythment.
89   Lord Justice-Clerk Grant in the appeal to the Inner House in *McKendrick* v. *Sinclair* was able to say only that "[t]he precise circumstances in which, and the procedure whereby, assythment could be recovered are, however, not entirely clear and probably varied and developed as time proceeded".
90   (1855) 17 D. 860.
91   at 864.

specifically mentioned in *Lady Leith Hall* v. *Earl of Fife*[92] and the equivocal nature of the term is also referred to by Lord Kilbrandon[93] and Lord Reid[94] in *McKendrick* v. *Sinclair*. Any discussion of its "decline" must bear in mind the two senses of assythment.

The main reason traditionally advanced to explain the decline of assythment, as stated earlier, is the decriminalisation, from the beginning of the eighteenth century onwards, of a range of conduct which had previously been assythable because it was criminal. It is thought that up until this time all bloodshed and homicide had been criminal irrespective of whether it was deliberate, negligent or accidental.[95] The reason given for this decriminalisation is "the pervasive influence of the theory that *mens rea* or dole was a condition *sine qua non* of criminal liability", which meant that "accidental or merely negligent mutilation or homicide was not criminally cognoscible". The "creative genius of the eighteenth and nineteenth century Scottish judiciary", through recourse to Roman law, we are told, filled the gap left by the decriminalisation of some wrongful behaviour.[96] The accuracy of this analysis may be doubted.

Sheriff Gordon writes:

> It was recognised as a general rule in the nineteenth century that culpable neglect of duty resulting in injury to the person was a crime; and this is still the law, although the standard of culpability necessary for conviction is now much higher.[97]

While in modern law for an act of injury to amount to a crime it must at least be grossly negligent, in the nineteenth century criminal liability was still equated more closely with the civil standard. For example, Hume says:

> It is culpable homicide, where slaughter follows on the doing even of a lawful act; if it is done without that caution and circumspection which may serve to prevent harm to others.[98]

---

92   (1768) Mor. 13904. The report describes assythment *in the more general sense* as reparation due for a criminal act. The decision appears to have been controversial and Lord Kames in his *Select Decisions* attributes this to "mixing the two senses of the word assythment, which occasioned much reasoning that was not applicable to the case" – see Lord Kilbrandon in *McKendrick* v. *Sinclair, cit. sup.*, n.88, at 121.

93   At 118 and again at 121 where he quotes Lord Kames as discussed in n.92 and also as saying that "Assythment has two senses: it is the punishment of a crime or it is solatium...We ought not to be misled by names. Had she [the pursuer] asked damages, there would have been no doubt. She asks assythment as damages. Why should there be a doubt?"

94   1972 S.C. 25, esp. at 53.

95   See McKechnie, *op. cit.*, n.26, at 272, although in respect of accidental homicide there do not appear to have been any cases of assythment.

96   Black, *op. cit.*, n.28, at 63.

97   *Criminal Law*, (2nd ed., Edinburgh, 1979), at 836, para. 29–55.

98   Hume, *Commentaries*, i, 233; Gordon, *loc. cit.*, confirms that the standard of negligence into the nineteenth century "is the same as the present day standard in civil law".

During the nineteenth century it seems that as a general rule negligent behaviour which caused injury or death was not decriminalised. Therefore there is no obvious reason why assythment could not successfully have been claimed in such cases.

The fundamental factor leading to the decline of assythment, we would suggest, was the separation of private from public wrongs which is reflected in the changing conception of the function of the law of delict. The idea that liability attached only to fault had been a feature of the *lex Aquilia* since its early days in Roman law, and, as we have seen, *culpa* was given a central classificatory position in their ideas of a legal system by the natural lawyers. The *ius commune*, in turn, exerted an important influence because it had transformed the Aquilian from a penal into a purely compensatory claim. These two strands of thinking are clearly discernible in the early institutional writers who saw, firstly, that only wrongful behaviour should create delictual or criminal responsibility, and, secondly, that a distinction had to be drawn between reparation for loss arising from wrongful behaviour which it was the right of the individual to claim and punishment of public wrongs which it was the responsibility solely of the state to prosecute. Assythment was an anachronism in the light of the new thinking because, although the claim was raised by the private individual, it was partly penal and, strictly construed, it lay in respect only of criminal behaviour. Importantly, assythment conceived as a composition to assuage outraged feelings was potentially also available to collaterals who need not show that they had suffered pecuniary loss as a result of the death of the victim of the wrongdoing.

To think of the demise of assythment as a linear process in which the general remedy for reparation introduced by Stair progressively came to prominence as a result of an equivalent decline of assythment is too simplistic.[99] There was in fact a period during which the claims of assythment and damage and interest became confused. In many cases assythment continued to operate perfectly satisfactorily as a claim to repair loss. Often we find that the issue of the criminality of the act which caused the loss was not raised or, at least, regarded as central to the claim. Thus, for example, in *Black* v. *Cadell* the pursuers argued that "assythment means neither more nor less, than payment of a private party's damages [which] is evident from all the statutes and law books in which the word is used". The idea that assythment was simply a reparative remedy is also found in Mackenzie and repeatedly in the case law where we find claims for reparation proceeding in the name of assythment alone, assythment or damages and assythment and damages. Since assythment was raised by the private individual, in a world where prosecution was now undertaken by the state, to most eyes it

---

99 Traditional theory adopts such an approach, suggesting that the general remedy was introduced following on from the progressive decline of assythment.

must have looked like a purely reparative claim and, as we have seen, the term was used in that sense. However, because the general obligation of damage and interest was founded on the accepted idea that the private individual has a right to compensation for loss arising from wrongdoing we also sometimes come across it in the case law, though in a subsidiary role. The question to answer is therefore how the general obligation, which to begin with had a very low profile in this context, asserted itself over assythment which was the established institution in the world of practice.

There are two main classes of case in which we find the general obligation being developed at the expense of assythment. Broadly stated, the common feature of these cases is that one party in a claim for reparation sees an advantage in presenting a feature of criminal assythment as part of their submission. The feature of criminal assythment which is relied upon is regarded as unacceptable in what is seen, in essence, to be a claim of reparation even if presented in the name of assythment. The result is that the criminal feature of assythment is either conceded but the claim before the court distinguished as one of damage and interest, or assythment is narrowly construed in favour of damage and interest in order, again, to defuse that part of criminal assythment on which one of the parties is relying. Assythment narrowly construed as arising from crime is not seen to be available in the cases in question for a number of reasons. For example, sometimes the wrong in question, although in law still criminal, is not of such a flagrant character as to have attracted prosecution by the state and sometimes the claim is against a corporate defender on account of the wrongdoing of an employee where the issue of the criminality of the defender was seen as doubtful or even inappropriate. Once assythment had been narrowly construed in terms of crime in a definitive manner, damage and interest replaced it completely because, for a long time, it had been appreciated that the right of the private individual was limited to a claim of reparation for wrongdoing and that punishment of crime was the responsibility of the state. The need to establish the criminality of an act was therefore not seen to be relevant in a claim of reparation.

It is helpful to illustrate these propositions with examples.

(a)

We find the general obligation being developed where in response to a claim which could be described as assythment in its broad sense the defenders saw an advantage in construing assythment narrowly as arising from crime. This led the pursuers in turn to plead their case in terms of the general obligation. Thus in *Black* v. *Cadell* we have noted that the claim was presented in the first instance as one of assythment conceived as a purely reparative claim. The problem was that the death had not been caused *directly* by a negligent act, but *indirectly* as a result

of a negligent omission to fence a pit. Two difficulties arose: whether
there was liability for this sort of negligent omission at all and whether
such an omission was criminal such as to found a claim of assythment.
In anticipation of the problem of crime the pursuers claimed that every
act inconsistent with personal safety was criminal. The assumption on
which they proceeded in this part of their pleadings was that Cadell's
omission was in its nature criminal but that a prior prosecution for
causing the death was not necessary to found assythment. In this context it is worth noting the observation of Professor Robert Black that
the Court of Session could and did hear evidence of the defender's
criminal guilt in assythment cases. He says:[100]

> [i]t would have been perfectly logical, and perhaps desirable, for
> eighteenth century Scots law to have required that a defender actu-
> ally be convicted by the appropriate Scottish criminal court before
> finding assythment due to the deceased's relatives. But it was not
> the law.[101]

Whilst this may be doubted in relation to cases of assythment in its
strict sense, cases do appear to have proceeded in the name of assythment without reference to an actual criminal conviction.

One problem with assythment was that, because of its traditional
association with crime, claims in its name always ran the danger of
being resisted on the ground that the behaviour in question was not
criminal because there had been no successful prosecution. Thus in
Black v. *Cadell* the defenders stressed that assythment lay only "on
account of the commission of crimes", and, by focusing on the word
"slaughter", that it could only be claimed where the death was caused
"by the act and deed" of the wrongdoer. This in turn led the pursuers to
plead in terms of the general reparative obligation which, because the
result was successful, led to an increase in the stature of the general
claim at the expense of assythment. There is no suggestion that the rise
of the general obligation in this instance resulted from the decriminalisation of wrongful behaviour. Assythment narrowly construed was
problematic because doubts could be raised as to whether the act was
criminal in the absence of a prior prosecution by the state and the pursuers could avoid these difficulties very simply by pleading damage and
interest.

(b)

A second category of case where we find damage and interest being
developed at the expense of assythment is where the pursuers saw an
advantage in founding on features of criminal assythment which were

---

100 *Op. cit.*, n.28, 69-70.
101 The judge at first instance in *McKendrick* also took the view that although
     assythment had to be based on a criminal act it was not necessary to have
     an actual criminal conviction and thus that it was perfectly competent for
     the whole proof to be in the Court of Session.

seen by the judiciary as out of tune with the precepts of a delictual action. These cases were those where collaterals sought to recover from the wrongdoer and where the judiciary defined the claim in terms of the general obligation in order to exclude the collaterals on the grounds that they could show no pecuniary loss resulting from the death or that they could show no obligation of support between the deceased and themselves. The judiciary in these cases defined assythment narrowly and extracted damage and interest from assythment in its broad sense in order to limit the range of pursuers in a delictual action, although the grounds on which they did this were not necessarily justifiable. The leading cases like *Greenhorn* v. *Addie, Eisten* and *McKendrick,* in which the "proper" content of assythment was narrowly construed in a definitive manner, all concern claims by collaterals which the courts wished to deny. In the case of *McKendrick* an additional factor in construing assythment narrowly was a reluctance to resuscitate a remedy which was thought to have been in disuse for nearly two centuries and which was seen as an anachronism.

The recognition of the general claim separate from assythment in its broad sense necessarily meant that the tensions in assythment as a reparative or a partly penal *quasi*-criminal claim were resolved in favour of a narrow construction in which the issue of the criminality of the act which caused the harm was again seen to be central. Thus the Inner House and House of Lords in *McKendrick* held that conviction or something analagous, such as a pardon, fugitation[102] or sentence of a court martial[103] was required for assythment. Lord Reid, even although he recognised its broader meaning, said:[104]

> To have allowed a case of assythment to proceed on mere averments that the defender had committed a crime would have gone a long way further than the court had ever gone.

The Rise of the General Action – The Case Law

McKechnie argues that:

> [i]f damages for non-criminal negligence by an act of omission were known to Stair it is inconceivable that the first action of that kind should have been (as is admitted in the *Session Papers*) *Gardner* v. *Ferguson* in 1795.[105]

But if, as McKechnie also suggests, the decriminalisation of offences otherwise assythable took place from the beginning of the eighteenth century, why was it not until 1795 that the "new" remedy appeared? Lord Kilbrandon in *McKendrick* observed:

---

102 See *Lady Leith Hall* v. *Earl of Fife, cit. sup.*, n.92.
103 See *Machargs* v. *Campbell* (1767) Hailes 192.
104 1972 S.L.T. at 113.
105 *Op. cit.*, n.26, at 274.

> While there is, as I have said, no evidence of an early acceptation by the courts of an action of reparation based on the civil law, nevertheless I am convinced that this development had already been foreshadowed by the institutional writers.[106]

Contrary to what has been assumed, there are in fact traces of the general remedy in earlier case law. The case of *Lady Leith Hall*, some twenty seven years prior to *Gardner* v. *Ferguson,* is an action of assythment which very clearly recognises a right to reparation for non-criminal negligence:

> If a man, who is culpable only, be liable in damages, what doubt can there be of his being liable when the damages are occasioned by his being guilty of a flagrant crime.[107]

In *Deniston* v. *Smith* in 1698, the summary in Brown's *Synopsis* states that the pursuer was entitled to a claim of *damages* for assault, though three years had elapsed and the offender had been prosecuted and fined.[108] At first sight there would seem to be no doubt that the case was one of assythment since it proceeds on a crime for which the defender had been prosecuted. Yet the claim is described as one of damages, not assythment, whereas every other entry in the section uses the term "assythment", with the exception of the report of *Macdonnell &c.* v. *Macdonald* (1813).[109] This again is described as an action for *damages* for assault, but there was no criminal prosecution for the assault. As the perception gained in strength that the interest of the private individual was purely to claim compensation it seems that the general claim was sometimes raised where the behaviour which caused the loss was clearly criminal.

Gardner v. *Ferguson* (1795) is traditionally presented as the earliest case where damages were given for non–criminal negligence. The pursuer had been injured by falling into an unfenced drain which had been left unguarded. He did not rely on assythment, and the action is described as one of damages. At first instance the defender argued that he could not be liable because he had no intention to injure, but later he argued the matter on the basis that he had taken reasonable care. The pursuer's argument was that although the defender had no intent to injure he was nonetheless liable on the basis of "a very great degree of *culpa*". The pursuer took the view that the principles of law which allowed him to succeed were sufficiently clear to require little reiteration on his part, although reference is made to the Civil law and the *lex Aquilia* in particular. This confirms that the general remedy was already familiar to the law of the time. Although the case was rejected at first instance, the pursuer was awarded damages and expenses on appeal.

---

106 *Cit. sup.,* n.88, at 120.
107 *Cit. sup.,* n.92, at 13905.
108 Vol.3, 2132; the report is in 4 B.S. 426 – Fountainhall
109 *Ibid.*; the report is in 2 Dow 66.

Gardner was followed in 1798 by *Innes* v. *Magistrates of Edinburgh*,[110] which arose out of similar facts. Here, the pursuer had fallen into a pit which was not adequately guarded. The action is once again described as an action for damages. The defenders, being responsible for the state of the streets, were found liable. The pursuer's argument was based on the great degree of negligence and culpability shown by the defenders in carrying out their duties. The general principle of law was stated to be that a person, failing to take precautions "must undoubtedly be liable for any damage that may be sustained by this improper conduct of his; for, as such conduct has been occasioned by his wrong or tortious conduct, he must...be bound...to make every possible reparation for it". This echoes the formulation of a general obligation to repair loss found in the institutional writers. Significantly, there was no argument about the applicability of the principles relied on by the pursuer. The defence proceeded on the basis that "great precaution" had been taken to prevent harm and that the accident should be taken as arising "*casu fortuito*", and could not, therefore, infer damages against anyone. The court took the view that "one of the most important duties [of the magistrates]...is to take care that the streets of the city are kept in such a state as to prevent *the slightest danger* to passengers. They are liable for *the smallest neglect* of this duty, and in this case, without some degree of *culpa* on their part, the pursuer could not have met with this misfortune" (emphasis supplied).

In *Black* v. *Cadell,* the facts of which have already been stated, action was raised for payment of expenses incurred and a sum "as a reparation to the pursuers...for the damage they sustained". The Lord Ordinary appointed condescendences to be lodged covering various issues including whether a claim was competent for reparation *or* assythment. As we have seen, the pursuers in the final analysis did not make out a case on the basis of assythment.[111] The issue of the dual approach to assythment was raised, however, for the pursuers point out that assythment is used to mean nothing more than a civil claim for damages, which has on previous occasions been sustained by the court. It is clear that the basis of their claim, ultimately sustained by the House of Lords, was the civil action of damages. An interesting feature of the case is the reliance of the pursuers on Voet to substantiate a claim for compensation from the wrongdoer for causing the death of a free

---

110 (1798) Mor. 13189.
111 Later judicial observation that a prosecution for culpable homicide might have been possible if unlikely to succeed has also been noted. It is interesting, however, that the papers disclose that the defenders had been prosecuted for failing to fence the coal pit and had been ordered by the Sheriff to fence it as a hazard. Such a prosecution may have been insufficient as a basis for a claim of assythment in any event as it was not a prosecution for the death itself, but it did render criminal the act which caused it, which could have been used as an argument. Yet it was not felt necessary to found on this.

person although they concede that no such claim is allowed by Roman law. The defenders sought to discredit Voet's standing by describing him as a (mere) "modern commentator".

These early cases were followed by others such as *Brown* v. *MacGregor*,[112] *Cooley* v. *Edinburgh & Glasgow Railway Company*,[113] *Greenhorn* v. *Addie*[114] and *Docherty & Ors* v. *Alexander*.[115] In *Brown* v. *MacGregor* an action for reparation and damages was brought by the widow and children of a man killed in an accident involving two coaches. The Lord Ordinary, to whose interlocutor the Inner House adhered *in toto*, awarded assythment. The court on appeal "were clearly and unanimously of the opinion that when damage was sustained by the *unskilfulness, malversation, or culpable negligence* of servants, the masters are liable" (emphasis supplied). The defenders' argument that the action could not succeed because assythment required a crime, and masters could not in any event be liable for the crimes of their servants was not answered, the court declaring that damages in general were due by the defenders. The main argument, however, was based on the fact that the servants had not been negligent, an argument which the court rejected. The award was for a sum to the widow for injuries sustained by herself in the accident, described as *solatium,* with a further sum for herself and the children by way of *assythment.* Yet there was no crime, or at least no prosecution. The case is reported under the heading of "Damage and Interest" – the name given by Stair to his general action.

In *Cooley* damages were sought by the children of a man who had been killed, this time in a railway accident. In the headnote, the action is called an action of "assythment and damages".[116] There was in this case a prosecution and conviction of the railway employees for culpable homicide,[117] but the case proceeds against the defenders on averments of negligence. Liability for negligence was in fact admitted, the only issue being whether evidence of the degree of *culpa* should be made available to the jury as relevant to the question of damages. On appeal, it was held (by a majority of both divisions) that it was relevant, and indeed material to the question of damages.[118] The case illustrates the confusion which had arisen at the time between the principles of compensation deriving from damage and interest and assythment. The Lord Justice-Clerk[119] conceived the claim as one of "reparation in an action of assythment" and argued expressly from the principles of

---

112 26th Feb. 1813, F.C.
113 (1845) 8 D. 288.
114 *Cit. sup.*, n.90.
115 1862 S.L.J. 40.
116 In the pleadings it is presented as a claim of assythment or damages or reparation.
117 *H.M.A.* v. *Paton & McNab* (1845) 2 Broun 525.
118 This approach was later disapproved.
119 (1845) 8 D. 288 at 294.

assythment to support the proposition that factors like the status of the victim and wrongdoer could be taken into consideration is assessing the level of *solatium*. He also recognised that there was some difficulty in reconciling this view with principle. Thus while it seems to have become accepted that the function of a delictual action was fundamentally compensatory[120] the rules on assythment were founded upon on this occasion to allow factors to be taken into consideration which might increase the amount of *solatium*.

In *Docherty and Ors.* v. *Alexander*, "damages and *solatium*" were awarded on appeal to the widow and children of a workman who had died as a result of an accident involving unfenced machinery. Liability was founded on negligence for failing to guard or fence the machinery in the face of probable dangers. Again the action is described as one of assythment and damages but there is no suggestion of there having been a crime. Similarly in *McLean* v. *Russell*[121] an action of assythment and damages is raised where there is no crime and in both *Lenaghan* v. *Monkland Iron Co.*[122] and *McNaughton* v. *Caledonian Railway Co.*[123] claims proceed in the name of assythment where there is no crime.

Greenhorn v. *Addie* raised the issue of the appropriate pursuer in cases of death. An action was raised by two brothers in respect of the death of a third in a colliery accident. The action is once again described as an action of assythment and damages, but the court did not entertain the claim on the ground of assythment in its criminal sense. It categorised the claim within the species of action where "we have recognised a right to compensation where there is no crime, in the stricter sense of the word".[124]

The court took the view that although assythment, in its "proper" sense, would have provided a remedy for collaterals, the general action for damages had so far been restricted to the widow and children of the deceased: "it does not appear that the right to sue for that civil claim has been in any case sustained to the same class of relatives or connections whose right has been recognised in the case of assythment in crime".[125] The door was not entirely closed to collaterals, for in this case there had been no question of loss of support, but only of *solatium* for grief at the death. The court left open the question of whether the claim might be sustained if loss of support was also involved. This question was the one that arose for decision in the case of *Eisten*, regarded as the leading case on the modern action of damages.

In *Eisten*, two sisters sued for damages for the death of their brother in a railway accident. The damages sought were not, as in

---

120 At 291.
121 (1849) 11 D. 1035.
122 (1857) 19 D. 975.
123 (1858) 21 D. 160.
124 (1855) 17 D. 860, *per* Lord President MacNeill at 864.
125 *Ibid.*

Greenhorn, for *solatium* alone, but included a claim for loss of support, as the pursuers had been entirely supported by the deceased for the preceding six years. It was argued, *inter alia,* on their behalf that the right of collaterals was recognised in assythment proper and accordingly that the pursuers should be granted a remedy, at least where the twin elements of *solatium* and loss of support were present. The court, however, took the view that even in those circumstances no claim could be maintained by a collateral in the general action. Lord President Inglis confirmed that in cases of death a civil claim was allowed to the husband or wife, or parent or child, as the case may be, where death has been caused by delict or *culpa.* He explained that "the true foundation of this claim is partly nearness of relationship between the deceased and the person claiming on acount of the death, and partly the existence during life, as between the deceased and the claimant, of a mutual obligation of support in case of necessity".[126] But the Lord President was not prepared to extend the right to claim in the general action to collaterals.

Lord President Inglis clearly addressed the issue of the nature of the action before the court. He contrasted the general action with assythment which he said arose only from crime:

> This is not an action of assythment, and it does not partake in any degree of such an action, for this, among other reasons, that no crime has been committed by the defenders. This is an *actio iniuri-arum* – a well known class of actions in the civil law. It is an action of damages to repair bodily injuries....[127]

The effect of this decision was to resolve the confusion over the different claims, and to establish the general action beyond doubt as a separate cause of action from assythment. We have already identified the reason why the court took this approach. It was probably only because of his status that Lord President Inglis brought the confusion surrounding assythment to an end. However, at the same time, by restricting the right to claim on death in a general action of damage and interest to a spouse or parent/child he limited this claim is an unjustifiable manner. Stair says that damages are available to one "entertained and maintained" by the life of the deceased, "as his wife and children". As has been shown, wife and children are one example only of persons who might claim, cited no doubt as the most common example of those "entertained and maintained" by the life of the deceased. The central principle governing the availability of the general action is that it is available to those who have suffered loss as the result of the wrongful act. The court in *Eisten,* partly swayed by reasons of policy, seems to have proceeded upon the following reasoning: assythment is available to collaterals, this is not a case of assythment, therefore no award can

---

126 (1870) 8 M. 870 at 984.
127 At 983.

be made to collaterals. Precisely in what is seen as the most authorita-tive recognition of the general action, the first inroad was made on the general principles which it expressed. It was subsequently recognised that the reasoning of the court was flawed,[128] and the law has since been changed to allow a claim for loss of support to an extended class of relatives and to cohabitees.

The general action was renamed by Lord President Inglis as the *actio iniuriarum*. In this he has been corrected by those who see it as an Aquilian action.[129] On one level it may be better to identify the remedy as an Aquilian action rather than as an *actio iniuriarum* but both these denotations are in fact misleading because they obscure the direct source and width of the true principle of liability. The action is one of damage and interest which expresses the general principle that there is a liability to repair loss caused by fault. Although expressed in the language and concepts of Roman law (*damnum iniuria datum*) the direct source of this wide principle is natural law doctrine.

Assythment was not abolished until 1976[130] after the unsuccessful attempt to raise the claim in *McKendrick* v. *Sinclair.* This action was brought at the instance of the sister and two brothers of a workman killed in an accident the circumstances of which, the pursuers alleged, amounted to culpable homicide. The normal action of reparation was denied them as collaterals following the decisions in *Greenhorn* and *Eisten.* The defenders advanced two main lines of argument; firstly that the action of assythment was no longer competent, either because it was obsolete or because it had been superseded by the modern action of damages; and secondly, that even if it were still competent, assyth-ment required a criminal act for which there had been a conviction.

---

128 In *McKendrick* v. *Sinclair,* Lords Reid and Kilbrandon in the House of Lords both suggested that the legislature should look at the matter of a remedy for collaterals, and Lord Reid went even further, saying "there seems to me to be no good reason for refusing redress to brothers and sis-ters (and it may be other near relations) of a deceased person in a case where his widow and children could recover damages, provided that they can establish financial loss. *Eisten* seems to me to be a policy decision...".

129 Lord MacMillan in *Stewart's Executrix* v. *London Midland & Scottish Railway Co* 1944 S.L.T. 13, whilst accepting Lord President Inglis' classification of the action as *actio iniuriarum*, said that "[i]t may be that the *utilis actio legis Aquiliae* was a nearer analogue of the modern action of reparation for personal injuries" and in *McKendrick* v. *Sinclair* in the Outer House, Lord Avonside referred to the modern action as that which "is popularly, though possibly inaccurately, called the *actio iniuriarum*". In the same case, in the House of Lords, Lord Kilbrandon goes further, saying "[i]t has been repeatedly pointed out...that the correct analogue is not the *actio iniuriarum*. This was truly based on insult or affront...The Roman ancestor of our action of reparation is the *lex Aquilia*..." for which he then cites various authorities in support. See also T.B. Smith, "Designation of Delictual Actions – Damn *iniuria* Damn", 1972 S.L.T. (News) 125–28.

130 By the Damages (Scotland) Act 1976 (c.13).

The defenders further claimed that the pursuers were not entitled to prove guilt of a crime in the Court of Session since that court had no criminal jurisdiction.

The judge at first instance, Lord Avonside, took the view that assythment remained competent, having neither been superseded by the modern action nor having fallen into obsolescence. He was also of the view that a criminal conviction was unnecessary. On appeal to the Inner House, Lord Avonside's decision was reversed, and the pursuers' appeal before the House of Lords was dismissed. The majority of the judges in both the Court of Session and the House of Lords took the view that assythment could not be rendered incompetent simply by long disuse, but nevertheless they regarded it as an outmoded concept which required a criminal conviction and upon which the pursuers had been forced to fall back due to the lack of any other remedy open to them. It was as a result of this case that, not without its mourners,[131] assythment was abolished in 1976. All civil reparation for personal injuries and death now rests on the general action for reparation originally introduced by Stair.

Conclusions

The results of this examination are partly practical in so far as they relate to questions like "who" is entitled to claim in an action of delict and "why". They are also partly historical. The development of a central part of Scottish private law, in our view, has been obscured by the fact that most modern commentators have not read the institutional writers against the background of the civilian culture on which their works drew in this context. We would suggest that the fundamental factor which led to the demise of criminal assythment was that it had to compete with a remedy which expressed what had come to be seen as accepted principles of private law; namely that the interest of the individual who suffered loss as the result of the wrongful conduct of another was limited to a claim of compensation for that loss which was recoverable irrespective of whether the wrongful behaviour was a crime or not and that such claims for compensation were not permissible to collaterals. However, assythment was clearly resilient and for a considerable period it assumed a dual *persona*. The confused relationship between assythment broadly construed and the general claim was finally settled by Lord President Inglis. Inglis, as a rule, stuck closely to Stair. On this occasion, almost certainly following Stair, the general claim was again recognised as a separate remedy from assythment which in turn made it possible for Inglis to construe assythment narrowly once more.

When modern commentators or judges have acknowledged the influence of Roman law in this field they have seen it in the form of

---

131 See Robert E. Mackay, "The Resuscitation of Assythment? Reparation and the Scottish Criminal", 1993 *J.R.* 242.

remedies which they describe as an *actio iniuriarum*[132] or an Aquilian *action in factum*. This obscures the direct source and width of the unifying principle of the Scots law of delict. In one sense it obscures the "Scottish" nature of this part of Scots law by secreting it behind a curtain of "Roman law". Scots law founded on the later civilian tradition represented *inter alia* by the natural lawyers and not strictly on the Aquilian liability of Roman law.

Erskine says that "every one who has the exercise of reason...is naturally obliged to make up the damage befalling his neighbour from a wrong committed by himself".[133] The ability of a legal system to express the essence of the law of delict under the general principle that loss caused by wrongful acts of the defender is recoverable was a product of sophistication which itself was a result of an immensely long legal development in which Roman law was merely one, albeit fundamentally important, part. This expression by the institutional writers of the essence of the law of delict in a single principle is a legacy of Scotland's civilian heritage which helps us to understand why it is sometimes said that Scots law has a system of private law based more on principle than the Common law. However, we should also remember that there have been many inroads made on this principle since its introduction – not in the pursuit of progress – but by people who did not know of its existence.[134]

---

132   We are grateful to Mr. David Sellar for the observation that the term "*actio iniuriarum*" had assumed a wider meaning in Scots law than that found in Roman law. See for example, *Cooley* v. *Edinburgh & Glasgow Railway Company* (1845) 18 D. 288 *per* Lord Fullerton at 292.

133   *Inst.*, 3,1,13.

134   We are grateful to Mr. Michael Christie and the Hon. Lord Davidson for their comments. We should also like to thank Lord Gill, who as then Keeper of the Advocates Library, gave permission to consult pleadings, and Kate Flett for invaluable help.

13. ROMAN LAW AND SCOTS LAW
– A BIBLIOGRAPHY

By WILLIAM M. GORDON

The following list attempts to include, arranged alphabetically by author within five-year periods, all references to articles bearing on the influence of Roman law on Scots law which have appeared since the later nineteenth century. It also includes specific discussions of that influence in books. It does not include writings on the general influence of Roman law which are, of course, relevant as background to the specific influence of Roman law in Scotland. There are undoubtedly omissions of incidental references. The list does not in general include references to the actual or potential influence of Roman law in books dealing primarily with Scots law although on particular rules or doctrines it is always worth consulting major treatises at least, such as Fraser's *Treatise on Husband and Wife according to the Law of Scotland* and *A Treatise on the Law of Scotland Relative to Parent and Child,* Rankine's *Law of Landownership in Scotland* and Gloag and Irvine's *Law of Rights in Security, Heritable and Moveable, including Cautionary Obligations,* to name some among the older treatises, and the volumes published by the Scottish Universities Law Institute in modern times. Reference should also be made to articles in the *Stair Memorial Encyclopaedia* and to the contributions on the history of the various branches of the law in *An Introduction to Scottish Legal History* by various authors (Publications of the Stair Society, 20, Edinburgh, 1958).

The following are useful bibliographical guides to Scots law and its history:

L.F. and W.H. Maxwell (edd.), *A Legal Bibliography of the British Commonwealth of Nations, vol. 5. Scottish Law to 1956 together with a List of Roman Law Books in the English Language,* (2nd ed., London, 1957), updated through *Scottish Current Law* and *Current Law.*

R.C. van Caenegem, "Les Iles Britanniques: Angleterre, Pays de Galles, Ecosse", Pt. C/5 of *Introduction Bibliographique à l'Histoire du Droit et à l'Ethnologie Juridique,* ed. J. Gilissen (Brussels, 1963).

The following article updates the bibliographies in *An Introductory Survey of the Sources and Literature of Scots Law* by various authors (Publications of the Stair Society, 1, Edinburgh, 1936) [hereafter *Sources and Literature*]:

W.J. Windram and H.L. MacQueen, "The Sources and Literature of Scots Law: a Select Critical Bibliography 1936–1982", 4 *Jour. Leg. Hist.*, 1–20 = *New Perspectives in Scottish Legal History* (London, 1983), 1–20.

H.L. MacQueen provides for members of the Scottish Legal History Group an annual list of articles on Scottish legal history which includes articles on the influence of Roman law.

Pre-1900.

R. Brown, "Assimilation of the Law of Sale", (1891) 3 *J.R.* 297–305.
H. Goudy, *The Fate of the Roman Law, North and South of the Tweed* (Inaugural Lecture, London, 1894).
W. Hunter, "*Conditio si institutus sine liberis decesserit*", (1891) 3 *J.R.* 289–91.
J.M. Irvine, "Roman Law", *Green's Encyclopaedia of the Law of Scotland*, ed. J. Chisholm, vol. 10 (Edinburgh, 1898), 376–88.
E. Jenks, "Scottish Land Law", (1896) 12 *L.Q.R.* 155–66.
A.J.G. Mackay, *Memoir of Sir James Dalrymple, 1st Viscount Stair* (Edinburgh, 1873).
– , "The History of Roman Law in Scotland", (1876) 20 *Jour. of Jurisprudence* 57–63.
T. Mackenzie (Lord Mackenzie), *Studies in Roman Law with Comparative Views of the Laws of France, England and Scotland* (1st ed., Edinburgh, 1862; further editions 1865; 1870; 4th ed. by J. Kirkpatrick, 1876; 1880; 1886; 1898; rept. 1911).
J. Mackintosh, "The Edict *nautae caupones stabularii*", (1891) 3 *J.R.* 306–24.
– , "*Actio personalis moritur cum persona*", (1893) 5 *J.R.* 375–79.
W.G.M., "General Disposition and Settlement and *conditio si sine liberis testator decesserit*", (1893) 5 *J.R.* 379–80.
J.B. Moyle, *The Contract of Sale in the Civil Law with References to the Laws of England, Scotland and France* (Oxford, 1892).
J. Rankine; G. Carle [trans. A.P. Goudy], "Professor Muirhead", (1890) 2 *J.R.* 27–32; 32–36.
R.M. Williamson, "*Actio personalis moritur cum persona* in the Law of Scotland", (1894) 10 *L.Q.R.* 182–84.
J. Dove Wilson, "The Sources of the Law of Scotland", (1892) 4 *J.R.* 1–13 at 4–9.
– , "The Reception of the Roman Law in Scotland", (1897) 9 *J.R.* 361–94.

1901–5.

H.H. Brown, "Sir George Mackenzie: a Study of Old Scots Crime", (1901) 13 *J.R.* 261–84.
W.C. Smith, "The Sources of Scots Law", (1904) 16 *J.R.* 375–92.

– ,   (1904–5) 12 S.L.T. (News) 118–19.
J.D.W., "Note on *Galliers* v. *Rycroft*", (1901) 17 *L.Q.R.* 109–12.
J. Dove Wilson, "The Study of the History of Law in Scotland", (1904) 16
    J.R 54–71.

1906–10.

H. Aitken, "The Present Position of Mercantile Law in Scotland", 1909
    S.L.T. (News) 5–8; 12–14.
J.R. Christie, "Joint Stock Enterprise in Scotland before the Companies
    Acts", (1909–10) 21 *J.R.* 128–47.
C.N. Johnston, "Environment and the Common Law", (1908–9) 20 *J.R.*
    178.
J. Mackintosh, "Curatory of Minors in the Civil Law", (1906–7) 18 *J.R.*
    18–29.
H. Burn Murdoch, "English Law in Scots Practice", (1909–10) 21 *J.R.*
    59–74.

1911–15.

D. Baird Smith, "William Barclay", (1914) 11 *Sc. Hist. Rev.* 136–63.
– ,   "John Barclay", (1915) 12 *Sc. Hist. Rev.* 37–59.
– ,   "Sir Thomas Craig, Feudalist", *ibid.,* 271–302.
T. Mackenzie (Lord Mackenzie), *Studies in Roman Law with
    Comparative Views of the Laws of France, England and Scotland*
    (Edinburgh, 1911, reprint of 1898 ed.).

1916–20.

H.H. Brown, "The Old Scots Law of Blasphemy", (1918) 30 *J.R.* 56–68.
– ,   "The Old Scots Law of Heresy", (1919) 31 *J.R.* 199–207.
W.G.M. Dobie, "Law and Lawyers in the Waverley Novels", (1920) 32 *J.R.*
    244–55; 317–33.
C.S. Lobingier, "The Value and Place of Roman Law in the Technical
    Curriculum", (1918) 30 *J.R.* 136–61.
T. Miller, "The Parochial Law of Tithes. Its Scottish Origin and Adoption
    by Europe and England", (1920) 32 *J.R.* 54–81.
D. Baird Smith, "*Teste meipso*", (1918) 15 *Sc. Hist. Rev.* 265–68.

1921–25.

A. Bérard, *La survivance du droit romain en Écosse* (Thèse, Paris,
    1925).
H.H. Brown, "Some Relations Between the Scots and Roman Laws of
    Contract", 1922 S.L.T. (News) 154–56.
– ,   "Ulpian's Definition of Jurisprudence", (1921) 33 *J.R.* 128–33.
D.M.G., "The N(otary). P(ublic).", 1923 S.L.T. (News), 103–6.
J.C. Gardner, "A Plea for the Restoration of the Law of Death-bed, 1925
    S.L.T. (News), 209–11.

H. Lévy-Ullmann [Trans. F.P. Walton], "The Law of Scotland", (1925) 37
     J.R. 370–91.
J. Mackintosh, "Henry Goudy", (1922) 34 *J.R.* 53–57.
A.R.G. McMillan, "The Scottish Court of Admiralty: a Retrospect", (1922)
     34 *J.R.* 38–44; 164–71.
T. Miller, "The Parochial Law of Tithes. Its Scottish Origin and Adoption
     by Europe and England", (ctd.) (1921) 33 *J.R.* 36–52; 109–27;
     (1922) 34 *J.R.* 45–52.
– , "Reception of Roman Civil Law and Roman Canon Law in Scotland
     in the Reign of David I", (1923) 35 *J.R.* 362–75.
– , *The Parochial Law of Tithes* (Edinburgh, 1924).
– , "Chirographs: their Place in the History of the Constitution of
     Scotland", (1925) 37 *J.R.* 1–14.
– , "Scotland in the History of Roman Law. The Notarial System",
     (1925) 37 *J.R.* 162–77.
W.G Roughead, "Plagium: a Footnote to 'Guy Mannering'", (1921) 33 *J.R.*
     18–35.
C.P. Sherman, *Roman Law in the Modern World* (2nd ed., New York
     1924), vol. 1, paras 359–60.
D. Baird Smith, "*'Teste meipso'* and the Parochial Law of Tithes", (1921)
     18 *Sc. Hist. Rev.* 36–43.
– , "A Note on Roman Law in Scotland", *ibid.*, 66–68.
– , "Roman Law and Political Theory", (1925) 22 *Sc. Hist. Rev.* 249–77.
J.F. Whyte, "Henry Goudy: an Appreciation", (1921) 33 *J.R.* 161–63.

1926–30.

J.H. Baxter, "Scottish Students at Louvain University", (1928) 25 *Sc. Hist.
     Rev.* 327–34.
W.J. Dobie, "Some Reflections on the *conditio si testator sine liberis
     decesserit*", 1930 S.L.T. (News) 9–10.
W. Duke, "Boswell among the Lawyers", (1926) 38 *J.R.* 341–70.
J.C. Gardner, "The Need for a History of the Law of Scotland", 1926
     S.L.T. (News) 29–32.
– , "The Origin and Nature of the Legal Rights of Spouses and
     Children in the Scottish Law of Succession: I – A Brief Survey of
     the Roman Law Relating to Wills and Succession", (1927) 39 *J.R.*
     209–16.
– , "II – The Origin of *jus relictae* and Legitim in Scotland", *ibid.*,
     313–44.
– , "III – The Origin of Terce and Courtesy in Scotland", *ibid.*, 434–45.
– , "IV – The Nature of the *jus relictae* and Legitim", (1928) 40 *J.R.*
     72–89.
– , "V – The Nature of Terce and Courtesy", *ibid.*, 89–92.
– , Letter to editor (replying to T. Miller), *ibid.*, 100.
– , *The Origin and Nature of the Legal Rights of Children in the
     Scottish Law of Succession* (Edinburgh, 1928).

A.D. Gibb, "International Private Law in Scotland in the Sixteenth and Seventeenth Centuries", (1927) 39 *J.R.* 369–407.

- , *International Private Law in Scotland in the Seventeenth and Eighteenth Centuries* (Edinburgh, 1928).

H. McKechnie, "The Notary Public and his Notebook", 1930 S.L.T. (News) 77–78.

J. Mackintosh, "Our Debt to Roman Law", (1926) 38 *J.R.* 327–40.

A.R.G. McMillan, "The Fusion of Scots and English Commercial Law", (1928) 40 *J.R.* 1–13.

T. Miller, Letter to Editor, (1927) 39 *J.R.* 472–73.

D. Baird Smith, "Some Notes on a Scottish Brocard", (1926) 38 *J.R.* 251–70.

A.M. Stuart, "The Liability of Common Carriers", (1926) 38 *J.R.* 205–12.

- , "Note on *Alexander's Trs.* v. *Preston*", (1928) 40 *J.R.* 187.

1931–35.

J.C. Brown, "The Origin and Early History of the Office of Notary", (1935) 47 *J.R.* 210–40 ; 355–417.

W.W. Buckland, "Casus and Frustration in Roman Law and Common Law", (1932–33) 46 *Harvard L.R.* 1284–1300.

A.L. Cordiner, "Interpretation of Wills", (1932) 44 *J.R.* 329–60.

W.J. Dobie, "The Law of Treasure Trove", (1931) 43 *J.R.* 300–10.

R.K. Hannay, *The College of Justice* (Glasgow, 1933) [reprinted, Stair Society Supplementary Series, 1, Edinburgh 1990].

J.M. Irvine, "Roman Law", *Encyclopaedia of the Laws of Scotland*, ed. Viscount Dunedin, vol. 13 (Edinburgh, 1932), paras. 147–84.

H. McKechnie, "An Eighteenth-Century Dumfries Procurators' Examination", (1931) 43 *J.R.* 337–48.

J. Mackintosh, *Roman Law in Modern Practice* (Edinburgh, 1934).

- , "*Nautae caupones stabularii:* Special Liabilities of Shipmasters, Innkeepers and Stablers", (1935) 47 *J.R.* 54–74.

Lord Macmillan, "Scots Law as a Subject of Comparative Study", (1932) 48 *L.Q.R.* 477–87.

T. Miller, "*Stipulatio'* in Sir James Darow's Protocol Book", (1933) 45 *J.R.* 32–48.

C. de B. Murray, "The Education of the Scots Lawyer", 1931 S.L.T. (News) 185–88, followed by letters in 1932 S.L.T. (News) 9–12, 28.

- , "Legal Education – Last Words", 1932 S.L.T. (News) 29–32.

T.A. Ross, "Servitudes in the Law of Scotland", (1933) 45 *J.R.* 151–65; 257–94; 344–58.

- , *Servitudes in the Law of Scotland* (Edinburgh, 1933).

D. Baird Smith, "Archibald Crawfurd, Lord of Session", (1933) 45 *J.R.* 166–78.

A.M. Stuart, "Will – *conditio si testator* – Right To Challenge", (1933) 45 *J.R.* 76–77.

T.C. Wade, "The Sea Law of Scotland" in *Miscellany Volume,* (Scottish Text Society, 3rd ser., 4, Edinburgh and London, 1933), 23–79.

1936-40.

A.I. Cameron, "Scottish Students at Paris University 1466–92", (1936) 48 *J.R.* 228-55.

A.H. Charteris, "Scotland and the Common Law System of Private International Law", (1937–38) 11 *Australian I.J.* 378-86.

A.D. Gibb, "The Inter-relation of the Legal Systems of Scotland and England", (1937) 53 *L.Q.R.* 61-79.

R.K. Hannay, "Some Questions regarding Scotland and the Canon Law", (1937) 49 *J.R.* 25-34.

S.G. Kermack, "Contract – *sponsio ludicra*", (1938) 50 *J.R.* 322-23.

W.E. Levie, "Bishop Elphinstone and the Law", (1936) 48 *J.R.* 107-22.

A.R.G. McMillan, *The Law of* Bona Vacantia *in Scotland* (Edinburgh, 1936), 5ff.

T. Miller, "Judge-Admiral James Graham of Airth (1702–1746), with Special Reference to his Civil Law Library", (1937) 49 *J.R.* 390-413.

R.J. Mitchell, "Scottish Law Students in Italy in the Later Middle Ages", (1937) 49 *J.R.* 19-24.

J.S. Muirhead, *Outline of Roman Law* (Edinburgh, 1937).

W.G. Normand [Lord Normand], "Consideration in the Law of Scotland", (1939) 55 *L.Q.R.* 358-74.

Lord Normand, *Scottish Judicature and Legal Procedure* (Holdsworth Club 1940–41, Birmingham, 1940).

D. Baird Smith, "Roman Law", *An Introductory Survey of the Sources and Literature of Scots Law*, (Stair Society Publications, vol. 1, Edinburgh, 1936), 171-82.

– , "Canon Law", *ibid.*, 183-92.

– , "A Note on *juramentum calumniae*", (1939) 51 *J.R.* 7-10.

1941-45.

J. Campbell, "Romanization of Scottish Law", (1942) 22 *Boston Univ. L.R.* 581-89.

T.M. Cooper [Lord Cooper], *Select Scottish Cases of the Thirteenth Century* (Edinburgh and London, 1944).

– , "A Scottish Law Student at Oxford in 1250", (1944) 56 *J.R.* 57-61.

A.I. Dunlop, *Scots Abroad in the Fifteenth Century* (Historical Association Pamphlet No. 124) (London, 1942).

J.C. Gardner, "An Historical Survey of the Law in Scotland Prior to the Reign of David I", (1945) 57 *J.R.* 34-51; 65-82.

W.E. Levie, "The Place of the War of Independence in Scottish Legal History", (1943) 55 *J.R.* 121-27.

F. Schulz, "The Writ '*praecipe quod reddat*' and its Continental Models", (1942) 54 *J.R.* 1-20.

1946-50.

E.J. Cohn, "The Nullity of Marriage: a Study in Comparative Law and Legal Reform", (1948) 64 *L.Q.R.* 324-40; 533-44.

T.M. Cooper, "Frustration of Contract in Scots Law", (1946) 28 *Jour. Comp. Legis.*, 3rd ser., Pt. 3, 1-5 = *Selected Papers* (1957), below, 124-32.

- , *The Scottish Legal Tradition* (Saltire Society, Edinburgh, 1949) = *Selected Papers*, below, 172-200 (reprinted, Saltire Society and Stair Society, Edinburgh, 1991).

- , "The Common Law and the Civil Law - a Scot's View", (1950) 63 *Harvard L.R.* 468-75 = *Selected Papers*, 201-9.

M.G. Fisher, "Scotland and the Roman Law", (1947) 22 *Tulane L.R.* 13-23.

W.G., "*Conditio si sine liberis*", 1947 S.L.T. (News) 85-87.

J.S. Muirhead, *Outline of Roman Law* (2nd ed., Edinburgh, 1947).

R. Powell, "Actual Military Service", (1949) 61 *J.R.* 172-85.

T.B. Smith, "The Durability of the Scottish Legal Tradition", (1950) 62 *J.R.* 1-17.

D.M. Walker, "Spuilzie", 1949 S.L.T. (News) 137-38.

- , "The Scottish View of Law and Equity", 1949 S.L.T. (News) 233-34.

- , "Solatium", (1950) 62 *J.R.* 149-68.

G.W. Wilton, "Pothier (1699-1772)", (1947) 59 *J.R.* 208-26.

1951-55.

A.E. Anton, "Medieval Scottish Executors and the Courts Spiritual", (1955) 67 *J.R.* 129-54.

A. Ashley, "Property in Relation to Marriage and the Family", (1953) 65 *J.R.* 37-68; 150-81; 262-93.

J.C. Barry, "William Hay of Aberdeen; a Sixteenth-Century Scottish Theologian and Canonist", (1951) 2 *Innes Rev.* 82-99.

A.R. Brownlie, "The Universities and Scottish Legal Education", (1955) 67 *J.R.* 26-61.

T.M. Cooper, "Scottish Students at Leyden and Utrecht", 1951 S.L.T. (News) 237.

Lord Cooper of Culross [T.M. Cooper], "The Scottish Lawyer's Library in the Seventeenth Century", (1954) 66 *J.R.* 1-5 = *Selected Papers* (1957), below, 276-80.

W.A. Elliott, "What is *culpa*?", (1954) 66 *J.R.* 6-36.

J.J. Gow, "Mistake and Error", (1952) 1 *I.C.L.Q.* 472-83.

- , "Some Observations on Error", (1953) 65 *J.R.* 221-54.

- , "*Culpa in docendo*", (1954) 66 *J.R.* 253-70.

R.W. Millar, "Memory Verses of the Romano-Canonical Procedurists", (1955) 67 *J.R.* 284-97.

J.S. Muirhead, "Notes on the History of the Solicitors' Profession in Scotland", (1952) 68 *S.L.R.* 25-36; 59-70.

H.G. Richardson, "Roman Law in the *Regiam Majestatem*", (1955) 67 *J.R.* 155-87.

T.B. Smith, "Scottish Marriage and Divorce Law", 1953 S.L.T. (News) 176-80.

– , "English Influences on the Law of Scotland", (1954) 3 *Am.J.Comp.L.* 522–42 = *Studies Critical*, below (1962), 116–36.

– , *The United Kingdom. The Development of its Laws and Constitution. Scotland* (London, 1955), 617–21.

P.G. Stein, "The College of Judges in Pavia", (1952) 64 *J.R.* 204–13.

– , "The *actio de effusis vel dejectis* and the Concept of Quasi-Delict in Scots Law", (1955) 4 *I.C.L.Q.* 356–75.

D.M. Walker, "Equity in Scots Law", (1954) 66 *J.R.* 103–47.

– , "Some Characteristics of Scots Law", (1955) 18 *M.L.R.* 321–37.

W.D.H. Winder, "Liability of an Innkeeper in Recent Cases", 1952 S.L.T. (News) 58–60.

1956–60.

A.E. Anton, "Scottish Thoughts on French Civil Procedure", 1956 *J.R.* 158–75.

– , "The 'Christian Marriage' Heresy", 1956 S.L.T. (News) 201–4.

– , "The Effect of Marriage on Property in Scots Law", (1956) 19 *M.L.R.* 653–68, esp. 653–655.

D.I.C. Ashton Cross, "Bare Promise in Scots Law", 1957 *J.R.* 138–50.

Lord Cooper of Culross [T.M. Cooper], *Selected Papers* 1922–1954 (Edinburgh and London, 1957).

J. Durkan and A. Ross, "Early Scottish Libraries", (1958) 9 *Innes Rev.* 5–167.

J.J. Gow, "The Roots of a Tree", 1958 *J.R.* 242–52.

– , "The Categories of Voluntary Obligations", 1960 S.L.T. (News) 107–8; 109–11; 163–4.

A.G. Guest, "Family Provision and the *legitima portio*", (1957) 73 *L.Q.R.* 74–88, esp. 74–78.

Law Reform Committee – Eighth Report (Cmnd 1017) 1960, Appendix I.

T.B. Smith, "The Common Law Cuckoo, Problems of 'Mixed' Legal Systems with Special Reference to Restrictive Interpretations in the Scots Law of Obligations", 1956 *Butterworths S.A.L.R.* 147–68 = *Studies Critical*, below (1962), 89–115.

– , "Master and Servant. Further Historical Outlines", 1958 *J.R.* 215–29.

– , "Scots Law and Roman Dutch Law: a Shared Tradition", 1959 *Acta Juridica* 36–46 = *Studies Critical*, 46–61.

– , "A Meditation on Scottish Universities and the Civil Law", (1959) 33 *Tulane L.R.* 621–30 = *Studies Critical*, 62–71.

– , "Strange Gods: the Crisis of Scots Law as a Civilian System", 1959 *J.R.* 119–41 = *Studies Critical*, 72–88.

P.G. Stein, "The Influence of Roman Law in Scotland", (1957) 23 *S.D.H.I.* 149–73.

– , "Legal Thought in Eighteenth Century Scotland", 1957 *J.R.* 1–20 = *Historical Essays*, below (1988), 361–80.

– , *Fault in the Formation of Contract* (Aberdeen, 1958), 171ff.

– , "The Mutual Agency of Partners in the Civil Law", (1959) 33 *Tulane L.R.* 595–606.

Various Authors, *An Introduction to Scottish Legal History* (Publications of the Stair Society, 20, Edinburgh, 1958), 4-5; 23, 30-31, 51, 52, 224, 234, 243-53, 265, 276-77, 280-81.

D.M. Walker, *The Scottish Legal System, An Introduction to the Study of Scots Law* (Edinburgh, 1959), 25-32; ch.3; 129; 254-55; (subsequent editions 1963; 1969; 1976; 1981; 1992).

- , "Legal Studies in the Scottish Universities", 1957 *J.R.* 21-41; 151-79.

- , "Legal Education and Training", 1960 S.L.T. (News) 41 at 43.

1961-65.

A.H. Campbell, "Diritto scozzese e diritto romano", *Bartolo da Sassoferrato: studi e documenti per il vi centenario* (Milan, 1962), vol. 1, 75-87.

W.Q. De Funiak, "The Legal System of Scotland", (1963-64) 38 *Tulane L.R.* 91-102.

- , "Legal Education in Scotland", (1963-64) 38 *Tulane L.R.* 361-70.

A. Giuliani, "The Influence of Rhetoric on the Law of Evidence and Pleading", 1962 *J.R.* 216-51, esp. 248.

J.J. Gow, "The Constitution and Proof of Voluntary Obligations", 1961 *J.R.* 1-20; 119-42; 234-52.

- , "The Categories of Voluntary Obligations", 1961 S.L.T. (News) 101-4.

- , "The Constitution and Proof of Real Contracts", 1963 S.L.T. (News) 125-27.

- , "Warrandice in Sale of Goods", 1963 *J.R.* 31-66.

T.G.I. Hamnett, "A Note on the Obligation of Nude Pacts in Canon Law", 1962 *J.R.* 256-59.

W.C. Lehmann, "John Millar, Professor of Civil Law at Glasgow (1761-1801)", 1961 *J.R.* 218-33.

K.H.O., "Common Calamities and the Presumption of Death", 1963 S.L.T. (News) 101-3.

D.B. S[mith], "*Characteres quorundam apud Scotos advocatorum*", 1961 S.L.T. (News) 73-75 at 73.

T.B. Smith, "Scots Law and Roman-Dutch Law: a Shared Tradition", 1961 *J.R.* 32-52 = *Studies Critical*, below, 46-61.

- , "The Influence of the 'Auld Alliance' with France on the Law of Scotland", *Studies Critical*, below, 28-45.

- , *British Justice: The Scottish Contribution* (London, 1961), Ch. 1. "Perspectives: Historical and Comparative".

- , "Full Circle: the Law of Occupiers' Liability in Scotland", *XXth Century Comparative and Conflicts Law. Legal Essays in Honor of Hessel E. Yntema* (Leyden, 1961) = *Studies Critical*, 154-67.

- , *Studies Critical and Comparative* (Edinburgh, 1962).

- , *Scotland. The Development of its Laws and Constitution* (London, 1962), 19-24.

- , *A Short Commentary on the Law of Scotland* (Edinburgh, 1962), 19-24.

–, "Trusts and Fiduciary Relationships in the Law of Scotland", *The Trust in Civil Law* (Toronto, 1962) = *Studies Critical*, 198-228.

P.G. Stein, "The Influence of Roman Law on the Law of Scotland", 1963 *J.R.* 205-45 = *Historical Essays*, below, (1988), 319-59.

–, "The General Notions of Contract and Property in Eighteenth Century Scottish Thought", 1963 *J.R.* 1-13.

W.J. Wadlington III, "Imputation of Payment: a Study of Obligations", (1963-64) 38 *Tulane L.R.* 31-52 esp. at 35-36.

D.E.R. Watt, "University Graduates in Scottish Benefices", (1964) 15 *Records of the Scottish Church History Society* 77-88.

I.D. Willock, "A Civil Lawyer Looks at the Canon Law", (1962) 11 *I.C.L.Q.* 89-107.

1966-70.

Anon, "The Notary Public" 1970 S.L.T. (News) 77-80.

J.C. Barry, trans. and ed. *William Hay's Lectures on Marriage*, (Publications of the Stair Society, 24, Edinburgh, 1967).

R.D. Carswell, "The Origin of the Legal Profession in Scotland", (1967) 11 *Am.J.L.H.* 41-56.

W.M. Gordon, "Roman and Scots Law – the *conditiones si sine liberis decesserit*", 1969 *J.R.* 108-27.

–, *Studies in the Transfer of Property by Traditio*, (Aberdeen, 1970), ch.12.

W.C. Lehmann, "Some Observations on the Law Lectures of Professor Millar at the University of Glasgow (1761-1801)", 1970 *J.R.* 56-77.

D.N. MacCormick, "*Jus quaesitum tertio:* Stair v. Dunedin", 1970 *J.R.* 228-46.

M.C. Meston, "Bastards in the Law of Succession", 1966 S.L.T. (News) 197-203.

A.F. Rodger, "The Praetor's Edict and Carriage by Land in Scots Law", (1968) 3 *Irish Jurist* 175-86.

–, "Molina, Stair and the *ius quaesitum tertio*", 1969 *J.R.* 34-44; 128-51.

P.G. Stein, "Roman Law in Scotland", *Ius Romanum Medii Aevi*, v, pars 13b (Milan 1968) = *Historical Essays*, below (1988), 269-317.

–, "The Source of the Romano-canonical Part of *Regiam Majestatem*", (1969) 48 *Sc. Hist. Rev.* 107-23.

D.M. Walker, *The Law of Delict in Scotland* (Edinburgh, 1966), 17-31, [2nd ed., 1981] 17-31.

N. Wilson, "The Scottish Bar: the Evolution of the Faculty of Advocates in its Historical Social Setting", (1968) 28 *Louisiana L.R.* 235-57.

1971-75.

R. Black, "An Historical Survey of Delictual Liability in Scotland for Personal Injuries and Death", (1975) 8 *C.I.L.S.A.* 46-70; 189-211; 318-43; and (1976) 9 *C.I.L.S.A.* 57-80.

R.C. van Caenegem, "History of European Civil Procedure", *International Encyclopaedia of Comparative Law*, vol. 16, chap. 2 (Tübingen, Paris, New York, 1971), sections 39, 58 and 73.

A.H. Campbell, "Legal Education in Scotland", *L'Educazione Giuridica. I – Modelli di Università e Progetti di Riforma* (Perugia, 1975), 147-67.

D.L. Carey Miller, "The Scottish Institutional Writers on Animal Liability; Civilian or Scienter?" 1974 *J.R.* 1-12.

– , "The Use of Roman Law in Scotland: a Reply", 1975 *J.R.* 64-69.

Hélène David, *Introduction à l'étude du droit écossais* (Paris, 1972).

R. Feenstra and C.J.D. Waal, *Seventeenth–Century Leyden Law Professors and their Influence on the Development of the Civil Law. A Study of Bronchorst, Vinnius and Voet* (Koninklijke Nederlandse Akademie van Wetenschappen. Afd. Letterkunde, Nieuwe Reeks, Deel 90. (Amsterdam and Oxford, 1975), 81-88.

W.M. Gordon, "Scots Law and Roman Law", (1972) 23 *Codicillus* 16-19.

Lord Hunter, "The End of Assythment", 1973 S.L.T. (News) 1-7.

B.S. Jackson, "Liability for Animals in Scottish Legal Literature: from the Auld Lawes to the Sixteenth Century", (1975) 10 *Irish Jur.* 334-51.

B.P. Levack, "The Proposed Union of English Law and Scots Law in the Seventeenth Century", 1975 *J.R.* 97-115.

K. Luig, "The Institutes of the National Law in the Seventeenth and Eighteenth Centuries" 1972 *J.R.* 193-226.

G.D. MacCormack, "*Culpa tenet suos auctores:* the Application of a Principle in Scots Law", 1973 *J.R.* 159-72.

– , "*Culpa* in the Scots Law of Reparation", 1974 *J.R.* 13-29.

I.S. Ross, *Lord Kames and the Scotland of his Day* (Oxford, 1972).

T.B. Smith, "Designation of Delictual Actions – Damn *iniuria* Damn", 1972 S.L.T. (News) 125-28.

– , "Authors and Authority", (1972) 12 *Jour. Soc. Pub. Teachers of Law* 3-21.

– , "Solatium", *Xenion. Festschrift für Pan J. Zepos* (Athens, Freiburg, Cologne 1973), vol. 1, 589-98.

– , "The Law Relating to the Treasure", *St. Ninian's Isle and its Treasure*, A. Small *et al.*, 2 vols., (London, 1973), vol. 1, 149-66.

– , "Exchange or Sale?", (1973-74) 48 *Tulane L.R.* 1029-42.

– , "The Age of Innocence", (1974-75) 49 *Tulane L.R.* 311-20.

– , "Mixed Jurisdictions", *Int. Encyclopedia of Comparative Law*, vol. VI – Property and Trust, ch. VII (Tübingen, Paris 1975), 115-36, 2-231 to 2-272.

D.M. Walker, "Equity in Scots Law", *Equity in the World's Legal Systems: a Comparative Study Dedicated to R. Cassin*, ed. R. A. Newman (Brussels, 1973), 187-204.

– , "Judicial Decisions and Doctrine in Scots Law", *The Role of Judicial Decisions and Doctrine in Civil Law and in Mixed Jurisdictions*, ed. J. Dainow (Baton Rouge, 1974), 202-23.

Various authors, *The Legal System of Scotland* (Edinburgh, 1975; 3rd ed. 1981).

A. Watson, *Legal Transplants. An Approach to Comparative Law* (Edinburgh, 1974), chs. 6 and 7.

W.A. Wilson, "Security and Corporeal Moveables - Scotland", *Security over Corporeal Moveables*, ed. J.G. Sauveplanne (Leiden, 1974), 43-48.

1976-80.

A.L. Brown, "The Scottish 'Establishment' in the Later Fifteenth Century", 1978 *J.R.* 89-105.

G. Donaldson, "The Legal Profession in Scottish Society in the Sixteenth and Seventeenth Centuries", 1976 *J.R.* 1-19.

B.S. Jackson, "Liability for Animals in Scottish Legal Literature: from Stair to the Modern Law", 1977 *J.R.* 139-63.

D.M. Johnston, "The Scottish Tradition in International Law", (1978) 16 *Canadian Yearbook Int.L.* 3-45.

F. Lyall, "The Maxim *cujus est solum* in Scots Law", 1978 *J.R.* 147-69.

K. Luig, *"Schottland", Handbuch der Quellen und Literatur der neueren europäischen Privatrechtsgeschichte, II.2. Gesetzgebung und Rechtsprechung,* ed. H. Coing (München, 1976), 501-4; 1431-45.

W.W. McBryde, "Frustration of Contract", 1980 *J.R.* 1-13.

G.D. MacCormack, "A Note on Stair's Use of the Term *pollicitatio*", 1976 *J.R.* 121-26.

J.J. Robertson, "The Development of the Law", *Scottish Society in the Fifteenth Century,* ed. J. M. Brown (London, 1977), 136-52.

T.B. Smith, *Property Problems in Sale*, (Tagore Law Lectures, London and Calcutta, 1978).

– , "Transfer of Property in Corporeal Moveables by *inter vivos* acts - United Kingdom - Scotland", *Essays in Honour of Ben Beinart,* edd. W. de Vos *et al.* (Capetown, Wetton, Johannesburg, 1978-79), vol. 3, 39-57 = 1979 *Acta Juridica* 39-57.

R. Sutherland, "Possession in Scots Law: a Comparative Response", *Perspectives in Jurisprudence*, ed. E. M. M. Attwooll, (Glasgow, 1977), 123-41.

D.M. Walker, *The Oxford Companion to Law* (Oxford, 1980).

– , "Legal Scholarship in Scotland in the Modern Period", *Essays Beinart,* above, vol. 3, 295-304 = 1979 *Acta Juridica* 295-304.

A. Watson, "The Rise of Modern Scots Law", *La formazione storica del diritto moderno in Europa. Atti del III congresso internazionale della società Italiana di storia del diritto* (Florence, 1977), vol. 3, 1167-76.

D.E.R. Watt, *A Biographical Dictionary of Scottish Graduates to A.D. 1410* (Oxford, 1977).

I.D. Willock, "The Scottish Legal Heritage Revisited", *Independence and Devolution: The Legal Implications for Scotland*, ed. J.P. Grant (Edinburgh, 1976), 1-14.

D.M. Yorke, "The Legal Personality of the Unborn Child", 1979 S.L.T. (News) 159-61.

1981-85.

P.B.H. Birks, "Six Questions in Search of a Subject - Unjust Enrichment in a Crisis of Identity", 1985 *J.R.* 227-52.

-, "Restitution: a View from the Scots Law", (1985) 38 *C.L.P.* 57- 82.

R. Black, "Practice and Precept in Scots Law", 1982 *J.R.* 31-50.

J.W. Cairns, "Institutional Writings in Scotland Reconsidered", (1983) 4 *Jour. Leg. Hist.* 76-117.

Lord Emslie, "The Law of Scotland - its Interest for the Comparative Lawyer", (1982) 35 *C.L.P.* 25-37.

Encyclopaedia Americana, "Scotland 5. Law", [T.B. Smith] (1981 and 1990 ed.), vol. 24, 414-15

A.D.M. Forte, "Must a Purchaser Buy Charred Remains? - An Analysis of the Passing of Risk on Civilian Principles", (1984) 19 *Irish Jur.* 1-14.

B.R. Galloway and B.P. Levack, edd. *The Jacobean Union. Six Tracts of 1604*, (Publications of the Scottish Historical Society, 4th ser., 21, Edinburgh, 1985).

G. Gorla, "Bell, one of the Founding Fathers of the 'Common and Comparative Law of Europe' during the 19th Century", 1982 *J.R.* 121-38.

A. Harding, "*Regiam Majestatem* amongst Medieval Law-books", 1984 *J.R.* 97-111.

P.C. Hemphill, "The Personality of the Partnership in Scotland", 1984 *J.R.* 208-42.

T. Ingman, "A History of the Defence of *volenti non fit injuria*", 1981 *J.R.* 1-28.

B.S. Jackson, "The Memorials in *Haggart and H.M. Advocate* v. *Hogg and Souter* 1738", *Miscellany II*, ed. D. Sellar (Publications of the Stair Society, 35, Edinburgh, 1984), 221-60.

R.D. Leslie, "*Negotiorum gestio* in Scots Law", 1981 S.L.T. (News) 259-61.

-, "*Negotiorum gestio* in Scots Law: the Claim of the Privileged Gestor", 1983 *J.R.* 12-35.

R.J. Lyall, "Scottish Students and Masters at the Universities of Cologne and Louvain in the Fifteenth Century", (1985) 36 *Innes Rev.* 55-73.

R.A. McCall-Smith, "Scots Law - another Mixed System", (1985) 1 *Lesotho L.J.* 283-93.

A. Murdoch, "The Advocates, the Law and the Nation in Early Modern Scotland", *Lawyers in Early Modern Europe and America*, ed. W. Prest (London, 1981) 147-163.

K.McK. Norrie, "Hurts to Character, Honour and Reputation", 1984 *J.R.* 162-84.

S. Ollivant, *The Court of the Official in Pre-Reformation Scotland* (Publications of the Stair Society, 34, Edinburgh, 1982).

O.F. Robinson, "Canon Law and Marriage", 1984 *J.R.* 22-40.

- , T.D. Fergus and W.M. Gordon, *An Introduction to European Legal History* (Abingdon, 1985), 377-384, 400-405.

T.B. Smith, "Law" and "Law, History of", *A Companion to Scottish Culture*, ed. D. Daiches (London, 1981), 201, 205.

- , "British Justice: a Jacobean Phantasma", 1982 S.L.T. (News) 157-164.

- , "While One Hundred Remain: Scots Law, its Historical and Comparative Dimensions", (1983-4) 50 *Aberdeen Univ. Rev.* 229-42.

P.G. Stein, "The Procedural Models of the 16th Century", 1982 *J.R.* 186-97.

- , "The Fate of the Institutional System", *Huldigingsbundel P. van Warmelo*, edd. J. van der Westhuizen *et al.* (Pretoria, 1984), 218-27 = *Historical Essays*, below (1988), 73-82.

R. Sutherland, *Lord Stair and the Law of Scotland* (Glasgow, 1981).

Various Authors, *The Legal System of Scotland* (3rd ed., Edinburgh, 1981).

D.M. Walker, *The Scottish Jurists* (Edinburgh, 1985).

A. Watson, *The Making of the Civil Law* (Cambridge, Mass. and London, 1981).

- , *Sources of Law, Legal Change and Ambiguity* (Philadelphia, 1984).

- , *The Evolution of Law* (Baltimore, 1985).

A.B. Wilkinson, "The Rule against Hearsay in Scotland", 1982 *J.R.* 213-36.

- and A.D.M. Forte, "Pure Economic Loss - a Scottish Perspective", 1985 *J.R.* 1-28.

S.E. Woolman, "Defaming the Dead", 1981 S.L.T. (News) 29-34.

1986-90.

P.B.H. Birks and G. Macleod, "The Implied Contract Theory of Quasi-contract; Civilian Opinion Current in the Century before Blackstone", (1986) 6 *Oxford J.L.S.* 46-85.

- , *The Institutes of Justinian* (London, 1987), 18-26.

A. Borthwick and H.L. MacQueen, "Three Fifteenth Century Cases", 1986 *J.R.* 123-51.

J.W. Cairns, "The Formation of the Scottish Legal Mind in the Eighteenth Century: Themes of Humanism and Enlightenment in the Admission of Advocates", *The Legal Mind. Essays for Tony Honoré*, edd. N. MacCormick and P. Birks (Oxford, 1986), 253-77.

- , "Blackstone, Kahn-Freund and the Law of Employment", (1989) 105 *L.Q.R.* 300-14.

– , T.D. Fergus and H.L. MacQueen, "Legal Humanism in Renaissance Scotland", (1990) 11 *Jour. Leg. Hist.* 40–69 = "Legal Humanism and the History of Scots Law", *Humanism in Renaissance Scotland,* ed. J. MacQueen (Edinburgh, 1990), 48–74.

M.P. Clancy, "A Further Note on *juramentum calumniae*", 1986 *J.R.* 170–76.

J. Durkan, "The French Connection in the Sixteenth and Early Seventeenth Centuries", *Scotland and Europe, 1200–1850,* ed. T. C. Smout (Edinburgh, 1986), 19–44.

R. Feenstra, "Scottish–Dutch Legal Relations in the Seventeenth and Eighteenth Centuries", *Scotland and Europe, cit. sup.,* 128–42.

T.D. Fergus, "Sources of Law (General and Historical): the Historical Sources of Scots Law (1) Roman Law", *Stair Memorial Encyclopaedia,* vol. 22 (Edinburgh, 1987), paras. 548–51.

– , *Quoniam attachiamenta* (Ph.D. Thesis, Glasgow, 1988).

A.D.M. Forte, "Reparation for Pure Ecomomic Loss: an Historical Perspective of Scots Law in the Seventeenth and Eighteenth Centuries", (1987) 8 *Jour. Leg. Hist.* 3–17.

– , "The Horse that Kills. Some thoughts on Deodand, Escheats and Crime in Fifteenth Century Scots Law", (1990) 58 *T.v.R.* 95–110.

D.R. Macdonald, "Mistaken Payments in Scots Law", 1989 *J.R.* 49–68.

H.L. MacQueen, "Pleadable Brieves, Pleading and the Development of Scots Law", (1986) 4 *Law and Hist. Rev.* 403–22.

– , "Scots Law under Alexander III", *Scotland in the Reign of Alexander III, 1249–1286,* ed. N.H. Reid, (Edinburgh, 1990), 74–102.

J.J. Robertson, "The Historical Sources of Scots Law (2) Canon Law", *Stair Memorial Encyclopaedia, cit. sup.,* paras. 557–86.

C.P. Rogers III, "Scots Law in Post–revolutionary and Nineteenth-Century America: the Neglected Jurisprudence", (1990) 8 *Law and Hist. Rev.* 205–35.

W.D.H. Sellar, "Legal History in Scotland", (1987) 9 Z.N.R. 74–87.

– , "The Common Law of Scotland and the Common Law of England", *The British Isles 1100 – 1500: Comparisons, Contrasts and Connections,* ed. R.R. Davies (Edinburgh, 1988), 82–99.

P.G. Stein, *The Character and Influence of the Roman Civil Law. Historical Essays* (London and Ronceverte, 1988), esp. chs. 5, 18, 19, 20, 21.

W.J. Stewart, "Smith's Question-mark, Walker's Exhortation and Quasi-delict", 1990 *J.R.* 71–82.

E.E. Sutherland, "Remedying an Evil? Warrandice of Quality at Common Law in Scotland", 1987 *J.R.* 24–37.

D.M. Walker, *A Legal History of Scotland, vol. 1, The Beginnings to A.D. 1286* (Edinburgh, 1988), 45, 91–92, 110–11, 249–50, 329–30, 341, 383, 394–95.

– , *A Legal History of Scotland, vol. 2, The Later Middle Ages* (Edinburgh, 1990), 13–17, 42, 254–55, 277–85, 372–74; 758.

D.E.R. Watt, "Scottish University Men of the Thirteenth and Fourteenth Centuries", *Scotland and Europe, cit. sup.*, 1-18, esp. at 8-9, 13.

1991-.

J.W. Cairns, "Rhetoric, Language and Roman Law: Legal Education and Improvement in Eighteenth-Century Scotland", (1991) 9 *Law and Hist. Rev.* 31-58.

- , "The Law, the Advocates and the Universities in Late Sixteenth-Century Scotland", (1994) 73 *Sc. Hist. Rev.* 171-90.

- , "The Origins of the Glasgow Law School: The Professors of Civil Law, 1714-1761", *The Life of the Law. Proceedings of the Tenth British Legal History Conference, Oxford 1991* (London and Rio Grande, 1993), 151-95.

- , "William Crosse, Regius Professor of Civil Law in the University of Glasgow, 1746-1749: A Failure of Enlightened Patronage", (1993) 12 *History of Universities* 159-96.

- , "'Famous as a school of Law, as Edinburgh ... for medicine': Legal Education in Glasgow, 1761-1801", *The Glasgow Enlightenment,* edd. A. Hook and R. Sher (Edinburgh, 1994), 133-59.

- , "From 'Speculative' to 'Practical' Legal Education: The Decline of the Glasgow Law School, 1801-1830", (1994) 62 *T.v.R.,* 331-56.

D.L. Carey Miller, "Stair's Property: A Romanist System?", 1995 *J.R.,* 70-81.

D. Daiches, ed., *A New Companion to Scottish Culture* (Edinburgh, 1993), *s.v.* "Law", "Law, History of", 175-82.

R. Evans-Jones, "The History of the *actio quanti minoris* in Scotland", 1991 *J.R.* 190-215.

- , "Payments in Mistake of Law - Full Circle", (1992) 37 *J.L.S.S.* 92-97.

- , "The *actio quanti minoris* debunked?", (1992) 37 *J.L.S.S.* 275-77.

- , "Identifying the Enriched", 1992 S.L.T. (News) 25-29.

- , "Unjust Enrichment, Contract and the Third Reception of Roman Law in Scotland", (1993) 109 *L.Q.R.* 663-81.

- and D. McKenzie, "Towards a Profile of the *condictio ob turpem vel injustam causam* in Scots Law", 1994 *J.R.* 60-77.

- , "Roman Law in Britain (sic) Scotland" (1994) 13 *Rechtshistorisches Journal* 494-505.

- , "Some Reflections on the *condictio indebiti* in a Mixed Legal System", 1994 *S.A.L.J.* 759-72.

- and J.A. Dieckmann, "The Dark Side of *Connelly* v. *Simpson*" 1995 *J.R.* 90-101.

J. Faber, "Rückforderung wegen Zweckverfehlung - Irrungen und Wirrungen bei der Anwendung römischen Rechts in Schottland", (1993) 1 *Z.Eu.P.* 279-97.

A.D.M. Forte, "Salvage Operations, Salvage Contracts and *negotiorum gestio*", 1994 *J.R.* 246-59.

S.D. Girvin, "Professor John Dove Wilson of Aberdeen", 1992 *J.R.* 60-73.

W.M. Gordon, "Scotland and France. The Legal Connection", (1994) 22 *Index. Omaggio a Peter Stein*, 557-66.

Lord Hope [J.A.D. Hope], "The Universities of Aberdeen and the Court of Session in Edinburgh", 1995 *J.R.* 5-19.

D. Johnston, "Sale and Transfer of Title in Roman and Scots Law", *The Roman Law Tradition*, edd. A.D.E. Lewis and D.J. Ibbetson (Cambridge, 1994), 182-98.

W.W. McBryde, "The Intention to Create Legal Relations", 1992 *J.R.* 274-79.

G.D. MacCormack, "The *actio communi dividundo* in Roman and Scots Law", *The Roman Law Tradition, cit. sup.*, 159-81.

H.L. MacQueen, "The Laws of Galloway: a Preliminary Study", *Galloway: Land and Lordship,* edd. R.D. Oram and G.P. Stell, (Publications of the Scottish Society for Northern Studies, 5, Edinburgh, 1991), 131-43.

- , *Studying Scots Law* (Edinburgh, 1993).

- , *Common Law and Feudal Society in Medieval Scotland* (Edinburgh, 1993).

- , "Unjust Enrichment and Breach of Contract", 1994 *J.R.* 137-66.

- and W.D.H. Sellar, "Unjust Enrichment in Scots Law" in *Unjustified Enrichment. The Comparative Legal History of the Law of Restitution,* ed. E.J.H. Schrage (Comparative Studies on Continental and Anglo-American Law, 15, Berlin, 1995), 289-321.

M.C. Meston, "The Civilists of Aberdeen, 1495-1995", 1995 *J.R.* 153-65.

J. Murray, "Potestative Conditions", 1991 S.L.T. (News), 185-88.

P. Nève, "Disputations of Scots Students Attending Universities in the Northern Netherlands", *Legal History in the Making,* edd. W.M. Gordon and T.D. Fergus (London and Rio Grande, 1991), 95-108.

K.G.C. Reid, "Unjust Enrichment and Property Law", 1994 *J.R.* 167-99.

O.F. Robinson, T.D. Fergus and W.M. Gordon, *European Legal History. Sources and Institutions* (London, Dublin, Edinburgh, 1994), paras 14.1.1 to 13; 14.5.1 to 8.

A. Rodger, "Potestative Conditions", 1991 S.L.T.(News) 253.

- , "Lord Macmillan's Speech in *Donoghue* v. *Stevenson*", (1992) 108 *L.Q.R.* 236-59.

- , "The Codification of Commercial Law in Victorian Britain", *ibid.* 570-90 = *Maccabaean Lecture, Proceedings of the British Academy* (1992).

- , "Roman Law in Practice in Britain", (1993) 12 *Rechtshistorisches Journal,* 261-71.

- , "Scottish Advocates in the Nineteenth Century: the German Connection", (1994) 110 *L.Q.R.* 563-91.

Scottish Law Commission, *Recovery of Benefits Conferred under Error of Law* (Discussion Paper No. 95, Edinburgh, 1992).

W.D.H. Sellar, "A Historical Perspective" in M. C. Meston, W. D. H. Sellar and Lord Cooper, *The Scottish Legal Tradition* (New enlarged edition, Edinburgh, 1991), 29-64.

– , "Forethocht Felony, Malice Aforethought and the Classification of Homicide", *Legal History in the Making, cit. sup.*, 43–59.

D.M. Walker, "The Province of Jurists Determined", 1991 *J.R.* 20–44.

– , *The Scottish Legal System*, (6th ed., Edinburgh, 1992), 35–40; 42–45; ch. 4; 155–56; 460–61.

– , "Legal Studies and Scholarship in the Time of David Murray, 1842–1928", 1993 *J.R.* 3–22.

– , *A Legal History of Scotland, vol. 3, The Sixteenth Century* (Edinburgh, 1995), 32–49, 827 and *passim*.

T.G. Watkin, "Saints, Seaways and Dispute Settlements", *Legal History in the Making, cit. sup.*, 1–9.

R.M. White and I.D. Willock, *The Scottish Legal System* (Edinburgh, 1993), 21–22; 82–83; 186.

N.R. Whitty, "Some Trends and Issues in Scots Enrichment Law", 1994 *J.R.* 127–36.

– , "Indirect Enrichment in Scots Law", 1994 *J.R.* 200–29; 239–82.

– , "*Ultra vires* Swap Contracts and Unjustified Enrichment", 1994 S.L.T. (News) 337–43.

INDEX OF SOURCES

ROMAN LAW

LEGISLATION

CASES

Scotland

Agnew v. *Ferguson* (1903) 5 F. 879: 218, 240, 241, 242
Allan v. *Cleghorn's Creditors* (1713) Mor. 11835: 33
Anderson v. *McCall* (1866) 4 M. 765: 131, 149, 169, 170
Arbuthnott v. *Paterson* (1798) Mor. 14220: 151
Armour v. *Thyssen Edelstahlwerke A.G.* 1990 S.L.T. 891: 152, 173
Arrol v. *Montgomery* (1826) 4 S. 499: 239

Balfour v. *Smith and Logan* (1877) 4 R. 454: 231, 232
Balfour v. *Pitcairne* (1540) Balfour's Practicks, vol. 1, 198: 25
Ballenden v. *MacMath* (1628) 1 B.S. 155: 30
Bell v. *Thomson* (1867) 6 M. 68: 218
Black v. *Cadell* (1804) Mor. 13905; (1812) Paton 567: 288, 293, 298, 299, 300, 303
Black v. *Incorporation of Bakers, Glasgow* (1867) 6 M. 136: 155
Black v. *North British Railway Company* 1908 S.C. 444: 287, 296
Boak v. *Meggett* (1844) 6 D. 662: 150
Bogle v. *Dunmore & Co.* (1787) Mor. 14216: 148
British Oxygen Company v. *South of Scotland Electricity Board* 1959 S.C. (H.L.) 17: 239
Brodie of Letham v. *Sir James Cadel of Muirton* (1707) 4 B.S. 660: 176, 188
Broughton v. *J. & A. Aitchison* 15th Nov. 1809, F.C.: 144, 169
Brown v. *MacGregor* 26th Feb. 1813, F.C.: 304
Brown v. *Storie* (1790) Mor. 14125: 166
Buchanan and Cochrane v. *Swan* (1764) Mor. 14208: 131

Cabbell v. *Brock* (1831) 5 W. & S. 476: 146
Came v. *City of Glasgow Friendly Society* 1933 S.C. 69: 269
Cantiere San Rocco S.A. v. *Clyde Shipbuilding and Engineering Co. Ltd.* 1922 S.C. 723, 1923 S.C. (H.L.) 105: 5, 8, 11, 243, 259, 265ff, 274, 275
Carrick v. *Carse* (1778) Mor. 2931: 218, 231
Charteris v. *King's Advocate* (1749–50) Mor. 7293: 260
Clark v. *Gordon* (1760) Mor. 13172: 197
Clark v. *West Calder Oil Co.* (1882) 9 R. 1017: 152
Connelly v. *Simpson* 1991 S.C.L.R. 295; 1994 S.L.T. 1096: 8, 10, 271, 273, 275
Cooley v. *Edinburgh & Glasgow Railway Co.* (1845) 18 D. 288: 304, 309
County Properties & Developments Ltd. v. *Gordon Harper* 1989 S.C.L.R. 597: 234
Creditors of Auchinbreck v. *Lockwood* (1758) Mor. 14129: 166
Cutler v. *Littlejohn* (1711) Mor. 583: 261, 262

Tuckers Land Development Corporation (Pty.) Ltd. v. *Hovis* 1980 (1)
   S.A. 645 (A):   58, 72, 77

University of Cape Town v. *Cape Bar Council and Another* 1986 (4) S.A.
   903 (A):   54

Van der Merwe v. *Meades* 1991 (2) S.A. 1 (A):   56, 73
Van der Westhuizen v. *Yskor Werknemers se Onderlinge
   Bystandsvereniging* 1960 (4) S.A. 803 (T):   59

Webster v. *Ellison* 1911 A.D. 73 (99):   47
Willis Faber Enthoven (Pty.) Ltd. v. *The Receiver of Inland Revenue*
   1992 (4) S.A. 202 (A):   65, 82
Winstanley and others v. *Barrow and others* (1937) A.D. 75:   68
Wolson v. *Gerber* 1954 (3) S.A. 94 (T):   64

Zuurbekom Ltd. v. *Union Corporation Ltd.* 1947 (1) S.A. 514 (A):   69

Australia

David Securities Pty. Ltd. v. *Commonwealth Bank of Australia* (1992)
   175 C.L.R. 353:   82

Canada

Air Canada v. *British Columbia* (1989) 59 D.L.R. (4th) 161:   82
Canadian Pacific v. *British Columbia* (1989) 59 D.L.R. (4th) 218:   82

Ceylon

Da Costa v. *Bank of Ceylon* (1970) 72 New Law Reports (Ceylon) 457:
   74

INDEX OF NAMES AND SUBJECTS